Making Room

Forty Years of *Room* Magazine

Room magazine
PO Box 46160 Station D
Vancouver, BC V6J 5G5
www.roommagazine.com

Caitlin Press Inc.
8100 Alderwood Road,
Halfmoon Bay, BC V0N 1Y1
www.caitlin-press.com

Text design by Meghan Bell
Cover art by Emily Cooper
Printed in Canada

Library and Archives Canada Cataloguing in Publication

Making room (Halfmoon Bay, B.C.)
    Making room : forty years of Room magazine / edited by the Growing Room Collective.

ISBN 978-1-987915-40-2 (softcover)

    1. Canadian literature (English)—Women authors. 2. Canadian literature (English)—20th century. 3. Canadian literature (English)—21st century. 4. Women—Literary collections. I. Growing Room Collective, editor II. Title.

PS8235.W7M33 2017   C810.8'09287   C2017-900073-X

The West Coast Feminist Literary Magazine Society (*Room* magazine) and Caitlin Press Inc. acknowledge financial support from the Government of Canada through the Canada Periodical Fund, the Canada Council for the Arts, the Province of British Columbia through the British Columbia Arts Council, and the City of Vancouver through the Cultural Grants Program.

 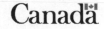

Funded by the Government of Canada
Financé par le gouvernement du Canada | Canada

Canada Council Conseil des Arts   BRITISH COLUMBIA   CITY OF
for the Arts   du Canada   ARTS COUNCIL   VANCOUVER
                                   An agency of the Province of British Columbia

Making Room

Forty Years of *Room* Magazine

Edited by the Growing Room Collective

First Readers (Longlist)
Meghan Bell
Terri Brandmueller
Candace Fertile
Taryn Hubbard
Lindsay Glauser Kwan
Alissa McArthur
Nav Nagra
Bonnie Nish
Rachel Thompson
Kayi Wong
Lisa Xing

**Second Readers
(Final Selections)**
Meghan Bell
Terri Brandmueller
Taryn Hubbard
Chelene Knight
Cara Lang
Nav Nagra

Proofreading
Lindsay Glauser Kwan
Brigid MacAulay
Nav Nagra
Rebecca Russell
Kaitlyn Till
Patricia Wolfe
Lisa Xing

Project Manager / Concept
Meghan Bell

Archives Coordinator
Nav Nagra

Marketing / Fundraising
Meghan Bell
Cara Lang
Kayi Wong

Graphic Design
Meghan Bell

Interviewers
Meghan Bell
Leah Golob
Lindsay Glauser Kwan
Kayi Wong

Forewords
Amber Dawn
Eleanor Wachtel

Afterwords
Meghan Bell
Chelene Knight

This project has been made possible by the Government of Canada.
Ce projet a été rendu possible grâce au gouvernement du Canada.

Thank You for Your Support

Donors ($50 or more)

Kathryn Alexander
Seonaid Andrews
Dilin B.
Karen A. Bannister
Joan M. Baril
Jan Barkhouse
Evelyn Battell
Rosanna Battigelli
Marilyn Belak
Douglas Bell
Marilyn Bell
Meghan Bell
Janet Berkman
Frances Boyle
Maureen Bradley
Terri Brandmueller
Connie Braun
Cullene Bryant
Shelley Burns
Clara Cristofaro
Jen Currin
Josette DoBrouwer
Jennifer Dellner
Anonymous

Mary Pat Detina
Laura Dilley
Andrew Dunn
Louise Dwyer
Anonymous
Taylor Brown Evans
Cynthia Flood
Elee Kraljii Gardiner
Chantal Gibson
Stephanie Hall
Lillian Henry
Susan Hufforth
Lynn Jacques
Carol Johnson
Sarah Kabamba
Amanda Leduc
Anonymous
Aviva Dale Martin
Chris Masterman
Bethmarie Michalska
Emily Morris
Erin Moure
Anonymous
Nav Nagra

Lana Okerlund
Kim Pittaway
Pat Preston
Jason Purcell
Paula Jane Remlinger
Anonymous
Anonymous
Erin Steel
Matthew Stepanic
Carol Stephen
Mollie Coles Tonn
Ayelet Tsabari
Anonymous
Deborah Vail
Anonymous
Jean Van Loon
KT Wagner
Valerie Chalker Whitfield
Linde Zingaro

For a complete list of donors, please visit roommagazine.com/anthology.

Funded by the Government of Canada
Financé par le gouvernement du Canada

Canada

The Growing Room Collective (2016 Collective Members)

Meghan Bell
Terri Brandmueller
Monica Calderon
Christina Cooke
Amber Dawn
Candace Fertile
Sierra Skye Gemma
Leah Golob
Taryn Hubbard
Nailah King

Jónína Kirton
Chelene Knight
Lindsay Glauser Kwan
Cara Lang
Mica Lemiski
Brigid MacAulay
Alissa McArthur
Rose Morris
Nav Nagra

Bonnie Nish
Dorothy Palmer
Rebecca Russell
Geffen Semach
Arielle Spence
Rachel Thompson
Kayi Wong
Lisa Xing
Jennifer Zilm

A special thank you to Mindy Abramowitz.

Founding Editors, *Room of One's Own*

Mary Anderson
Laurie Bagley
Pat Bartle

Penny Birnbaum
Lora Lippert

Gayla Reid
Gail van Varseveld

Table of Contents

❧

THE SECOND DECADE (1988 – 1997)

THE THIRD DECADE (1998 – 2007)

THE FOURTH DECADE (2008 – 2016)

COVER ART

AFTERWORDS

Foreword

ELEANOR WACHTEL

WHEN I MOVED TO VANCOUVER IN THE FALL OF 1975, along with trying to carve out a career, I wanted to meet feminists. In some ways, it's hard to imagine how things were then. I'd recently returned from East Africa, where I'd written a paper, "The Mother and the Whore: The Image of Women in Post-Independence Kenyan Fiction," published by the University of Nairobi. I noticed that a talk was being given at UBC called "The Mother and the Whore" (with a different subtitle that I can't quite recall now) in the Fine Arts department. I got in touch with the prof, Avis Lang, and we've been lifelong friends, even though neither of us lives in Vancouver any longer.

Given my time in Africa, I was reading whatever I could find by Canadians who'd lived there and written about it. There were a few: Margaret Laurence, Dave Godfrey, Dorothy Livesay, Audrey Thomas. At the annual meeting of the Canadian African Studies Association in Victoria that year, I spoke about Audrey Thomas's compelling fiction that drew on her experience in West Africa. Her work interested me especially because I knew she lived in B.C., on an island, and that sounded romantic. I sent the piece off to *Canadian Literature*, the first quarterly devoted entirely to the criticism and discussion of Canadian writing, founded by George Woodcock. He sent it back, suggesting I try *Room of One's Own*. (It's not until I read the interview with Gayla Reid in this book that I learned that Woodcock, the admirable anarchist, had supported this publication right from the beginning.) So like any conscientious contributor, I went to a bookstore to have a look at the magazine and saw that there was a notice seeking volunteers to join the collective. *Feminists*, I thought. *Perfect*. In fact, it was Gayla Reid who phoned me—I couldn't quite place the Australian accent—and we've been lifelong friends too. Just to come full circle: ten years later, when I was involved in the creation of a special issue of *Room* on Audrey Thomas, I received a note from George Woodcock praising my extensive interview with her that appeared in the issue. And incidentally, my article about her African-inflected fiction did appear in the magazine way back when. (It hadn't occurred to me until this moment to wonder why Woodcock rejected it for *Canadian Literature*. Would it have had something to do with our being women?)

Back in the mid-'70s, there was a growing world of feminist periodicals—right across the country. There was so much to say, such a hunger to communicate and understand, to question, unravel, debate, reveal. In providing room, a space, for women's writing, we also decided to celebrate the work of particular Canadian women authors as well as focus on opening up certain themes, such as science fiction and fantasy (issue 6.1, 1983, edited by Susan Wood) or women in theatre (issue 8.2, 1985).

I remember with particular pleasure my involvement in these special issues—for instance, photographing Dorothy Livesay (issue 5.1, 1982) or Marian Engel (issue 9.2, 1986) or Audrey Thomas (issue 10.4, 1987). Or meeting Montréal writer Nicole Brossard, the co-founder of the literary periodical *La Barre du jour* (and then, *La Nouvelle Barre du jour*) to discuss how we could translate and publish some of the writers who'd appeared in a special feminist issue she'd edited. The result was "Québécoises!" (issue 4.1, 1979), one of the first publications to introduce writers such as Louky Bersianik, Monique Bosco (p. 69), France Théoret, and Brossard herself (p. 98) to English Canada.

The last special issue I collaborated on was devoted to Carol Shields (issue 13.1, 1990). This was when I moved to Toronto to work full time for CBC Radio, and before she won a Pulitzer Prize. I interviewed Carol for my program, *State of the Arts*, and then for *Room*'s special issue—a luxury of a conversation which took place over two days. (Dare I say we, too, became lifelong friends?) In the full circle department, years later when Carol died, it was in *Room* that I contributed an essay, "Scrapbook of Carol" (issue 29.2, 2006), that became the germ of my book, *Random Illuminations: Conversations with Carol Shields*.

It is with amazement and pride that I congratulate the current team on their dedication to paying tribute to the past and continuing to offer expansive and inviting room for women writers and artists of the future.

You hold in your hands a remarkable anthology.

—Eleanor Wachtel, December 2016

Overturning Scarcity: Forty Years of Abundant Change

AMBER DAWN

THROUGHOUT MY FORTY-TWO YEARS OF LIVING, I've spent a lot of time with shame. But I've only felt ashamed of my writing once. It didn't take volumes, or even pages, to provoke this feeling. All in all, it was only a few words within a poem. I had changed the pronouns in a love poem from "she" to "he"—making the poem's narrative appear decidedly heteronormative.

I wasn't exactly a new writer at the time; however, the goal of building a writer's CV was new to me. Getting published is what we do, right? We get the work out there. We garner literary magazine publications, as many as possible, eventually leading to that coveted first book deal.

This vocation wasn't going so well for me. My work was, and still is, a three-pronged praxis of queer identity, individual and systemic trauma, and sex work justice, themes drawn from my own lived experience and cultural knowledge base. While this made me something of a unique darling on the poetry stage and an "it girl" at book parties, I had been rejected by almost every Canadian literary magazine, coast to coast.

Publications with the staff or volunteer capacity to include a personal note alongside their rejections were seemingly encouraging—I was always invited to submit again because the writing I had sent was "not a fit" for their magazine. After a fair few of these notes, the phrase "not a fit" became less and less sharp, and more and more curious.

Was it my effusive use of words like "rape" or "cunt" or "slut" that was not a fit, I wondered? Was it my sexuality? Was it me? I investigated by un-queering a poem, altering only the pronouns, so that the female narrator in the poem was speaking to a male recipient of her desire. With this pronoun change I resubmitted to the same Canadian literary magazine that had previously rejected me, and that year I saw my first professional publication. Except I don't refer to it as my first professional publication (that sounds like a cause for celebration). I refer to it as the poem that was edited by shame.

I grew up white, poor, and surviving trauma in a small village that frequently winds up the list of Canada's poorest postal codes. I was educated in scarcity, by the idea that there simply isn't enough for all of us to have resources or space or value. I learned that scarcity is both physical and psychological. For example, for a good part of my childhood, my single mom and I lived in an attic where neither of us had bedrooms. We could not afford physical space; we could not afford rooms of our own.

A psychological example? Well, those examples are endless. For the purpose of brevity, I'll pick one memory. When I was an awkward, runty teenager in 1989 the federal government vowed to eliminate child poverty by the year 2000. I distinctly remember the pending changes to the mothers' allowance program (a welfare program adopted by five provinces during much of the twentieth century) because my ma was crying as she filled out the new application form. Would the new program be any better? Would she still receive a monthly government cheque? In our village, the cluster of single mothers that it is, my ma wasn't the only one with questions. As the questions spread, they snow-balled into scarcity conflicts—with mothers of colour and Indigenous mothers and white mothers and newcomer mothers systemically pitted against each other. (Many unemployed men in the village were already incredulous toward mothers for receiving government cheques in the first place.) I remember how these scarcity conflicts trickled down into schoolyard gossip and tension. I cannot report on who actually collected welfare and who didn't, nor would I want to. All I can say is that the year 2000 has come and gone and child poverty in Canada has risen. The personal anecdotes I share with you are in no way unique. In fact, statistics show us that scarcity is growing.

Sometimes I try to imagine these estimated 1,331,530 poor children, as individuals, and also as a growing population of people psychologically conditioned by scarcity. Some of them will grow up to be poets, like me. Maybe they will send their work out there, like I did. And if and when they receive rejections with messages that their work is "not a fit," will those messages feel so painfully familiar, like they did when I received them?

When I was a not-so-new, but unpublished writer, I discovered that CanLit wasn't all that different from the village I grew up in. It is a landscape of scarcity. There are simply not enough publishing opportunities (or book reviews or grants for writers or invitations to literary festivals) to go around.

It may be a distant parallel, but I nonetheless have drawn an apt comparison between my ma crying while filling out a new welfare application (an origin story of my shame) and me editing out my queer truth in a poem so that CanLit might accept me.

While I am currently grateful for my decade-long run of seeing my work published, I can still say with great assurance that scarcity shapes CanLit. And who receives the bulk of rejections or messages that the writing is not a fit? Women of colour, Indigenous women, queer and trans women, and women whose writing explicitly explores trauma or difference.

I've witnessed literary agents, editors of large Canadian publishing houses, and creative writing program chairs alike try to address the glaring gap in diversity in our literary communities with bewilderment and defensiveness. Each time I see a literary professional with some degree of power respond to "why does CanLit lack diversity?" like it is a dirty question, I feel that same scarcity panic, that shame.

For the many women authors who read this, and for those readers who believe that there is an unjust bias in CanLit, you will hardly be surprised that change is occurring, because diverse writers are creating our own opportunities. The incredible thing about psychological conditioning—like the very idea of scarcity—is that we also have the capacity to learn new messages and to create change. For forty years *Room* has been at the forefront of this change.

Room changed CanLit when Cyndia Cole's groundbreaking "No Rape. No" (p. 24) was first published in the 1970s. *Room* has shown CanLit that women's complex bodies are indeed a fit, with fiction like Juliane Okot Bitek's "The Busuuti and the Bra" (p. 109) and with poems like jia qing wilson-yang's "trans womanhood, in colour" (p. 376). *Room* continues to recognize that trans and non-binary gender narratives are an inherent and esteemed part of feminist literature by calling attention to Ivan Coyote's "My Hero" (p. 195) and Lucas Crawford's "Failed Séances for Rita MacNeil" (p. 364). By honouring work like Doretta Lau's "Best Practices for Time Travel" (p. 388) and Eden Robinson's "Lament" (p. 221), *Room* challenges tired notions that social justice and Indigenous speculative fiction are anything less than synonymous with great literature.

As you read this anthology, you will undoubtedly regard it as a timely collection of seventy-eight exceptional literary works. Please, also take a moment to marvel at how scarcity and shame have not claimed a single page, not a single line or word of this anthology. You, dear readers, and I, and the seventy-five remarkable contributors are both teaching and learning a new message, right now. Say it with me. There is *Room*. We do fit.

—Amber Dawn, November 2016

The First Decade

 ❧

Volumes 1 – 10 (1975 – 1987)

Riding the Wave: An Interview with *Room* Co-Founder Gayla Reid

LEAH GOLOB

Originally from Australia, Gayla Reid played an active role in Canada's feminist movement by editing *Kinesis*, a national feminist newspaper, and co-founding *Room [of One's Own]* in 1975.

ROOM: How did you, Mary Anderson, Laurie Bagley, Pat Bartle, Penny Birnbaum, Lora Lippert, and Gail van Varseveld come to form *Room of One's Own*? What kind of work were you doing professionally around that time?

GR: *Room* grew out of a non-credit evening course on women in literature that I'd started at Vancouver Community College. The very first evening of the course I met Gail van Varseveld and the two of us adjourned for coffee to talk more about women's writing. Soon we were making plans for a feminist literary journal. Lora Lippert, Laurie Bagley, and Penny Birnbaum all came to that course and wanted to be involved in planning and producing the journal. And then we roped in some friends. What we had in common was this: we were reading women's literature as if our lives depended upon it. It was 1975, the International Year of Women, and we managed to obtain federal project funding for one year.

I don't think any of us thought of ourselves as having a "profession." Our working lives were way more tenuous than that. Laurie was the mother of two very young children, Lora was working at a small press, and I was getting by on LIP grants (Local Initiative Projects with short-term federal funding). I had been doing a PhD at UBC, but I'd dropped out. Gail was just back from England, where she'd been active in the women's movement—she found a job in hospital planning.

ROOM: What was the literary landscape like around 1975?

GR: The literary landscape, male dominated from the beginning of time, was undergoing tectonic shifts. And in Canada it was a moment of nationalist surge. Alice Munro already had her first two books out, Margaret Laurence was huge. In England, Margaret Drabble was bringing out a major novel every few years while Doris Lessing remained a towering figure. The early '70s also saw an outburst of feminist magazine publishing. In the U.S., *Ms.* magazine put out its first issue in 1972, and in England, *Spare Rib* began in 1973. There were a few feminist literary magazines around, such as *The Second Wave* and *Aphra* in the U.S. We wanted to be part of all that. To say it was exciting is an understatement.

ROOM: What was your vision for the magazine?

GR: We felt very much that we belonged in the feminist landscape. High time that women had their own space to write about whatever we wanted. Women's voices needed to be heard. Silent no more. There was no requirement that submissions should explicitly address sexism. We wanted to publish writing by women that was good writing, and we were convinced that there would be a lot of it around—and there was. At the time, writers typically got started by publishing in a little literary magazine (usually edited by men). So, *Room* would be a place where women could get started. Our voices could be heard, we could emerge, develop, blossom—all those growing images.

ROOM: I think it's very interesting that the collective was named the Growing Room Collective, as the magazine has continued to evolve over the past forty years. Did you ever imagine that kind of longevity? Why did you call yourselves a collective as opposed to an editorial team?

GR: Writers were the focus. We were thinking about the need to give women writers a space to grow, right now. We were not thinking about what might happen to *Room* in the future; we didn't look down the track beyond a year or two at most. We believed we should work collectively as opposed to hierarchically. Collectives were the feminist norm: there were daycare collectives, health collectives. The impetus came from the left and it was very much part of the times.

ROOM: Did you face any challenges in the first few years?

GR: It was a challenge to be starting a magazine as rank amateurs, but we didn't see it like that. Starting things was what feminists were doing—starting transition houses, starting rape relief organizations, starting women's centres. Why not start a literary magazine?

We ran on deeply felt enthusiasm. We had the International Women's Year funding for a year only. At the end of that year, George Woodcock, renowned author and anarchist, wrote a stellar letter for our first Canada Council application. I suspect it opened doors. And the Canada Council officers were unfailingly supportive. For special issues, we sought and received funding from the Koerner Foundation. We used funding for three things only: printing, contributor honoraria, and mailing costs.

In political terms, *Room* was challenged by its own lesbian members to promote greater visibility of lesbian content. Were we making choices driven by homophobia? Learning to identify the sneaky ways in which homophobia can assert itself was a challenge right across the women's movement, and *Room* was part of that. In addition, there were tensions you find in any group about who is using up the most oxygen, and how to integrate new members. And given that the work had glamour features (such as relating to authors), and housekeeping features (such as maintaining subscription lists), there were occasional tensions about who was doing what work.

ROOM: How were you defining feminism in the magazine's first decade? Were there any key themes or trends your contributors were writing about during the late '70s and early '80s?

GR: I'd say we subscribed to the broad women's movement understanding in that we demanded equality, full voice, full participation in every area of life, including the ability to express ourselves in writing in whatever way we chose. Members of *Room* and its contributors included feminists from the left, lesbian separatists, and mainstream feminists. All three streams were for the most part made up of white, middle-class women. Very few were women of colour or Indigenous women. As for key themes among contributors, it seems to me that women were writing about their experiences of relationships, of love and loss, and of the struggle to establish one's own identity and to be part of social change. All of that.

ROOM: Were you primarily seeking out specific Canadian female writers or choosing from works that were submitted to the magazine? What kinds of literary writing were you looking to publish?

GR: At first we were busy choosing from submitted works. After a few years, we also sought out specific Canadian female writers. The first adventure we had in this area was a special issue on Québécoise feminist writers [4.1], which was tremendously exciting because we did not know their work—very little of it was available in translation.

In terms of literary writing, I'd say we were most often looking for what Doris Lessing called the "small personal voice," which is what poetry and short fiction writing is particularly good at rendering.

ROOM: The magazine developed the tagline "a feminist journal of literature and criticism" and included a review section called "By Women Writ," as well as other critical essays. Why was the focus on criticism so integral to the magazine?

GR: We saw re-evaluating literature and how it was read as being an important part of the feminist project. Simone de Beauvoir, Kate Millett, and Germaine Greer had all provided tremendous insights by looking at how male-centred authors objectified women.

We were interested in publishing criticism that saw female characters through a feminist lens. It looked at how women wrote about women, and at how women challenged the patriarchy. Feminist criticism seemed to be a powerful tool, but as it turned out we did not receive many submissions and therefore did not publish a great deal of it. (At first we thought *Room* was going to be about a third poetry, a third fiction, and a third criticism.) Gender criticism and queer theory, as you well know, had not yet emerged.

ROOM: When you look back, what are some of the more rewarding memories of working with the magazine?

GR: The friendships are what count, some of them lifelong. As for memorable moments, I recall sitting in the late Gail van Varseveld's living room, which was our regular meeting place. Her rented apartment was on the top floor of a house in Kitsilano, with windows facing west. On certain summer evenings, golden light would be streaming in and we'd all be working together—shoulders to the wheel—and I felt I was exactly at the centre of the life I most wanted. We were making history. We were riding the wave.

Editorial

FOUNDING MEMBERS, *ROOM OF ONE'S OWN*

Virginia Woolf, one of our most distinguished novelists and critics, was the first to explain the lack of a strong female tradition in literature. In her now-famous essay of 1928, she asserted that "a woman must have money and a room of her own if she is to write . . ." Since women have been forced by custom and by law into financial dependence upon fathers and husbands, few ever acquired the freedom or the privacy necessary for artistic achievement. Working-class women had a further handicap: they were so busy trying to make ends meet and caring for their large families that they seldom had any time at all for themselves. Privacy and free time were luxuries denied to all but a very small minority of women.

As a result, early women writers produced few literary works of major significance. And the absence of a female tradition in literature was itself a deterrent to the development of such a tradition. Woolf points out that even such authors as the Brontës and Marian Evans published their novels under male pseudonyms. Without feminist writers to serve as models, and lacking the self-confidence to devise distinctive modes of expression, most women who wrote at all conformed to overwhelmingly male conventions and stereotypes.

Although the problems of the female artist in the male-dominated culture have not yet been resolved, a tradition of women in literature is developing at last. Women writers, encouraged by the women's movement of this century, are now insisting upon the validity of their feminist perceptions. Determined to tell their stories in their own ways, women of every economic and social class are turning out literature of every kind. Women writers once considered eccentrics now command respect for their role in society, as well as for their individual artistic achievements.

But the actual literary process, difficult and important as it is, is only a first step. Once she has arranged a time and a place to write, the beginning author wants to feel that other people will be interested in her finished work. Access to publication is absolutely essential if a writer is to develop her skills and her confidence.

The woman writer needs not only a private place in which to create but also "room" in publications where she can communicate her ideas and feelings to others. We of The Growing Room Collective hope that *Room of One's Own* will serve as a forum in which women can share and express their unique perspectives on themselves, each other, and the world.

Mary Anderson
Laurie Bagley
Pat Bartle
Penny Birnbaum
Lora Lippert
Gayla Reid
Gail van Varseveld

1975

No Rape. No.

CYNDIA COLE

the man who raped me
was called my lover
and so it took me
long years to name it rape.
how many sisters
join me in such
mind fuck?
i cried through the rape testimony
of other women.
cried at the court house
in the cold november rain
two years ago
that day i said
with confidence
"i have never been raped."

to have named rape love
is a heinous crime,
a tearing and twisting
of my mothertongue.
a perversion
turned against me
so devastatingly,
i do not want to believe it.
NO NO. not me. this did not
happen to me. to other women,
to my sisters, not to me.
yes, rapists attack us on the
streets, break into our homes
trap us in their stranger cars
but No No not a story of
a known man, my lover's housemate,
who i take breakfast in bed
after minding his child all

morning so he can sleep in
and he will not take breakfast
but takes me instead.

no. not rape. not really.
after all
i didn't fight back.
i didn't say no.
and weeks later he
fucked me again and then
regularly for a long time,
how could
i have possibly allowed myself
a relationship with a
man after he raped me—
a relationship begun in rape?

i did.
i was taken in.
i did not believe i could say no.
i was afraid to say no.
i knew no way to fight back.
i allowed what was against my will.
i pretended i liked it.
i did.

and it was rape.
he raped me.

i who thought myself
inviolate
suddenly know
i have been
trampled
in a cattle stampede
i once called love.

my tongue is bloated
with burning sores
from this mutilation of naming.
i cannot speak
such twisted sounds.

Grade Three

LEONA GOM

> *"We had to make the quilts fast*
> *so the children wouldn't freeze. We had to*
> *make them beautiful so our hearts*
> *wouldn't break."*   —a pioneer woman

this man is painting a picture. he is
producing *art*. this man is playing a
piano, that one writing a book. this
is also called *art*. this woman is
making a quilt. this is called a *craft*.
this woman is painting an Easter egg,
that one crocheting a tablecloth. these
are all called *crafts*. tell me
the difference again, teacher, the
difference even a child
can understand.

Was That Malcolm Lowry?

SANDY FRANCES DUNCAN

WHEN I WAS EIGHT MY FATHER DIED and my mother bought a shack on the beach at Dollarton. It was green and had painted in a white horseshoe shape on the front door: DUCUMIN. The outhouse was also green and its door invited one to BIDEAWEE, which, when I deciphered the curving unspaced words, delighted me with its scatalogical daring. It did not delight my mother however, and she threatened at least once a month for as long as we owned the shack to paint both doors, but she never did, and the shack passed out of our hands four years later still weather-beaten green, still inviting one to DUCUMIN and BIDEAWEE.

In spite of its having a name we never called it anything but "the shack," never beach house or cottage or summer camp; my mother was a respecter of connotations and our shack would have had to be larger, neater, or more decorated to qualify for another noun. It was one of the long line of squatters' shacks stretching west from Roche Point light along Burrard Inlet and north from the light up Indian Arm to Dollarton and Cove Cliff. Ours was the third shack west of Roche Point directly across the Inlet from the railroad tracks and the oil refinery's stack of constant fire.

It was possible to drive halfway from the highway to the shack down a rutted double track so narrow the thimbleberry, salmonberry and cedar branches whipped in the open windows of our '49 Prefect and left scratches on its paint. We parked in a clearing so small that only a Prefect could turn and then loaded our food, clothes, toys, cat, bathing suits, and gumboots into a battered black baby buggy my mother had procured at a second-hand shop to solve this final transportation problem. Past my favourite climbing tree and down the trail which, in fall, the maples littered with leaves like giants' splayed footprints, winding down and down, the buggy forcing back the bushes which gained revenge on our faces, the incline gradually lessening until suddenly we stood, always newly delighted, on the narrow, grassy bank between the forest and the beach.

One of the marvels of the shack was that it stood right there as well, from its back windows appearing rooted to the forest, permanent and safely anchored, yet from the front we saw nothing but water and hills across the Inlet, and the shack became a houseboat; one flip of a mooring line and it could drift forever. There was a short board-walk from the grassy verge to the veranda and if we had arrived at highest tide when the water tried to reach the grass and missed by only inches, the boards became a gangplank and we could see crabs scuttling among the newly washed and sparkling pebbles.

I see us now on the bank, the buggy stuck on some unseen rock, my mother jiggling the handle, me holding down a struggling cat while trying to lift up the front end. The cat scratches and leaps away, the buggy bounces over the rock and onto the boards and what I remember of this, even more than how I licked the small beads of blood from the scratch, what I remember are the smells. They are still stored pure and strong in some area of my brain, recorded by an olfactory nerve not jaded with smoke and drink and aging: the tangy hot and coolness of a forest, sun on cedar, on stones, on small wild strawberries, rotting, growing earth and roots, bleeding hearts and huckleberries, all damp and acrid and warm; and then on the narrow bank exchanging this pomander of rain forest for that of the beach: shock of hotter sun on me, on pebbles, on barnacled rocks, on the sea, salt, salt, do not breathe deep at first but test with gentle whiffs, rotting crabs and fish, a dead gull perhaps, seaweed dry and peppery-crackly jilted on the beach, slimy kelp strands the tide still plays with, lush and foam-collecting, woodsmoke from some shack, oil and gas from a passing boat, a piece of rusted boom chain smelling like the city; then back to us, my mother's lavender, the buggy's cracked and tangy warming leather, and, if we stand here too long, the smells of cake and apples and red-running juicy beef.

Up onto the veranda then, unlock the large padlock always stiff and unyielding with its unquenchable thirst for oil; it had come with the shack and is loathe to admit us. That time for me, while my mother turns the key and pulls the lock, squeaks back the hasp, pushes hard on the moisture-swollen door, is as long and jiggly-footed as Christmas Eve, but the door grudgingly opens and I dash in to check all three rooms and relief stills my impatience, allows the curled-up ball of time to once again relax into the infinity of summer.

There is a special sort of mustiness in a closed-up place by the sea that is not shared by lakefront cottages nor damp cellars in the city, an acrid salty sharpness, an awareness of fecund origins and destinies perhaps. It permeates the walls and floors and furniture, pricking nos-trils as the brain sorts out and rediscovers: ashes in the stove, oil cloth, linoleum, sheets and blankets, old clam and oyster shells now used for pins and paper clips, lexicon, dominoes, comic books, and popsicle sticks piled on shelves, last year's shorts and bathing suits, too-small sneakers, water-whitened; odours take on shape and solidity, becoming part of a child's primeval response to a wild and changeless place.

And now quickly outside to turn the stiffened, salt-caked clasps and remove the heavy shutters so light can help explore the shack. Four windows, one in each bedroom on the side, one at the back over the dishpan sink, one at the front looking over the veranda, all with smaller panes of glass, washed inside and out and again next day salt-sprayed, so even on sunny midsummer afternoons the shack inside was cool and dark.

The main room had a large black stove which insatiably emptied the woodbox and challenged my mother to bake cakes in its unpredictable oven, counter, table, and untidy shelves all covered with worn, red-printed oil cloth, small pantry at the back which once the cat used for a bathroom, and everywhere unmatching chairs, wood-backed or wicker.

A double bed filled each bedroom, a foot perhaps of floor space on three sides, more bed closets than rooms, old sheets on rods for doors. My mother had one and I the other, except when we had guests and then I shared her bed as I had done when my father was ill before he died. Or when we had a lot of company we children slept in blankets on the veranda, giggling, coming untucked, listening to the water lap the pebbles, to the thump and creak as the tide bunted a log into the pilings, mystified by grown-ups who preferred to sleep in beds.

Time at the shack stretched straight and sunny, marked by the coming and going of friends, and each day when the water crept up the hot beach, we swam. The beach consisted of potato-sized rocks, barnacled sharp and slippery with lime-green algae. We wore old sneakers or special bathing shoes whose rubber soles whitened and cracked with the salt and the sun. Sometimes one came off in the undertow and I hobbled and paddled to shore, trying not to place my foot on barnacles or crabs or some hungry, tickley fish. Days later the tide might deposit the lost shoe, a curled-up cadaver in the line of jetsam, and I would retrieve it triumphantly, placing it to dry with others on the veranda railing.

At high tide we could swim in front of the shack, letting ourselves into the three feet of water from the railing in the space of time before the rotted screening was replaced, a biennial chore close to the ocean.

We helped the screen's disintegration, poking at tender spots with surgical precision, the fine metal giving way under our fingers, not thinking we were being destructive, but rather hastening the time a hole was big enough to scramble through onto the railing. There we crouched, turned around, dangled over the edge, feet scraping the shingles, escaping from pirates, knives between our teeth, or jumping noisily from the burning warship, white-knuckled until our numb fingers slid off the railing and we splashed into the sea, that cold, clear salt water locating scraped knees and barnacle cuts with the unerring ability of a medieval torturer.

The beach sloped steeply so we did not have to go out very far at high tide to be up to our necks, but at low we could not go past our waists for fear of the sudden drop-off into the boating channel with its undertows and whirlpools, so frequently we went around the Point to swim where the beach was pebbly as if a philanthropist had raked away the rocks. We were cautioned to stay away from the line in the water which snaked directly from the lighthouse toward Ioco—it was a rip tide.

I certainly never went near it; Rip Tide could have been some Ogo-pogo relative who lurked just below the surface, his thrashing tail the line in the water, waiting to eat the legs of a child who went too close. Still, I learned to swim with my eyes open underwater, hoping to catch sight of Rip Tide from a distance; I never did for he was canny, slipping away when his invisibility was threatened. I did not have a face mask or snorkel; had I, I would have seen all the fearful length of him like Leviathan or Nessie, would have felt the chill thrill of terror, kicked for my very life back to the beach certain the trailing kelp's tickle was his touch—or else I would not have seen him, would have discovered Rip Tide to be only the prosaic meeting of two swirls of water, and underneath that surface turbulence only the usual and unterrifying denizens: starfish, rock cod, anemones, mussels, and the omnipresent, irritating barnacle. Had I discovered this, I might not have been con-sidered an obedient child, trusted after one warning to stay safely east of the Point.

My mother lay on a blanket against a log protected by a large, striped canvas beach umbrella, reading Agatha Christies, Mary Rob-erts Rineharts, or Georgette Heyers while alone, talking to the other adults when we had company. After some time she would get up and advance slowly into the water, standing with the skirt of her bathing suit floating around her, glaring at my teasing attempts to splash her, then launch herself forward into a personal combination of dog paddle and sidestroke, carefully keeping her hair out of the water. I loved it when my mother swam. I'd swim beside her with my head above the surface but I always floundered in a stroke or two; my head belonged in water as much as the rest of me. She was a good swimmer in spite of her idiosyncratic stroke—strong, steady, and enduring. She'd lived in English Bay and had swum each day before school, frequently across to Kitsilano and back. "In the winter too?" I'd ask, hoping to spur on these unbelievable reminiscences, but "The water was warmer then" was all she would say, and laugh.

I was rarely given the opportunity to see my mother as an endurance swimmer for as I swam alongside, moving my legs and arms twice for each of her strokes, she'd invariably announce, "You must be freezing, your lips are turning blue," and around she would turn and head for shore, ignoring my protestations, which were false bravado, for "blue lips" was nearly as terrifying a pronouncement as Rip Tide. How long would it take the rest of me to turn blue? Would I stay blue? If lips could turn blue and Anne's hair green, what other colours might the body break out in? And how could it happen without a person knowing it? Blue lips were associated with freezing, as in "freezing to death"; could I freeze to death without knowing it? I obediently trailed out of the water, but waited a few seconds to show that "blue lips" didn't bother me.

Because we were not swimming directly in front of the shack, technically we had "gone to the beach" and that entailed a picnic. I stood shivering in a towel wondering how the air had cooled so much when the sun still shone, and watched my mother put out the food. It was packed in square glass containers with carved daisies on the sides and matching lids, potato salad, devilled eggs, lettuce and tomatoes, buttered raisin bread, and I remembered a time before my father went to hospital, before he was moved into my bedroom to die, a very long time before the shack, when the three of us had gone to sandy city beaches with these same containers. I knew my father had not liked sandwiches at a picnic; it was that sort of knowledge one has always had about one's family. I assumed my mother had told me. Or maybe, now I wonder, because of the way that sort of knowledge gets confused, if it was my mother who did not like sandwiches, for although she had given away my father's suits and sword and revolver from the war, she continued to use the glass containers.

As distinctly different as the times of high and low tide were the times of having company and the times of being alone. I couldn't have said which I preferred, no more than I could place a value on the tides. Both had good aspects and bad; at low tide clams and crabs and starfish were exposed for tormenting, but high tide transformed the pebbles into jewels and brought the phosphorescence up the beach. What I did not like, however, was the change from one state to another, from low to high tide, from companionship to solitude. No more does my daughter now; to get ready to go out or to leave to come home provokes an irritated outburst and I still do not like the transition between holidays and routine.

Then, at the shack, the arrival of company meant my solitary activities were interrupted by noisy, excited children who claimed the forest and beach in undisciplined forays, perhaps unwittingly trampling the seedling I was nurturing into a West Coast beanstalk. But a week later, the exodus of this same company left the forest echoing with boredom and loneliness, left no pirates with whom to jump into the sea, no noisy, nightly games of snap or cheat, no cowboys and indians and so no reason to rebuild the fort.

After I had grumpily waved goodbye I informed my mother so petulantly and continuously that there was nothing to do, she lost patience and I could retaliate in anger. With her lips pressed together she stomped to the shack, already reclaimed by the cat, and her interrupted reading, and I stomped to my favourite tree, a cedar with bushy, low-growing branches which overhung the path. I climbed as high as my fear of heights allowed and sat in a green cave, peeling strips of bark off the trunk, crushing needles one at a time until my nostrils were filled with pungency, knowing the world to be a cruel and unfair place and my mother its inimical manifestation.

Slowly, as the branch turned my leg first frizzy-feeling and then numb, I remembered the hole I'd been going to dig, or the candies left in the box the company had brought, or that I'd not been able to climb my favourite rock or read my comics in peace, and maybe the fort would make a better hermit's cave than Wild West outpost.

I opened the door and my mother looked up from her book. I studied her face; guilt prompted my apology. "Yes," she usually said, sounding impassive, but she held out a hand and I advanced and put my head on her shoulder, my face in the softness of her neck. "You have your father's temper, you must learn to control it, he did, he was a gentle person." I vowed I would learn, but then, with greater guilt now he was dead, thought he could have left his daughter better gifts than red hair and temper, he could have left her height and slimness.

After the inevitable mention of controlling my temper, I could feel her neck muscles tighten into a smile. I stepped back and smiled at her and we shared the remaining candies—one for her and one for me, whether there were two or nine and if the number was uneven, I got a knife and divided the last—half for her and half for me. Still hungry, I offered to make her a sandwich as well but she usually declined, still smiling, and I got out the bread and peanut butter and the other most important ingredient, pickle or apple or lettuce or cucumber, whatever was my fancy of the week.

At home my mother made popsicles in flat, coffin-shaped aluminum containers, out of strawberry, lime, or cherry Kool-Aid, and once, only once, out of tomato juice. She never made popsicles at the shack; we had no electricity, no ice, no running water. We washed dishes, clothes, and ourselves in the ocean with cakes of special salt-water soap which never seemed to lather. Occasionally I and whatever children were visiting were made to take the soap with us on our swims. Those were the best baths, washing each other's hair, the soap bar skipping out of our hands, rinsing our hair by diving for the soap, sometimes finding it before the undertow dragged it to the middle of the Inlet, where I imagined some mother fish delighted, her babies not. It did not float. We lost a lot of soap.

We brushed our teeth in the sea as well, the company children trying to use their Colgate or Ipana, spitting white blobs among the phosphorescence we stirred up with our toothbrushes until either the taste or my mother convinced them salt water was a better cleanser than their commercial products.

My mother must have had some deep alliance with the ocean— which she called "salt chuck" with West Coast pioneer familiarity—for there was not an ailment it could not cure, not a mineral it did not contain, not a beneficence it could not bestow. Scraped legs, cut hands, gouged knees, all were sent into the chuck, where the iodine, she said, was a better antiseptic than bottled Mercurochrome. Headaches and mild fevers were cured by brisk swims, although the sufferers were watched to ascertain that in their weakened state they avoided the clutches of both Rip Tide and "blue lips," and if the ailment were too severe—though I cannot imagine what that might have been—pneumonia perhaps?—a good dose of brisk salt air was next best.

My mother's trust in natural cures might have been consolidated by Rena. For the three years before his death my father had been in and out of hospital, which necessitated my mother's return to work and a succession of housekeepers who cooked and cleaned and looked after me. One was Kate from Switzerland, whose idea of making toast was to cook only one side of the bread, but it was Rena, a short, fat, Eastern European woman of indeterminate age but determined ideas, who might have influenced my mother's naturopathy.

I fell when I was seven, pretending I could ride a friend's two-wheeler, and exchanged half the gravel of the road for the skin on my arm. Rena's cure was plantain which she picked from the boulevard in front of our house and I attended school in utter mortification with green leaves peeking out of the gauze bandage. Every day when she changed the limp leaves for fresh ones she dragged me to my mother saying, "See, Missus? Real good now, God gives us best," and my mother was so impressed by the cleanliness of the wound she ignored my pleas that Johnson & Johnson's cure, if not more efficacious, was at least less obvious, and off to school I went to have my pride hurt worse from laughter than my arm had hurt from the fall. Definitely the cure over-shadowed the ailment and I finally understood my mother's expression "adding insult to injury."

The salt chuck could not provide drinking water and it was my job to trek up the trail, up the rutted, bumpy road and along the highway to a gas station, where I could also buy real popsicles, the most surprising of which were root beer and blueberry.

Years later at friends' cottages in Northern Ontario when we emerged from cool woods to hot, hot highway, my mind was unwillingly assailed by those early emergences from cool to hot, pails clanking against my legs, and then, on the return trip, from hot, tar-sticky macadam to the relief of the forest trail, pails now pulling my shoulder muscles, digging into my hands, slopping water on my sneakers. In Northern Ontario I squelched the unwanted memories, but sometimes wondered at their constant rise from the basement of my mind, for the birch and spruce and pine, lakes and rocks of Ontario were so unlike the cedar, maple, fir, gentle rotting humus and salt tang of Dollarton; only the contrast of hot and cool remained; was that enough, I wondered, to return me with phoenix-fullblown-ness to this earlier time?

Once, coming down the trail in the early morning, the water pails slipping and slopping from a stick across my shoulders, I surprised a deer. I stopped, but must already have made too much noise, pails rubbing bushes, feet clicking rocks, for it dashed away immediately. After that I stalked everywhere slowly and silently, a deerhunter, but although I was allowed within five feet of birds, the deer always eluded me. So did the raccoons and, fortunately, the bears. I caught slow salamanders on the muddy path, and tried for a while to salt a crow's tail, followed our cat on mystery tours, short because I lost him or grew bored while he sat.

Once I found an injured squirrel and carried it to the shack rolled up in my T-shirt. It lay so still I was afraid it was dead but then it twitched and I knew I could save it, held it gently against the warmth of my chest, and showed my mother, whispering as one does near the ill. But she said it was dead, and I said, "No, it moved," and she said that happened—an after-twitch. I didn't believe her and wanted to say so, but the last time I had was on top of my memory. "Your father is dead, he died in the night." "I don't believe you, you're lying," and I'd run to my room. It was empty. "Where is he?" I'd asked and she'd told me they'd taken his body in the night. Now I wanted to ask if he'd twitched like the squirrel, if everything twitched when it died, but there are some things not safe to ask, some things one does not want to know.

The squirrel was stiffening and there was blood on my shirt so I found an empty candy box, dug a hole and had a funeral with a doll and a Mortimer Snerd puppet for pallbearers. We sang "Onward Christian Soldiers" as we had at my father's funeral and then "Hark the Herald Angels." I covered the box with earth and made a popsicle stick cross on which I carved *SQUIRREL R.I.P.* Later I dug up the box and poked the squirrel to make sure it was really dead.

Company at the shack consisted primarily of women and children, friends of my mother who came for a week, leaving their husbands at work in the city, or career women like her who had married late and been widowed early, who had only children about my age. These women, social workers and nurses, were the dominant decision-makers of my youth, the hewers of wood, wielders of machetes and hammers, and men were the background shadows, loved, enjoyed, considered, and occasionally deferred to—as were the children. It was the natural order to me that King George would die and the Princess become ruler of Canada with all that televised pomp and ceremony. I doubt I had even heard of St. Laurent.

Both my parents had large families and I had many uncles who came to visit and whose questions my mother's frown made me answer politely before I was dismissed to play. Later I was summoned for leave-taking, which consisted of a kiss and a quarter, but my uncles had military moustaches and moist lips and the latter gift barely compensated for the former. Once I ran away from an exiting uncle, trying to appear for my mother's sake, teasing and silly, but clearly aware that if left to me, I would not return to submit to the rape-like humiliation of that kiss. Just as clearly, however, I was aware that a man's kiss was something women put up with, like dirty dishes and dust, soon disposed of and worthy of no further attention in the real business of running the world. I returned, I submitted.

Men might have seemed strange creatures with unpleasant demands but boys were my favourite company. Some of the girls who came to the shack were afraid of snakes, bothered by sandflies and crabs, preferred to stay inside reading my comics—although they complained there were too many Superboys and not enough Katy Keenes. The girls sometimes cried when scratched by bushes or barnacles, but the boys saved their tears for importances, fights usually initiated by me—with boys not only did I not have to control my temper, it gave me enough strength to push and kick them to the ground, in one instance to rip the shirt off my friend's back, buttons popping in Clark Kent fashion.

We played complicated games involving knives and sticks, forts and axes, that went on for days, then with sudden consensus switched to the beach where we constructed boats out of scrounged wood, nails, popsicle sticks, and string for railings. Sometimes the warships were elaborated into houseboats with the addition of curtains attached so they really opened. The boys, away from their neighbourhoods, would play with my dolls, but here their imaginations flagged, and we usually switched to cars in the dirt at the edge of the forest.

I don't think I thought of myself as a boy, but neither particularly as a girl. I was fully aware of the anatomical differences which we had discussed and illustrated far away from the shack, but other than that minor and obvious difference, which I thought more a nuisance for a boy than a lack for a girl, I regarded us as the same, and whether I felt closer to boys or to girls depended on our activity: pirates or dolls, warships or houseboats. However, I must have wondered what it felt like to be a boy or thought that with practice I could compete in the forest, for once, early in our time at the shack, I walked into BIDEAWEE, pulled down my pants, thrust my hips forward, and tried, as I had observed, to direct the stream forward. I then had to wipe the seat and floor and reach the shack unnoticed, there to change my shorts, pants, socks, and shoes. Even the fact that no one knew my failure did not lessen the humiliation that there was something I would never master, no matter my desire or practice. It was after that I deliberately turned my back when boys had to pee in the woods, and told them they were disgusting.

Later, perhaps the following year, my mother introduced a further complication in my denial of sex differences by insisting I stop running around in public without a shirt. I stared hard at the boys' chests, cool and free in the sun; my nipples no longer looked the same. From then on I wore an undershirt as well as a blouse or T-shirt, began to hunch my shoulders, continued to beat the boys in fights or races, continued to try to believe there were no differences, but when my conviction waned or reality impinged, I was, for a very long time, angry that this was the way it was.

Although my remembered images of the shack are always bright with summer sun, we did spend Thanksgivings and winter weekends there as well, and then the grey waves beat up the beach, inexorably chewing at the rocks' thin snow cover until all lay nude and abject under the vanquisher's retreat. We walked along the beach at low tide, around the Point as far as the Dollarton pier then back again, our feet growing numb in cold gumboots, but this discomfort ignored in the delights a winter sea threw up: seaweed of course, brown kelp, green sea lettuce, dark purplish dulse, and mixed with this glass floats from Japan, old fish net, corroded boom chain, rubber boots and summer sneakers, things from houses and wrecked boats—red and yellow chairbacks, mugs, plates, shirts, unidentifiable metal pieces, rusting stoves, and dishpans.

On these beachcombing expeditions we saw the permanent denizens of Dollarton, a private group of people who shunned the summer residents. One man and woman we met quite regularly, at first only risking a smile above our acquisitions—a glass float, gnarled driftwood, or chairback—and then, later, stopping to talk. The man wore a red and black tartan mackinaw and the woman a faded, green knit hat. They lived, we thought, in the shack with window-box geraniums—the only window box on the beach. They were friendly; the woman and my mother talked, the man smiled at me, but I always walked away, continuing our search if we had just set out or heading home if we were done, for the man had a moustache like my uncles.

After that I seemed to see them everywhere, singly or together, as with the selective perception of learning a new word which then jumps into the air from every page or conversation.

As well as a favourite tree, I had a favourite rock, one of two left behind on the beach by a retreating glacier. It was about five feet high with handholds and a gentle upward slope. The tide reached it first and I frequently sat until the rock was an island and water had inched up its barnacle skirt, sat looking across the Inlet until the water behind me had climbed as far up the beach as I could jump.

The other rock, farther to the west and from the water, was nearly seven feet high with steeper and smoother sides. A taller, older company child had claimed it as her rock and truly it was, for I could not scale it without help and that was only grudgingly and occasionally forthcoming.

Every few months when she was not around I attempted to climb the rock; one day, cold and raw in the fall or spring, the man was suddenly there. He said, "Shall I give you a leg up?" and held out his hands cupped together. I must have been concentrating on my scrabbling failures for I had not heard him approach and I jumped with shock and fear. The rock hid both of us from sight of the shack and there was no one else on the beach. I wanted to run away but I would have had to dash by him and risk his grabbing me; more than that, I would have had to manifest my fear and I knew somehow, as with my uncles' kisses, that to let the enemy know my fear would increase its power over me. Still, I could neither let him touch me nor accept his help, and silently I shook my head and with a gargantuan struggle made easier from the force of fear, I gained a previously unnoticed toehold and threw myself on top of the rock.

From there I could see the green shack, smoke from the chimney, a corner of BIDEAWEE behind, could look down on my old favourite rock and the man. He still stood there, smiling. He said, "Good for you," as if he understood, and I smiled back, embarrassed in case he understood it all.

Untouchables: A Memoir

AUDREY THOMAS

WHEN I HEARD MY MOTHER SAY IT, "grass widow," I imagined her to be the very best sort of widow, a *summa cum laude* widow, who went faithfully to the cemetery every day to water her husband's grassy grave. Although I was still very young I knew quite a lot about cemetery etiquette, for we regularly visited two, one for each side of the family. We took along pruning shears and a trowel and spicy-smelling geraniums in brown cardboard wraparound containers. My father and mother would get to work on the graves (his father and mother in the Ross Park Cemetery, her mother out in Corbettsville) while my sister and I wandered along the paths, reading inscriptions, sighing over little cement lambs (sure sign of the death of a baby), daring each other to push open the doors of mausoleums.

But the way my mother said it, "grass widow," with an introductory sniff and a toss of her head, seemed to contradict my romantic image of the absolute in wifely devotion. "Oh, she's only a grass widow." Only. This to my father, who had just come home from work and was standing in the kitchen with his coat on.

My mother had a lot of expressions which interested me. If someone burped or belched she always said, "Pardon me, Mrs. Astor." (When I asked who Mrs. Astor was, I was told she was "one of the Four Hundred" and then had to ask who they were.) If, on one of our Sunday drives along the Chenango Canal, the car went over a pothole our mother said we'd just hit a "thank-you ma'am." She called "spineless" men "milk-toasts" (after the comic-strip character Mr. Milquetoast) and used words like "gumption" and "spunk" to refer to people she approved of. She called having your period "falling off the roof."

"What's a grass widow?" I asked. I was setting the table in the dining room. My mother did not answer. Little Pitchers weren't supposed to hear. The fact that she did not answer meant that it probably had something to do with sex. It was no good looking it up in our abridged desk dictionary and I was too shy to ask the librarian downtown. I wasn't stupid. If it had to do with sex she'd never tell me. And she would probably tell my mother that I'd asked.

Once I had read in the evening paper about a child molester. But I got it wrong, or I got the idea almost right but I got the word wrong. I thought it said "mole-taster," a child mole-taster. And then my father came home so I didn't have a chance to read the article again. It sounded so disgusting, this mole-tasting; and as I had a very prominent and rather pretty mole on the left side of my neck I went around in terror for weeks, knowing there was a mole-taster at large, wearing my coat collar turned up whenever I had to go outside. Finally I went to the big dictionary at the library. It wasn't there. "Mole" was there, all three kinds, and "molecular" and "molecule." I was trembling with fear. The crime was so disgusting it wasn't in the dictionary. Then I saw "molest," which I realized was the word I'd actually seen in the *Press*. Meddle hostilely or injuriously with (person). It was all quite vague but I felt such relief to think it had nothing to do with moles, my kind of mole, that I didn't really care. I had not noticed the librarian, who had come up behind me.

"What are you looking up, dear?" she said in her rather unctuous voice. (The truth was that she didn't like the children in the library, especially when they ventured out of the children's section.) I closed the book with a slam and blushed furiously.

"Nothing," I said.

"It has taken you a long time," she answered sweetly, "to look up nothing. There may be other people waiting to use the dictionary."

There weren't, of course, but I could tell by her face she thought I'd been looking up dirty words. After that I was always aware that she was "keeping an eye" on me. Every Saturday, as she checked out my books, she read the titles aloud, as though she expected to find *Forever Amber* or *The Chinese Room* among them.

So I finally let that one drop—the meaning of grass widow, and yet it remained at the back of my mind for over thirty years, and the other day I heard myself asking a great friend of mine who is of my mother's generation, although English, not American, if she had ever heard the phrase "grass widow."

"Oh yes," she said. "I think it has something to do with India—going up to the hill stations to escape the heat." With India? To escape the heat? I had heard the expression in a small town in New York State. We didn't know anybody who'd been to India.

"Are you sure?" I said.

"Oh, I think so. The women and children were sent up into the hills when the weather got too hot, and the men often had to stay behind." She is English, and of the last days of the Empire, and yet it worried me.

"I don't think that's what my mother meant. I think it meant something nasty—at least to my mother."

We looked it up in her *Concise Oxford*. "A wife temporarily separated from her husband; a divorced woman; a discarded mistress." We were both right.

It was one of the last two that my mother was talking about, a divorced woman or a discarded mistress. But how did grass get involved in it? Were these grass widows (second and third sense) put out to pasture like old horses? Had they "gone to seed"? Had they "taken a roll in the hay"? Words fascinate me. I like to go right back to their beginnings. It delights me to discover that a tulip, so eminently Dutch, is related linguistically to a Sikh's *turban*, that our common daisy was named after an Anglo-Saxon kenning for the sun, *daeges eage* or "the eye of day." It becomes addictive, looking up words. So the next time I was at the public library I sought help from the *OED*.

> *grass widow*
> *1) an unmarried woman who has co-habited with one or more men; a discarded mistress (obs.)*

And there I found Oliver Goldsmith, in *The Goddess of Silence* (1760), making a character say, "I have made more matches in my time than a grass widow."

Dialect dictionaries, says the *OED*, often give this old meaning, but the *modern* meaning is:

> *2) a married woman whose husband is absent from her*

And it is, indeed, an expression which seems to have originated in Anglo-India. So we have a man named Lang, writing in *Wandering in India* (1859), "grass widows in the hills are always writing to their husbands when you drop in on them." Poor Mr. Lang! Or Lady Dufferin, in *Vice-Regal Life in India* (1889), mentioning "the expectant husbands [who] come out to meet the 'grass widows' who have travelled with us."

So, one's wife was sent to the country, "turned to grass," went away on a holiday, lived, temporarily, "the rustic life." All that is perfectly clear. But one suspects that meaning 2) came out of meaning 1) and those Empire Builders were having their little joke. At any rate, no dictionary has yet told me how the expression originated, although it goes back in print to the early sixteenth century and was not "obs." in New York State in the '40s. I have more research to do. I still don't understand, with the older meaning, why "grass." I did find a "hempen widow" explained: that was a woman who was unfortunate enough to have been married to a man who was hanged. I suspect that the "roll in the hay" idea is close to the truth. A "bastard" is really a child born of the saddle, a *fils de bast* (i.e. not a "child of the bed") and a grass widow may be a woman whose "marriage" took place in a haystack or convenient field—a greenwood marriage, if you like.

If my mother meant simply a divorced woman (although I don't think so) then she may have been referring to Mrs. Cowan, mother of our best friend Margaret. Divorcées (Di-vohr-says, as my mother made a point of pronouncing it) came in for her strong disapproval.

Mary Cowan had lived in our town all her life and had gone to high school with my father. (My mother was a year ahead of them and I think it always embarrassed her to admit she married a younger man.) Her husband (ex-) had been in my mother's class. My mother was very torn in her attitude to Mrs. Cowan, who lived just down the street. Mary Cowan had been a Whitehead and the Whiteheads were a "good" family. Indeed, until old Mr. Whitehead's death they had owned half of the town's best department store. Margaret could still go in and buy something, adding the magic words "stockholder's discount please" to the clerk behind the counter. We, on the other hand, usually put things on layaway with a couple of dollars down. But Mary Whitehead had married Scottie Cowan, handsome as a prince but no good, a drunk who squandered Mary's family's money. ("Handsome is as handsome does," said my mother.) In the days before the actual divorce, at which time Scottie went "out west" somewhere to live and eventually die, I can remember seeing him fall out of taxis in front of their house. If we were outside playing hopscotch with Margaret, on our front walk or theirs, we tried not to look. Sometimes the taxi driver helped him up and to the door; sometimes Mrs. Cowan, who must have been waiting behind the front room curtains, rushed out and helped him up the steps. Eventually she divorced him and I guess that would have been acceptable to my mother (although it was then, as it is still to a large degree, the woman's "fault" if a marriage failed) but Mrs. Cowan started having boyfriends. She wasn't a particularly pretty woman but she was small and trim and wore clothes well. I suppose she was in her mid-thirties when she finally got rid of her husband. She, too, "drank" (no one drank anything in our house except some Virginia Dare in the fruit cocktail on Thanksgiving and Christmas) but she didn't have a "problem." Or if she did she was very discreet about it. I seem to remember her always with a glass of something or other in her hand, and sometimes she wanted to carry on long, rather meandering conversations with us if we were playing cards in the living room or once again rearranging all the furniture in the big old doll's house which stood on the first floor landing. But I thought she was quite nice, as mothers went. She would let us touch the crystal stoppers of her perfume bottles to the backs of our ears (I remember her once telling me that when I was a "big girl" I should always remember to put a dab of perfume behind my *knees*, something I still haven't tried), or let us play dress-up with her discarded gowns, shoes, and hats. Margaret called her mother's boyfriends Uncle this and Uncle that, and she was babysat by the cleaning woman whenever her mother went out with one of the uncles.

"*Hmnpf*," my mother would snort, "'uncle'! In a pig's eye!" (This was another one of my mother's expressions which interested me.) Mrs. Cowan never married any of these men, so maybe there really wasn't anything going on; but the fact that she was divorced and going out with a lot of men could have given her near grass widow 3) status, I am sure, in my mother's eyes. "And with a daughter, too!" My mother, generally speaking, did not like people to "have fun," and parents, particularly, were not supposed to "have fun." When we came home smelling of French perfume we were told to go and wash immediately and my mother would wonder aloud to my father if perhaps we should be stopped from playing there. My father had no opinion whatsoever. He wasn't meant to. Most of my mother's "conversations" (as opposed to fights) with my father were really soliloquies.

One day, shortly after he disappeared beyond our ken forever, I came home from school to find Mr. Cowan swaying back and forth in our kitchen, totally smashed, a bucket of smelts in his hand. He was trying to persuade my mother to accept them, as a gift, and she in her turn, arms covered with flour and a leprous patch of flour on her fore-head, was trying to get him to go home. She wasn't frightened of him; indeed I was surprised to see that she was laughing, for she laughed seldom. He kept insisting that she take the smelts "for old times' sake" and she kept telling him to go home or she'd have to call the paddy wagon.

Then when she saw me her manner changed and she became much more forceful and businesslike. She had him out of the house in no time and he stood in the street, still swaying, still carrying the bucket of smelts, calling her name, until she stuck her head out the door and told him she really would call the police if he didn't go home. She was truly angry by now, and he knew it, and went off home. I don't think I ever saw him again after that.

But worse than a grass widow or a divorcée, the worst thing you could possibly be, was an Old Maid. It was a far, far better thing to have had a man you couldn't keep than never to have had a man at all. My parents had terrible and regular fights, my mother often threat-ened to leave (once she even went as far as Scranton but came back and phoned from the depot for my father to come and pick her up). They slept in separate rooms and always had, for as long as I could remember. Sex was not only not mentioned in our household; it really didn't exist. Even our dog was spayed before she ever had a litter of puppies. But better unhappily married than not married at all. We lived in terrible fear (I think just about every girl of my generation did) that we might never marry. Then we would never have the won-derful post-war kitchens promised us in *The Ladies Home Journal* or *The Women's Home Companion*. We would never have the option of wearing Mother-Daughter dresses with our very own little girl. There would be no engagement ring ("She's lovely; she's engaged; she uses *Pond's*"), no wedding or baby showers, no silver pattern or Quaker Lace tablecloth. We knew that Old Maids didn't live in "homes." They lived in boarding houses or dreary apartments, or in the worst rooms (peeling wallpaper, windows with broken sashes) in other people's homes. They wore sensible shoes, ugly black or brown lace-ups with minimal heels, because they had to walk or take buses to the places where they worked for a living, as teachers or librarians or "compan-ions" to elderly invalids. Those sensible shoes were the outward and visible sign that these women had to "stand on their own two feet." In the game of Old Maid (which is still played, alas) it didn't matter that the odd Queen was a queen; what mattered was that she was alone, a solitary bird in a gilded cage. Everybody knows that if you get left with the Old Maid you have lost, you *are* the Old Maid. (And everybody knows that this sort of card game is usually played by little girls.) In Hoyle's *Book of Rules*, in the section called "Games for Children," where Old Maid comes between Slap-jack and Pig, it says: "The games in this section are recommended for children because they are simple enough to be understood by the very young, not because they are without interest to adults." My daughter has an up-to-the-minute version of the game called "Fussbudget." On the back of the package it says: "Don't be left holding the Fussbudget card when all the pairs have been played." And just who is the Fussbudget? Why Lucy, of course, of *Peanuts* fame, standing there with her mouth wide open, its interior as black as the Black Hole of Calcutta. "Fussbudget," my ass. All the other *Peanuts* characters are there in pairs. Lucy, like the cheese, like the odd Queen, stands alone.

When I was at the public library looking up grass widow I couldn't resist taking a peek at what the *OED* had to say about Old Maids.

1) a woman who remains considerably beyond the marrying age; an elderly spinster; usually connoting habits characteristic of such a condition. [Such as being a fussbudget.]

2) a name of a bivalve mollusc of the family myidae, *also called Gaper or Gaping Clam.* [Oh Lucy!]

3) a West Indian name of a plant.

4) a simple round game at cards in which one card (usually a queen) is removed from the pack and the rest distributed among the players, who draw cards from one another till all are paired except the odd one, the holder of which receives this title.

In 1673, in a book or play called *Lady's Calling*, it is remarked that "an Old Maid is now looked upon as the most calamitous Creature in nature." And in 1874 somebody said, "Chastity, cards and scandal, the solid comforts of Old-Maidenship."

"To stand on the maid," of a woman meant to remain single, and the English equivalent of the guillotine was called "the Maid." But a maid was only a "maid" until she got married. If she *passed* "the marrying age," then she became an Old Maid. People write songs about maids and maidens, poems too. The closest thing to a poem about an Old Maid (a "celebration of such a creature") would be T.S. Eliot's poem about his aunt.

Everybody used to have at least one "maiden aunt" in the family. Our family was long on Old Maids of this kind.

"All paired except the odd one," says the *Book of Sports and Pastimes* (1891). That was part of it, of course. Old Maids were "odd" in the other sense as well. They were fussbudgets, sharp-tongued, or too nervous, given to dark unattractive dresses and those sensible shoes. And why were these women odd? Because they didn't have husbands, had never had them (unlike widows and divorcées), didn't even *pretend* to have had them (unlike certain grass widows). They had been passed by and passed over. (The idea that any of them might have turned down a man—except under extreme parental pressure—was unthinkable. The idea that some of them might have preferred to live alone was likewise.) I have heard a contemporary of mine, a very intelligent man who teaches literature at a university, say of an unmarried female colleague of his who was causing some trouble in the department, "Oh well, she's over forty and under-fucked," a phrase not original with him but a clever "modern" way of saying that she was behaving like a classic Old Maid. In my youth no one would have put it so bluntly. The fact that our three maiden great-aunts and two maiden ordinary aunts had no sex life was never mentioned, at least not in my hearing. It was lack of husbands as status symbol, not husband as fucker, that made my aunts the object of my mother's scorn. Looking back now I see that my mother used *exactly* the same tone of voice, the same note of contempt, the same snort, for grass widows, divorcées, and Old Maids. So, in her eyes, you were damned whether you did or didn't ("she's only a grass widow," "she's only a frustrated Old Maid") for the only acceptable state, the only *respectable* state, after the age of about twenty-two, was marriage. No matter what other accomplishments these women may have had, what honours they may have achieved, they had failed miserably in a woman's primary task—to find a husband, any husband—and to keep him. (Later, in my cynical twenties, I would come to think of this as the "half-a-loaf" theory of marriage.) The search for a husband was basically materialistic, however much the stories in the ladies' magazines might try to disguise it. I have some old *Saturday Evening Post*s from the 1930s and '40s. One of my favourite advertisements is for Oneida Silverplate. A young, Joan Crawford-looking woman, in a satin dinner gown, is leaning across a candlelit table saying, "How handsome you are tonight, Jim, almost as handsome as our Oneida Silverplate." Marriage was an economic and social armour which protected you not only from the slings and arrows of outrageous fortune, provided you with Oneida Silverplate and a Philco Radiogram, but also from the barbed tongues of the World at Large.

One of my great-aunts died when I was so young that I do not remember her; but I remember the other two quite well. They lived someplace upstate, Oneonta or Syracuse, and they were both retired schoolteachers. They came once a year to have a visit with my father, their dead brother's son, but they didn't stay with us, they stayed at the Arlington Hotel, a very respectable hotel within easy walking distance of the station. They came to tea but never, that I can remember, to supper, and brought us our annual presents of new and rather expensive dresses which were always beautiful but not always in the right size. I remember one which I adored from the minute I took it carefully out of the tissue paper. A middy dress with a white lanyard at the end of which dangled a little silver whistle. All agreed that it really did not fit while I, red-faced from sucking in my breath, kept insisting that it did. The aunts wrapped it up and took it back home with them, and I was sure that I would never see the like of it again, but wonder of wonders, a package arrived within the week and there was an identical dress, complete to lanyard and whistle, in a size more suitable for a girl who had been so thoughtless as to "shoot up" in the past year.

I do not remember the faces of these aunts and wonder if I would recognize them from photographs. I do remember *their* dresses, which were of black crepe, the sort of dresses my grade schoolteachers wore, only without the powdering of chalk dust. And their shoes, black and sturdy, and one of them, I think it was Aunt Aggie, whom my mother liked much better than her older sister, Katherine, had wonderfully slim ankles, rather like the slim "legs" one sometimes sees on a heavy, old-fashioned sideboard. They had both retired when I "knew" them (of course I didn't really know them at all, except from what my mother chose to tell me), although Katherine had risen to be superintendent of schools, in her district, before she left the system. My mother told me that Aunt Aggie had wanted to marry but the family put a stop to it, so she became an RC (the way my mother told it there was a definite link of cause and effect). Aunt Katherine was the Old Maid with the sharp tongue and she and my mother barely tolerated one another; Aunt Aggie, in spite of her loyalty to the Pope, was "the sweet one." That's all I remember except that one of them fell off the pier while waiting for the Staten Island ferry and although she was rescued, she failed rapidly after that. They were both enormously stout and I remember thinking how she must have looked in the water, my great-aunt, bobbing up and down in the water and crying for help. Even when she was dry you could see all the ridges of her corsets. I was embarrassed for her, hoped no one laughed, and was very glad I wasn't there.

There was another aunt, Aunt Gertrude, whom I think was only called "Aunt" (the way English children call their mother's friends Aunt this and that) and whom I never saw. She lived somewhere in New Jersey and may or may not have been a distant relative of my mother's. Being the little materialist that I was I remember her only because she sent us delightful presents at Christmas, things like a dozen pencils with our names printed in gold, a piece of the Blarney Stone with an accompanying legend, a lucky rabbit's foot, Scottie dog magnets. She probably ordered by mail from the backs of magazines and I'm sure the presents didn't cost very much, but they were always the sort of thing a kid would like. My mother, fond of imparting genealogical information as well as her personal history at the slightest excuse, must have told me who "Aunt Gertrude" was, but I have lost it, that information. She had cataracts, that I remember, and we children could not decipher her Christmas notes.

And then there were Aunt Hazel and Aunt Grace.

My father had a brother, younger, and an older sister. This sister was also an Old Maid. She was much younger than the great-aunts, naturally, but as my parents had me and my sister in their forties she was probably at least forty-five when I first begin to remember her. She was a brilliant mathematician and rose to be a full professor of mathematics at a good college upstate. For a long time she was a house-mother in a sorority house and I believe she was very popular with the girls. She actually owned the house we lived in, her father's house—a fact that galled my mother—and we paid her a nominal rent. She also bailed us out financially whenever my father was in a jam. She, like the great-aunts, used to come for an annual visit, although that visit often ended in a fight.

I have a couple of really bizarre memories associated with Aunt Hazel. One concerns a year we spent in Ithaca while my father was getting a master's degree at Cornell. We rented a huge, drafty, old house and had very little money. At some point or other I had a smallpox vaccination (I was then about four years old) and my mother, who had a small cut on her hand, became infected. I remember, or *think* I remember, that there was a possibility she might have to have her arm off. Could that have been so? Could my sister really have said to me that if mother did have her arm off it was ALL MY FAULT? At any rate, she had to go to the hospital and I was sure *that* was my fault. Did I not have the itchy scab on my own arm to prove it? My father, totally involved in his studies, could not manage and my aunt came up and looked after us for several days. Eventually my mother, both arms still attached, came home.

I remember nothing specific about my aunt's stay except that it is associated with the fear that I had caused my mother to lose her arm (would they saw it off and throw it in the garbage?) and I knew that my mother would never forgive me. I was not a child who told people what I was thinking (I had learned very early that that was usually the quickest route to trouble) but perhaps I did break down and tell my aunt, for she and I always seemed to have some special relationship toward one another.

The other thing I remember is my mother standing in the doorway to the dining room—I must have been about ten when this took place— and tearing up a twenty-dollar bill my aunt had given her about half an hour before. I can't remember any of the words of that particular quarrel. Probably it started for the usual reasons—my mother felt that my aunt, because she was always willing to come to the rescue, kept my father a perpetual "mama's boy"—but I remember being horrified at the sight of my mother screaming and tearing the money into smaller and smaller bits. Twenty dollars was a lot of money in those days.

But still Aunt Hazel made her annual visit. We went down to the bus depot with my father, who hurried along, not liking to be seen with all those people minding cardboard suitcases and parcels done up with string. He would try and get there just after the bus pulled in, grab her suitcase and move off fast toward the exit, she and the children hurrying along behind. My father was a Mason; Masons didn't take buses, they travelled by private car or train. When I was a teenager my aunt went all the way out to California on the Greyhound and sent back a lot of postcards saying she was having a wonderful time. "*Humpf,*" went my mother, who was born in New Jersey but hadn't been out of New York State in years except for a brief family trip to Massachusetts and an even briefer one to Buffalo and Niagara Falls. My aunt, for all her solvency, her Phi Beta Kappa key, her friendships with the sorority girls, was an Old Maid, forever and ever amen, a real fussbudget (this term was actually used) who put too much emphasis on religion (High Episcopalian), wore gabardine skirts in dull colours and couldn't remember where she had put her folding umbrella or the return half of her bus ticket. "Typical Old Maid," my mother would say after she left, "typ-i-cal." Once my mother hinted darkly at something about my aunt being beaten by her father and that's why she was the way she was. But I didn't really believe this then nor do I now. She was simply a brilliant, determined, rather plain woman who never married, probably never was asked, but who led a life that was, I suspect, infinitely richer and happier than the life my mother led. That is how I look at it now. But I got the message then. I too was bright, very bright. I was good-looking but not what you'd call pretty. I was too critical. I had better be careful. And I am ashamed to say that I fell for it, all the propaganda about Old Maids. I never gave my aunt her due.

But the very worst Old Maid of all was my mother's own sister, Aunt Grace. She did not live in our town and I don't think I ever saw her until I was fifteen or sixteen and she came back to "look after" my grandfather, who was in his eighties. ("Just *who* is looking after *whom*," said my mother.) By then she had become a horrible legend, a cautionary figure, a brilliant and beautiful girl who took a small inheritance and went to Europe in her early twenties, came back and enrolled at Barnard College, but didn't really have enough to live on. She became very "queer" and one day my mother, who was also in New York at this time, studying at Katharine Gibbs, I think, got a call that her sister had drunk iodine and was out on a window ledge, threatening to jump. She was taken to Bellevue (for how long I don't know) and eventually my mother went with her to some resort while she recovered.

I still don't know what it was all about—the iodine, the window ledge, they seem such desperate acts—but my mother's version was that my aunt had "tried to do too much," wanted to "have her cake and eat it too," but didn't even have enough for adequate daily bread, had starved herself and had a nervous break down. I would look at the sepia print of the smiling, ringleted three-year-old and feel nothing but pity and horror. Wasn't it *awful*, my mother said with relish, when she had been the beautiful one, the brilliant one with naturally curly hair and a lot of zip. The one all the boys had wanted to walk out with. But she got too big for her boots and now where was she? "Where" in those days, when I was still a child, was a women's reformatory in Massachusetts where she worked as some kind of social worker. "Where" was the First Church of the Nazarene, where she had been "born again" or "Saved" (I think "Saved" was the word she used). The Nazarenes weren't a "real" church at all, said my mother. All that stuff about being Saved and shouting "Yes, Lord!"—all that kind of thing would not do. My aunt sent me my first Bible, *Illustrated: Questions and Answers,* and my name printed across the front in gold. I was six years old and did not doubt for one minute that there was a God and that the Bible was "true." Most of the illustrations were of men doing heroic things—Daniel, David, Shadrach, Meshach, and Abednego, but I liked best the picture of Solomon being confronted by the Queen of Sheba. She is sumptuously dressed and a bearer holds a state umbrella above her head. A lot of the men in Solomon's court are bowing down and the King himself has three-quarters risen from his chair. Underneath it says: "She came to prove him with hard questions—I Kings 10:1." A real queen, she, who came with camels and spices and gold and a full retinue and did not go away empty-handed. It never occurred to me to wonder where her consort was.

When I finally met my aunt she did not look very crazy to me. Just a thin, middle-aged woman in a red-checked house dress and gold-rimmed spectacles. She did wear sensible shoes (by their shoes shall ye know them) and she did talk a lot about the Lord—even preached at the City Mission from time to time—and was a vegetarian. (Ours was a meat and potatoes family; vegetarians, married or not, were definitely "queer.") I did not like her because she was always criticizing me and my family (it was all very well for *me* to do it, that was another thing) and because she had caused to leave, or be fired, my very favourite of all the housekeepers my grandfather had had in the years since my grandmother had died. Much to everyone's surprise she got married not long after she returned home. I met her husband once, a nice enough man who had also been Saved one night, when, coming across a field on his horse, dead drunk, he had fallen off and then tried to carry the horse (at which point he'd been roundly kicked in the head). He realized he was as far down as he could go and gave himself to the Lord (and subsequently to my aunt). I can only assume they've been very happy. Marrying late, like that, didn't really count. It was "only for companionship," said my mother. In her eyes my aunt was still an Old Maid.

My youngest daughter is twelve years old (oh yes, I married young, I made sure of that). She wants to be a trumpeter and a journalist. She is very aware of boys, of their power over her and hers over them and the awful bargains men and women sometimes make with one another out of their deep fear of being alone. Yet she has already picked out the names for her children and knows that she will probably want to marry. Why not? It's natural. But let us hope that she has the option not to and still remain respected, or admired. Let us hope that we really do live in an age where that is possible. Let us hope that the words "Old Maid" will become as obsolete as "reticule" or, perhaps more to the point, "grass widow." I think of all those women who were put down by other women (never mind men), a lot of them gifted and even brilliant, probably far more interesting than at least fifty percent of the women who looked down upon them. But however that may be they were of course aware that society looked upon them as inferior, as misfits, as objects of pity and scorn. Has that changed, I wonder, has it *really*? Or is it just that the "marrying age" has now been extended to thirty, or even thirty-two? After that one is in danger of becoming what? A "career woman"? What phrase will be used?

I think of my own generation. I do not know the percentage of our graduating class at Smith who never married, but one is always surprised to see, in the Class News, somebody with only one last name instead of the mandatory two. (Laura James Riley, Mary Kennedy Smith—you know the sort of thing.) And I remember very clearly our graduation day. The ceremony was held out of doors on a perfect June day. The *summa cum laudes* (a handful) went up for their degrees, the *magnas* (also a handful), the *cums* (more here). Everyone applauded loudly, fond parents and classmates alike. Under our black gowns we all wore white dresses, like girls at first communion, like brides, like the pure gem-like flames that most of us still were. The girls on either side of me, in my row, had become engaged that week (as had my roommate the month before, as had dozens of girls). As they applauded, their diamond rings sparkled in the sun. We were twenty-one or twenty-two years old. We were pretty well (let's leave Radcliffe out of this) the cream of the cream. We wanted to get married and have babies. Those of us without rings felt curiously naked and alone. We dreamt of being the wives of senators or famous men. Even those of us who wanted to write or dance or act or discover a cure for cancer did not imagine doing these things alone. We wanted to be half of Lunt and Fontaine, Rogers and Astaire, Leonard and Virginia Woolf, Anne Morrow and Charles Lindbergh, Pierre and Marie Curie. And the message was very clear—we had learned our lesson well. The first priority was always to find a husband. Most of us, to the great relief of our mothers (not to mention ourselves) were married and had children—at least one—by the time we were twenty-three.

Musing with Mothertongue

DAPHNE MARLATT

THE BEGINNING: LANGUAGE, a living body we enter at birth, sustains and contains us. it does not stand in place of anything else, it does not replace the bodies around us. placental, our flat land, our sea, it is both place (where we are situated) and body (that contains us), that body of language we speak, our mothertongue. it bears us as we are born in it, into cognition.

language is first of all for us a body of sound. leaving the water of the mother's womb with its one dominant sound, we are born into this other body whose multiple sounds bathe our ears from the moment of our arrival. we learn the sounds before we learn what they say: a child will speak babytalk in pitch patterns that accurately imitate the sentence patterns of her mothertongue. an adult who cannot read or write will speak his mothertongue without being able to say what a particular morpheme or even word in a phrase means. we learn nursery rhymes without understanding what they refer to. we repeat skipping songs significant for their rhythms. gradually we learn how the sounds of our language are active as meaning and then we go on learning for the rest of our lives what the words are actually saying.

in poetry, which has evolved out of chant and song, in riming and tone-leading, whether they occur in prose or poetry, sound will initiate thought by a process of association. words call each other up, evoke each other, provoke each other, nudge each other into utterance. we know from dreams and schizophrenic speech how deeply association works in our psyches, a form of thought that is not rational but erotic because it works by attraction. a drawing, a pulling toward. a "liking." Germanic *lik-*, body, form; like, same.

like the atomic particles of our bodies, phonemes and syllables gravitate toward each other. they attract each other in movements we call assonance, euphony, alliteration, rhyme. they are drawn together and echo each other in rhythms we identify as feet—lines run on, phrases patter like speaking feet. on a macroscopic level, words evoke each other in movements we know as puns and figures of speech (these end-less similes, this continuing fascination with making one out of two, a new one, a simultitude). meaning moves us deepest the more of the whole field it puts together, and so we get sense where it borders on nonsense ("what is the sense of it all?") as what we sense our way into. the sentence. ("life"). making our multiplicity whole and even intelligible by the end-point. intelligible: logos there in the gathering hand, the reading eye.

hidden in the etymology and usage of so much of our vocabulary for verbal communication (contact, sharing) is a link with the body's physicality: matter (the import of what you say) and matter and by extension mother; language and tongue; to utter and outer (give birth again); a part of speech and a part of the body; pregnant with meaning; to mouth (speak) and the mouth with which we also eat and make love; sense (meaning) and that with which we sense the world; to relate (a story) and to relate to somebody, related (carried back) with its connection with bearing (a child); intimate and to intimate; vulva and voluble; even sentence, which comes from a verb meaning to feel.

like the mother's body, language is larger than us and carries us along with it. it bears us, it births us, insofar as we bear with it. if we are poets we spend our lives discovering not just what *we* have to say but what language is saying as it carries us with it. in etymology we discover a history of verbal relations (a family tree, if you will) that has preceded us and given us the world we live in. the given, the immediately presented, as at birth—a given name a given world. we know language structures our world and in a crucial sense we cannot see what we cannot verbalize, as the work of Benjamin Lee Whorf and ethnolinguistics has pointed out to us. here we are truly contained within the body of our mothertongue. and even the physicists, chafing at these limits, say that the glimpse physics now gives us of the nature of the universe cannot be conveyed in a language based on the absolute difference between a noun and a verb. poetry has been demonstrating this for some time.

if we are women poets, writers, speakers, we also take issue with the given, hearing the discrepancy between what our patriarchally loaded language bears (can bear) of our experience and the difference from it our experience bears out—how it misrepresents, even miscarries, and so leaves unsaid what we actually experience. can a pregnant woman be said to be "master" of the gestation process she finds herself within—is that her relationship to it? (see Julia Kristeva, *Desire in Language*, p. 238.) are women included in the statement "God appearing as man" (has God ever appeared as a woman?) can a woman ever say she is "lady of all she surveys" or could others ever say of her she "ladies it over them"?

so many terms for dominance in English are tied up with male experiencing, masculine hierarchies and differences (exclusion), patriarchal holdings with their legalities. where are the poems that celebrate the soft letting-go the flow of menstrual blood as it leaves her body? how can the standard sentence structure of English with its linear authority, subject through verb to object, convey the wisdom of endlessly repeating and not exactly repeated cycles her body knows? or the mutuality her body shares embracing other bodies, children, friends, animals, all those she customarily holds and is held by? how can the separate nouns mother and child convey the fusion, bleeding womb-infant mouth, she experiences in those first days of feeding? what syntax can carry the turning herself inside out in love when she is both sucking mouth and hot gush on her lover's tongue?

Julia Kristeva says: "If it is true every national language has its own dream language and unconscious, then each of the sexes—a division so much more archaic and fundamental than the one into languages— would have its own unconscious wherein the biological and social program of the species would be ciphered in confrontation with language, exposed to its influence, but independent from it" (*Desire in Language*, p. 241). i link this with the call so many feminist writers in Québec have issued for a language that returns us to the body, a woman's body and the largely unverbalized, presyntactic, postlexical field it knows, postlexical in that, as Mary Daly (*Gyn/Ecology*) shows, with intelligence (that gathering hand) certain words (dandelion sparks) seed themselves back to original and originally related meaning. this is a field where words mutually attract each other, fused by connection, enthused (inspired) into variation (puns, word play, rime at all levels) fertile in proliferation (offspring, rooting back to *al-*, seed syllable to grow, and leafing forward into *alma*, nourishing, a woman's given name, soul, inhabitant).

inhabitant of language, not master, not even mistress, this new woman writer (Alma, say) in having is had, is held by it, what she is given
to say. in giving it away is given herself, on that double edge where she
has always lived, between the already spoken and the unspeakable,
sense and non-sense, only now she writes it, risking non-sense, chaotic language leafings, unspeakable breaches of usage, intuitive leaps.
inside language she leaps for joy, shoving out the walls of taboo and
propriety, kicking syntax, discovering life in old roots.

language thus speaking (i.e., inhabited) relates us, "takes us back" to
where we are, as it relates us to the world in a living body of verbal
relations. articulation: seeing the connections (and the thighbone, and
the hipbone, etc.), putting the living body of language together means
putting the world together, the world we live in: an act of composition,
an act of birthing, us, uttered and outered there in it.

Ten Sketches

CAROLE ITTER

I.

I WANT TO GET HOME TO MY LITTLE GIRL but that's not entirely true, true only when the idea comes into my mind. That is, time passes when I don't think of her, do not remember her, and that now pleases me. How old is she, a measurement more of my life than hers, for me, sixteen months. When I think of her I can't think of anything to say about her.

The train is going south and soon I will see her. Four times in the days just past, tears have come, rushed in, as I thought of her. A few times each day I have squeezed milk from my breast into a glass and then I think of her. It's her milk or milk for any baby that should come along. His mouth was too large and his lips not used to the sucking action and I saw that it wasn't milk for him, and he didn't want it and was doing it to relieve me.

I drank the first ounce from a Dixie cup in the toilet of the train ride north. What seemed most distinct was not the taste, but the temperature of it. When I have sucked my blood from a cut finger, I recall the taste as being distinct, what it does in my mouth and the salivary action, but not the temperature. The milk seemed weightless in my mouth.

I didn't drink the milk in the glass. Every few hours I would add another ounce or two. At the end of a day, or when it came to mind, I would dump the milk into the sink drain at the motel. Sometimes there was a creamy layer on the surface.

I suggested squirting some into his mouth from a few feet away, as I became more expert at expressing it, when it was spurting out easily in three or four narrow streams. I aimed for my own mouth and tiny droplets of warm milk landed on my face, weightless and without temperature. I knew they had landed only by the instant coolness as they evaporated.

I was trying to remember my daughter. Looking down at the floor of the train, I began to feel nauseous and thought only of that, then looking up to the sky I forgot again. Focusing directly ahead to the front of the coach, I saw parts of passengers' bodies in my immediate vision. I would look around to any unexpected noises, wanting to know what was happening there, behind me. Everything seemed okay and in my peripheral vision, a glorious landscape rippled in the plate glass window.

II.

Thinking about my daughter, her age measured in months still, not years, I am beginning to know what to say. It is becoming easier to think not of what there isn't to say about her, and that's something that can be said.

I am awed by how much she knows. That is something I can say about her. I am astounded by how well she knows me, sometimes scared. She wakes in the night if I begin to think about her. Writing this will probably wake her. If I pause to think that maybe I am making too much noise and that it might wake her, then it happens.

She doesn't want me to talk, only to listen, as she is listening, not talking yet. She will sit on my lap as my guide. She sees me walk out of a room into another and follows, and doesn't like that I should leave. She is asking me to sit still.

I see her eyes in the back of her head, that sense of knowing if I am watching, by her turning to see me. I am learning to stop watching. She tells me not to talk at her but to her. I see her being taught, taunted, to be saucy, a smart aleck, to "toughen her up" and I am unsure what it means.

What goes through the umbilical cord, is it ever cut, why isn't this examined, who dares to, she doesn't.

III.

I see her looking for me in front of my eyes. She follows me about to find out who I am and where it is I am going. I am saying, somewhat too urgently, that she shouldn't, shouldn't look at me or look to me, but what choice does she have.

I find it easier to say something about her because I am beginning to hear her, not hearing what others say, and not hearing her speech which hasn't happened yet. She calls by reaching out her hand, reaching to everyone from their sitting position into the ring. Ring around the rosie. She laughs hard when we all fall down, so hard that sometimes she loses her new-found balance and falls down too. She calls by shouting, that something isn't right, isn't working, has hurt, can't be reached, and she knows exactly what she wants. She calls by bringing something to me, something tiny, in her hands, something that usually she has had enough of, had done everything possible to, and doesn't know how to get rid of it, to stop using it. In the morning she calls when she wakes and I climb into her crib while she arranges her blankets about me, patting my head.

I am learning to leave her alone. That is the hardest part. She is standing on a chair at the sink, washing the chair with a dripping face cloth, her bare feet squishing two turds into a puddle of water on the seat. I wipe up the turds and dress her. She screams to leave her alone.

I am looking for her as she is for me. I understand her less than anyone else seems to, yet I'm the one she stands nearest to.

IV.

I lead her to the stream, not exactly that, but what I imagined I was doing. I was walking to the stream to refill the water buckets, walking quickly to get ahead of her, down the steep bank and into the creek then carrying the heavy full buckets up the bank, all done before she arrived, done so that I wouldn't have to carry her as well as the full buckets up the bank. She was crying as she tried to catch up. I was impatient, wanting to get it over with, the chore. I carried the buckets back to the cabin, the chore done, she still crying, following some forty paces behind me. She had never seen a stream, and it was by this measure that she followed me, or, I led her there.

After supper while it was still light out but raining lightly I walked to a special place by the stream, carrying her in a backpack through the dense forest. About a foot from the edge of the stream I placed her on the ground, moved back and squatted. She looked and pointed and laughed and squealed at the fast running water. After some minutes she turned to me and said so much as "Look at this!" in her own particular syllables.

The next time we went to the place she was restless, a little less interested. In order to call her back to the stream, I dropped a tiny stone into it. (Look at this!) She, without hesitation, picked up all the nearest stones, one by one, and dropped them in. It made a muddy mess in the clear water. She began to shout in frustration when she tried to lift the heavier stones, and we left.

Another time we took a visitor and her four-year-old daughter. The child wanted to wade in the stream, took off her shoes and socks and stepped in. She, eighteen months old, wanted her shoes off, wanted to wade, the stream cold, she complaining soon enough.

Each time we go to the stream a more direct contact with it takes place. I have been going to the place for years, never intentionally changing a thing, noticing how little it changes from season to season, year to year.

I led her to the mouth of the stream at the ocean. We walked on the sandbars, she didn't see for its size, the water. I continue to lead her to things, learning so slowly, when will it come, to give her the lead.

V.

I want to be the baby. I like to be taken care of. I like taking care. I want to be the mother too.

A low table for eating, cut back the salmonberry bushes, a low bench for sitting, a meeting place where the morning sun reaches, where she can reach onto any plate, eat all the food she wants, let her. Leave her alone.

I was wanting her to like this place as I do. We moved into the cabin, a shack, a woodchopper's shanty, a few weeks ago. The move, a getting away, the getaway, my getting way.

I tell him, them, what it was we did when I return. I am asked if I had a good time. "Oh yes," I reply, "We did this, this, this." But I should say, "Oh yes, I had a good time, I did this, this, this." There. And then to her, "And you, did you have a good time?" She does not understand the past, time past, does not recall enjoying the time past, the past that is trained, conditioned into us. She looks directly at the questioner, eyes big, listening, what is happening. The question is then directed to me, keeper of the records of time gone past and I reply, "Oh, *we* had a great time," (meaning *she*), "we did this & this & this." (Meaning *she* did.) Me telling, talking at, training.

I grovel in some pit that looks for improvement, to whom, to her, not to her, yes to her, to whom, to him, not him, yes him, to them, not them, yes them, not yes, by god, yes. Show me, let me show you says the teacher in despair. Teacher, student, each wanting to be the other; baby, mother, wanting each the other.

She can be the mother, I'll be the baby. "Okay, it's your turn, I'm the baby," I suck her tits, she laughs and laughs.

VI.

Thinking to the days preceding her birth, and the day of her birth, the time measured by her growth, and the occasion thought of less as she grows older. I am trying to forget the disillusionment, wanting the memory to become hazy and softer, less brittle than the birth was. I wonder if her struggles, vibrant temper, shyness, fears and demands are only her recovery from the trauma of that birth, of being born, but almost of not being born, and not being born at home but being born seventy-two hours later, not at home but within minutes moved to a sterile room of tile and chrome. She was tugged out, forcefully tugged out.

He saw her born, he said he doesn't need to see another birth. Her birth was our first failure. I was unable to give the birth, as the doctor observed, the word "give" the key, the place where hell rides high, and I still allow it, seem determined to keep it.

She came out wrong. Not easily, not by standard patterns, but by her and my own peculiar rhythms, and they were distinctly not in sequence; not she and I working together but not against either. Not without rhythm, but arrhythmically. The hours of controlled breath, the control of the sexual gasp, the force of the uterus, the thunderbolts, the dance he and I tried to do, couldn't do, the need for one another.

Leave me alone, oh don't, trust me but don't, touch me, oh don't. I didn't want to push, the doctor asked me to, I had to push, he said don't, he said to push, I couldn't.

VII.

Where was I, somewhere high, not here, giving, grasping, taught in the body, tense in the head.

We step in and out of the stream; one washes dishes, another crosses it, gets lost, found, one cries in excitement. Mirrors reflecting generations to come, those past. I see her frustrated, whining, crying, lonely, for something, anything other than what is nearest, me. I look at her, thinking "Hey, little girl, slow down, there's time enough." She looks at me. "Sit down, mom, I'm tired."

Or whatever we are, she, I, whoever. She is torn between us, she is torn between, she is tearing, tearing, tearful.

They say she is strong, by saying reassuringly, "She's strong," meaning she'll get by, get through, tear away, from me in spite of me, not because of me. She'll make it without me, does it mean that, what does it mean?

I was in a corner of the garden, she went looking for me. I heard a faint cry not distinct from the sound of the stream. She was standing at the edge of the bank, crying, calling. She had come to find me.

My pace is always fast, governed by the weight of the water in the buckets, the strain on my shoulders and back, the wish to get it done, walk the distance, put down the weight.

VIII.

I am paralyzed by time, by beginnings and by endings, by comings and by goings, starts and finishes. She moans in her sleep, turns over and by the motion I anticipate her waking. I'm frozen, standing still, waiting to see what to do next, to move or sit still.

When we start together then everything falls into place and time is less essentially measured. Sometimes my timing is kinky, out of time and hers will follow. It is at the same time awesome and intolerable that my rhythms can also be hers.

I am learning the meaning, the way to grace, to be graceful, gracious. Her names: great-grandmother Grace; her great-grandmother, Catherine; Lian; the sisters, she is called Lara, (The Milky Way). She came from the stars, her sign is fire. "Fire in heaven, first what is difficult, then what is easy." Lara: Roman daughter of the river God Almo. Lara: Latin, shining famous one.

loodle	doodle	da	da		
loodle	doodle	da	da		
loodle	doodle	da	da		
me	mom	me	mom	me	mom
me	mom	me	mom	me	mom
me	mom	me	mom	me	mom
nee-ow		nee-OW		NEE-OW	
loodle	lew	doodle	lew		
loodle	lew	loodle	lew		
loodle	lew	loodle	lew		

om	boom	boom
om	boom	boom
om	boom	boom
OOO — LA!	o o o — LA!	O O O O O O — LA!

IX.

She can go all day, in and out of, up and down through, she doesn't know what not to go means. She doesn't like going to sleep, stopping. When she wakes, awake is slow to come, it comes through anger, to get going, awake is somewhere, what was sleep. I say hello and she draws me to her:

ahh	maa	mee
ahh	maa	mee
	OOO — LA!	
	eeeeeeeeeeeee	

Cookie?

She lies down again, watching to see if I am watching, but I do not watch as far as she can see or so I think I see. Her cryings are to her the silences I take for myself, a resorting. Sometimes I interrupt her in my excitement to show her something, something from my silence. I hear the cry become whine become chant become song become silence, the centering in.

X.

When he returns we are three, before it was she and me; when I return we are three, before he and she. She is the constant of the three, she doesn't leave, doesn't return, she is where he and I meet. Wherever she'll be, one of us will be, the other will meet the two at some given time, an hour from now, Thursday at noon, sometimes unexpectedly.

One is often checking on the other, taking care, seeing how the other is doing, what is there to do. She once made seventeen consecutive trips from the bedroom to the kitchen, checking on each of us, taking care, seeing what each was doing.

Two will come looking for the one, she is always one of the two, always looking. Only one going looking for her, seeing what she is doing, checking on, taking care. One asks things of the other two, the other one asks the two, or one and one. Two plus one is the three; three takes away one from the two, one makes three plus the other two, three is made by one and one and one.

When I am the one, the centre shifts, direction shatters. What I do is more strenuous than if she were here, or he were here, or he were her, or her, he—the list of what to do in my pocket, forgotten to do, phone the other two, meet somewhere, become three.

Hysteria

HELEN POTREBENKO

I wanted too much, I know.
I wanted to go to Bowen Island.
I wanted to walk on the beach
one night when the moon was full.
I wanted to walk around Stanley Park.
Women always want too much.

I wanted a proper stove,
with burners, an oven,
each turning up and down
as well as off and on.
Women always want too much.

I wanted people to be on time.
If someone said—see you at 6,
I'd expect to see them before 8.
Women always want too much.

Sometimes even, I'm ashamed to say,
I wanted a baby.
A small baby with a fuzz of hair
that would grow fat and sassy inside me
then go breathing on its own.
I wanted to measure time by height marks on the wall.
Women always want too much.

to Karen

BETSY WARLAND

we
we are
we are so
      careful
           with each
      other
      careful
not to
      touch too long
not to
      look too long
not to
      smile too
not to

we
we are waiting for a storm heavy in the air
hanging over there
we
      tease it
      bait it
          to come
             shake
             the
             sky
a wild thunderous
flashing bizarreness
             that makes our own
                  seem
                    small

Mooring~Buoy/Moored~Body

MONIQUE BOSCO

WITH WHAT REAL, invented, imagined words should we treat this body? This body, you said? The only body I know is the moored-body, the buoy, precious to sailors. Berth, anchor. With what ink should we conjure it up? In the depths of the sea, they let it slide down. Immobility achieved at last, reunion. Woman's body ought to be thus at rest. Buried. Let us once more bury the moored-body there. Let us once more take refuge in the sea-womb. There, in the hollow of wave and belly. In a ball. In stone. In the family way. In the stone family of saints. Glass ball. Slow swell. And already there's the nausea of the wave. Swirl and sway. Remorse. Re-moored. *Re-mort*. At the heart of this surf of salt and blood. Precious and bitter waters. Depths.

But the sea soon casts up this foreign body. Ultimate revolt of the body in labour. This girl who bears such a disgraceful resemblance to her mother is quickly expelled. Exit the daughter. Mother-child or child-mother, this filiation doesn't matter since, in any case, disorder reigns in this couple. The breast turns away from this red and raging bubble that puffs up with screams and cries. Scream, daughter, you're right. *Bitch*. There, you're christened with the only dirty name common to all girls.

Make yourself small. Be good. Be clean. Be quiet. Be nice. Take care of your small brothers. Play little mother. Smile. Look pretty. Be quiet. Don't venture asking stupid questions. You'll know everything soon enough. Everything, I tell you. Everything and nothing.

Know what? Know nothing. Silly foolishness of the tales. Snow White and Cinderella.

Mirror, mirror, tell me I'm the prettiest.

How fine, right and good it is that at least in the children's stories, the stepmothers, far too beautiful mothers, are already afraid of their ugly duckling daughters.

Rivalry. Soon the girl too young, too thin, too stupid and naive will be this ingenue who dethrones all the coquettes. After much haggling. You're too young, too small, too fragile. Wait.

How many more years still before I supplant you? Horrible duels. Always rivals. Cruel childhood prolonged and humiliating.

Plaits or curls. Lace dresses. Smockings.

Stay in the hollow of the nest. Play dolls.

Silly daughters. Spoiling mother. So many treats. Sweets. Rotten teeth. Coated with sweetness.

What a screen between life and us.

Ignorance. We're dying of ignorance and boredom. In such a long childhood, like Agrippine, you make us rot and languish.

Feverish growing pains. Nice medical invention. Madly feverish to grow, stretch, beat it, away from this cocoon. Grow up, fast, like Alice. That our breasts fill up. Hope for the buds of this first spring. Rounder hips, longer legs. Everything must be perfect.

Nothing will ever be too beautiful. Lengthy stops in front of mirrors. Merciless inspections. The die is cast, no more bets. There's too much. Not enough. At the wrong place. How to pass through the needle's eye and join the elect. How dreadful to be this thankless girl in all the meanings of the word. The buds awaited for such a long time to change into wretched pimples. Humiliation for this body that doesn't know where nor upon whom to fall.

You want to stand on your own feet? They'll rape you at the first opportunity. What fears right from the beginning. What terror. What envy since the mists of time.

Let them rape me so that I learn at last what is happening on the other side of the wall. Let them rape me then like a poor man steals a precious and rare object that he can't afford otherwise. Isn't it the proof that I'm irresistible? What I vainly try to give freely must be taken by force.

Tie me up like in the stylish movies. I consent. I'm happy. Let him run the risk of going to jail and hanging, this unfortunate fool, to get me out of my jail, cheerless cage where I'm cooling my heels.

I'm fading at the bottom of this well of repressed and indistinct desires. Who will take me, to the broad daylight of desire? Burning sun. Fountains. At last drink to satiety, till no more thirst, no more hunger. We're also like Narcissus, on the edge of all the ponds. Trying to scrutinize, closely, this vague and uncertain face. But I'm still young? You think so?

If you believe, little girl, little girl, if you believe.

She shouts it, beautiful Juliette, in all the cellars of St. Germain. Alas, no, I don't believe that it's going to last. At sixteen I'm already crying about my fifteen years during which nothing happened.

I will not allow anyone to say that twenty is the best time of life exclaims Nizan, who keeps on rebelling.

Everything threatens to ruin a young man.

And us? And us? Twenty is not the only awful age for us.

Everything is too soon, too late, too fast. Everything threatens us, us too.

How do we make do with this body when everything foretells us that it has vowed us to perdition. It is sung the better to lament its fragility.

Feminine body that is so soft

Adorned, sweet, so precious

Poor female body. If we give ourselves, we're damned. If we refuse, we condemn ourselves to regrets and sterility. You only have to listen to the Ballads of La Belle Heaulmière. Horrible. Decrepitude of the old women. Abandon. Abandon.

If this body comes to grief, fails, gets out of shape, it's all over for us. Who takes us out, in, or loves us for our noble soul? No soul could be hiding in this old carcass, of course not.

Poor body despised as soon as it stops being desired or desirable, as soon as it's no longer cherished. Tricks. Marvellous miserable tricks. Rouge. Dresses. Veils. Clever pleats. Everything is tried. All the gold in the world. Endless tortures. Evermore exhausting confrontations. Mirror, mirror, tell me that I can still come, go, perhaps, even dazzle, especially when the light is subdued!

Only a few women have known that we were well, free, and happy only in the splendour of free nature and brightness of the sun.

Hurrah Sand. Respects to wonderful Sido.

When the mirror falls silent or no longer gives comforting answers, one must turn to the oracles of books. Page after page, to find the secret, the recipe, the infallible magic.

Where are the witches of old? Our prosaical mothers only offer us examples of restraint or renouncement. After having told us time and again that we had plenty of time, they are delighted to find that in our turn our time's up. *Do your time*, like the unfortunate draftee on fatigue-duty. Then cast aside. Shelved. With some mending and embroidery to pass the remaining time, precisely, like the veterans.

Messages from the older sisters. What a good thing it would be to find in them which road should be followed in order to escape being totally caught up in the machine. Yet for them too, everything seems to be already settled.

Our reckoning is settled for us. Atrocious countdowns. All the woes of the second sex recorded, precisely, from adolescence to menopause, without mentioning the throes of old age.

And Violette complains, from one book to the next, about this ugliness which she lewdly and niggardly enumerates, each new insult. And Anaïs examines herself closely and gazes at herself, from mind to navel, drapes herself in sumptuous capes, embroidered dresses, soft chiffons.

Alas. We've all really been had.

And yet, how I've loved and tried to be like the heroines begotten by men. Those are my true models. Indeed, I must admit it. There I took my crudest lessons. By heart, wholeheartedly. How do you escape from such a magnetic hold? There I thought I had understood how one must love, suffer, rebel, but above all conform to delightful precepts of moderation and sublimation. Not a trap or pitfall I didn't try, avidly, plunging into, headfirst.

Rebellious women of Corneille, Camille, or Emilie. Enamoured women of Racine. Wonderful creatures of Stendhal, always ready to follow their maddest and noblest folly to the bitter end. Holy women of Claudel, Jouve's mystic Paulina or mysterious Catherine Crachat, Bemanos's Mouchette. I wanted to take each and every one of them as models. Such a good pupil, I can assure you.

How can you be otherwise when you are sung, understood, and loved in such a way? There, at last, justice and honour are done to us, faults are confessed, rapes, deceptions, and betrayals reported.

On these ostentatious models, honestly, I've made my own movies. On the small stage of my room, I thought I was living great tragic passions. You wake up, one day, years later, distressed.

The broken woman, yes. *Back Street* should be read in its time. You need humour, indeed you do, to finally accept that you've been a sucker for so long.

Feydau created the Dindon. I am the Turkey of my own farce. Let's laugh then, in chorus, oh romantic and naive sisters to find ourselves smack in vaudeville after believing for so long that we were in the seventh heaven of passion.

Mystified woman, yes, indeed, for certain.

But to hell with passion, now. It is a time to listen to our rebelling sisters. To hell with love on a pillow. From now on, we will follow our own roads, free at last to go wherever we see fit.

Today's little girls finally refuse their yesterday role of lovely good little girls, always ready to curtsy in every living room.

The world is vast and beautiful. And even if the earth is round, I'll go play at its four corners. To be granted *half the sky* is not enough, I want it all, earth and sky, undivided, in full abandon.

No, I will no longer be this moored-body that sinks and comes to a standstill in the depths of the ocean.

Moored-body? Cormorant rather, eager to fish and catch, plunging only to better rush again at new conquests.

And don't quote to me the Book of books. *God is not a nigger* as in Ferré's songs. God is a male. And from the beginning of time, he has known, wanted, and accepted that David might defeat Goliath. And yet, David himself wasn't afraid to break the law. And after going to Bathsheba, he nevertheless dared compose this psalm for his God:

Make me hear joy and gladness,
That the bones which thou hast broken may rejoice.

For us, too, the hour of joy has come. The time of the wise ants is over.

It's cicadas' season. Songs and dances alternating. Never again oppressed and crushed under man's ruthless law. We are free now. Strong and courageous. Seeing all the adventures through. Free and alone. Death can indeed approach.

Yes, death can indeed approach. I refuse to fear it. And so what if I must revert to dust. I finally accept my fate and my body. Let it then, at last, be reduced to dust, this poor body. So be it, I will be only dust. But such fine and light dust that it will dance at the smallest breath of the wind.

No, never again will I be this moored-body burying itself forever in the sea, bitter mother, source of all life and death. At last, I accept, that at the end of the journey, this defeated body be again laid down into the rich and black mother-earth. Let them bury me in it, at great depths, so that I better take on life again and root.

And I swear to give birth, in turn, to new and wonderful flower-girls.

Moored-body, cast off body.

Just a simple story. Always the same, with the same stale words. Essential repetition. Like ruminating air, intolerable rancour. Always the same phantasms, the same scene to watch. Useless productions. Everything is perfectly connected. Everything is imprinted there, on the centre of the cornea. From birth to death. Set eyes. Everything's already inscribed. Alas. You only need being born. Being only that, this body. This girl's body. Defenceless.

Nausea. Milk too thick. To think that I came, with great difficulty, out of this belly. Such hard passage. I'm choking. I'm being strangled. Always held, head too low, legs bundled up in swaddling clothes. Lumpy gruels. Tough apprenticeship of maniacal and sanctimonious cleanliness. What a sorry rag doll I make. Limp rag. That gives up walking, cooing. No game. I barely exist. I am but sly fear and whispered excuse. Just about excuse myself for breathing the air of the house. What house? Nothing's mine. Everything's theirs, organized according to their order. I keep on choking under my sheet. How do I hide. Fear and hatred. And so much love too. What to do to appear lovable? But I'm not presentable, it seems. Either too shy and timorous, or haughty and boorish, they say. Can I still be legitimately concerned about such ancient slights, I ask you.

My very own life. The old refrains should be repressed forever. To please, at any price, to survive in this bear-garden. Wouldn't I be a giant, a three-headed calf. I'm only myself and that's never enough. I cling to this breast. I'm thirsty. I'm dying of thirst and hunger. They maintain that they alone know the extent of my needs. Everyone decides what is good for me. I survived nevertheless. Tough little girl, tenacious and stubborn. How mulish I had to be. My very own head. Hard as a coconut. I pound it in the dark, to be reassured about its resistance. So many many times already. I'll be thick-headed. Wooden marble. I roll as I please. I escape. Everything escapes me. I bring up this vile and tasteless food which you force-feed me like a goose. I'll be skinny. And small. So small. Ever ready to run off like the fine silk stockings of our mothers, in olden days. Marvellous ladders. I slide on them. I run away. There is no more good little girl here, who works herself to death to make others love her, or at least accept her.

Yes, the ruthless training that comes after that must also be described. Only the men serve their apprenticeship, as they please, with the craftsman of their choice. They break us in, chastise us, curb us. To mould us, of course. Strange deformation, carefully graduated, like these espaliers in our grandmothers' beautiful orchards. That will give good pears, later on, luscious as one would wish, juicy and sweet. Delights for the lovers of good fare. Similarly we are raised for the discerning consumption of the buyers of fresh meat for the coming seasons. For now, we are being watched. Nothing escapes the eye or the ear of the gossips around us. They even finger, on occasion, to make sure that they're not being cheated about the goods. Already formed. Quite regular. Shocking inquiries. The searches of the jail matrons are not more severe. How I've hated that season. Cruel and thankless season. Years like centuries. Everything is whispered and mumbled with vulgar chuckles. Nothing's spared to break us in, to break me in. *Mater dolorosa.* Because our exasperated mothers complain about our rare outbursts. Under a bushel, the girls. Let's sing small. And don't you speak in undertones among yourselves. Who will come and get me out of this stupid demolition business? Let's watch the boys. Stealthily. What a sly teenager. Nothing is as foolish as the schemes of that age.

Pressed, they have scuttled off, the others, in tulle clouds, orange blossom wreaths over the head. Wedding or funeral? Flowers and crowns. Enbalmed, the pretty things, in wax and lace. Good bees. Patient needlework. They sew and knit. Mend old dreams. Everything's so peaceful. No need to think. Everything has been anticipated. How nice and well to have crossed the threshold, the barrier. They are now safe from the spinsterhood of solitude. The dreaded stage, the last entrance examination passed with popular approval, just a few more efforts are required. So few, I can assure you.

There, madness was avoided. Returned to the ranks. Two abreast. Like in school years ago, along the covered playground, after recess. But there's no longer the uncontrollable laughter, the silly laughter of the girlfriends of old.

Two abreast, as for Noah's ark. Male and female. And forward, reproduction. May the species multiply. Good wife, accomplished. Excellent mother.

How these kids do scream constantly. That's strange, in the long run. Is it possible that history is repeating itself?

My daughter hates me. This male child that I have hits with foot and fist so violently that it's terrifying. I can already see him, helmeted and booted, sowing terror wherever he goes. New wars will have to be invented, other territories invaded, in order for him to display the scope of his talents and strength.

How I do dream about what could have been. So many snares avoided, but so many stupid traps I fell for headfirst. All or nothing, I had said. And I've only had the mediocre betwixt and between of those who hesitate and waver between fear and hatred, thinking they can find love there. What abysses of non-love. I've wanted, with dogged foolishness, the idiotic semblance of the silliest romance stories of another age. I mistook the century, upon my word. Always behind history, living counter-current, suffering, on the other hand, with the alacrity of an addict fleeing this very day to Kathmandu.

My former companions slave at industrious orgies of production: curtains, embroidered tablecloths, carefully simmered dishes. They're praised and honoured. I stay in my corner, at my naked window, watching for the one who never comes in time.

So many many hours. Penelope without courtiers, tapestry, or legitimate hero. I polish, in silence, old, shoddy arms. Who would take me seriously? Where are the convents and cloisters which received in the old days the madwomen like me? It would be good, though, to share with gentle feminine companions the hours of expectations of madness and mirage. Rage. Distress to the end of sight and soul.

Anne, my sister, don't you see anything coming? What to see? Who? What is there? There's nothing. Phantasms and phantoms. Stupid desire and huge desert. I've loved in vain, for nothing, a vain and conceited man. A twitty man or twenty, what's the difference, I ask you. Who loves, here, if not the imagination of the madwoman dwelling here. And there's no dwelling and madness, also, has fled. Gone. *Pfuit.* There's nothing anymore. Not even a tear to be shed to erase a little more cleanly, the slate.

You're hurt, darling, poor little girl. Blow on it and it will go away. It's all gone, with the current. Nice little boat. Sink or swim, without making waves.

Be quiet. Blow your nose. Like the candles are blown out and snuffed, with great whacks of the extinguisher. In this church or chapel, no need for a chair-attendant or a verger. Everything has taken place. The service is over. You've played your part. You can leave the service or go into service as a totally different part. There's always room, as extras, for elderly women. Utility. Broom and rag. In vain, you turned your apron in years ago. You can take it back, wrap yourself in it, drape yourself in it with dignity if that suits you. Anything is better than the idleness of premature retirement.

Oh sisters, what a disgraceful mess. All these botched struggles. All this time lost that no quest or search will ever give us back. Quick, it's time to go. Leave everything. Like the snake sheds its old skin.

Quick, find again the innocence and strength of the first revolt. Heart throbbing, palms bared, move as if it were the dawn of the first morning and the creation of another world, in a garden made only in our own and radiant image.

translated by Josée M. LeBlond

Women as Poets

DOROTHY LIVESAY

IT HAS OCCURRED TO ME that since so many Canadian poets review each other in incestuous fashion, one might go a step further and review oneself. An occasion presents itself, here and now: I shall review my own editing of *Forty Women Poets of Canada*. It will be a kind of preface after the event.

Let me say first that as a teacher I am opposed to the whole idea of anthologies. How then did it come about that I agreed to edit an anthology limited to female poets? To begin with, I have always been fascinated by the role of the woman as writer. But only recently have I become aware that although the work of Canadian women writers can be found in current Canadian publications, their representation is rarely equal to their worth or their numbers.

This was brought home to me when I examined several Canadian poetry anthologies. In the Oxford University Press collection edited by Gary Geddes, for instance, only three of the *Fifteen Canadian Poets* are women. In the League of Canadian Poets' anthology published by Oberon Press (and edited by Douglas Lochead and Raymond Souster), *Made in Canada*, only ten of the sixty-four poets are women. In *Storm Warning*, edited by Al Purdy and published by McClelland and Stewart, only four of the thirty poets included are women. This imbalance was unrealistic. Surely there were as many interesting female as male writers, but the women had not been given a hearing. And so, when the publisher and editor of Ingluvin Press, Montréal, asked if I would consider editing a book by women poets only, I felt it was a necessary step, a challenge.

The most vociferous response to the proposed anthology came from women themselves . . . several women poets who did not want to be "put in a ghetto." They felt, with some justification, that women should appear alongside men without fear or favour. They insisted that men as well as women should be represented. (This was also a common criticism among male critics and poets.) My reply was that women are already in a ghetto! Too many women poets of solid calibre had been left out of the previous anthologies; I wanted space for all of them.

In choosing forty poets from among the sixty who submitted work, I had several considerations in mind. First, I wanted as wide a geographic spread as possible. A second consideration was the need to see how women's poetry reflects the woman's view of life and art. I concluded, with Gwendolyn MacEwen, that ". . . no man could write Avison's poems, no woman could write Cohen's. The sexual difference is vital . . ." It was also important, I felt, that the poems be contemporary, by living writers, reflecting the immediacy of the scene in which we live. One reviewer complained that "[w]ith few exceptions . . . the poems are wry, agonized, despairing. The subjects chosen are suffering, dark, hurt, lonely. There is very little joy. One wonders why." I think one knows why. This is the world we live in, the world from which women must free themselves.

It should go without saying that my last criterion was also the most important: Do the poems communicate through beauty of language, intensity of feeling, technical competence? Although some of the work by new poets was slight in volume and impact, the spark was there, the likelihood of development. And so I believe that readers will be reassured when they see the freshness, vitality, and individuality of the poems chosen. In *Forty Women Poets of Canada* and in my more recent collection *Women's Eye*, it is obvious that Canadian women poets are writing as strong people, concerned not only with the traditional female role but also with the complete range of human issues. And if that is the case, then the publication of this book has been a leap forward.

Nothing is Private

DOROTHY LIVESAY

Men have never been
subjected to physical scrutiny
as have women
What is private?

For a man
not face   not torso
not (nowadays)
the scrotum with its pointing
flower design
seen in all ancient art

But for a woman
What is private?
Not the breasts   the nipples
not the rippling hips
not the small forest
covering that incredible cave
whence mankind springs

For a woman
nothing is private!
she is invaded
night after night
has only the soul's essence
through which to believe herself
human, and right

The Smell of Sulphur

MARIAN ENGEL

THERE WERE TWO GIRLS IN THAT FAMILY, Tess and Junie, six years apart. Tess was the little one, named after her mother's cousin Maria Theresa Brown, who worked at the *Toronto Star* and gave her namesake a silver locket. Only Theresa was a Catholic name and wouldn't do, so she was called Tessa Marie. She was six that summer and Junie was twelve. Junie called her Tillie the Toilet, after the comic character and her own feelings.

What happened was that when their father went to his ulcer doctor in Brantford in March, the doctor said, "Frank, you've still got that house-on-wheels thing of yours, and when school lets out in June, I tell you what you're going to do and it isn't a suggestion, it's an order. There's a place called Star Bay about five miles from my cottage up the Bruce. All the land there is owned by a family named Ellis and I know them well. Nobody much is going up there now because of gas rationing, and what you're going to do is save up your gas ration, drive up there and park your trailer where the hotel used to be and spend two months fishing."

Frank went back later and was told that a man who taught boys to fix cars wouldn't have a hard time laying hands on a boat; they'd needed a mechanic up there the last ten years. The two men talked bass and pickerel and glowed.

Maudie got out the sewing machine and started running up seersucker outfits for Tessa. Junie ordered hers from Eaton's catalogue, she was that age.

Tessa had few talents, and her greatest one was being sick in the car. Once it was over with, Junie was the one who suffered. Tessa sat high in the back seat of the Studebaker Commander, Queen of the World as the landscape rushed by her, changing at her command. The trailer had, her father said, the best hitch in Christendom, and, her mother said, this made them snails with their house on their back. Tessa looked and smiled and babbled and nobody listened. Julie practised her Deanna Durbin imitations.

It took a long time to get there, and where was that? First the road was all farms, then it was cottages with bits of lake glistening between them, but that wasn't where they were going. They entered a flat, desolate landscape, where there were grey stones and sheep and scrubby bushes. The road was very straight. There wasn't any traffic: they were the only ones who had been provident enough to save their whole gas ration. You had to hand over a coupon the way you had to for butter, but they were a different colour and shape. It was about the war, but Tessa didn't care: the day the King came on everyone had looked serious and told her not to talk in competition with the radio.

"Now girls, look out," their mother, Maudie, said from the front seat. She had black hair and she looked happy with a kerchief around her neck. "We're turning at a place called Mar, and the first one to see the sign gets a nickel."

"I do," Tessa shouted, "right up there."

"Moth—er!" Junie groaned. "You're going to have to turn this kid in to the cops."

"No, June, she's right, there it is," said Frank. "We turn left and in about two miles we drive over a causeway over Sky Lake."

"It's a hot day," said Maudie, "and a long drive for you, Frank."

Mar, Mar, Mars, thought Tessa. Mars and Sky take us to Star Bay.

"I see Sky Lake!" Junie shouted, straining through her spectacles. And she did. And it was full of lily pads. And the causeway rumbled as they drove over it.

They had hung over Dr. Arnold's map night after night at home, and Tessa, who was put to bed long before Junie, lay sleepless, dreaming of it: up the Peninsula to Mar, to Sky Lake, down a road through the bush to Star Bay. And Dr. Arnold had promised them the perfect place, and he would know, because he was special: he was curing their father. He'd even made him stop smoking, and that other time they went away he sent huge bottles of thick, pink medicine in wooden boxes with dovetailed ends, lined up like chocolate boxes with padding, that would have made good doll beds, only they had to send them back. That was when she was four, and they sat watching the men carve the Presidents on Mount Rushmore, looking like ants on irritated faces (she kept waiting for the noses to twitch) until this job came up.

The Snail Family at Large, she thought. She was already a reader.

After the boggy lake, the road turned south. It was narrow and twisting, and the woods shouldered in at them on either side. Father blew the horn before every little rise and turning: they had a big car and a big trailer, and everyone needed to be warned.

"It looks like nothing," the doctor had warned. "It takes a while to find out it's heaven."

It was the last day of June, and hot, though somewhat cooler as they proceeded through the woods. The road turned from gravel to sand and they had to turn right—"toward the lake," Frank said to Maudie, who never knew where she was. They went through scrubby cedar bush hedged by snake fences, past a tumbledown farm. "That'll be Ellis's, we'd better stop."

"No!" cried Tessa. "I want to get there."

"Shuddup, kid," said Junie, because her parents were already out of the car. She got out too, and Tessa was going to, but when she went to open her door, there was a big sort of duck there staring at her and hissing. The sound was dreadful, dry, and angry. The creature had a thick yellow tongue but it didn't stick out, it curved meanly up. It took Tessa a long time to learn to hiss like that.

They found her cowering. "Oh, I know what you mean, Tess," said Maudie. "I always hated geese. And did I tell you about the time my brother Will found me down in the barnyard and the turkey cock was pecking at me?"

"Not exactly friendly," the father said.

"No, but she likes to rule her own roost."

"I thought she was very interesting," said Junie.

"She has a boy about your age," Maudie said.

Junie huffed and puffed.

It was only a little way now: the lake was already there, looking grey because the sun was so bright. There wasn't a road along the beach, they just turned and humped along a track, past two cottages, big ones, and then two little ones, and over a log bridge. "There it'll be," Frank said.

"Oh," said Maudie, because what she was looking at was nothing. A dump of old cans, a half-fallen chimney. "You can get out, girls," she said.

Junie got out her side, and went into conference at once with the adults. Tessa finally wrangled her door open, found no goose-guardian, and stepped into her world. A stony beach, thin, shallow water with well-spaced grasses growing in it and look—but nobody was there to look, they were parking and levelling and doing whatever they did with the trailer so they could open the door without having it slam right into their faces—look, there are tiny little fish, there. And then there was a big island, and farther out, a paradise of little islands. Tessa took off her shoes, and then her socks. She put them neatly down on a rock, tucked her new seersucker shirt into her new seersucker shorts, and set off to find her world.

She didn't have to go far. She just lay down on the sand and began to stare into the water. Very small fish nipped from reed to reed: it was enough.

"Tessa . . . Tess—a."

They had done their things now, even had the two folding chairs and two folding stools in a row facing the beach and parallel to it. "It's your job to get the flowers," her mother said, "and, oh, put on your shoes."

New Sisman Scampers.

What could the flowers have been that June? Because later she remembers cinquefoil and pearly, everlasting fireweed. But they are August flowers. And when do the harebells, leafless and blue, come out?

The trailer door faces inland, and when Tessa returns with much-praised flowers the table is already set, Junie has been sent somewhere to get a pail of water, and the naphtha gas stove is lit and Maudie is scrambling eggs. Soon enough, they seal the place up against mosquitoes and they're lying in their bunks in the last glow of the Coleman lantern. If Tessa remembers that it was because she couldn't keep her fingers off the rainy tentsides that they got the trailer, she doesn't remind herself. She dreams of touching the glowing, forbidden mantle of the lamp.

Does she hear her mother whisper to her father, "But there's nothing here, Frank, nothing"? If she does, she doesn't care. Junie, who is elderly and responsible, turns heavily in her sleep.

All the years of summer in heaven run together and who can tell how many there were? Two? Three? Five? Junie got big in the summers there, and pretty enough to get the better of her glasses, and modest enough to hide with a flurry that knocked the upper bunk down on Tessa's head the night Joey Ellis came late with the ice. Tessa was never big, there, never awkward (though old Mrs. Ellis kept saying, "Don't send that Tessa for the milk, she's that clumsy she'll fall into the spring"), never fell out of heaven.

Because even her talent for vomiting became an asset; even the war became her ally: once they got the use of a boat, or whichever boat her father was fixing up for whichever cottager, Tessa was firmly left on shore and for what seemed wonderful eternity she was in possession of paradise.

They got up early, slipped into their bathing suits or their seer-sucker costumes. Mother went out and got their washcloths off the line and they went down to the water to wash their faces. There was drama if the Pike boys from Detroit, whose mother was supposed to be a German spy, had been along first and tied garter snakes to the clothesline, which was a tow rope. Then Maudie had to decide whether to be merciful and untie the snakes, be sluttish and let the girls go dirty, or go in and fry the eggs. Frank was already off tinkering with something somewhere: how he spent his life.

Then suddenly everyone was gone, there was no one to call her Tillie the Toilet, there was nothing to do and everything to do. No other kids—the Pike boys weren't kids, and they only wanted to get a look at Junie and hand out snakes—no one her age: only Tess and the beach.

She ran and ran and ran. She outran sandpipers and caught their babies, holding the fuzzy balls in her hands before she let them go again, being careful not to hold too tight, because last spring on Uncle Will's farm . . . she outran Popeye, Joey Ellis's black and white dog, and nobody believed her but when she threw a stick in the water for him down farther by the big dock where the fishermen's boats were, threw it good and far out into the water, the dog swam after it and his green coating of fleas rose from the water and hovered over him, hopping on through the air. Nobody believed her, but it happened

There were a fair number of cottages, most empty. The two next to them belonged to the Pennypackers from Buffalo. Then there was the Crow's Nest, owned by a man named Crow who never spoke. Past the creek where the live box was, there was Sovereigns's place: they had a niece called Dorothy Crown. Over the road from there was a man called Grimes and even though his cottage was empty Junie and Tessa went mad with embarrassment when their mother sang, in her church contralto, "Old Grimes is dead, that dear old man" as they passed it when they took a stroll in the evening.

But the evenings weren't the best time: the lone mornings were: running alone on the beach, king of the castle on every rock, and *no one to see!* No one to say, don't, Tessa.

There was only one rule. It all ends if you swim alone. It was like Uncle Will's farm: it all ends if you try to get on a horse. You can be, but you can't do. A bad rule for later life, it turned out, but she couldn't have known that.

Probably, they could always see her from where they fished. But she did not feel watched.

There was lunch when they got back; then a nap; then swimming. She learned to swim, but so did her mother, the very same day, and scooped her. They all except Junie, who got something prettier from the catalogue, had woolen bathing suits. Her father's had big holes in the sides. Hers took the skin off her thighs: it was pink.

If she stayed too long in the sun she got sick, disgusting them all with her vomiting. Mostly she remembered to keep on her hat.

There was much to see, and when they were swimming she lay in the shallows and felt the minnows nibbling at her with their soft, puckering, little mouths. One year when the water was low she and June swam out to the island, but she got scared when she turned out to face the open lake and had to be rescued.

The islands out there were called the Fishing Islands and there were certainly a lot of fish. Every night they had bass for supper. Tessa went to the live box with her father and helped to pick them out, big, sturdy fellows, all over eight inches because that was the rule. Among them sometimes there were beautiful little baby fish that had hatched in the creek, but it was against the law to take them home and put them in a jar, Frank said.

Then he sat in the grove of cedars by the trailer and filleted the fish with a special knife he had bought in South Dakota for trout. The nasty part came when it was Tessa's job to take the cleanings out on an aluminum plate to the seagulls. She hated it, it was a rock she played King of the Castle on she had to set the plate on, and the gulls were always expecting her and swooped down greedily. Their wings were beautiful and they looked as if they could knock your head off; they were sharp and clean as a shining knife. She never got out of the job. Or failed, later, to eat as many delicious slivers of bass as she could obtain.

She must have grown up: one summer two English children came, and she hated them, and they hated her, and that was that. She collected a whole Campbell's soup can of baby toads and fixed them in the crotch of a cedar tree, to have someone to talk to, but the wind blew it over. Her mother said. Once a week she was allowed to overturn a certain board in the clearing and watch the ants carry their Rice Krispies away. In the evenings they sat in a row outside, listening to the nighthawks boom and cry. They mewed like cats sometimes. A bat took up residence inside the window by Junie's bunk, and they didn't dare open it all summer: they lay and watched him hanging upside down. He had an evil-looking nose, but he was very shy.

When the mosquitoes got bad they went indoors and went through the ritual of watching Father light the Coleman lantern. (Father was the most important person in the world: nobody else could control naphtha gas.) Then they played rummy, trying to beat him, but he could remember the cards. Then they went to bed and lay in their beds singing "Redwing" and "When It's Springtime in the Rockies," and (Tessa was patriotic and the war was still on, always on) "There'll Always Be an England." "The White Cliffs of Dover" was too high for Mother.

Tessa got old enough to go up to the spring house for milk, through the woods instead of up the road, because she hated, vividly and personally, the geese, who hated her, surrounded her when she tried to take a step. Once, dreaming, swinging the tin billy can, she walked straight into a cow and ran home so fast that she spilled not a drop, and it took her mother an hour to get a description of the monster.

Junie must have had another life, but sometimes they went somewhere together. Once up to the Big Sand Pile, a strip of dunes inland toward the forest road. There were other children with them, and they threw themselves down the hillocks of fine white sand screaming and crying and rolling as if it were snow: then a rattlesnake slithered across the bottom of a dune, its tail sizzling like dried peas in a gourd and they fell silent and after it went home, they went home.

Other things happened: she took up catching baby leopard frogs for fishermen. One of them paid her in stale humbugs instead of money and her mother taught her about business. Her father made friends with a fat man from Buffalo, a cooper, who admired a mechanical man and invited them to come to his cottage for steak and ice cream from Mrs. Ellis's cows, churned in a big vessel with a crank. One of June's friends rubbed poison ivy on her face to see what would happen. Tessa made a friend, and then she went away.

How many summers? Who can tell? Tessa has tried to ask June, June has tried to remember: neither of them knows. They lead different lives, and Star Bay wasn't important to June. she had no leopard frog business, she had other things on her mind, the time just went.

Once they went into the woods together, the forbidden woods, and June was the leader, and June, with her mother's gifts, got lost. "We must sit and wait, Tess, until they come and find us," she said piously. "That's what Daddy said."

Tess sat on a log as long as she could, a whole minute. "Look, June, the sun sets over the lake and it's afternoon and there's the sun so if we walked we'd get to the beach, see?"

"Tess, we are to sit and wait until we are rescued. Otherwise we will walk in circles. People die that way."

Tess, conscious as June that she was the great-grandchild of pioneers, extended her arm. "Look, Junie, you stick out your arm and at the end of it are your fingers, and you put them between the sun and the horizon: each one is fifteen minutes. It's only about three o'clock."

"Tess, stay there."

"Well, you can stay there. I'm going to the beach, and when I get there I'm turning left." She skittered off, leaving Junie, scared, in a mossy cathedral of a clearing, trying to decide how best to be elderly and responsible. Reluctantly, she followed Tess.

They came out somewhere they'd never been before and even Tess was scared for a minute, but she knew home was left. She danced ahead and June followed sulkily. "Look," she cried finally, "we're on the other side of the clearing, look!" Junie, stubborn and humiliated, looked down instead of ahead and saw that rarest of treasures, a leaf-coloured whippoorwill on her nest. They sat down and worshipped, not daring to breathe. The bird's whiskers twitched, her eyes rolled with fear, she was as quiet as they were. When they got up and tiptoed home, she flopped off, but only a little way, for a little while. When they looked back she was back with her eggs. They went home hand in hand and told their adventure.

Then something happened: their father was given a job teaching on an army base. He couldn't turn it down: his First War service record put him in an excellent category (though he wouldn't join up and be a Captain, once was enough, he said, and civilian staff got better pay); everything about the job was advantageous, especially having a sergeant to handle the discipline. They moved. Junie set out to conquer her eleventh school. Tess was no longer thin and faster than a sandpiper. There were only two weeks' holidays, and Father's ulcers were cured.

They never went back. Frank and Maudie didn't believe in going back anywhere. And anyway, wouldn't Tess like to go to summer camp with the girl next door? They could afford it now. So Tess went to camp and her parents took the green trailer somewhere by themselves. Junie was fruit-picking.

It might even have been thirty years later that Tess and her husband were driving down the Bruce from Tobermory, arguing who had overspent on the holiday. There was a big green sign, "Mar" on the highway, and Tess, who never learned to drive said, "Oh, please." He gave her his kismet look and sighed. "We can have lunch there." The children were asleep in the back of the car.

She began to bounce. "Sky Lake," she said. The way he looked at it, she knew it was a plain patch of swamp. The road through the bush had been widened, but he honked for her pleasure. The children didn't wake.

At Ellis's, she said, "I'll just get out and get a quart of milk."

He said he'd stay with the kids, but got out of the car and stood against the fender, not unpleased to find himself beside a tumbledown farm in a sandy wilderness.

She asked for a quart of milk in the store, which was a farm kitchen, then confessed, "We used to come in the summer. We had a trailer."

"Oh, you're the Chalmers girl, you write for the papers and you married a Jew. I heard about you. Well, it's not the same place, we sold off a lot of cottage lots. And don't you try to put up your tent or your trailer: we don't allow that now. People aren't what they used to be." She went on for a bit about how they didn't eat what was put before them, either, and how she'd married Joey's brother and taken over the store from the old lady, who died a couple of years ago, she was a hundred.

Tess, conscious of Sam out there waiting, said well, it was nice to see her, and where was the milk?

"Don't you remember? Why, it's out where it's always been, in the spring house, by the road. And don't fall in." Then she told her how her husband had had a foot cut off because of the diabetes and the other one would soon have to go, which was a pity because for a while he was Township Reeve.

Tess felt guilty going down the path, as if, like Elmer Ellis, she'd eaten too many chocolate bars. Sam was still by the car, but she couldn't quite remember where the spring house was, and she was tense; then she thought, it's the geese and the old woman, I was scared of the geese and the old woman.

Right at the bottom of the path, where the wire fence with pressed iron maple leaves between its scallops left off, there was a wooden shed. It was open to the road, so she had only one gate to go through. She walked in: it was new inside, all concrete, but there was a funny smell. There was a concrete floor, and it had certainly been earth before, and there were wire baskets containing waxed-paper cartons of milk, not billycans or bottles or whatever there were before, and she half-closed her eyes and reached forward.

Then she remembered: because around each carton there was a garter snake coiled. And the smell was sulphur because it was a sulphur spring. She took her milk and half-ran to the car.

"Home?" Sam laughed.

"Sort of. Oh, look, two rows of cottages, like a subdivision. That was the Little Sand Pile. It was always full of cow pies."

"Glamorous." He wasn't particularly urban, but he had gone to more expensive camps: he expected his wilderness to be up to a certain standard.

They got down to the lake. There was a new dock, but not a very good one. The ice house had collapsed. Sovereigns's and Grimes's and Crows's cottages were exactly as they had been before. "That's Sunset Island," she said, pointing at it. It looked terrible: a mud blob in a mercury pool. The day was so hot everything had flattened out.

She got out the food box and set about making some sandwiches. The children woke up and were so overheated she set them down in their shorts in the shallow water. Nobody wanted any milk. The children paddled in the water and pronounced it yukky. Sam told her to go for a walk; he would babysit.

She set out. Mrs. Ellis had told her the Blue Cottage was for sale. She went past it and Pennypackers's and came to their own clearing; it was exactly the same. The cedar grove was still the shape of a woodshed or a living room. She might find the aluminum plate for the fishcleanings if her parents had been the sort of people who ever left an object behind. But they had littered with memories, and she had become the sort of person who picked them up after them. And if she went looking for the board with the ants under it, or the can of toads, or the scars of the towrope against the tree, or the whippoorwill's nest, what wouldn't happen? Anyway, she was too big to be King of the Castle anymore. She heard her mother's voice, "You won't remember, but that first day up there, I thought, what's happening to us now, what is this place, how can we bear it?"

She turned back toward Sam and the children and saw in the distance because she was still long-sighted a tall athletic woman walking, and remembered a certain woman, another non-Canadian, a minister's daughter from California who used to organize games on the beach. She pelted back to Sam. "Let's pack up. There's someone coming."

Ten years after that, she thought, would it have helped if I had said something artistic like "Od und leer das Meer"? And laughed, and plunged her hand in again among the cold bottles and the cold snakes and smelled sulphur.

Still Life with Nude

LORNA CROZIER

On this beach everyone
wants to be skinny
except the Rubens nude
sleeping in her flesh on the pier.

The sun is too small, her skin
consumes it. The movement of one foot
is answered by her whole body, ripples
rising up her thighs and belly,
the waves of her hair.

When she gathers the light, billows
past the young women, she is a bright
silk tent breathing in and out
with wind off the water.

Inside its walls a cat licks sweetness from an empty cup. Flies
dip their feet in the pulp of figs.
On white cushions a man kneels by a woman
who lifts her buttocks
round and glistening with sweat
in the perfumed light.

Sea Gifts

CONSTANCE ROOKE

THIS—THE ORANGE AND IRIS COLOURED SKY—is the first sunrise I have looked at since Caitlin's death. The others (for I have been awake so early and have passed windows) would bring tears so instantly, bring back the old mornings at the beach when I had fed her in my arms and from my body, bring them so entirely that looking was not possible. And now? For three months there has been only pain, waves that would take me away just a short, familiar distance—return me again until it was night and I lay exhausted, rehearsing waves in my sleep. At the beach, in my rocking chair before the long windows, I could ride such different waves in perfect happiness. It was all easy. Each wave was mine, they were real—we were clouds together, I and my daughter and the sea. I was not wet, I rarely saw the milk then, and there was no salt. The gulls were behind the glass—but it was all real. I was in the sea. The sky was orange and iris coloured, and then it was blue like the sea. I will go out today. I will have breakfast, then I will go out.

She was Chinese-looking at first, my baby. She was magical and loose as a trail of ivy in my arms. I could never think of a name beautiful enough for her. I knew there was one name that belonged to her, that she would smile in a new way when I found and gave it back to her. In the meantime I called her Caitlin, and she forgave the error. She always seemed generous, as if when she had heard enough of my language she would tell me what the language had never been made to say before. She would choose an ordinary moment—and then what she said would be in phrasing and rhythm quite different from my speech. She would have done this. Before the time came she died. Before she had told me her name or what I would become she left. They called it a crib death. I thought that was a very stange name for Caitlin's going. A disappearance act with the shape of her body still there, with the lashes resting on her cheeks. Her cheeks began there really, just under the eyes. Little black lines resting on her cheeks, I thought she meant them for goodbye. Sweet lashes, pen-strokes: my milk and my tears ran together to find her.

Gift Number One. "Yes, Miss? Can I help you?" Her voice is like cream. "May I try the pistachio please?" There is a sign saying you can try anything, and a supply of little wooden paddles. I have come all this way to Baskin-Robbins to find myself unsure whether it was for pistachio ice cream or some other kind. But the sign allows no disquiet. Does it see that I am to be treated tenderly, and is that why the girl's voice is so unworldly, so good to me? Before I came out today it was all arranged. I can see that now. "This is wonderful," I tell her, and she smiles as if she knows everything. I imagine her feeding it to me forever, smoothing my forehead with her cool hand and never speaking.

Gift Number Two. There is a place where the tan metal shelves go on for miles, where the lights are out. There are no books in that part of the library. Yet today one light is shining, and the gloom is altered. An old woman there on the floor is eating sandwiches. Above her, my gardening books are waiting: it has been five months since my last visit, and still they have not been moved. "I'm sorry, these are yours?" she asks. "I'll get them for you." She rises, and I show her the bougainvillea. Now in my car I sit trembling because this has happened.

You leave messages, Caitlin. My sea-child, my giving-bird. I will hear the sea.

Sleeping Together

SUSAN MUSGRAVE

In my dream you have become
a fisherman. You are going fishing
in my sleep.
"Sharks come to light and blood,"
you whisper, as if you have always been
a fisherman. A shark surfaces beside me;
still I cannot stop dreaming.

In your dream I am a bird,
I am trapped inside your house.
I flap my wings, beat on the windows.
"My house has no roof," you say.
Still I cannot get out.

You touch me, very gently.
You want to make me happy.
You say so, over and over.
You want me to stop dreaming.

In your dream I am dead.
You have made sure of that.
Still I am stronger than you
and more confident.
My hand does not tremble as yours does
when you twist, again, the knife.

In my dream you have become an
undertaker. You are syphoning my blood
under a cold light.
"Sharks come to light and blood,"
you whisper, as if you have always been
an undertaker. Still I go on dreaming.

You touch me, very gently.
You want me to make you happy.
You want me to stop dreaming.
You say so, over and over.

A shark is swimming towards us;
still, we sleep.
"Stop dreaming," you whisper; he surfaces
beside me.
"Stop dreaming," you shiver; he nudges your
blind windows. The shark has become a bird,
like me. Trapped inside your house we are
flying, flying.

"My house has no roof," you cry,
but the shark, too, is dreaming.
Like me, he does not want to stop dreaming.
He does not want to stop dreaming.

State of Rescue

ERÍN MOURE

The sky dark & she is under it,
behind the house
lifting her baby on his birthday, into the home
of her arms;
her body wide in its winter clothing,
her car open & yellow lit
In the house the father roars, cutting up the furniture,
shaking the white crib with his beard;
his wild arms
drunk on whisky, shut up like a jar

The woman is holding the baby into the cold air
beside two policemen at 4 a.m.,
putting his diapers into the car,
warming its engine
scraping ice from the windshield
As the woman moves out, she rescues
herself from fear, rescues
the child whose eyes are caught
in the coat of terror, of furniture breaking in the night
waking the neighbours

to the voice of his father
who is not in heaven, whose name is not clear
whose will is his child
one year old
too frightened to cry till the policeman held him
Safe in his mother's car, its engine
a soft sigh in the neighbourhood,
the car's warmth
a red thermal line on the city's scanners,
driven
to a sister's house, & sleeps   now
whatever the sky brings, wherever the father is,
whoever he wants to be

The Face She Makes

NICOLE BROSSARD

ANALYSIS: SO THAT THE LIPS APPEAR AGAIN TO ME as a motivation to follow mouths full of affinities. In that, I work at ending the convulsive habit of initiating girls to the male like the usual practice of lobotomy. I *in fact* want to see women's form take shape in the trajectory of the species.

March 1977

I've finished the book *L'Amèr* or *Le chapitre effrité*, but *I imagine that everything will start over again*. The temptation for more or tender nourishment in the abode of thrilling spaces. Face facts. Inclined toward reality. Ardour should not be confused with pleasure or the double delirium of women lovers. Let us refer to the present.

Which body is it all about on the horizon, low tide, there's hardly any excuse to forget that it concerns us in the hard mould of conditioning. Mould, mould, crack running after the words to grasp one's share. Strange participation of *the pebble girl* at the will of the sea. Let us refer to the present. The tasks are numerous (breeze while embracing still) in the forging of lives when emotion rouses the voice, experience; in thinking that only the guile used to camouflage the breasts is real, permanent breast heavy with consequences for the bearer, nipple negates me, still me.

The face she makes! Devouring in the reading the recurrent foetuses. Going away, which drifting body is it all about?

It's in the hollow of the hip, in the waistlines with terror, entering cold into the imaginary as one freezes on the spot, tears, tears, *cheek*. Consent near the belly. I look at my undertaking: I must write then.

I'm surprised. *The surprise of my life*. Unexpectedly, something at the beginning, quick remember *it is not the same it is never the same*. That makes all the difference in the world. The part that's hatching. The ready-made one.

Blotting the flux, I implicate myself: read, write, clitoris, fleeting ink my arms. To the sisters, all out speed, our bodies, our morals: "Try and guess what's happening to me."

Death is sometimes so foreseeable at the centre of the eyes that it alters forms. Renders them sterile. It also happens that the corner of the mouth goes up, *to better grasp* and that the saliva makes it. Starts to formulate the active stages of the grasped body. The face she makes then, suspended in time between her girlish past and let us refer to the present from the side of sisterhood.

Sunday and my mother so routine. On what would then depend the urgency to write, to see myself so fertile in describing the meeting of crystals, in dreaming the colour of pebbles, the white embraces in the sunlight. So differently, so tirelessly with women. A certainty watches for me in the night, radical presence. Tender in my mouth. I imagine with my tongue what's happening to me.

To have in mind the long and systematic history of our mutilated bodies that value reality as well as life, rankles too much in the heart. Be strongly tempted to resort to the image of the fist just as you make up your mind to act with your body. But in the word what can really happen to my body that it doesn't already know or is aroused by. I can in the word tell how with this body. Whose breasts.

It's thus night always at night because we constantly watch. Drowsy in our bellies. By the forms, easy to substitute. "I'll go mad" not anymore "I've killed the belly" horizon. "But the terror, says she, that we find daily in books and in bed, like at the bedside, lead feet." "It happens to me where does it get me?" The beautiful desire of our arms thought she in the early hours.

I don't want to go round in circles to write down the virtue of books It touches me constantly. Open the book on carnal identities where in the seduction zones we appropriate with clarity *a vision*. Cycle. Cycle. The synthesis of relationships.

And then in the spring we don't have to think that there are suicides in the trees.

Now, everything relates to this when someone says "you, woman" and consequently "me a woman" suspended like a vague shape right at the height of emotion. In the throat, sensitive and rising tide. I want us rigorous ones to undertake the proceeding, the coincidence of seeing ourselves politically favourable to assertion. Feel that the eye undertakes to feed the inside of what it stares at, the vital form of the feminine. Prolong fiction, *in reality*, I look at things straight in the eye.

The face she makes at the other end of her body. The body she makes when from her belly *it has flowed* like an expression between her legs. It is then that her mouth opened up.

This cry at birth, exploring it, covering it up with words, she has begun to translate her body. It is then that her mouth opened up. Even if she must during all that time politicize her belly haunt it like the fiction that goes through her. Have her way.

With words, I redeem the births I give. I take back the child, echo the cry. In exchange for a text like a text. Raving madness. That's indeed the point *the face she makes* it's when *I realize* really my body put into words. Breach in the break like producing positive energy. Maybe then start anew the blinding cycle of desire. The dense projectory of bodies, it'll soon be noon, perhaps dream the kiss like a superfluous word in the double mouth. Or the political pebble to better project the voice.

Agitation. Full of risks. Is giving battle down to earth. "I'm hungry thirsty hot it rains don't go away." Can everything be started over again? The tangible afternoons of the flesh looking for its words.

Head in hands, so, a fragment of life. She thinks, pliant like an earlobe, in her hand, the thought, a vision of the world. Her hands on the temples, heartbeat. Daily rhythm, thought, acts, any act—I'm so vulnerable then in this posture in front of the window. For certain I deviate. Violently. Violently an *IDEA* in mind. To cross my own matter, the fluids, one and collective, full of numbers: beautiful agitation. The idea I have of myself in person and woman. Idea: form one body in the city, eye aflame in the cycle of inscriptions. Because all that time, it was a question of writing to avoid that a woman's eye, that the sea erases the signs of the hand. *City in the water* the A the Origin the Alphabet the phantasm, without restraint, engulfed, am I possible then and tolerable in the city, me met at the height of ardour who trace mark write leave leave the blotting paper when you happen to lose your head moving your lashes between life between death Atlantis pebble girl.

Surface: emerge radical from the waters.

Women lovers: I put my mouth with your sex is it revelation to see us slow to live sharing in the same agony like trembling members of which only the brightness will be talked about in any eventuality. Either foolishness, subversive jugglers we entering the city true to life. Can we think relationships otherwise than in the form that we adopt. Or in the posture.

To be in position to with an intention. I want to leave the enigma with *a price on my head* so that the superstitions and *the fruit of thy womb end.*

The face she makes. It is then that her eyes opened up without hallucination and the fiction the more coherent.

"Don't go away."

translated by Josée M. LeBlond

Straight Talking

CAROLYN SMART

The women around me are my friends.
They speak like poets, and when I think poets,
I think men, and the way they speak like women,
and I can understand them. And these women,
sometimes I take them in my arms;
they are swimmers, they dance
and they are swimmers.
They are afraid of the same things
and sometimes not. And their hearts
beat against the windows like pigeons.
Some nights they think of flying,
the perfect freedom without lines
and their eyes become whole again in the light.
Their dreams are bad and good
and it feeds their days, everything becomes food
for my friends are always hungry
and allowing others to feed with them, of them,
for through this they become filled.

The Second Decade

Volumes 11 – 20 (1988 – 1997)

This Is Not Chick Lit: An Interview with Editor Mary Schendlinger

LINDSAY GLAUSER KWAN

From 1982 to 1989, Mary Schendlinger was an active member of *Room*'s editorial board, the Growing Room Collective. She has a long history of working in publishing, including for the 1970s feminist magazine, *Makara*. She went on to co-found *Geist* magazine, where she was Senior Editor for twenty-five years. Mary is also a writer, a comics maker (as Eve Corbel), and a retired teacher of publishing. Lindsay Glauser Kwan spoke with Mary about *Room* and feminism in the late 1980s.

ROOM: What were the types of behind-the-scenes conversations that [the Growing Room Collective] was talking about at that time? I mean, right now, we are talking a lot about diversity and how to increase the diversity in our pages, and new ways of thinking of that, but back then, it was a different context.

MS: Yeah, it was completely different. And we were so un-diverse [*laughs*]. You know, you were white or you were something else, you were gay or you were straight. That was the extent of it and so, I mean, again, this was unpaid work. It was like whoever had a few hours to throw in every month and who would stagger up to the plate and do it, and we published, I think, a better variety than what was represented in the collective, but you know, it's just how things were. And we were certainly talking about those things. In that phase of the women's movement, there were workshops on class and race and gender and things like that. Not nearly to the extent that there is now, but we were sure talking about it. We didn't think of ourselves as single-issue feminists, as they say, but it was white women who were doing that stuff because we had the skills and wherewithal. There were some publications where it was just beginning, to go out of our way to invite women and to bring them along, right around that time.

ROOM: We find today that our collective tends to be younger—we have a few people with children—or also mostly older and without those responsibilities. Does it seem like an issue for a lot of women that caregiving is a big barrier to their participation?

MS: Yeah, it's just the fact of it. In fact, I almost feel unauthorized to say anything about it because things were way, way easier for us than they are for women now. When my kids were small and in daycare in the early '70s, we had an NDP government. We had subsidized daycare. I mean really subsidized daycare. We took one hundred women and children to Victoria in a protest one fine day because they wanted to cut off the hot lunch program for kids and we knew it was very important—particularly for low-income families. For them to have that service in daycare. We had to take the government to court to even get our permit to run the daycare where my kids were. It was all so new, and families were changing.

ROOM: So it was more accessible for you, even though you had to fight for a lot of issues.

MS: Yes, that's right, and the fact that you could get a chicken for a dollar. I was living in housing that was well subsidized. You know there's still housing co-ops now but they're closer and closer to market rent. It was Brian Mulroney who pulled the first rug out from under that. So it was different for us. We had resources that you guys don't have. And you can't imagine doing that now, when one of the incomes in the household has to all go for child care. It's different.

ROOM: You were on the collective during the late 1980s. How did you—or the collective—define feminism at that time?

MS: Well, we talked a lot about that. Certainly in the second half of the '70s and into the '80s, there were events, workshops, any number of potential spots in which to have debates about these issues. There was this idea that feminism was for white middle-class women—the *Ms.* magazine feminism, it was called. I don't know if you've read Gloria Steinem's memoir that she wrote recently at age eighty. But you know, everybody should. She was never a single-issue feminist—never, never, never, never. But it got that reputation because that's who could afford to buy *Ms.* magazine and who could be a voice of women in the United States. And it was largely those women who could achieve some power politically, who could do some good. White middle-class women. There was a lot of work done on other issues—class and race particularly, starting in the late '70s, that I knew about anyways; there were workshops on sexuality, and this is when the Women's Health Collective was getting going and we were all, you know, looking at our own cervixes with mirrors. And then we were taking self-defence workshops and stuff like that. So all this is swirling around, swirling around, swirling around and there were extremists who were lesbian women who were separatists. And who, if you had a son, you gave your son to the father or some men and just, you know, you were or weren't a woman-identified woman. So there was all this stuff flying, flying, flying around.

I think that in general, in the groups that I hung around at least, there were many, many definitions of [feminism]. Lesbian feminists had their own issues, and then there's women of colour who had their own issues, and there was the takeover of the women's press that happened. And then there was the great split about the rape groups, that was Rape Relief against WAVAW [Women Against Violence Against Women], and it was a huge public meeting of feminists, and it was just people ripping people's guts out. It got so awful, you know—should we be more political or just keep scraping women up off the street? I'm oversimplifying but these things were all up for grabs. It was as if we had a few years and got our legs under us, like oh we're women and we are worth something; it doesn't matter what everybody in our life is telling us—every part of our culture.

When I moved to Vancouver in 1970 with my young husband and my baby, he was in school and I was working, and I went to Woodward's to get a charge card because they had a food floor. We were poor, and I thought if we could just have some credit. I wasn't really identifying as a feminist at this point; I had a pretty feisty outlook on life but not particularly political. And they said no you can't have one because the male in the family isn't working. Like what difference does it make? So yeah I'm getting paid, I was paying bills. No they wouldn't give me one. Well, I mean, that was my education; so I'll just cut to the chase—I got my card [laughing].

So that's what it was like in 1970 and then a few years later, there was a movement. And you could feel the moment and you could be part of the movement, but it was all quite new at that point and all these issues were still quite embryonic and we had kids to raise and, you know, husbands to leave, and communal houses to live in, and my God, just speaking with people who weren't related to me, we were redefining the family. So I'd like to give you a short answer. But my memory of it and when I paw back into my journals—because I've been keeping journals obsessively for many years—it's just like question, after question, after question. And how did I feel about it. Everything, almost all my values as a girl growing up were on the table to be reassessed and to be rethought.

ROOM: Yeah, that's a really good answer actually because I had another question about the feminist climate of the time. It reminded me a lot of this job that went viral in recent months [because] it said that they wanted this woman for a secretary. And you know, everyone, went crazy! [*laughing*]

MS: It's just not acceptable anymore.

ROOM: Yeah, and then when I posted it with my friends and family on Facebook, [some of] my aunts came out with these stories about how they had experienced something like this in the workplace and it was pretty astonishing—like about not getting a job because they were pregnant, for instance. For [my generation], we kind of take it for granted, but we see parts of this as well—like with maternity leave. There is an unconscious bias against women, right, even though [employers] are not technically allowed to say it because of the movement before us, but it's still there. So it is nice to have those reminders, of what it was like.

MS: You're so right about that and that is why we can never, never, never let down our guard. [Because] the rights we have, we will lose them if we don't keep working. We will lose the right to a safe and legal abortion. We will lose the right. If we are not on the case every minute, they will take it away! [*pounds fist on table, laughing*]. We know they will; they've done it. And you're absolutely right about that.

These Hips

KATE BRAID

Some hips are made for bearing
children, built like stools
square and easy, right
for the passage of birth.

Others are built like mine.
A child's head might never pass
but load me up with two-by-fours
and watch me
bear.

When the men carry sacks of concrete
they hold them high, like boys.
I bear mine low, like a girl
on small, strong hips
built for the birth
of buildings.

The Busuuti and the Bra

JULIANE OKOT BITEK

I'LL TELL YOU WHY THEY ARE FLAT AND LONG AND DRY. I'll tell you why no bra can help me. And I'll tell you why I will not stop wearing sleeve-less, round-necked blouses even though they do not flatter my chest. I'll even tell you, my young daughter, why I will not do anything about it. No. No breast enlargement, no pump-up bras, no nothing. I want to tell you why I love my breasts the way they are.

A long time ago, it seems like a long time ago, way back when my chest was flatter than flat; yes, long before I even knew about training bras, my grandmother, Min Aton, came to stay with us for a while, and she talked to my sister and me about breasts.

Before then, I had never given thought to breasts, or bras, or boys, the way you do now. My sister and I were more interested in being the best at skipping, running the fastest at seven stones, hiding the longest at hide-and-seek. It was Min Aton who first brought the idea of breasts to our attention. And it's not as if we knew completely nothing about them. We did. We just never thought about them. We knew that grown women had breasts, and that little babies suckled at them. We knew that overweight men had something of breasts, some fat babies did, too. And we even knew that most boys did not have breasts. Other than that, we did not know the difference.

One afternoon, Min Aton called my younger sister and me to her bedroom. We entered the room and ran straight to her bed. I've told you about Min Aton's bed. It was the softest, the warmest, the deepest, the best place to be. It was a place you never ever wanted to leave. We had dived into the blankets and we were already giggling inside.

"Get up."

We were not about to listen to that now, the fun was just beginning.

"Get out of there, girls, I want to talk to you."

We sat up with the blankets drawn up to our knees.

"I want to talk to you about growing up. Do you know that one day you are going to be grown women?"

We giggled nervously. We did not know what to expect.

"I just want you two to grow up into strong, beautiful women. I want you to know what to do when the time comes. What do you know about growing breasts?"

What did we know about growing breasts? One of the girls we played together with was growing them. She could no longer catch balls thrown at her chest, the way we still did. She could no longer practise diving in the long grasses outfield, when we fantasized about real diving and real swimming. And she could not run very fast any more. She said that they hurt.

"They hurt," we said at the same time.

"Well," Min Aton smiled. "There is a little more to it than that."

Why didn't I tell you this story before? Sometimes I wish that I had. I guess I thought that these times did not warrant such stories. But let me tell it to you now.

"Look at my chest. Do you see anything?"

My sister and I squinted. We were not sure of what we were supposed to be looking for. No, we did not see anything. Min Aton laughed.

"Your mother. Your mother and your aunt. They both sucked me dry."

We were hugging the blanket tightly around our knees. This did not seem like it was going to be a traditional folk story with a chorus and an end. Besides, it was not yet evening, and we had not yet had our supper. We could hear the playful screams of other children outside, but they began to fade out as we saw Min Aton's hands go up to the buttons of her *busuuti*.

You do not know what a *busuuti* is. It is, well, it used to be the national dress for women in Uganda, like the sari in India, or the kimono in Japan. It is very hard to describe—you have to see one. But I can tell you that it is stately and elegant. My own mother never wore one, because she said that it made her bum look too big, that it was too long, too bulky, that she could not move in it, she had no occasion to wear one. It was the only thing that Min Aton wore.

Let me try to describe a *busuuti* to you. It has a square neckline, with two big buttons that open up between the shoulder and the right breast. The sleeves cap, then fall to the elbows. The *busuuti* is belted at the waist with a stiff, thick cloth that ties in a knot below the belly button. The rest of it flows to the ground. But who can describe a *busuuti*? No, no. It is a dress that brings out the dignity of the woman that wears it. But let me tell you this story.

We were still concentrating on Min Aton's hands as they fumbled with the buttons. It became dead silent. There was a kerosene lamp on the shelf. Yes, we had electricity, but Min Aton did not trust it. She thought it was too bright. It "did" her eyes. It drained her energy, made her feel weak. Min Aton could come up with any excuse not to turn on the light in her room. But that was only part of what made that room so special. It was never too bright. And at this point, the flame in the lamp was perfectly still.

"I want you both to look at me again. What do you see?"

Min Aton eased her arms out of the top of the *busuuti* and let it fall to her waist. She was wearing an old petticoat inside. It was so old that the lace was tightly wrinkled and the original beige colour had turned a dirty brown with time. Its neck sagged so much that Min Aton's chest was naked to her stomach. Why did she still wear it? Habit, maybe?

We watched her as she lifted out her braless breasts from the petticoat. Her breasts were very long. She pulled them out, one by one, and let them fall back down to her lap. No, I am not exaggerating.

Just listen.

The breasts were dry. Not flaky-skin dry. They were dry dry. They had no life in them. Limp. Like that. Wrinkled skin bags. Her nipples were soft and tired as they lay in the cradle of her lap.

"Wow."

My sister just stared.

"These fed your mother and your aunt. You see them today, this is not the way they always were. They have been through a lot. And I am proud of them because my children would not be where they are today without them."

We knew that there was a whole lot more coming.

"I was a young girl, right before the great World War, newly engaged to your grandfather." At this point, Min Aton spat. *Ptah*! She always spat whenever she mentioned my grandfather. He had left her for giving birth to two "useless girl babies, one after another." Now he was married to a small-breasted woman, not much older than my mother. He'd had six "strong sons" by her.

This was definitely not a "once upon a time" story.

"There was talk of a great war coming. Talk that the strongest and bravest men were required to go and defend freedom. Freedom! *Ptah*!"

She spat again. Freedom and my grandfather made her spit. No, she was not a woman's rights activist or anything like that. She was Min Aton. That's all she was, more than many of us women today can be.

She went on. "There were recruitment centres growing like weeds all over the place. Men of strength, men of integrity, men of conscience—they all lined up to fight the white man's war. The lineups were long and slow. They were asked questions, filled out forms, were measured for weight and height, were allocated battalions, given guns, made to swear allegiance to the king and empire, and then sent to die. I watched them go. Your grandfather? *Ptah*! Of course he did not go! That coward? He didn't go! He got medical records that said that he was not healthy—epilepsy, something like that. He still is. Look at him."

Our mother had warned us not to believe everything (from experience that translated into most things) that Min Aton said about our grandfather. We were not to defy her word against him, not to interrupt when she went into these tirades about his flaws that seemed uncountable.

"Nobody knew that man like I did. I spent six years of my life," she held up the last three fingers of each hand.

"Six years! I knew him when he was nobody with no son to boast about." She went on. "We lived near the recruiting centre close by the market. There were always young men in the area. Where there were young men, there were young women. Where there were young women, there were suitors, there were lovers. Everyone was looking for everyone. It was a lusty time. Hah! It was a time that everything that mattered depended on the physical, at least the war did. Women walked about with sharp, angry breasts, fighting for space with the cotton bras that was fashion. And men, they walked about with spears in their pants."

For a long time, I thought that spears in pants was a very clumsy idea, but by the smile on your face, I see you know what she meant.

Min Aton continued.

"The breasts I had then were not like what you see now. I did not want to wear a bra. I did not need one. My breasts were strong and free. They stood in my chest with no restrictions. And when your grandfather used to say that his blessing was his curse, I thought he meant that he had too much of a good thing with me. That what he loved about me was what other men wanted me for. I told you, back then what mattered was the physical. I was young then. I laughed and was warm and content with that. We got married. Then he wanted me to stay in the house all the time. He said that my breasts would get me into trouble, and I learned to hate them because they imprisoned me. No, no. I had a wonderful figure. I did. But I became convinced that I was ugly, and I hated myself. Now that I am old, my figure is gone and I am alone, I love myself more than I ever did."

She held her hands to her chest, her left hand on the left breast and the right hand on the right. Then she got up, her breasts hanging out as she stood, then lying flat against her chest. She walked across the room and picked up the kerosene lamp from the table where it had been sitting. Our shadows danced against the wall as she walked with the lamp and placed it on the bedside stand. We could feel the glow from the flame as we listened to Min Aton.

"After we got married, your grandfather decided that craziness was going to be his nature. Yes, I said *decided*. He knew what he was doing! He used to go to the market to listen to the radio at the market corner. It was the thing that men did. Well, those men that did not fight for freedom, listened to that radio. And at the end of the day, they came home and spouted out news about the war in Europe—the advances of the enemies, the victories of the Allies, the bombings, losses, spoils, the politics. The radio was all-important. More important than money for rent or salt for food. I say this because when I wanted to go out and buy salt, or sell vegetables from the garden in the market, your grandfather said I wanted to sabotage his plans to go and get the facts about the war for freedom. I wanted to spoil his name, embarrass him by showing off my fantastic figure. I was a married woman now. I should be happy staying at home to take care of things. He would take care of everything else, and he never did. *Ptah*! It was the radio that sapped what little reasoning he had. The radio and the war—freedom. *Ptah*! And in those days I listened to him and believed him.

"After your mother was born, my breasts became heavy and swollen with milk. Your grandfather claimed that I was taking some kind of medicine to make them grow bigger, attract more attention. How could I attract attention if I was in the house all the time? He wanted me to tie up my chest so that my breasts lay flat. And he tied them up himself, before I stepped out of the house. I began to faint frequently as a result. He said it was a ploy to get his attention. By the time your aunt was born, I was no longer the beautiful wife. I was now a witch, he said, giving birth to other witches like me. The only extent to which I was a witch was that I let dark thoughts crowd my heart, and I hated myself even more. And you know, he is now living with that woman, young enough to be his daughter, and he thinks he is happy, *ptah*! I never told you how your grandfather . . ."

Min Aton had a talent for zigzagging stories. In a story there were several stories, several experiences. And with each, her face went through the range of utter disgust to unabashed ecstasy. My sister and I were always entranced. We were the perfect audience.

Then Min Aton smiled. And when she smiled, who didn't? She had a huge gap between her upper front teeth. The gap was so big that it could have taken another tooth. I see you are grimacing. I always wished I had a gap like that. Then I wished that when I had a daughter, she would have one just like that. You know, in some places, that is considered a sign of beauty. Not here. Not these days either. Now it can be "fixed" at the dentist. Fixing beauty, hiding it, closing it, tucking it in, tying it up.

When Min Aton smiled, she was not responding to you showing your teeth. When she smiled, she smiled with a part of your body that rose in the form of a warm glow from your toes, tingled at your fingertips and embraced you. No, I am not kidding. When you were a baby, you responded to Min Aton that way that I have described to you. It did not matter that you were feeling cranky, or sick and burning with a fever. Min Aton used to make you smile and laugh out loud with tears still running down your face.

Min Aton held her limp breasts in her hands.

"These are not for beauty. These are for life. Would your mother and aunt be alive if I had not fed them? Would you?"

She laughed.

"I see you don't quite understand. I don't want to confuse you. But, hah, I spent so much time suffering over this body of mine, I don't want the same pain for you." Her smile faded as she continued to explain. "When I thought that breasts were for beauty, I was miserable, I was not nearly as happy as I am now, knowing that my body is mine to enjoy. So, don't ever let anyone make you feel either way, on account of your breasts or any other part of your body."

The story was not interesting anymore. We started fidgeting.

"I want to tell you something else. When I was a young girl, my mother told me to massage my breasts so that they would remain perky."

"How?"

"Do you want to be here all night long, and tomorrow and the next day, too?"

We were paying attention again.

"I will show you another time. I just wanted to tell you that I massaged them for a long time, in search of the perfect breasts, and I did get them. But I want to be honest with you. I want you to know that it is not important what shape your breasts come in. You are my children, and all my children are beautiful."

Min Aton stood up and slapped her thighs with open palms. "Oh, oh, oh, what time is it?" She pulled the curtain back. The sun was setting. "Girls, you better go and have a bath. It will soon be time for supper. Come on, get up, out, out, out!"

Min Aton tickled us out of her bed, and we scampered out laughing. As usual, it had been deeply satisfying to be there. Then we all stood in the middle of the room, feeling the warmth from the flame, and our tie with this woman, Min Aton. Our grandmother. I have felt that way only once since. It was when I first saw you, my love.

So, don't tell me about fashion, about bras, about length, shape, size, or whatever numbers you have been taught to believe are relevant in breasts. No breasts, no part of me makes me any less than I am. I am Min Aton's daughter, and I am beautiful the way that I am, and like all the women in time, so are you, my love, so are you.

from The Cancer Year

DOROTHY ELIAS & barbara findlay

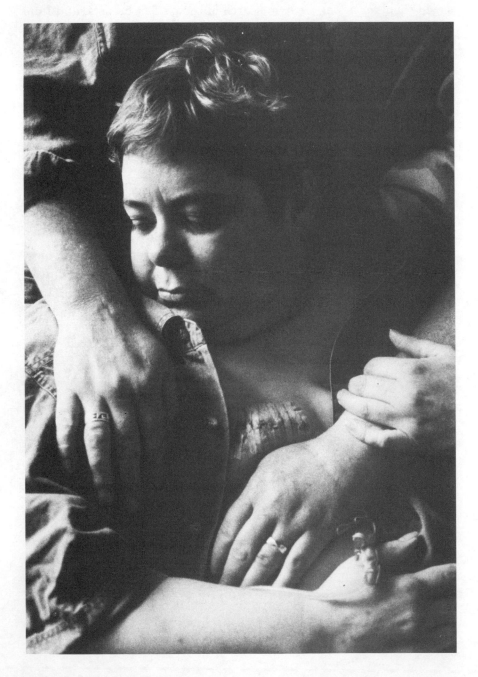

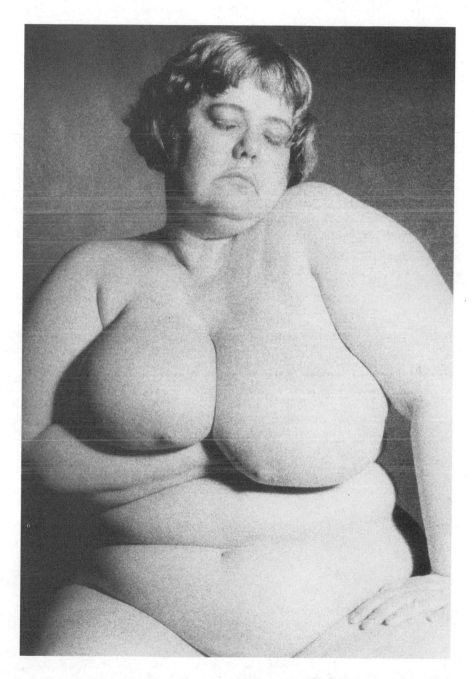

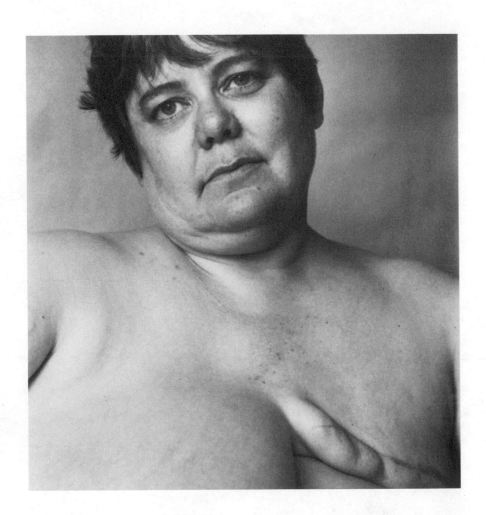

Dorothy Elias & barbara findlay

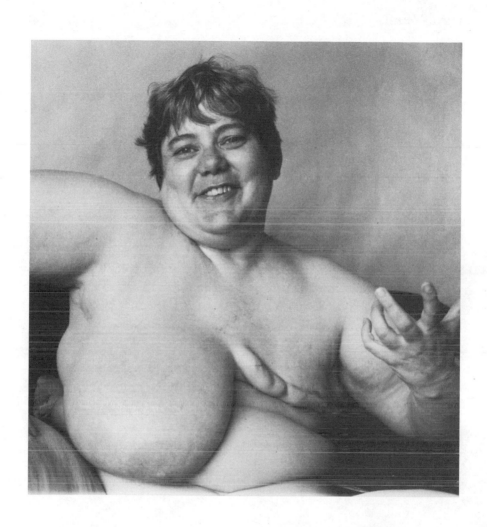

The Japanese rock garden I will have when I am an old woman

MINDY HUNG

then, I will choose smooth
lake stone, rounded shoulders curved
with years of washing.

La Guerra

VERA MANUEL

What do I know
about war.
and grandmothers
and babies
being killed.
Massacres,
blood, and
permeating fear.

I know
about love
and life.
I've known
safe places,
in spite
of where
I've been.

"Those *puta* soldiers
kill
everything,
mothers
babies . . ."
you cry.
And I can't
imagine
how it felt
to watch.

What do I know
about the war
that rages
in your mind?
that spills out
into my life?

I'm really scared
of you,
sometimes

"My family—
todos
everything wiped out,"
you say,
"And my babies
gone
I don't know where."

I
who've never
experienced
the death of someone
close.
What do I know
about
being empty,
alone?

I want
to run,
to hide,
to find
a safe place
to be,
away from you.

Then
I want to stay
to rub
that fear
out
from
your mind
to send you home
again
to die,
free.

WHEN WE FIRST MET, I never intended to stay this long and, I suspect, neither did you. What were we looking for? A good time, someone to fill up the spaces. I know I didn't intend to fall in love with you. This last year—during the hard times—I couldn't help but think we should have kept our romance in the bar, where we met. That way it could have stayed uncomplicated and extricable. We've come too far for that now, but always I go back and trace over in my mind those complicated paths we took. I remember everything.

How many times this past year have I wakened you from your tormented sleep and heard you muttering, "*Maldito suenos* (damned dreams), those *puta* soldiers trying to kill me," your body trembling and bathed in sweat? Then every time I planned my escape I'd wonder and worry if anyone would care enough to wake you from your dreams. They were always such ugly dreams, you never had nice dreams. "I was running trying to get away," you'd say. "There were soldiers everywhere. I came into this clearing and this soldier stepped out from the trees, he had a gun pointed right at me. I know he was going to kill me. I know I was going to die." Or, "They were chopping my legs with a machete. I was fighting and fighting, trying to get away, but there was blood everywhere . . . my blood," you'd cry.

Other times you wouldn't tell me what it was about. You'd light a cigarette and never say a word, then the rest of the night I'd hear you tossing and turning or prowling around the room, afraid to go to sleep. They you'd start drinking for days and you'd tell me that this was the only way you could sleep without dreams. I'd listen to you retching in the bathroom, with ugly scenes of the night before imprinted on my mind and I'd think and think of how I'd have to get away from you and that ugly war.

But I knew I'd made a decision to stay, that first time I invited you to my house. We weren't used to seeing each other away from the beer and the noise of the nightclub. My Spanish was about as good as your English and we stumbled along, making small talk, shy with one another. "And your family, are they all still in El Salvador?" I asked. You answered so matter-of-factly, as if we'd been talking about the weather. "My family is all dead. I have two sons, I don't know if they are still living." And that, I believe, is precisely the moment that took me inside your life, when all my defences dissolved and you came into mine.

Those first few months were the most difficult. We fought about everything. The distance between us was immense, filled with dark shadows and pain that I naively believed my love had the strength to lighten and heal. I kept a bag stashed in my car and a change of clothes in my sister's closet. I kept all my school books in a box in my car, in case I had to make a quick getaway. I don't know when I began to be afraid of you when you drank. For a long time I couldn't understand your violence or how anyone could be so full of anger. Yet I had great dreams about our future together and I was often hurt and couldn't understand why for you there was no tomorrow, only today and always yesterday. How many times did I want to yell, "If life was so great in El Salvador why in the hell didn't you stay there?" Your anger exploding, flying off in different directions, wounding me, as if somehow you believed I was to blame for you being here. But I did yell, often, "If Latina women are so perfect, why in hell didn't you find one? There are plenty of them up here. Why did you have to come bothering me?"

But there were more good times than there were bad. I don't remember how many times you told me you were sorry, that it would never happen again. I guess about as many times as I believed you. Then when you quit drinking, everything changed. Our arguments became deeper, the wounds we inflicted on each other were more penetrating, mortal wounds. Then I, too, began to think that maybe there wasn't a tomorrow.

You became more serious, withdrawn, brooding and often you built a wall around you that I couldn't penetrate. You couldn't talk to me about yourself, but you'd quote me statistics and tell me facts about the war, about Central America, but never enough so that I could understand. I was like a detective searching for clues. Trying to piece together your life. Hoarding and unravelling bits of information, initiating conversations with your friends, using things you said as bait. There was too much unsaid that I had to know. Then you withdrew from me completely. I went to Carlos, your friend, your confidant, because I knew you told him things you couldn't tell me.

"What is wrong with him lately?" I asked. "He's so unhappy. These last few weeks I don't know who he is anymore. He's having bad dreams again. He listens to those records of revolutionary songs all the time. When he's home he barely speaks to me. He's full of rage, and I don't know why. I don't know how to stop it."

Carlos responded by telling me about you. About the "you" that is your enemy now—that struggles with you. About the revolutionary you that I think I will never know.

"You shouldn't let him listen to those records," Carlos said. "You must tell him to take them back to Mario. That's who he borrowed them from. If you tell him to take them back, he will. We've talked about them and he knows they are bad for him. He says they make him remember everything. There is so much about that guy that you don't know. He has so many reasons to be angry. We both fought in that war, I know what it was like.

"He told you that the army killed his family. They killed everyone in the village and that is how he found them. You can't imagine what that is like. To come back to your village and find everyone dead. Bodies everywhere . . ." his voice trailed off to erase the image. "He always talks about revenge. That is what he lives for, is revenge. Maybe he can forget for a while, but I don't know if it will ever leave him completely. Maybe he has to go home. Maybe he has to kill soldiers until one of them kills him. But he can't go back now. The minute he steps into the country he will be dead. Someday, when we win the revolution, we'll all go back. That is what we dream about, all the time. But those songs," he said, "they're songs about the life of the guerrilla fighter and when he listens to them he remembers and wants to be there. You have to stop him from listening to that music."

I try not to think about that time when you will leave. But when I'm miserable, when I'm unhappy, I wish you would leave today. "Will you come with me when I go back to El Salvador?" you asked me once. "Yes," I said. But I know there will be no place for me and you there. I think in your heart you know that too. When we first met you were not strong as you are now. Now every day I see you growing stronger and as you grow stronger you grow farther and farther away from me.

Yet there is much that I do understand, probably more than you will ever realize. An Indian from this land knows what it means to struggle. We were born with that knowledge in our heart. We know what it means to love our land more than life. My people too have suffered. I've never seen them slaughtered like cattle, but I've walked down East Hastings Street late at night and I've seen their spirit dying, slowly, a more subtle way of death. So when you talk about going my heart shudders and it takes all my strength not to say, "What about me? Are you just going to go off and leave me? What about us?" because I know I would do the same. I'd do whatever I had to do to make peace inside.

"He was one of the best," Carlos told me. "He knew everything about guns. In our country he was the equivalent to a Green Beret in the United States. They nicknamed him "Junta" because he fought like a dozen men. Myself, I never fought up in the mountains, I was an urban guerrilla fighter. I was attending university during the daytime, and at night we would fight. Some days some students never made it back into the classroom and we never saw them again. He fought up in the mountains all the time, for five years. You know, to stay alive in the mountains for that long a time, you had to be one of the best. He barely got wounded. But you can imagine what it would do to your head to be fighting for that long a time. To see so much killing. To do so much killing—and to be so hungry all of the time.

"Oh yes, he has a lot of reasons to hate those soldiers and that is why I tell you he lives for revenge. He was never a really political person, but he was a good guerrilla fighter and he knew what it meant to be hungry. In our country only a few people are rich and they own all the land. Most of our people are starving. That is why there are people like us. We can't sit by and watch while our people are suffering. It is more difficult for people like us to be here in Canada, because we know no matter how tough it is here to survive, it can never be as bad as it is back home. Our government has to kill people like us or make sure we never return."

But I have a life too. My people are struggling too and they need me. I can't live like this forever, you know. My life in some kind of limbo, determined by your moods. I have no future with you, with only today, a day at a time waiting for that war to end. Maybe it will never end.

When we moved into this new co-op I thought we'd be happy here. "People in my country live like sardines in cardboard houses," you said. "They have no running water and toilets. Only rich people live in apartments like this." And I don't know what to say. When I was a child, six of us grew up in three rooms in a dismal little shack on the reservation. That's how all Indians lived. In the winter the freezing winds would blow right through those houses. That's how a lot of Indians still live today.

One time you told me about your baby. Your eldest son, the other was just an infant when you left. You never talk about him anymore. You used to talk about him a lot, when you believed he was still alive. You had no picture of him. Only that image of him crying after you that last time you left.

"He wore a bright red shirt the day I went away. Really, really red like that dress you're wearing now," you told me. You faltered, stopped, and started speaking again, carefully. "I think maybe he knew we would never see each other again. He was only four years old when I left and he told me, *I want to come with you, Papa. I'll get a gun and come with you. I'll kill lots of soldiers, Papa.*"

And I watched you smile at the memory of such a courageous son.

"I told him no, *no you can't come with me. You have to stay here. I'll be back soon*, and I held him and rocked him but he wouldn't stop crying. I set him down beside his mother's house. I told him to stay, and walked away. I kept turning to look back for as far as I could see. I could see him with his red shirt, his head in his arms against the house, and he was crying over and over again, *Papa, Papa, take me with you, Papa. I want to go with you*, and in my heart I was sore. Then his mother came out of the house and carried him inside. That's the last time I saw him."

When you looked at me with all that pain in your eyes, it was difficult for me to speak. That memory haunts me now as it does you.

"I'll have to go back and get him someday soon," you said. "When he is twelve, the soldiers will come and force him to fight in the army. If he doesn't fight in the army he will have to go up into the mountains to join the guerrillas. When I go to get him his mother won't want me to take him, but I'll have to take him anyway. I'll tell her that I'm going to take him to the city to buy him clothes and then I'll tell him to come with me. He will want to come anyway. If I bring him here, will you love him too and take care of him?" you asked.

But while I nod my head, I know that this too will never be.

I remember one night lying in bed listening to the rain and wind outside against the window. You holding me close, wrapping your legs around mine. Still, silent, listening . . . "There were many nights in the mountains when we'd have to sleep out in the rain," you said. "Sometimes a *compañera*, one of the women fighters, would come and lie beside me. It was nothing sexual, sometimes we'd just need someone to hold because it was cold, or we were feeling lonely. Sometimes we would sleep like this,"—you'd show me, lying scrunched, burrowing your face into the bed—"so the rain wouldn't fall on our face, holding our gun like this, we'd sleep."

When I go back over it in my mind, it plays on my memory like some sporadic, sad melody. It's there all the time now, haunting us, but we try to pretend it's not. We get up every morning and go to school. I, to the university to study the history of my people; you, to learn to speak English well enough so you can survive in this country. In the afternoon you go to visit Mario or one of your other friends so you don't feel so alone. When you come home we have supper and talk. Then you watch TV or study and I work on my papers until we go to bed. After a good day we lie for a long while, talking, joking in the dark, laughing; happy, I think. Until our entwined legs and arms let go, relaxing, we drift away to sleep. On good nights there are no dreams.

Another day I notice you've slipped away from me again. There is no conversation with our meal. There are shadows on your eyes and you don't look at me. You don't touch me. One night you don't come home from school and I sit and wait and wait for that damn war to end.

Oh God how I love you. I love the way your cheekbones lie high upon your face and how your eyes slant upward in every shade of dark. I love the way the gold flashes in your teeth when you smile. I touch your face often because it's my favourite place of you; and your body lean and hard from so many years of discipline and endurance . . . but it's not enough.

Some late nights you come home drunk and raging. The shell inside cracked along the edges, spilling out all the vileness of your life. You've gone away and in your place, in the battleground of my living room is the guerrilla fighter who has nothing to do with love.

Why have you come so far away from your war? Wouldn't it have been better to die? Tell me, does the death of a guerrilla fighter have more meaning than your life here?

"We were attacking one of the garrisons of soldiers," you tell me. "We used to do that all the time. We would surprise them, and for hours we would fight and on signal we would stop. We'd go off in different directions and later on we would make our way back to a meeting place. It was very dark that night, and I had to be careful I didn't get separated from the others by the soldiers. It was always dangerous when we travelled at night. I knew where the soldiers were, and I kept moving trying to keep my bearing. I knew if I walked in a straight line, soon I would be among my *compañeros*. Then something stopped me, I don't know what. I wanted it to end, I wanted to be out of there, the fighting, I was so tired. I looked behind me, back in the direction of Guatemala, Mexico, the United States. I lay down my gun and I turned and walked away. I walked and walked, I can't remember what I was thinking. Maybe I was thinking about running away. Then it was like I woke up. I didn't want to leave my *compañeros*, my babies, my country; I turned and ran back in the direction I'd come. I found my gun and slipped it back over my shoulder, but it was too late. The soldiers were fanned out in front of me, cutting me off from my *compañeros*. If I had tried to get back in they would have killed me. I had only those few minutes to decide. I wanted to leave and by the time I decided I wanted to stay, it was too late.

"All the way through Guatemala, Belize, Mexico, Texas," you tell me, "until I was arrested and sent here, I kept looking back. I kept thinking I'd return . . ."

Twoscore and Five

CYNTHIA FLOOD

WE WERE ALL THEN IN OUR TWENTIES.

Jack was a painter. So was Marjorie. At the back of their dark small Kits apartment was an unexpected door into a north-lit studio where they really lived; nothing blocked their view of the North Shore mountains. They had not even a houseplant on the sills. Jack was "macho" (the term was not then in use). Present or absent, he dominated conversation with Marjorie. His asthma required attention. Marjorie talked, cooked, cared, smoked. He painted far more than she. The point is this: she knew. To her women friends she spoke openly of her efforts ("struggle" was not used then either) to believe in her own work's importance and to act on that belief. Her preference, which ran counter to received radical artistic opinion of the day, was for small canvases. She would not marry Jack. Well. While I was away in library school in Toronto she left him and took a studio of her own. Her postcard with this news pleased me; many of her friends were pleased. In my next letter I told her how I looked forward to hearing of the progress of her work. Would she plan a show soon? But she did little painting in the new workplace. I had not expected that.

Then she suddenly left Vancouver, with Leo, whom we had all known in university. He had been close to forty then, glamorous with age, poems in print, critical articles, affairs with students and junior faculty. "Leo's latest" was a sought-after position. What is the desire to be defined thus? He was now almost fifty. His poetry was in my opinion undistinguished. Nobody knew his wife; evidently Marjorie was her last straw. The house was sold, the children distributed, and Leo was off to his new job at U of T, with Marjorie. She turned out to be a poet. We remembered then, discussing the event: she had written poems in college, off and on, and she had always given her paintings unusual titles. Formed as lengthy phrases, they were suggested routes for the viewer to travel into the work. They returned to the mind.

She and Leo had rented a lovely old house in the Annex. I was living as inexpensively as possible, in one room, in order to save even small amounts toward my garden and my house, and found it most pleasant to talk with Marjorie in her turret study—"Yes, it's really a room of one's own"—and to look out over the spreading, abundant foliage of the beautifully mature maples and oaks that border the streets there. Marjorie and Leo did little with their garden. Admittedly the exposure was difficult. Marjorie said herself that to work was not easy for her. Although the child was Leo's, Marjorie was the adult at home when Jake got out of school. Leo was the established writer, she the roadie; considerable entertainment was required to establish him socially at the university.

Leo lasted seven years, the same as Jack. I had been back on the coast five years by then, and although I was still working at the Collingwood branch I was about to be transferred downtown, to the main branch. My savings were accumulating. I viewed houses in Kitsilano and Dunbar regularly, having particular blocks of particular streets in mind for the best possible combinations of terrain and outlook. A southern exposure was essential. Marjorie wrote that the worst part was leaving the boy. They had apparently become close. Leo placed severe restrictions on her contact with Jake. She thought Leo resented her refusal to marry him. It is certain that he did nothing for her as a writer, in spite of all his connections. In spite, I suppose. Only a handful of her poems had appeared in little magazines (I checked the new issues regularly as they came into the Literature section). She created some striking images. One poem presented a train journey east from Toronto, in winter. Glancing up from her newspaper, the speaker of the poem saw at the grey lake's edge, just in from the stony beach where the white ice-sludge crashed and waved, an apple tree, bare-limbed of course, but still carrying half a dozen frozen apples. They were no longer scarlet, but blackish, like dried blood.

When I wrote in response to the news of Marjorie's departure from the Annex house I praised this poem, expressing the hope that her new situation would permit the writing of many more of such quality. I got a note back almost at once. I had not expected that. Customarily, weeks and even months passed without a word from her. Then would come a long, long letter, its various parts written on different dates and kinds of paper with different writing implements, its content so miscellaneous (recipes, work in progress, Jake, the English department, jokes, weather reports, comments on the biographies she was always reading) that I found it as difficult as it was absorbing to read. Or postcards would come, mailed on successive days and forming a serial message like the old Burma-Shave commercials, or a beautiful card of paper handmade by an artist friend. Often her writing not only covered the designated areas of the page but also ran clear over whatever printed message there might be, or into the space intended for the address. Sometimes Marjorie even wrote on the backs of envelopes. I myself wrote to her once a fortnight, regardless, on regular bond and the typewriter—or, in the last year or so of her time in Toronto, on my computer.

This time Marjorie had painted a card herself: a beautiful watercolour illustration of a skunk cabbage. They were thick in the marshy parts of Stanley Park just then; by chance I had walked there only the previous day, and their strange colouring, gamboge and brilliant green, was sharp in my mind. Here it was again. Such accurate rendering of detail is not often found outside specialized botanical publications. Marjorie wrote that she had found a design job with a firm of medical publishers and planned to write on her own time. She added, "Dear M, your steady letters and steady love help keep me going. Have a drink! Start smoking! Love as ever, Marjorie." I was unreasonably pleased, though puzzled.

That year was the first Christmas I went to Bermuda. People at work thought I was going for sunshine. In a sense that was accurate, for my desire was to observe the vegetation of another climate, the fruits of another context of soil and atmosphere. I wished to see that other life, to see for example the indigenous Bermuda cedar that I knew only through photographs; it is really a juniper, and nearly died out earlier in this century. Stopping over in Toronto to visit Marjorie, I found her full of stories about a doctor she had met through her job, who was setting up a community clinic in her neighbourhood. She was painting murals for the reception area and writing leaflets. When I thought subsequently about our conversations, I realized she had evaded my questions about her poetry. Instead, she had heard the story of the difficult and dangerous events which had led to my new job in Acquisitions, and learned my timetable for buying my garden and my house. I had not expected that. I was not surprised, though, when Marjorie wrote that she and Gordon were living together. Discussing the news with mutual friends, I realized that Marjorie's life was like a story, or, more precisely, a story retold several times in different ways. I do not object to this in fiction (I have noticed that some of the major novelists tell and retell essentially the same tale) but the clinic ate up every hour Marjorie chose to give it and asked for more, was Gordon's far more than hers, formed the basis of their social life.

He was not an unpleasant person, Gordon. I spent time with them each December in the four years they were together, and found him gentler and kinder by far than the other two. He was no gardener—only a couple of spider plants and an African violet sat dryly on the kitchen window sill of their apartment over the clinic—but he took at least an amused interest in my plant-smuggling from Bermuda, recommending ways to calm myself physically before the encounters with Customs. When I finally made the purchase of my garden and my house he also made some useful suggestions about shelving; many of my books on gardening and botany and natural history are outsize or otherwise unusually shaped, and so required me to create custom shelf designs, and these in turn needed to complement the type of wood used in their construction. Fiction of course fits easily onto store-bought shelving.

Gordon ended it, though. Marjorie would not have a baby. She had always been clear that she did not want children, first because she was painting and then because she was writing poetry. I do not know what reason she gave Gordon. Her letters did not say. She was apparently in pain. How is it possible to give up a known person for a hypothesis?

After Gordon, Marjorie came back to Vancouver. My promotion to assistant department head had just been confirmed. I felt strong in victory. Marjorie looked ill and was. A Toronto doctor had recommended a hysterectomy—discussing this had generated the break with Gordon and a Vancouver doctor confirmed that diagnosis.

Marjorie would have the surgery and would then come to my house to recuperate. Unlike our other friends, I could offer her no children, no pets, no men. Of course a very great deal remains to be done in the garden, even at the level of basic design, for I have had just two growing seasons here and am only now becoming familiar with the variations in the soil, the drainage, the disposition of the existing trees and shrubs, the angles of light in the twelve months, the ways the shadows fall from house and garage. This year the new greenhouse and solarium will introduce yet more variables, and although I of course made extensive calculations when designing and locating these additional structures, I have learned, with difficulty, with reluctance, that for me at least it is not possible to predict the activity of plant life. What I can only term bizarre capacities are present, for growth, for refusal. Bermuda made me see that first. Perhaps the sight was easier in another climate. To work deeper into such difficult garden-seeing is like going from reference to cross-reference, shelf to shelf, text to text, in search of an answer. Extraordinary developments, though, can take place in greenhouses. This Christmas I plan to bring back some begonias. I have tried nothing so ambitious yet. The deception at Customs unnerves me, brings me into risk, the narrow airless corridors at night and the men with shining glasses, but I want to attempt those exquisite Bermudan begonias here, to try my best to make them accept as theirs another climate. The delicacy of their colouring is remarkable.

Whatever the external weather, in the solarium there is always light and green. As I told Marjorie before her surgery, she could be in the solarium all day if she chose, comfortable, healing, neither overheated nor damp nor chilled, reading the catalogues and watching the bulbs come up while I did the spring pruning. She wept. "God, Mary, it'll be wonderful. I could use a lifetime of that." That is exactly what I have.

In the meantime I visited her daily in the Vancouver General. She looked small, frail. Grey was coming in at her temples because a tinting was overdue. I thought of all she had done for Jack and Leo and Gordon. For several days Marjorie's pain did not permit conversation. She lay, I sat and held her hand. Then she entered the bored, irritated stage of recovery, unable to abandon herself any longer to hospital passivity and equally unable to read or talk seriously. She ordered me to start talking.

"I can't just lie here, Mary, I'll go nuts. Tell me about your job, or something. What are those things people have? Hobbies."

Well. Although "restraint" brings many dramas to the administration of public libraries, I have never been able to make the intricacies of budgets interesting to friends. So instead I told Marjorie about the risks people take in libraries: the men who expose themselves in the Boys' and Girls' sections, the patrons who use X-Acto knives to slice sections out of illustrated reference books and take them home, the patron who, before we caught him, went through four shelves of Shakespeare using a fluorescent yellow felt marker on every appearance of "breast." (There are many.) Having told these brief tales, and having established that Marjorie still did not play bridge, I cast about for something more substantial.

"What about your lovers? Tell me about them."

"I don't have lovers, Marjorie." Technically this was not so. I do on occasion share a bed. But that is all I have felt like sharing. She closed her eyes and moved her head restlessly, turning toward the window. The sun shone on her upper body. The weatherbeaten skin of her throat and chest stopped, and below was silken cream. From where I sat, the cream met the yellow of the budding daffodils I had picked for her, and this colour in turn met the blue air over the North Shore mountains.

"Well then, tell me what your life is about, at forty-five. What do you do when you're not alphabetizing or chasing old men out of the Heidi section?"

"Forty-four," I said, and knew. "Marjorie. I'll tell you about—about A and B and C."

A decade ago, an intelligent and highly qualified woman I worked with lost a promotion to a foolish and underqualified man. She and I never thought of the library the same way again; we had not understood that merit was relatively insignificant in the matter, and had waged no campaign. We have since more than regained that lost ground. At that time, I developed a slender but firm link with a women's organization in the city. To energetic activists, keeping periodicals and clippings and books and pamphlets in order (alphabetical and otherwise) is not an appealing task, but some of them do recognize it as essential. Twice a month I go into the office, more often if there has been a flurry of feminist activity in Vancouver. I feel odd in that office, yet I like it. The young women are friendly, although or perhaps because I do not appear to be like them. I listen to their conversations as I work among the files and shelves. Doing so, I am reminded of browsing; I rarely browse now, knowing the classification system as well as I do, but many library patrons of course do, dipping into a page here or there to sound out a book, to know if they want to enter further. I like to watch them. Sometimes I bring flowers, which the young women always welcome. I believe most of them do not habitually observe the natural world, absorbed as they are in their interactions with each other and with various opposed and allied organizations. That is why I bring only cut flowers.

The story I now planned to tell Marjorie I had learned through overhearing at the women's office; I had heard it in instalments, as it were, over the year or so the narrative had taken to play itself out.

"What kind of story? I didn't know you were a libber, Mary." Marjorie turned from the window and looked at me critically.

"Political, really."

She closed her eyes again.

"It isn't boring, Marjorie. It's about three young women."

"Oh Mary, you're not going to call them A and B and C, are you? If you must tell me this tale then I'll think of names for the characters."

Impatiently I waited, because the more I thought about my story the more I felt it was perfect for Marjorie now. Jobless, manless, babyless, stripped of routines and entertainments as of her own always distinctive clothing, my old and dear friend could now observe her own naked lineaments and design her own life, not one predicated on someone else's design for his. Marjorie could grasp that certain emotions are insubstantial bases for decision-making; that if you do not act in your own interests, others will impose theirs on you; that—

"Alicia, Beatrice, Caroline."

"Why such old-fashioned names?"

"Because mine is. I like it, and I've spent years defending it against people who want to call me Marge. So start, Mary."

The previous spring, the women's organization had decided to publish a monthly magazine and for this task had initiated the formation of a collective. Of this, Beatrice and Caroline were members and Alicia was not; she did fundraising work for the organization as a whole. Shortly before the first issue appeared, the collective discovered that the woman who had agreed to solicit advertising had not done so.

"Actually what they said was that she had fucked up."

"I've never liked that expression," said Marjorie crossly. "It makes fucking equivalent to a mistake. Go on, Mary. This isn't interesting so far."

The collective gratefully accepted Alicia's offer to do a one-shot job of selling ads. She did so, very well, and came to a collective meeting to report and hand over her files. When she left, Beatrice rose and excoriated Alicia for having usurped the functions of the woman who had originally assumed the task.

"But—"

"Yes, obviously. Everyone reminded Beatrice of what the process had been. But Beatrice said she had been talking to the woman—"

"What was her name?"

"Oh Marjorie, surely we can just call her D."

"Daphne."

"If we must. Beatrice said many things that began with 'If Daphne were here I know she'd say . . .' She would not stop. Then Caroline spoke up, defending Alicia. Beatrice became angrier still. The argument drew in the whole meeting. The women never reached the rest of their agenda."

"There was something else going on," said Marjorie, "there must have been. All this emotion." She opened her eyes.

"How did you know? Beatrice and Alicia had been lovers previously, and now Caroline and Alicia were lovers."

"Complicated." Marjorie giggled, and winced. I did not see why she giggled; there had also been giggles when I had first heard this part of the story. I had felt uneasily that such hearing was an invasion of privacy, but neither the teller nor the other listeners had apparently even been aware of me sitting next to them. Perhaps they assumed I would not comprehend, even not hear. Many professionals assume their conversations are incomprehensible to the layperson.

"To continue. Beatrice and Caroline worked together in the magazine collective, arguing all the time. I should explain that all three women lived in the same communal house, along with other members of the organization. The collective used the basement to do the magazine layout."

"Even more complicated. What did these women look like, Mary?"

"I never met any of them, Marjorie."

"Oh well. I'll just use my imagination."

Why, when the obvious question was this: How could anyone by choice enter such a situation? But I went on. The magazine was well received. Beatrice and Caroline fought; they had full opportunity to do so, for Beatrice was deeply involved in the production process and Caroline as deeply on the editorial side. Alicia and Caroline were happy.

Then came the Thanksgiving weekend, for which the lovers planned a trip to Seattle, where they would stay at the home of an absent friend, attend a Holly Near concert, browse through the university bookstore, eat Mexican food.

"A little honeymoon," said Marjorie approvingly.

"I suppose. When they were about to leave—Alicia was in the car, with the engine running, waiting for Caroline—Beatrice came rushing out and asked, no pleaded, to stay at the house in Seattle with them. Another women's trip had fallen through, and Beatrice had a chance at her air ticket and concert seat, but she could not possibly afford a hotel. And Alicia—"

"Said yes without asking Caroline!" Marjorie burst in, half-rising on her elbow.

She was right, again. But again I could not give Marjorie the detail she wanted: How had Caroline reacted? What had the weekend in Seattle been like for each of the women? I knew only that after "a lot of hassle" Alicia had assumed the mantle of peacemaker. ("What an operator!" murmured Marjorie.) She urged that when they all got back to Vancouver, Beatrice and Caroline should meet formally, perhaps even with a mediator, and reach an understanding. "For the sake of the magazine as well as for their own sakes," I added, repeating the phrasing as it had come to me.

"Yes, well." Marjorie sniffed. "Do get on with it, Mary. Did they meet?"

"They made a date. Some weeks away—"

"Who was stalling?"

"I am sure I do not know, Marjorie. They were both very busy. You have no idea how active these young women are. They go to meetings constantly."

"Boring."

"On the day of the dinner Caroline developed the flu. It was November; raining of course, and cold. But she was not able to reach Beatrice at work and cancel, so she dressed and got herself out to the agreed-upon restaurant."

"Beatrice never showed." Marjorie smiled, and scrabbled in the bed-side table for her cigarettes.

"You shouldn't do that."

"I know I shouldn't." She lit up. "This is the first one that's tasted good since the op."

Difficulties were developing with the magazine. The springing vigour of the first few issues had metamorphosed into a regular production cycle, wherein financial and editorial problems grew monthly larger. Beatrice and Caroline disagreed yet more sharply and frequently ("Well of course they did," Marjorie said with irritation). At the New Year, the collective did a self-evaluation. The analysis was that more members were needed.

"Alicia!" Marjorie waved her cigarette.

"Well—yes. She had done hours of volunteer work for the magazine, and that was a recognized way to become eligible. But Beatrice said she could not work with Alicia under any circumstances. She refused."

"And she reminded everyone about poor Daphne." Marjorie inhaled with delight.

"Marjorie, how can I tell this story if you keep on trying to tell it?"

"I'm just telling you more about it while you tell it. What then? What reasons did Beatrice give?"

"She said that Alicia was 'too bourgeois.' A quite incorrect use of the term; they use political terminology so carelessly—oh, very well. But that made no sense, Marjorie. There were other well-off women in the group and Beatrice had never objected to them."

"They hadn't taken away her lover."

The meeting failed to resolve the issue. Everyone left for home exhausted.

Over the next few days Caroline phoned round to various group members to say that in the interests of the collective she thought both she and Beatrice should leave. An emergency meeting took place. Would the collective not expand but shrink, and at that lose two of its most hard-working members? Caroline recanted. Believing that she did not bear the major responsibility for the dissension, and that she did have a useful contribution to make, she would remain. Beatrice said, "I resign, on political grounds," and walked out.

"Oh dear." Marjorie thoughtfully stroked the sheet over her incision. "Poor thing. She still felt she had to put it that way. And Madame Alicia was waiting in the wings?"

"Well, yes. She came right in with the other new collective members. They proceeded with the agenda. There was such relief, you see."

When Alicia and Caroline got home that night Beatrice had moved out of the communal house. She left her job the next morning and the women's community saw her no more. Someone said she had gone back to Alberta.

Shorty after this the organization, concerned at the way the magazine ate money, decided to pull back to a simple gestetnered newsletter. The collective dissolved itself without argument. Alicia and Caroline moved forward to other projects. A new group formed for the smaller newsletter task, and when the letter from Beatrice came no one at first understood what it was about. Who was this woman on the prairies who claimed the collective had slandered her, had put about a rumour that she'd been expelled? She wanted a retraction, in print. The new group couldn't see the point. They put Beatrice's letter—it was quite long—in the "Hold" file. When the long-distance calls came, various women in turn said they were really sorry but there was no one who could help.

Marjorie sighed. The sound indicated both sadness and satisfaction. "So it was Beatrice who made the magazine be."

"Marjorie! She wrecked everything."

"Oh Mary, that's not how it was, you've told it all wrong." Marjorie sat right up, wincing and looking stronger than since her return to Vancouver. "It's a love story, Mary, you must see that, it's about the power of love to move people, change things. Oh, Beatrice must have been very much in love to be so strong. Fighting with Caroline so as to stay bonded somehow to Alicia. Keeping even a little separation between the two lovers by fending Alicia off from the collective. And living in the same house! Probably she had to overhear them making love. Oh, such determination, such a fight for her love, don't you see? It's quite clear. Beatrice's emotion was the power. The magazine lived on the tension she created. Of course her leaving meant collapse."

Marjorie lay back smiling on her pillows and turned away from me to the window, where pigeons flapped in the brightness. The mountains were brilliant, the snow a harsh dazzle. What to say? Haphazardly I visualized the possibilities for my rock garden: alyssum of course, sedum, potentilla, aubretia in its subtle shades, snow-on-the-mountain, perhaps cotoneaster or another prostrate. Attempting such growth is risky because just there, in the only place where the rockery can be, the soil tends to clay and will need careful treatment before planting, close attention after. I know already that some of the plants will fail to thrive, for reasons I will not be entirely sure of, and similarly some will do extremely well.

"God, it's good to see those mountains again," said Marjorie. Her voice shook. I had not expected that. "She didn't quite get out in time, did she. The letter, the phone calls. Poor Beatrice. Over the edge a bit. You have to learn to get yourself out in one piece." She looked again at me and showed the tears. "I know her, Mary. I've not been in the exact situation but I've felt it all happen. When did Alicia and Caroline break up?"

"Did I say they broke up?"

"Well of course they did, without Beatrice."

"As a matter of fact it was just recently, when Beatrice was telephoning."

Marjorie took another cigarette. I did not speak. She blew smoke reflectively. "Soon it'll all start again for them." She seemed neither sad nor happy in saying so.

"Surely not Beatrice and Alicia?"

"Oh no no, not that specific pairing. The pattern." I considered this. In university we had had to write essays concerning novels and plays. "Do you mean that in Beatrice's life there will always be an Alicia and a Caroline, and that in Alicia's—"

Marjorie wagged her cigarette in agreement. "Yes, that's right. You do see, Mary, really?"

I was pleased. "A and B and C." Perhaps even now I could make my point.

"Oh Mary, what will you do with the rest of your life?"

"I was about to ask you the same thing."

"No, you were going to tell me what to do, Mary. I can feel what you think of my life, my dear, it's all in how you hold yourself. So stiff in the chair there. Well. Probably quite soon I'll fall in love. Oh no, I'm not over Gordon. I never really get over them. Not Jack or Leo either."

"They are compost, perhaps." I had not meant to speak aloud, but Marjorie reached for my hand and gave her lovely smile, unaffected by the lines and the altered texture of her face. "Yes Mary, I can feel that I'm ready to love again. A man wandered in here yesterday looking for a patient who'd just been discharged, and we got chatting for a while. I wouldn't be surprised if he came back to visit me. He's an architect."

"You're certainly making your way through the professions." I tried to take my hand away.

"Mary, do try to understand. I've got so much from each one, lived in such different ways—I've almost been three different people. Four, counting me. You've misunderstood me, you know, I don't have it in me to be a great poet or painter or anything like that. I have a bit of talent, enough to give me and a few others some pleasure, that's all. It isn't really what I'm about." Marjorie stubbed out her cigarette and clasped my fingers now with both hands. "Oh Mary, I wish so much you'd take a chance on a person. Garden, books, bridge. You know what you should do, Mary?"

"What should I do?" Marjorie seemed unaware of sarcasm. Her eyes focused brightly on her idea.

I thought of the vegetation in Bermuda, how fantastical and strange it first seemed to me, so luxuriant, enveloping; but I went back, again, again, and came to know those plants, travelled to some familiarity with the casuarinas, the bougainvillea, the lovely trailing vines, and the myriad begonias. I do not truly know them. I doubt even the possibility of real knowledge. But I rely, yes, I rely upon that annual visitation to another country.

Marjorie was bursting. "Look out the room door, and the next man that comes along, go after him and say, 'You're so handsome, I just had to speak to you. Come have a drink.' Look, let's see who comes." Laughing, she peered round me to the hospital corridor. For half a minute no one passed. Then came a tall youth, perhaps eighteen, carrying freesias. He strode by and out of sight.

"There he is, Mary!"

"Marjorie, hush, for heaven's sake. He's probably visiting his girlfriend."

"No, his mother or an aunt. The wrapping's from the hospital flower shop. For his girlfriend he'd have gone to a real florist, and got bigger flowers too. Go on!"

"Marjorie, freesias do not need to be any bigger than they are." I turned from the door and clasped my other hand over hers. Marjorie leaned back again, flushed, relaxed, alive with smiling humour, and we looked at one another, two middle-aged women friends, each gazing at the mystery of the other's life.

helpful hints

barbara findlay

I.

so, lady: you asked. here's how it goes. incest, at 40. the
memories bubble into the day in seismic shifts, or like
indigestion.

suicide, feasible at 20 when you last tried it, is out of the
question. you Know Too Much—you've learned to say that
the pain is old pain, that it's safe to feel it now; that it hurts,
but that's just old fear. why, if you committed suicide now
you'd be the laughing stock of the neighbourhood.

no melodrama. that's basic. it's ok to cry at poetry readings,
weep over your journal at la quena, sob going down the drive
arm in arm with your support person. but you're old enough
to know better than to act out. no agoraphobia, no intrusive
obsessions, no inappropriate rage. it's fine to *talk* about
those things . . . provided it doesn't become a bore.

it is important to strike the right tone. acknowledge your
Commitment to the Work you need to do to
Discharge/Release/Unlock/ Access yourself. but don't let it
interfere with previously scheduled meetings or birthday
parties.

books and support groups are in. drugs (prescription or non)
are out. writing is in, most therapy is out. body work is ok
in some circles, check it out first.

and after you've spent the weekend Dealing with the Incest,
move on to something else.

II.

shame, little girl, shame
for wanting what is not yours
the right to speak, and be heard

III.

rapists have feelings too.
raping a woman is an event in the day
along with eating mashed potatoes
brushing teeth
reading the paper

going to church.

rapists get their hair cut
play with their children
change the oil in their cars
have birthdays

the rape of a woman is an everyday event.

IV.

it is hard to carve from silence
silence.   nothing
is its counterpoint

V.

some women learned how to cry from their mothers
i was not one
i was suckled on silence and dread

now, i clear my throat
to wail
and my voice is small, reedy, caught
in a high register.

VI.

mama

what do you tell yourself
about me?

> i know what you tell the minister,
> the bridge club, the relatives:
> my daughter the lawyer/professor
> at ubc, you know/ in montréal this
> weekend/national convention
>
> i know what you don't tell
> the minister the relatives the bridge club:
> my daughter the lesbian/crazy
> you know/mental hospitals/in surrey
> doing an unlearning racism workshop

but what i don't know is
what do you tell yourself
about me

mama

VillainElle

LYNN CROSBIE

Come now, do this, my soul! No secret murder
earns renown; proclaim in people's eyes
your cruel and bloody skill.   —Medea

I painted a picture for Arlene, & wrote
across the moon & stars, pick a dream/
any dream, longing here, for her
consultant fingers, an arcana of cards
splayed over my desolate body.
empêchement, déplaisir, une lettre,
une brune, la mort. she says she
wishes she was a magician & she would
get me out of here, keys sewed in her
palms, she would pull silver from my
ears, my mouth. she is my last chance,
I asked her to help me, *I need to change*
before I fall. I have killed seven men.
each time, I flagged them down & *I put them*
out of their misery. I would stand by the
topless bar, by the highway & smile & say,
hello handsome. hello baby, could I get
a lift? & kiss them & empty their pockets
& strip off their clothes. take it all off,
I said, & shot them dead. Arlene, I wrote,
you are way too kind/ to get to know my kind
of mind. but if you listen, a silent novena,
I will tell you where it ended & I began.

Was there another Troy for her to burn?

seven marks on the wall, seven shadows.
I know that I left Troy, Michigan,
behind me. but their faces interface,
the men I grew up with, brother stepfather
grandfather. my corner of the yellow house
was draped in pink chenille, a daisy
clock, a baby doll that cried & cried.
they would circle my bed, & I buried myself
under the sheets, percale smooth & frayed
from my teeth, my screams! suddenly,
he pushed my hands behind my back & covered
my mouth. I can't remember, the grass the daisies
leave orange silt on my legs & the sky is
black. the sky, my mother, is a cold
compress & his tongue his pores his eyes
are not there. nothing, but the pain &
that never goes away, *I have to stop the
pain.* his low growl, the hair raised on
his neck, picking her bones, fleece, muscle,
she is lost & far from home & when she hears
them in the wind she is afraid.
I turned mean back then. listen you old
bastard if you ever touch me again, I'll
tear you to pieces & eat your flesh. I
imagine a bloody trail, ear eyelid thigh
foot that leads to the seashore. taking
his magic, my magic & I leave, with a dragon at
my heels & their voices, calling

In Florida the living is easy. I pull on
my stockings dress & stiletto shoes &
stand on the corners, where the palm trees
are. their serrated leaves fringe your
picture Arlene, & lizards hang on the
windowpanes, I said, do you feel lonely,
or would you like some company? but it
wasn't the work, it was their faces,
destitute & barren. without her,
I would have killed them sooner, *earthly*
words cannot describe how I felt about
her. beautiful Tyria, I cherish the night we
met at the Last Resort & she nailed my slip
to the bar & we danced until we were breathless.
why don't you do something, she said. if you
can't stand it any more. my hate was palpable,
something between us. & I know you can't understand,
but the first time, seeing him crumpled beside me,
I just fell in love.

I became careless & they found me, & combed my
apartment & found glass cleaner, bullets,
tattered neckties, but I never surrendered.
& so, you found me here, in the last place
I'll ever live, in these pious chambers.
you touch me through the mesh & bars, &
wonder, at the danger. does your skin burn,
on contact? I think you are enamoured of
my history, you wear my death like pendant
earrings. & never ask, I lived in the forest
once, when I ran away. & dreamed below the
poplars, in the ferns & moss. it is there that
I perfected my *cruel and bloody skill*, & it
is here I am devoted to the memory. you want
to save me, so I'm asking you. to slip in at
night, & take my clothes. the shapeless grey dress,
the embroidered numbers. & cover your face,
I will leave, as you, & drive away. you can
hope & pray, as they strap you into the electric
chair, but I will be gone, long gone, as the
smoke plumes from your temples & your eyes bake
under their metal vices. I will be cruising,
slowly along the highway, smiling at your grief,
your error. I never cared, Arlene, & I never will;
I'm strange that way.

Notes on the Sexual Division of Labour

CARMELITA McGRATH

So you were there
when the body played out
its eventual nature
its drive

on a long table: my legs were frozen

you were not there—not really:
how could you be?
you saw them cut through me,
so how could you be there; people who witness
such things must be somehow absent.

I had already become a concentration of breath and waiting arms:

had lost two-thirds of my body
to the absence of sensation.
I might as well be a caryatid
holding this crazy scene up,
I said to the anaesthetist, but
he was already laughing
at my outrageous reaction
to something as normal as birth:

those legs are marble: they are not mine.

Then out of the dead marble, they lifted
our daughter. She pissed on the doctor
and closed her eyes against
the thousand blazing suns around her.
And two hours later,
her long eyes roving under the shield of a blanket,
I felt the sensation: marble made flesh.

Nights later, you lay next to me, but keeping your distance.

I touched my legs, once marble, felt
the abdominal flesh where nerves were cut
through. It was a long time
before this body wanted anything: night after night

it expressed only a craving for itself.

What She Tells Them

GAIL ANDERSON-DARGATZ

SHE HAS TOLD EVERYONE NOW.

She has told Barbara, her friend from high school, her closest friend. She told Jennifer, the woman with the long straight hair and white, white skin who lives in the apartment next to hers. She phoned her mother the morning after it happened and cried over the phone. Her mother said, come home for a while. She said no, there was work. She couldn't get time off.

She told David, the man from work who buys her coffee every noon hour, at the trendy Cheeko's cafe on Robson. She told Ted, the man she loved for a while. After she told him, they slept together, once.

She told them all, and told them all again. She brings up the subject in almost every conversation. She fits it in, even when it doesn't fit. She tells them even while she sees their faces turn from attentive to fidgety, even while they clear their throats and cough. She goes over each detail, picking the story apart, looking for clues. She has told them all more than they want to hear, more than is the truth. Because what really happened wasn't enough.

She was alone, she says, standing near the dance floor, sipping a shooter. The drink is different each time, depending on who she is telling. For Barbara, she tells the truth. Barbara was there. Barbara saw. She was drinking a tequila shooter. For Jennifer she says white wine. For David she says coffee and Amaretto. She told her mother brown cow. Her mother knew what that was. She told Ted the truth. Ted knows what she likes.

She tells them she was watching Barbara dancing on the floor with the good-looking lawyer friend of Ted's. They ran into him at Kit's. She was standing there watching, not playing the games. Barbara would back her on this. She was not looking for anyone. She was watching the dancing, that's all.

He came and stood next to her, not looking at her, just standing close, holding his drink, watching the dancers. He even waved at a girl, a nice-looking girl. The girl waved back. She makes a point of telling this, to prove she had no cause to think he was some weirdo. He had friends there. He was probably attached. That's what she thought when he waved at the girl.

Then he turned and talked to her. He asked for a light, for his cigarette. She didn't smoke, she told him. Yeh, he said, bad habit. She smiled. No, not trendy, she said. They both laughed then, because they saw how ridiculous it was. He started smoking because it was trendy, now he had to quit because it wasn't. She tells them this.

They talked for a while. Then he asked, would she go for a coffee? Too loud in here, he said, for talking. She said yes and caught Barbara's eye and signalled she was going. Barbara nodded okay. So they went, to a little well-lit place around the corner and drank cappuccinos and talked about the ozone crumbling to bits. Chicken Little, she called him. He laughed. She tells this, about the ozone layer, to prove he seemed up on things, he seemed bright. He got her joke about Chicken Little. Maybe he was a writer. In fact she didn't ask him what he did. She didn't ask the usual questions. She asked what colour his underwear were. Did he like croquet? She giggled. She doesn't tell them this.

She says he was a writer. What kind, Ted asked. She said she wasn't sure. She told Jennifer he was a fiction writer. He wrote a book. *The New Invisible Man*, she said it was called. Jennifer asked, what was it about? She said she didn't know. There hadn't been time to ask.

When she drank half her coffee, she started to come down, feel heavy. She thought she might be sick.

She told him she would be right back and went to the ladies' room and sat on the cold toilet. Her underwear were around her knees. She remembers thinking about what colour they were, pink and grey, and how they fit.

She sat there until the nausea passed, then stood and patted her clothes in place. She washed her hands. She looked in the mirror and saw a small pimple had worked its way to white at her eyebrow. She decided to leave it.

What she tells them is that she went into the bathroom to comb her hair and when she came out he wasn't there.

The waitress said he paid for the coffee. She doesn't tell them this. She tells them she paid.

There was a lineup at Kit's. She couldn't get back in to get Barbara to take her home, so she went to the bus stop. She hoped the buses were still running. She didn't have a watch on, but she didn't think it was that late. She hoped it wasn't that late. It was drizzling.

She sat on the bench at the bus stop. No one walked by. She was afraid someone might. She doesn't like waiting. Sometimes she adds that a group of punkers were standing at the corner, talking and laughing. She says she was afraid of them. She has told everyone this part, at some point.

After a time she no longer felt sick. She stood and walked around the bench. She warmed her hands together. She whistled. She looked around. She thought about the man she had coffee with. She wished he would come by. She wished she had got a ride home with him. She wished the bus would come.

After five minutes, the man did come by. He said he was sorry he had to leave. He said he realized the time and had to tell the people he came with where he was. He hoped she wouldn't leave before he got back and could explain. He was sorry. Would she like a ride home?

She said no, she would catch a bus. He said it was too late. The buses were no longer running. She tells them she believed him.

He took her home. He insisted on walking her up to her apartment. It was late. She tells them she appreciated this. She thought he was a gentleman for doing this.

She invited him in. She took his coat. She poured them both high-balls, coke and rum. She drank hers quickly. He drank his slowly. He told her he liked her apartment. Did she live alone? She said yes, would he like another drink? He said no. She poured herself one.

She sat next to him on the couch, facing him. Was she seeing anyone? She said no. He told her she was pretty. She thanked him. Music, what kind of music did he like? David Bowie. She stood and put on *Never Let Me Down*. She sat in the armchair. She drank her drink. He was still drinking his. Would he like another? No. She stood and put on the kettle, for tea. She leaned over the counter. She tapped a spoon against the arborite. He stood and put a hand on hers. She stopped tapping.

The kettle whistled. She made tea and poured it into a cup for herself, but didn't drink it. She said she was tired. She wanted to sleep. He said he would tuck her into bed. It was late. Could he stay the night? He would share the bed, that was all. He was pleasant. She said yes.

She went to the bathroom and removed her contact lenses. She left her makeup on, and brushed her hair. When she came out, he was in her bed. His clothes were on the floor. He said a funny thing. He said, now you can see what colour my underwear are. She didn't understand at first. Then she remembered. She laughed, a little.

She took off her clothes and put on a nightshirt, a man's nightshirt she picked up at Sears. She did this with her back toward him. He said something she didn't hear. She said, pardon? He didn't answer. She got into bed.

The light went out. She felt his arm go around her. But at the same time, he said goodnight. She fell asleep.

Later in the night, he woke her.

She does not tell them he stayed the night. She does not tell them that in the morning he ate breakfast with her, drinking coffee and talking about Rick Hansen's wedding. It was on the front page of *The Province*. She does not tell them that when he left he said he would call her. She does not tell them that she nodded and smiled.

She does tell them that after he was gone she stood under the shower until the water went ice cold.

Then she tells more.

For Jennifer she adds in details. She talks about pain. She says there were bruises. She says she's thinking about going to the police. Twice during the telling she has cried.

She told Barbara that she ran to the balcony, but he caught her. Barbara asked, would she have jumped?

When she phoned her mother, her mother said she didn't have to go on. She understood. Would she write?

She phoned in sick Monday. David phoned at noon. Was she all right? Yes, she was fine. Then she told him, just what she told Jennifer. He wanted to come over, so she had someone to talk to. She said no. Then she phoned Ted. He stayed the night.

The next day Ted was gone before she woke. Ted worked in Coquitlam. It was a long drive. She understood. She looked for a note.

The month has gone by quickly. They have all phoned again, and everyone has come to visit. And she has told them all the story, a little different each time, so that now she's not sure which story she's told who. Now she's not so sure just how it really happened. The truth, it seems, is in the telling. And she keeps on telling, even as they grow restless, even as they cough and look the other way.

The Orange Fish

CAROL SHIELDS

LIKE OTHERS OF MY GENERATION I am devoted to food, money, and sex; but I have an ulcer and have been unhappily married to Lois-Ann, a lawyer, for twelve years. As you might guess, we are both fearful of aging. Recently Lois-Ann showed me an article she had clipped from the newspaper, a profile of a well-known television actress who was described as being "deep in her thirties."

"That's what we are," Lois-Ann said sadly, "deep in our thirties." She looked at me from behind a lens of tears.

Despite our incompatibility, the two of us understand each other, and I knew more or less what it was she was thinking: that some years ago, when she was twenty-five, she made up her mind to go to Vancouver Island and raise dahlias, but on the very day she bought her air ticket, she got a letter in the mail saying she'd been accepted at law school. "None of us writes our own script," she said to me once, and of course she's right. I still toy—I confess this to you freely—with my old fantasy of running a dude ranch, with the thought of well-rubbed saddles and harnesses and the whole sweet leathery tip of possibility, even though I know the dude market's been depressed for a decade, dead in fact.

Not long ago, on a Saturday morning, Lois-Ann and I had one of our long talks, about values, about goals. The mood as we sat over breakfast was sternly analytical.

"Maybe we've become trapped in the cult of consumerism and youth worship," I suggested.

"Trapped by our Zeitgeist," said Lois-Ann, who has a way of capping a point, especially my point.

A long silence followed, twenty seconds, thirty seconds. I glanced up from an emptied coffee cup, remembered that my fortieth birthday was only weeks away, and felt a flare of panic in my upper colon. The pain was hideous and familiar. I took a deep breath as I'd been told to do. Breathe in, then out. Repeat. The trick is to visualize the pain, its substance and colour, and then transfer it to a point outside the body. I concentrated on a small spot above our breakfast table, a random patch on the white wall. Often this does the trick, but this morning the blank space, the smooth drywall expanse of it, seemed distinctly accusing.

At one time Lois-Ann and I had talked about wallpapering the kitchen or at least putting up an electric clock shaped like a sunflower. We also considered a ceramic bas-relief of cauliflowers and carrots, and after that a little heart-shaped mirror bordered with rattan, and, more recently, a primitive map of the world with a practical acrylic surface. We have never been able to agree, never been able to arrive at a decision.

I felt Lois-Ann watching me, her eyes as neat and neutral as birds' eggs. "What we need," I said, gesturing at the void, "is a picture."

"Or possibly a print," said Lois-Ann, and immediately went to get her coat.

Three hours later we were the owners of a cheerful lithograph titled *The Orange Fish*. It was unframed, but enclosed in a sandwich of twinkling glass, its corners secured by a set of neat metal clips. The mat surrounding the picture was a generous three inches in width—we liked that—and the background was a shimmer of green; within this space the orange fish was suspended.

I wish somehow you might see this fish. He is boldly drawn, and just as boldly coloured. He occupies approximately eighty percent of the surface and has about him a wet dense look of health. To me, at least, he appears to have stopped moving, to be resting against the wall of green water. A stream of bubbles, each one separate and tear-shaped, floats above him, binding him to his element. Of course he is seen in side profile, as fish always are, and this classic posture underlies the tranquillity of the whole. He possesses, too, a Buddha-like sense of being in the *right* place, the only place. His centre, that is, where you might imagine his heart to be, is sweetly orange in colour, and this colour diminishes slightly as it flows toward the semi-transparency of fins and the round, ridged, non-appraising mouth. But it was his eye I most appreciated, the kind of wide, ungreedy eye I would like to be able to turn onto the world.

We made up our minds quickly; he would fit nicely over the breakfast table; Lois-Ann mentioned that the orange tones would pick up the colours of the seat covers. We were in a state of rare agreement. And the price was right.

Forgive me if I seem condescending, but you should know that, strictly speaking, a lithograph is not an original work of art, but rather a print from an original plate; the number of prints is limited to ten or twenty or fifty or more, and this number is always indicated on the piece itself. A tiny inked set of numbers in the corner, just beneath the artist's signature, tells you, for example, that our particular fish is number eight out of an existing ten copies, and I think it pleased me from the start to think of those other copies, the nine brother fish scattered elsewhere, suspended in identical seas of green water, each pointed soberly in the same leftward direction. I found myself in a fanciful mood, humming, installing a hook on the kitchen wall, and hanging our new acquisition. We stepped backward to admire it, and later Lois-Ann made a Spanish omelette with fresh fennel, which we ate beneath the austere eye of our beautiful fish.

As you well know, there are certain necessary tasks that coarsen the quality of everyday life, and while Lois-Ann and I went about ours, we felt calmed by the heft of our solemn, gleaming fish. My health improved from the first day, and before long Lois-Ann and I were on better terms, often sharing workaday anecdotes or pointing out curious items to each other in the newspaper. I rediscovered the girlish angularity of her arms and shoulders as she wriggled in and out of her little nylon nightgowns, smoothing down the skirts with a sly, sweet glance in my direction. For the first time in years she left the lamp burning on the bedside table and, as in our early days, she covered me with kisses, a long nibbling trail up and down the ridge of my vertebrae. In the morning, drinking our coffee at the breakfast table, we looked up, regarded our orange fish, smiled at each other, but were ritualistically careful to say nothing.

We didn't ask ourselves, for instance, what kind of fish this was, whether it was a carp or a flounder or a monstrously out-of-scale goldfish. Its biological classification, its authenticity, seemed splendidly irrelevant. Details, just details; we swept them aside. What mattered was the prismatic disjection of green light that surrounded it. What mattered was that it existed. That it had no age, no history. It simply *was*. You can understand that to speculate, to analyze overmuch, interferes with that narrow gap between symbol and reality, and it was precisely in the folds of that little gap that Lois-Ann and I found our temporary refuge.

Soon an envelope arrived in the mail, an official notice. We were advised that the ten owners of *The Orange Fish* met on the third Thursday evening of each month. The announcement was photocopied, but on decent paper with an appropriate logo. Eight-thirty was the regular time, and there was a good-natured reminder at the bottom of the page about the importance of getting things going punctually.

Nevertheless we were late. At the last minute Lois-Ann discovered a run in her pantyhose and had to change. I had difficulty getting the car started and, of course, traffic was heavy. Furthermore, the meeting was in a part of the city that was unfamiliar to us. Lois-Ann, although a clever lawyer, has a poor sense of spatial orientation and told me to turn left when I should have turned right. And then there was the usual problem with parking, for which she seemed to hold me responsible. We arrived at 8:45, rather agitated and out of breath from climbing the stairs.

Seeing that roomful of faces, I at first experienced a shriek in the region of my upper colon. Lois-Ann had a similar shock of alarm, what she afterwards described to me as a jolt to her imagination, as though an axle in her left brain had suddenly seized.

Someone was speaking as we entered the room, I recognized the monotone of the born chairman. "It is always a pleasure," the voice intoned, "to come together, to express our concerns and compare experiences."

At that moment the only experience I cared about was the sinuous river of kisses down my shoulders and backbone, but I managed to sit straight on my folding chair and to look alert and responsible. Lois-Ann, in lawyer-like fashion, inspected the agenda, running a little gold pencil down the list of items, her tongue tight between her teeth.

The voice rumbled on. Minutes from the previous meeting were read and approved. There was no old business. Nor any new business. "Well, then," the chairman said, "who would like to speak first?"

Someone at the front of the room rose and gave his name, a name that conveyed the double-pillared boom of money and power. I craned my neck, but could see only a bush of fine white hair. The voice was feeble yet dignified, a persisting quaver from a soft old silvery throat, and I realized after a minute or two that we were listening to a testimonial. A mystical experience was described. Something, too, about the "search for definitions" and about "wandering in the wilderness" and about the historic symbol of the fish in the Western tradition, a secret sign, an icon expressing providence. "My life has been altered," the voice concluded, "and given direction."

The next speaker was young, not more than twenty I would say. Lois-Ann and I took in the flare of dyed hair, curiously angled and distinctively punk in style. You can imagine our surprise: here of all places to find a spiked bracelet, black fingernails, cheeks outlined in blue paint and a forehead tattooed with the world's most familiar expletive. *The Orange Fish* had been a graduation gift from his parents. The framing alone cost two hundred dollars. He had stared at it for weeks, or possibly months, trying to understand what it meant; then revelation rushed in. "Fishness" was a viable alternative. The orange fins and sneering mouth said no to "all that garbage that gets shovelled on your head by society": "So keep swimming and don't take any junk," he wound up, then sat down to loud applause.

A woman in a neatly tailored mauve suit spoke for a quarter of an hour about her investment difficulties. She'd tried stocks. She'd tried the bond market. She'd tried treasury bills and mutual funds. In every instance she found herself buying at the peak and selling just as the market bottomed out. Until she found out about investing in art. Until she found *The Orange Fish*. She was sure, now, that she was on an upward curve. That success was just ahead. Recently she had started to be happy, she said.

A man rose to his feet. He was in his mid-fifties, we guessed, with good teeth and an aura of culture lightly worn. "Let me begin at the beginning," he said. He had been through a period of professional burnout, arriving every day at his office exhausted. "Try to find some way to brighten up the place," he told his secretary, handing her a blank cheque. *The Orange Fish* appeared the next day. Its effect had been instantaneous: on himself, his staff, and also on his clients. It was as though a bright banner had been raised. Orange, after all, was the colour of celebration, and it is the act of celebration which has been crowded out of contemporary life.

The next speaker was cheered the moment he stood. He had, we discovered, travelled all the way from Japan, from the city of Kobe— making our little journey across the city seem trivial. As you can imagine, his accent was somewhat harsh and halting, but I believe we understood something of what he said. In the small house where he lives, he has hung *The Orange Fish* in the traditional *tokonoma* alcove, just above a black lacquered slab of wood on which rests a bowl of white flowers. The contrast between the sharp orange of the fish's scales and the unearthly whiteness of the flowers' petals reminds him daily of the contradictions that abound in the industrialized world. At this no one clapped louder than myself.

A fish is devoid of irony, someone else contributed in a brisk, cozy voice, and is therefore a reminder of our lost innocence, of the era which predated double meanings and trial balloons. But, at the same time, a fish is more and also less than its bodily weight.

A slim, dark-haired woman, hardly more than a girl, spoke for several minutes about the universality of fish. How three-quarters of the earth's surface is covered with water, and in this water leap fish by the millions. There are people in this world, she said, who have never seen a sheep or a cow, but there is no one who is not acquainted with the organic shape of the fish.

"We begin our life in water," came a hoarse and boozy squawk from the back row, "and we yearn all our days to return to our natural element. In water we are free to move without effort, to be most truly ourselves."

"The interior life of the fish is unknowable," said the next speaker, who was Lois-Ann. "She swims continuously, and is as mute, as voiceless as a dahlia. She speaks at the level of gesture, in circling patterns revived and repeated. The purpose of her eye is to decode and rearrange the wordless world."

"The orange fish," said a voice, which turned out to be my own, "will never grow old."

I sat down. Later my hand was most warmly shaken. During the refreshment hour I was greeted with feeling and asked to sign the membership book. Lois-Ann put her arms around me, publicly, her face shining, and I knew that when we got home she would offer me a cup of cocoa. She would leave the bedside lamp burning and bejewel me with a stream of kisses. You can understand my feeling. Enchantment. Ecstasy. But waking up in the morning we would not be the same people.

I believe we all felt it, standing in that brightly lit room with our coffee cups and cookies: the woman in the tailored mauve suit, the fiftyish man with the good teeth, even the young boy with his crown of purple hair. We were, each of us, speeding along a trajectory, away from each other, and away from that one fixed point in time, the orange fish.

But how helplessly distorted our perspective turned out to be. What none of us could have known that night was that *we* were the ones who were left behind, sheltered and reprieved by a rare congeniality and by the pleasure that each of us feels when our deepest concerns have been given form.

That very evening, in another part of the city, ten thousand posters of the orange fish were rolling off a press. These posters—which would sell first for $10, then $8.49, and later $1.95—would decorate the rumpled bedrooms of teenagers and the public washrooms of filling stations and beer halls. Within a year a postage stamp would be issued, engraved with the image of the orange fish, but a fish whose eye, minaturized, would hold a look of mild bewilderment. And sooner than any of us would believe possible, the orange fish would be slapped across the front of a Sears flyer, given a set of demeaning eyebrows, and cruelly bisected with an invitation to stock up early on back-to-school supplies.

There can be no turning back at this point, as you surely know. Winking off lapel buttons and earrings, stamped onto sweatshirts and neckties, doodled on notepads and in the margin of love letters, the orange fish, without a backward glance, will begin to die.

Kiss Me or Something

JANE EATON HAMILTON

THE FIRST THING THAT HAPPENED was that Dorianna took me into our bedroom and after waffling around some said, "I'm pregnant."

"What?" I said.

Dorianna couldn't suppress a half smile. It happened to her out of nervousness. Now was not the time for smiles; her smile offended me. She picked at the bedspread, breaking into this sheepish grin, ducking her head as if pleased by my obvious shock, how my face—I felt it—drained of colour.

"Those stomach aches? The back aches?" she said, staring up out of her bangs. "The doctor says I'm pregnant, Liz."

I shook my head as if the sweep of it back and forth would stop Dorianna's news from reaching me.

Dorianna waited a second before burbling on. "Thank God I wasn't sick. Thank God it wasn't anything serious."

As soon as I heard this, I almost laughed out loud. A baby, not serious?

"I mean, it could have been cancer, Liz. We thought about cancer." When I didn't respond, when my mouth only opened and closed, Dorianna added, "Honey?"

I said, "This was . . . we were—"

"And now we have!" Dorianna cried happily. She smoothed her hand across her belly. She wanted me to be glad.

I was staring hard at her. I could feel how cold my eyes were.

Dorianna said, "I want you to be happy. I thought you'd be happy. Happy I'm not sick. Happy about the baby." Her voice was tentative, almost pleading. "Sweetie?"

I made a sound like spitting and left the bedroom. Dorianna scrambled after me, following me to our tiny kitchen. I was standing by the fridge, staring at the cartoons we had taped up there. Dorianna touched my back. "We have to talk."

"Leave me alone."

"Don't punish me," Dorianna said. "Honey, please? Don't punish me. I did it for us."

I turned to face her. I felt a bitter coldness, a new contempt rising inside me. I grabbed my jacket and stomped down the stairs.

Dorianna and I had been a couple for three years. It had happened, all things told, very quickly. Dorianna, an artist, met me, an elementary school teacher, at a ballroom dance class. Since I was learning to lead and Dorianna to follow, and since there weren't enough men to couple the women in class, we danced together. It was Dorianna who suggested taking it further. At first, it was just espressos after class and walks in Stanley Park Sunday afternoons. Then, one day, Dorianna asked me to take her to a lesbian bar. I resisted.

"Aren't there lesbian bars?" she asked. "You must go somewhere."

"Sure there are," I admitted. We were walking along Robson Street after a slow, sweet lunch where Dorianna admitted she was "curious." Something about how she'd mowed through men by the bushel and wasn't there something more, wasn't there? I had told her I wasn't the person to ask; I'd been gay all my life.

"I want to meet your friends," Dorianna said. "Why won't you take me? Are you embarrassed to be seen with me?"

In fact, this was true, or partly true. I hadn't admitted to my friendship with Dorianna at all; my friends would think Dorianna was simply another straight woman aiming for some thrills until the next boyfriend came along. Which I thought was as likely as not. "Look," I told her, "it's not like we're exhibits, you know. Sometimes straight women just love us and leave us."

Dorianna stopped and pulled me to a stop. Crowds of Sunday browsers flowed by us. "If *I* loved you," she said earnestly, "I'd never leave you. Kiss me or something, would you?"

I kissed her. Two weeks later Dorianna moved her stuff into my house, taking up the spare bedroom as her art studio.

After we became lovers, Dorianna began a series of paintings of women. Men disappeared completely from her work. She went to the bars with or without me, and joined the Lesbian Centre so she could attend a coming out group. Fiercely, she told her mother she was gay, hoping, I thought, that her mother might disown her. Instead, her mother joined a parents of lesbians and gays group and gave her a labyris for our first Christmas together. My own parents, who lived across the country and who'd known about me since I was fourteen, still refused to acknowledge my lesbianism, suggesting each time they called that there was still time to settle down with a "nice young man."

After a couple years, when we were still together and still happy, I thought maybe Dorianna was a lesbian after all. She hadn't left me; there were still no men on her horizon.

I started to relax and Dorianna started to talk about having a family.

I was thirty-eight. Dorianna was thirty-five and thinking about her clock. I had to tell her frankly that I'd never considered having children. Or, rather, that I'd considered it and ruled it out. I'd never had the urge women speak of. Parenthood was a lifetime commitment I wasn't prepared to make, that I was, in point of fact, too selfish to make.

Of course lesbians can't go out and just do it, just get pregnant. The children have to be planned. Lots of our friends were either planning them or past planning, in childbirth classes together having used some sort of insemination, a turkey baster or a clinic. With HIV, a turkey baster seemed pretty risky to me, but Dorianna thought a straight man whose sexual history she knew would be safe enough. Talk like this, the actual bones of the thing, how we could do it, brought me around. When I came around I had to admit the idea of making love with a pregnant woman was about the sexiest I'd ever had. The thought of Dorianna, pregnant, made me almost swoon.

Let me describe this woman: Dorianna had curly hair that splashed in ripples and wavelets almost down to her waist. When we danced, as I spun her out in underarm turns, it sometimes whipped across my cheeks like pelting rain. In bed, when we finally got there, she used her hair like a lovemaking appendage, taking clumps of it in her hands and tickling them over my breasts or across the tender skin of my inner thighs. When she grew braver, when we'd been lovers a few months and she knew the territory, she'd have me lie naked and stock still on the bed while she made love to me with only her hair for what seemed like an hour, until I was beyond myself, until I couldn't help grabbing her up.

Dorianna was small, only five-foot-two.

I remember our first morning after: I was sitting at my desk in my living room, preparing school lessons, when she appeared naked in the doorway. She grinned at me, leaned against the door frame with her arms up so her breasts raised and her waist thinned. I thought she was the most beautiful woman I had ever seen. Then and later, I admit I was full of pride to be seen with her.

I ended up calling Pat from a pay phone on the corner. Pat's been a friend of mine since junior high; back then, in fact, she was my first lover. We stayed friends after it ended and by now have seen each other through what we call "too many women."

"Pat," I said when she picked up, "Dorianna's pregnant."

"My God!" she said. "Congratulations, you old goat."

"You don't understand," I said and added faintly, "it wasn't . . . it isn't mine."

"It's yours, though, Liz. I mean you knew it couldn't be, biologically."

"I don't mean that," I said. "I had no idea she was—" I started crying.

"What? What?" Pat kept asking.

"She's gone back to men," I finally got out.

"You're not saying she left you?"

"She's having an affair! I wish she had left me! God, that would be easier to handle."

"Don't be maudlin, Liz. You always said Dorianna wanted a man. Is she leaving you?"

"I don't know!" I wailed. "I walked out."

"Well walk back in, for heaven's sake. Find out."

After I hung up, I didn't want to go home to ask the necessary questions, to hear whatever Dorianna had as answers. I didn't want to know who the father was, though possibilities steamed in my brain. I didn't want to hear she was leaving me, that she and this father were in love, that she wasn't, after all, a lesbian. I didn't even want her to say the child was ours, when I hadn't participated in conceiving it. When I'd finally agreed to have a baby, when I'd accepted we someday would, I began to entertain a fantasy of the two of us achieving it together, a fantasy where, in a clinic, we held hands and gazed soulfully into each other's eyes. If at home, I imagined inseminating her just at the pinnacle of our lovemaking.

There was never any question but that it would be Dorianna who carried our child. Dorianna was the mother. We weren't taking turns, first her, then me. Dorianna was the mom. I was . . . what the hell was I? I knew what I should've been—her partner, by her side.

I decided to go to Stan's, a straight bar Dorianna wouldn't find me at in a thousand years. We all have our secrets, I thought ruefully as

I slipped onto a bar stool and ordered a draught. I used to come here, before Dorianna. Sometimes the lesbian community was just too small and cloistered. What I wanted, when it closed in on me, was strangeness, and unless I went over the border to find new women, a straight bar was as strange as it got. Which was pretty well strange enough. I watched the reflections of women dancing in the mirror above the bar and thought how many lesbian hearts they could break.

A man came up and asked me to dance. I thought again of Dorianna and then thought, what the hell, and said, "Sure." Everything about him was foreign to me: his height, his body, his shaving stubble, his beery, male sweat. What did Dorianna see in this, I wondered as I danced. It wasn't that I didn't like men—I had friends who were men; it just never occurred to me to feel sexual about them. Looking at this man, a mid-size guy probably pushing forty and balding slightly, I had a sudden, painful image of him as the father of Dorianna's baby, of the two of them in bed together. It was only partway through the song but I stopped dead and stared at him, then wheeled around and left the dance floor.

I was surprised when he came after me.

"Lady," he said above the music, taking my elbow and spinning me to face him, "you all right?"

I shrugged him off.

"You got a boyfriend?" he said, bending down. I got a face full of his breath.

"Something like that," I said. Then I relented, adding, "Don't take it personally."

When I showed up at home again, I was as drunk as I could remember being. I still hadn't wanted to face Dorianna, but I'd figured it would be easier pie-eyed. At first I thought she wasn't there—everything was dark and the silence was palpable—but I found her in the bedroom. Even in the half-light from the street lamps, I could see she was crunched over in a fetal position, crying. I didn't say hello. I turned my back and started undressing.

Finally she said, "You smell like a brewery." Her voice was humid and deep from crying. "Where were you?"

"Out," I said shortly.

"I was worried," Dorianna said. "You didn't take the car . . ."

"This isn't going to work, Dorianna," I said. My chest expanded as

I circled to face her. I felt sure of myself, righteous. I'd get out. Now, before I got hurt worse.

"Liz, I—"

"Dorianna, I don't want to talk about it. I still don't want to talk about it. Okay? I'm drunk. I went to a bar and I got drunk. I'm glad I'm drunk. If I had to be sober, I'd jump off a bridge. You're pregnant—"

"I just found out today." Again, her unavoidable note of pleasure.

"—and I don't know how you got that way except I'm your lover, and I'm probably the one person on this earth who should be absolutely sure, and I'm not. And so what do I ask myself? I ask myself what kind of relationship this is where such a thing could happen. I ask myself if you love me. Or, no, if you feel anything for me at all. Or whether you're straight." I lowered my voice menacingly. "That's it, Dorianna. Because really, I know how you got that way."

"It just happened, Liz. One time, I swear it. Just once and I never even thought I could get pregnant."

I'd still half-believed I'd been wrong, that she hadn't slept with someone, a man, that she'd gone to a clinic alone. What she said about just the once took my breath away.

"I never didn't want you, Liz." She moved onto her knees and bent slightly forward, gesticulating with both hands. "I never stopped loving you or believing in us, never. I love you."

"Am I supposed to believe that?"

"I was just curious. Can't you see that? After all these years I wanted to know what it was like again."

"You're straight," I stated flatly.

She cried, "I'm not. I'm not!"

I'd really opened a wound. I pressed my advantage. "You always were and you are now and always will be."

She was up off the bed and trembling in front of me. "You're so cruel," she said, lowering her head in transparent pain.

A silence hung precariously.

I didn't think of myself as cruel. I was scared, suddenly, that she did. That she possibly could. "You're the one who's screwing around, Dorianna, not me," I said. I always called her by her full name. I wondered if her boyfriend had a nickname for her, Dory or maybe Annie.

"It's *our baby*," she said, "the baby we've wanted."

"You've wanted," I corrected dangerously.

She reached for me. "Feel my belly, Liz. In here we've got our daughter or son growing."

I snatched my hand away. "Your daughter or son. I can't love a woman who'd betray me."

"I never meant to betray you. Honestly. I just wanted to see—"

"That's what you said about me, Dorianna. You were just curious with me. At first."

"And then I fell in love with you."

I reached for my shirt. "I think I should leave."

"Don't," said Dorianna. "Don't. Don't go."

"No," I said. "I need time. I've got to think." I pulled on my jeans.

"If you walk out of here again, I'll tell him," Dorianna said, her voice low and threatening. "I'll tell Jake I got pregnant."

"Jake?" I said. I hadn't thought to ask who it was. In all this fighting it hadn't once occurred to me.

"Jake. The sperm donor."

"Father," I said belligerently.

"Father," she said and nodded. She backed up and sat on the lip of the bed.

I could make her out more clearly because my eyes had adjusted to the dark. Her face was in shadow, but I had no trouble seeing the parenthetical sweep of her hair on either side of it. I saw her bent neck and the hunched yet somehow hopeful posture of her back. I asked, "Who is he?"

"A guy at the gallery. I mean, a guy who bought a painting. You remember. A couple years ago, my first show? It was the only painting I sold."

I remembered him; I remembered being jealous because he was all over Dorianna at the opening and she flirted back. It was another time I thought: This woman is no more a lesbian than I am a mole.

"I'm sorry. Good God, Liz, I'm so sorry." She floated off the bed and took my face in her hands. "I made a terrible mistake and I need your forgiveness. Please, let's stop and celebrate the good that can come of it. Honey, I mean it, it was just the once. While I was doing it, I hated it, hated him. I missed you so much. He wasn't half the lover you are. Please, Liz, please."

How could I resist her? She kissed my cheek and my chin, small, adorable kisses, and I folded my arms around her, pressed myself against her still taut stomach. I groaned.

"Please," she whispered. "I'm so sorry. Please forgive me."

Now I knew who it was, I wanted Dorianna in a territorial way. I wanted to mark her, claim her, leave my scent on her, fight Jake and win her. Drunk and confused and overcome by instinct, I felt like an animal. I pushed Dorianna down on the bed and made love to her like a beast, without taking off my clothes, lost in a haze of insane, itchy, carnality.

When Dorianna left me for Jake some two months later, no one was as surprised as I was. I think all our mutual friends, even all my friends, saw it coming. They'd been taking me aside and asking things like "Are you sure she's not still seeing this guy?" and I'd been telling them I was positive Dorianna wasn't, that Dorianna and I had forged a new relationship out of the tatters of the old and out of our upcoming maternity.

Some of them wanted to know how we were planning, legally, to arrange things, and I'd blithely replied that between lesbians shared parenting was based on trust. Actually I was hoping to adopt, not because I thought Dorianna would ever try to cut her losses and run, but because I wanted to be held responsible for little him or her.

At home, we called the baby Georgie. In bed, as Dorianna began to show and then the baby to kick, I put my hand on Dorianna's tummy. Each night I slept spooned around her, cupping our daughter or son in my hand. Sex between us was warm and funny and wonderful—Dorianna was often so happy she burst into laughter. At the obstetrician's, I listened to the fetal heartbeat. We signed up for prenatal classes. We discussed cribs and strollers and getting a bigger place so Dorianna could still have a studio, or renting a studio somewhere else. We pushed her painting supplies to the middle of the room and painted the nursery walls a soft green. That's when she told me. She was wearing old jeans and a man's white shirt and was speckled and smeared with paint. She had the roller in her hand and was pushing it up and down the third wall—I was edging with a brush, standing on a step stool—when she said, "Liz, get down. I can't do this anymore."

I thought she meant painting. The fumes or maybe she'd overexerted herself.

"It's Jake, Liz. The thing is, I'm still seeing Jake."

I really didn't think I was hearing her correctly. I heard the words, of course I heard them, but because they didn't make any sort of sense, I didn't appreciate there was a message in them for me. When it hit me at last, I threw my paint brush at her. It clipped her head and clattered to the floor leaving drips of green in all her blond curls.

"Don't throw things," Dorianna cried. "Haven't I tried to make it work, Liz? Haven't I been here with you, trying? But now I know I have to be with Jake. He's the baby's *father*, after all."

I couldn't believe she said that. I got down off the stepstool, marched over to her and took the roller from her hands. I wanted to say everything, but there was too much and nowhere to start. I put the roller in the paint tray, loaded it and rolled it over Dorianna's face. She was so shocked she just stood dripping as I rolled it lower, all the way to the belly that now stuck out too far to be fit into ordinary clothes. I rolled it down and then up. Then I looked her in the eyes, coldly.

"I don't care," I said.

Two months later, I received an invitation to attend a baby shower. I hadn't heard from Dorianna since the night of our breakup, although of course her mother sent some men over to clear out her things, and of course I heard tidbits about her from friends—like she and Jake weren't planning to marry, like she'd had a test and knew the baby was a girl, like she thought she was gaining too much weight—and of course I kept track of how far along she was, six months, seven months, eight months, but from Dorianna herself I'd heard nothing, which was pretty well the way I wanted it. The way it had to be.

The shower invitation was pink, with a cascade of embossed green and blue balloons falling over the inked-in information lines. I didn't at first understand what it was, that it was something from Dorianna or that it was about the baby. I was distracted because of problems at school with our principal—I was the staff rep and it was my job to find solutions—and I stared at the invitation for the longest time. When it finally sunk into my brain, when I grasped that I was invited to Dorianna's baby shower, as if I had no more to do with the child than her sister or her best friend did, when I realized that I was supposed to show up with booties, maybe, or a year's supply of diapers, I uncapped a beer and commenced stewing.

After spending a morose and stupid weekend—apparently I begged my friend Pat to go to bed with me—it became obvious to me that I couldn't go on the way I had been, in this sort of suspended animation, where despite putting up a good front I was still deeply hooked into Dorianna's life—which, admittedly, I generally thought of as "our" life.

Which is not to say I was prepared to take her back. That's not to say I thought she'd ever offer me the option.

I also knew I could not go on drinking, so after work on Monday, instead of driving to the bar to spend another night watching women who love women being loved back, I took myself to Oakridge shopping centre. I walked around the Bay's baby department. I noticed a pregnant woman absent-mindedly rubbing her belly as she tried to decide between crib mobiles. It made me flash hard on Dorianna and made me furious. I grabbed the thing I was closest to, a collapsible stroller, and marched to the cash register.

I should have had the gift delivered to Dorianna from the store. That would have been the right, the generous, thing to do. Instead, I walked outside into the rain and dark, leaned the stroller up against the car parked next to mine and drove away without it.

What I sent Dorianna by FedEx was the half-full cans of green paint from the nursery, paying extra for a guarantee that they would be delivered during the shower. A couple days later, Dorianna called me.

"It's me," she said when I picked up.

"Dorianna?"

"I just want you to know I'll still think of you as this baby's other mother. Even though you're being mean to me."

"Dorianna," I repeated.

"No, listen to me. I did what I had to do. You did what you had to do. Everybody's sorry. I just wanted—"

"I'm not sorry," I interrupted.

"Well, I am. I'm sorry it couldn't work between us."

"It *was* working between us," I said dryly.

"For me, then. It wasn't working for me." There was a silence. Dorianna said, "I cut off my hair."

There was another pause.

"Well," she said, "no hard feelings, right? I just wanted you to know Jake and I don't harbour any ill will. He understands perfectly."

I thought of Jake, understanding perfectly. Not for the first time, I had a moment of utter humiliation at how he must twist and distort what Dorianna and I had shared.

After I hung up, I wandered into the nursery, Dorianna's studio, which I now made some effort to call the spare bedroom. There were still drop cloths covering the floor, the way there had been since Dorianna had moved her art supplies in. The walls were still partly white and mostly green. The clothes Dorianna had worn the day she left, that I'd painted, were in a heap on the floor exactly where she'd taken them off. I picked them up. They were crusted into a ball. Slowly I pulled them apart, trying to refashion them into garments, the way I'd tried to refashion Dorianna into a lesbian. When I had them unstuck, I lay down on the floor. I remembered how Dorianna had looked when she stripped the clothes off. The paint I'd rolled on had gone through her shirt, so a patch of her belly was green. So was some of her hair and most of her face. I thought of her now, bigger, with short hair, and tried to imagine what she looked like. I didn't even have a picture of her pregnant. I picked up her shirt and put the uncrusty back of it to my nose. I couldn't smell her; I couldn't smell anything. Somehow the day the baby came was easy to imagine: Jake and Dorianna in the hospital, Dorianna's face screwed up with labour, Jake panting to show her how. Maybe, I thought, this was how things were supposed to work out. Maybe she's counting her blessings for making the choices she did; maybe she's happier like this. She used to say she'd never been as alive as when she was with me. She probably said the same thing to Jake, in bed, whispering it in his ear.

I rolled on my side. I heard the phone ringing, but I didn't get up to answer it. The drop cloths were heavy cotton, tarpaulins, and under them I could feel the nap of the carpet against my cheek. After a while, I rose and began to pull them, balling them into a pile in the centre of the room. Finally, moving slowly as if I were easing myself through toffee, I picked them up and carried them out to the trash. I stood under my upstairs windows as if I was a stranger. I don't know what I thought I'd see there. Maybe I thought if I looked for long enough, Dorianna might appear. But of course she didn't, and eventually I got in my car and drove off.

At the paint store I came to, I picked rust, a colour I was lukewarm about but that I knew Dorianna hated. I went home and put on Dorianna's clothes, which were huge around my waist and too short on my arms and legs, and started painting the room, inch by inch. The light was dimming by the time I finished covering the green. I was tired but satisfied. For a minute, I stood at the window looking at the waning sunset and the sparkle of city lights, and at the mountains in the distance. By this time next month, I thought, I'll be a decade older. Forty. I wondered if forty would bring wisdom. Usually January brought snow—maybe snow was enough.

the way my mother (although first of many children) never

WASELA HIYATE

she workstudies
nibbles at her inside her
cheek gets slapped by her ma
(dont read those books theyll
give you fancy ideas)

she workscrubs floors
craves chocolate when shes
17&beautifugly pregnant by
my dads parents bought her
for a coupla sheep

she workscrapes carrots she will cook
                              coo s over baby
(in india the prize is a firstborn son)

she worksintowntall buildings hurt the sky
nibbles her litlegirlhabit cheek gets
called down to the bosssmiles &pats her
cheek you do (one day he will tell firstborn watch out for
them marriage is never the mansidea) fine work and youre up
for promotion

she worksatwork the boss pretty eyepretty eye &jokes the way
dad never did she laughts
&types   types&types & types &   types&

she workswith cosmetics first time in
her life when she is most beautiful

she workscleans tubs is a goodmom (makes
4 separate chicken meals
4 separate children
            be good girls
is up all night when her daughters go dancing

then she works in th morning   she works &she works and
works &she worksheworks &she
worksand quickshe workswell &she works quicks and she
in th morning in th quicks&she work s ideas
theyll give you a firstborn idea workshe works and
she worksand watchout the quicksand the mansidea neverth
prize the mansideathe she
works& works &she nvershe never   she   never   gets
                                                      angry

Trips to the Basement

SU CROLL

come quickly
say what you want to say
say it quickly
say it in parentheses
making it notational   knowing
there are notes
toward understanding

all that relentlessness

RITUAL OVERBOARDING   our little girl
faces stuffed   pork hocks and cold greens
stuffed in to keep us   bless us and keep us
quiet   scotch taped lips and hair
that won't curl   cutting tangles out or contests
for holding hands over flame   this is not
what you are interested in   these are not things
that can make up a text   that can seek
validation in this or any other language
known to man

that's women's work

THAT'S WOMEN'S WORK AND YOU DON'T WANT
anything to do with it   don't want to hear about it
don't want to know how you got her feet
into those little lotus shaped shoes
don't want to know how long she stayed locked
into that chastity belt   tightening into sainthood
that's women's work   that's between
mothers and daughters   *that's between*
you and your mother

what did you think
all those trips to the basement were about

last time he gave it to me there was a star in the east

MAKE ME EAT   make me
take these words in   I need to eat them
searching for a sensation not unlike that fish
hooking the last light in some poem you don't want
anything to do with   another fishing story
the usual density of reference   say what
you don't want to say
say that quickly too

yes we went to church but we didn't understand
the words couldn't make
the responses
what did you think

there's a voice existing below the rhetoric
but we can't hear it
the whole time there was a cross on the wall
what did you think

he's not the kind of god you can hold in your mouth

worship begins at home and how else
are we to praise this god   how else are we to raise
our bodies in prayer   raise our bodies from the dead
but this raising of his staff of life

WHAT IS BEYOND THAT FIRST SITTING
first straddling of the narrative with its usual
density of reference

is that what you would prefer
would you prefer to be reminded of what has been buried
in language   words losing meaning
until we cannot recognize ourselves
until we cannot know how to name ourselves

we cannot get back to the basement
of language

IN THE WRITING WORKSHOP HE SAID
we should be salty   we should be taking a piece
around with us   taking the taste of the ocean around with us
in our open mouths maybe   he told me
to keep myself pure   douche with vinegar and kosher salt
to keep quiet until I had something to say
something sensible something rational something
he could understand
he was very big
on science
as an everyday part of our existence
can't argue with a tree he said
and was proud to say it
proud that he was older   a kind of grand
daddy of language and he told
he told us we should be tight enough
not to be
argued with

HE SAID AN AUTHOR DOESN'T KNOW THE TRUTH
but embodies it he said and was proud to say
proud to claim he was looking for the genuine
the simple the sensual
but when we pulled out our suppers   being working women
working all day at our women's work
and at night coming quickly
to learn to write   to learn to embody language
when we pulled out our suppers   not having eaten all day
he turned away   he could not bear to see people eating
could not bear to see women
eating   their jaws working   their mouths swallowing
and swallowing

so we are stuck straddling this top floor narrative
being made to prefer being tight enough
being made to embody
a poem that would feel less used
more virginal   more willing
to open up   more willing
to be pried opened

SWITCHING THE CONTEXT OF SCREWING
his ageing narrative   wondering how long
it can hold up   how long he can hold on
stay hard   how long
can language stay hard   hold water
hold ground and when can we ever be
holding our own
ground   our own place
for expression of our own language

you don't want anything to do with
another fishing story
you might prefer something about culture and nature
you might prefer not to smell us
in heat   that's women's work
and who wants anything
to do with it   you don't
want to hear about it   all those trips
to the basement of our gendered lives

BETTER TO BE STRADDLING THIS NARRATIVE
a woman a writer a piece of salty natural scenery a poem

yet there is still sitting on that stiff
staff of life
this literary one coming
to life inside

all that nature that makes us up

all that flower imagery that you've read about for years
and years   gladioli and amaryllis giving over
more seeds than literature can ever harvest
a whole poetic tradition crammed in
and I reshape you with every thrust
poetry
language
emerging
lotus shaped
as a broken rose

all those peach trees
coming to life inside me
peach coloured tulip shaped cock
coming out daffodil
coming up roses

I know

I know my lines
should be tight enough
not to be argued with
but what did you think
those trips to the basement
were all about

The Third Decade

～

Volumes 21 – 30 (1998 – 2007)

Are We Feminist Enough? An Interview with Editor Lana Okerlund

MEGHAN BELL

Lana Okerlund is a partner at West Coast Editorial Associates, and a former *Room* collective member. In this interview, Lana discusses *Room*'s identity crisis in the early 2000s and the rebrand that followed.

ROOM: How did your five years at *Room* affect your editing career?

LO: Well, I can't say that it *made* it, but I think it made it more possible. I moved here from Winnipeg in late 2001, because I wanted to go back to school to explore this idea of being an editor. I was a business consultant. I found out about *Room of One's Own*, and I went to an anniversary reading they had, and met Virginia Aulin, who encouraged me to apply. The people I met became early mentors of mine, and just to be taken under some of those wings gave me more confidence. A few years later, I had an opportunity at the Vancouver Art Gallery, and I brought the editions of *Room* I had edited to the interview, these things I had done as a volunteer, but they were the best portfolio pieces for that particular job. I think that's what got me that gig. As my career developed, that gallery experience was really important and it led to other things.

ROOM: What were some of the challenges the magazine faced?

LO: So, back when I started in 2002, the kinds of things they had just done—they had just put the subscribers in a database—

ROOM: [*laughing*] Oh my god, how were you keeping track [before]?

LO: I don't know! I just remember them saying at one of my first meetings, *Oh, we're so happy we have this database now.* They had just done all of that! It was very different. Steady coming and going of people [on the collective] has probably always been a challenge. Sometimes there were fit issues, or there were people trying to change things too quickly. Then, [around] 2003, we started to get some Canada Council feedback that made us concerned that they might discontinue our grant, or reduce the amount they granted us, if we didn't address the issues they raised.

They were concerned about the quality of some of our production values, in particular of interior artwork. We didn't have [a] cohesive acceptance process, we had some spotty issues, and we were told there was a kind of "sameness" to the issues. Some former collective members like Mary Schendlinger [gave] us really frank feedback. And we weren't on the web at all; I mean, we had a website, but it was just a static brochure, and we weren't using it to promote the magazine. So those were some of the main challenges. And addressing all of that took money and time, and we didn't have much of either.

ROOM: I've always wondered about the rebrand in 2007. In *Room* 30.1, a question is posed: "Do women still need a room of their own? Or has feminism become the new "F" word—too divisive to be associated with a magazine that celebrates women writers and artists." In the last issue as *Room of One's Own* [29.4], you write: "Come the 1990s and 2000s, feminists—and we here at *Room*—have been tangling with what feminism even means. The puzzle of feminism's identity in the so-called third wave has been reflected in this magazine and some may even have concluded that *Room* isn't 'feminist enough' anymore." Can you elaborate?

LO: You know I'd have to go back and look at some of my records to really understand and pinpoint when and why we felt the need to rebrand. We were going through quite a bit of soul-searching to address those Canada Council issues—I said the word "sameness," [but] I think it also felt like there was a *safeness* about *Room*. As women who had inherited the work of early feminists, we were kind of coasting. [On the collective], we were mostly middle class, not very diverse, and there was this feeling like maybe we were not doing anything very important anymore, like *Room* was becoming irrelevant. We had many discussions about our mission; we didn't just need to clarify it with Canada Council and with our readers; we needed to clarify it for ourselves. We started to ask all these questions.

I remember one session [where] we really started to get into it. And somebody said, *I don't know, I don't really want to be involved with a crisis dialogue in our magazine all the time. I want it to be entertaining!* The minutes from one of the sessions even records that we didn't want *Room* to be attached to the word "feminism" anymore. It was a real identity crisis. And I think that's also us reflecting where feminism was too. We had this naive perception that the work was done. But I know now, and I knew very soon later, that that wasn't the case. There are still so many struggles; we're not at all equal yet. Look at the [U.S.] election that just happened. We all know this is still an issue.

And so ten years ago, when *Room* was rebranding, we were like, *We need to knock this around and freshen things up*. And although *Room of One's Own*, the title, was important to our history, it seemed outdated and confining. We wanted the magazine to move forward and initiate conversation and literally give writers and readers the *room* for that dialogue. So we decided to use the short form, which everyone already used to refer to the magazine anyway. We got a very negative letter from someone who had long admired and been involved with *Room*, and she said she thought that we were really doing damage to the magazine by rebranding it. But we also got positive feedback. And I think it was a really important pivot. I feel like I'm seeing with [*Room*] now that it is taking more risks, that it is not just the same old, same old.

ROOM: In the last five years, tons of feminist or women/trans-inclusive lit magazines have emerged. Ten years ago, were [there] others like *Room*?

LO: I don't know if there were or not. Certainly there weren't many of these other inclusive magazines that you're talking about.

ROOM: Has *Room* always been trans-inclusive, as far as you know?

LO: No! I remember a very heated discussion about it, actually. Because we'd always accepted pieces by women, and through this process of accepting—you needed to have three people saying yes—and through that three-reader process, a piece was accepted by a trans individual, and one of the members was really against publishing it. I don't know if that was the first time *Room* addressed that or not, but it was certainly the first time I was party to it. And we published it.

ROOM: [*laughing*] That's good! That's the right decision. Way to be on the right side of history.

LO: Yeah, the discussion was about, well, do you have to be born one gender or another in order to qualify? It was really bizarre—yeah, it was bizarre. That's what I mean, we were sort of becoming a safe, beige thing. And had we [continued to go] in that direction and had there not been pushback to that, then maybe *Room* wouldn't be around anymore.

ROOM: It's interesting, ten years ago [people said], *Oh, maybe we shouldn't use the word feminist, it might be too extreme*, and now it's so embraced that *Room* is one of six literary magazines in Canada [with] this mandate.

LO: Oh wow. There's a real resurgence. Many in my generation—we were just kind of holding the fort. Not really doing anything. I don't know, I think this is a bigger issue. Sorry, I interrupted the question.

ROOM: Oh, no, that was the question—what has changed?

LO: Well, I don't know. You may have a better idea than me. Culturally, it seems like there's increasing objectification of women, there's still this enormous gap in political leadership and in who holds power in general. And so I think there's a swelling—I feel it—of frustration. And that tells us that there's still a lot of ground to go.

I went to see *Star Wars* last year when that series rebooted, and everyone was talking about Rae, who was this amazing feminist role model. And I remember coming away from that saying if Rae, and the guy who ended up playing the new Darth Vader in town, Kylo Ren, if he was a woman, and [they] had an epic lightsaber battle and nobody noticed and commented on the fact that it was two women, that's when it's done. It's the no commenting on it that's important. It's the not noticing. We're so far from that. And I don't think it'll be in my lifetime.

Room was founded because women's writing wasn't being published as much. It was going to give women at least this space. *We will take your work. We will take it because we're only taking that kind of work.* So whether we still need this women-only space, I don't know, but we certainly need a space for that conversation.

ROOM: It's funny—one of the reasons I brought up the other magazines —I was at a conference last year, and there were two sort of alarming conversations. A woman came up and said she only submitted to feminist, women-only literary journals now, and I said, *I don't think that's the point.* That sounds so fundamentally wrong to me, that wasn't what I wanted to hear. And then the second one was, we did this women of colour issue last year, and a woman came and said she got an encouraging rejection from [it]. I said, *That's awesome, submit to us again, it means we liked it.* And she said, *I didn't think I had a chance at another issue of the magazine, I thought I only had a chance at this issue.* And I [said], *Well, that's not the case.* But that was the attitude, from two different angles, and to me that seems—is that a step back? I don't actually know.

LO: I struggle with those same kinds of questions. Again, it's about the day that we arrive at a place where you don't notice that there is a women of colour issue because it mostly is and it just happens to be that way because that was the strongest work. And there were so many women of all sorts who could contribute this strong work, and it was all equally validated because there were people of all sorts reviewing it. It's about the whole ladder. But it's not fairly distributed right now. The people who've had the social capital in the past pass it on to their children, and so you continue to have this power structure. And—it's beyond me, and it's probably beyond this interview. I struggle with that same thing. Anytime you have to denote something as a particular—then, you know, isn't it important that men read the stuff in *Room*? How many men subscribe?

ROOM: I think about five percent. Less? Less.

LO: It's a really small number. And so it's just one more echo chamber. Maybe we're just talking to ourselves, and frustrated with the lack of change. Increasingly in our world, everyone's just talking to themselves and the people who already believe them [*laughing*]. I don't know. I don't know what the answers are. It's never-ending—we need to continue to chip away at it. But think about how far things are now. Our mothers' generation, or their mothers' generation, they didn't have the same opportunities we had. It's measurably better.

I was going to say—back to your very first question—I did want to mention that the very first issue that I edited, I worked on it with a woman named Melva McLean, and, honestly, I was so proud when I held the finished magazine in my hands. I was so happy about the accomplishment [that] I bought the painting [on the cover].

ROOM: That's amazing.

LO: Yeah, so, for me, it really marks the beginning of my editing career. It means a lot to me.

from 14, as More Than Just a Number—Montréal Massacre

ANNA HUMPHREY

For Genevieve Bergeron, 21

Because you bled one week of every month.
Because you wanted to build bridges and towers.
Because you weren't at home dusting the den.
Because, for no reason.
Because "The gunman suffered a brutal upbringing."
Because the world has gone mad, gone sad.
Because you were there.

For Sonia Pelletier, 28

Your body was found underneath a cafeteria table,
trying to hide

just like you used to duck behind the sofa,
conceal yourself in the closet
with your feet in a pair of boots
and a jacket wrapped tight around you

Ready or not
here I come

like you used to hide your toothbrush
so when eight thirty came
and you wanted to stay up
you could waste time
searching,
then ask for a glass of water,
another kiss goodnight,
one last hug.

Exactly like they told you to do
in event of an earthquake.
"Sit in a doorway,"
they said,
"or under a table.
While the floor shakes
and the drywall cracks
around you

you should be safe there."

For Annie Turcotte, 21

Probably not how you imagined
your funeral

On an icy day with
3,000 plus in attendance

And 14 hearses
gliding past
with white numbers on their sides
and all in a row
1 and 2, 3, 4

And a sunken-cheeked woman on the street corner
holding her daughter's hand
and
5, 6,
7, 8

and the daughter not understanding
9, 10, 11,
and
12
13

14
saying to her mother,
"Why are you crying,
if you didn't even know them?"

For Barbara Daigneault, 22

Later, they talked about the men
and the guilt

He was smaller than me,
I could have jumped him.

Could have
Should have
Would have

Could have been the hero
Should have hit, kicked,
slugged him hard,
sprayed a fire extinguisher
in his eyes.
Would have, if only
I'd thought of it in time.
Could have bashed his teeth out
Should have thrown him through
the wall.

For Helene Colgan, 23

At 5:30, the paper says,
on Dec. 6
he began to roam the halls
hunting humans

with two ammunition belts
criss-crossed on his chest;
a semi-automatic,
and a knife
and his eyes—cold
and his hands—steady

And in the paper they quote,
"It was just like Rambo."

But what would you say, Helene,
if you could say?
Probably just
that it wasn't fair;
that Rambo
only shot
the bad guys;
that your gunman
was shorter,
much scrawnier,
and no kind of hero.

For Anne-Marie Edward, 21

21 is very young
only 17 + 4.

21 should be camping in the Gatineau
backpacking, hitchhiking,
meeting the man of her dreams

21 drinks cold coffee and works
late into the morning, on drafts
of a paper
she really should have started
last month.

21 drives with her music
turned up loud
and worries where
she's going
with this life of hers
and whether or not
she can pay off
the phone bill

21 thinks of a house
in a quiet neighbourhood
and a wedding dress
with a nice headpiece
or veil
not too fancy,
and not too soon,
but not so very far off either.

My Hero

IVAN COYOTE

WEBSTER'S NEW SCHOOL AND OFFICE DICTIONARY defines a hero as a man of distinguished courage, moral or physical; or the chief character in a play, novel, or poem. Her name was Cathy Bulahouski, and she was, among other things, my uncle John's girlfriend. She had other titles, too—my family is fond of nicknames and in-jokes—she was referred to as the girl with the large glands, and later, when she left John and he had to pay her for half of the house they had built together, she became and was remembered by the men as "lump sum." The women just smiled, and always called her Cathy. Cathy Bulahouski, the Polish cowgirl from Calgary. I've wanted to tell this story for years, but never have, because I couldn't think of a better name for a Polish cowgirl from Calgary than Cathy Bulahouski.

I remember sitting in her and John's half-built kitchen, smell of sawdust all around us, watching her brush her hair. Her hair was light brown and not quite straight, and she usually wore it in a tight braid that hung like a whip between her shoulder blades. When she shook the braid out at night, her hair cascaded in shining ripples down her back to just past the dips behind her knees. She would get John to brush it out for her, she sitting at one end of a plain wooden table, he standing behind her on their unpainted plywood floor. I would be mesmerized, watching her stretch her head back and show the tendons in her neck. Brushing hair seemed like a girl-type activity to me, but John would stroke her hair first with the brush, then smooth it with his other hand, like a pro. My father rarely touched my mother in front of me, and I couldn't take my eyes off of this commonplace intimacy passing between them.

The summer I turned eleven, Cathy was working as a short-order cook at a lodge next to some hot springs. She was also the horse lady. She hired me to help her run a little trail-ride operation for the tourists. My duties included feeding, brushing, and saddling-up of the eight or so horses we had. And the shovelling of shit. I wasn't paid any cash money, but I got to eat for free in the diner, and I got to ride Little Chief, half Appaloosa and half Shetland pony, silver grey with a spotted ass. Cathy and I were co-workers and conspirators. Every time we got an obnoxious American guy she would wink at me over his shoulder while he drawled on about his riding days in Texas or Montana. I would saddle up Steamboat for him, a giant jet-black stallion who was famous both for his frightening bursts of uncontrollable galloping and for trying to rub his rider off by scraping his sides up against the spindly lodgepole pines that lined the trails.

I always rode behind my aunt. Her horse would plod along at tourist speed in front of me, and I would try to make my legs copy the way Cathy's moved, the seamless satin groove her hips fell into with every swing of the horse's step. Sometimes we would ride alone, and she would whistle and kick the insides of her boots in and race ahead of me. Little Chief would pick up the pace a little like the foot soldier he was, and my heart would begin to pound. Cathy would ride for a while and then whirl her horse around, her long braid swinging around and hanging down her front as she rode back toward me.

One day we were lazily loping along the little road that led back to the hot springs when one of Cathy's admirers came up from behind in a pickup. He honked hello as he and his road-dust drove by, which spooked Little Chief and he bucked me off. On impact, tears and snot and all the air in my lungs were expelled. I lay on the hard-packed dirt and dry grass for a minute, bawling when I could catch little pieces of my breath. "Get on," Cathy said, hard-lipped as she rode up beside me. "Get back up on that horse right now. Go on, do it now, or you'll be too afraid to later." She was tough like that.

One Christmas shortly after she and John had finished drywalling, our family had turkey dinner out at their place. We were each allowed to open one present on Christmas Eve, and my mom had suggested I bring the one shaped just like a toboggan from under our tree at home. The coolest thing about Cathy was how she would gear up in a snowsuit in thirty below in the blue-black sky of a Yukon night (which begins at about two in the afternoon around winter solstice) and play outside with the rest of the kids. Not in a grown-up, sit-on-the-porch-and-smoke-cigarettes-and-watch kind of way, but in a dirty-kneed, get-roadrash kid kind of way. Right after I ripped the last of the wrapping paper off of my gleaming red sled, she was searching through the sea of snowboots by the door for her black Sorels and pulling her jacket off the hook behind the door. "Let's go up the hill behind the house and give it a try. Not much of a trail in winter, but we'll make one."

I suited up right behind her, followed by my sister and a stream of cousins with mittens on strings. It was so cold outside that the air burned arrows into the backs of our throats and frost collected on our eyelashes above where our scarves ended, which would melt if you closed your eyes for too long and freeze on our cheeks. We packed as many of us onto the sled as we could so everyone could have a go. We rode and climbed, rode and climbed until our toes began to burn.

"Once more, everybody goes one more time, then we should go in," Cathy breathed through her scarf. She pushed her butt to the very back of the sled, and motioned for my little sister to shove in front of her, between her legs. I jumped in the front, and my little sister's snowsuit whistled up against mine as she wrapped her legs around me. The toboggan's most alluring feature was the two metal emergency brakes on either side, with the black plastic handles molded to fit the shape of your hand. I tried to grab both and steer, but my sister also wanted to hold onto one, and started to whine.

"You can each have one," Cathy ordered. "You steer one way and you can steer on the other side. Don't fight about it, everyone else is waiting for their turn. Let's go." About halfway down we flew off a bump. My little sister hauled on her brake and we screeched off the path and smashed into a tree. Cathy's leg hit first and I heard a snap. By the time we rolled her onto the sled and pulled her back to the house, her face was glowing blue white and her teeth were chattering. John came running out with a flashlight. He gingerly pulled up the leg of her snow pants, and dropped it again, his face changing from Christmas rum red to moonlight white.

"Jesus Christ. Get the kids in the house and pull the truck around. And get her a blanket, she's going to emergency. Pat, are you okay to drive?" A weird silence took over the house after they left. I fell asleep in my clothes on the spare bed and barely woke up when my dad carried me out to the truck hours later.

"Did Cathy live?" I whispered into his ear. He smelled like scotch and shampoo and his new sweater.

"She's fine. She's asleep. She's got a cast and a bottle of painkillers. You can call her in the morning."

I told my friend Valerie all about it the next day, bragging like it was me. "I tried to save us, but my sister is too little to steer. Cathy's bone was poking right out of her leg, and she never cried once. There was even blood. Now she has a little rubber thing on the bottom of her cast so she can walk a bit, plus she has crutches."

"My dad cut the tip of his finger off with a saw once. They sewed it back on," she reminded me.

"Yeah, but you weren't even born yet. Besides, a leg is way bigger than a finger. Hurts more."

Later that winter the wolves got hungry because the government sold too many moose-hunting licences and dogs and cats started to disappear. Cathy phoned me one Sunday morning and told me that they had found what was left of Little Chief at the bottom of the mountain the day before. "I didn't tell you yesterday because your mom told me you had a hockey game. I know you're sad, but horses and wolves are animals, and they follow different rules than we do. He had a good horse life, and now the wolves will make it until spring. You were too big to ride him anymore anyway, and your little heart will get better in time. Wolves are wolves and men are just people." She was tough like that.

When she left John, she was tough too. She took her horse, one duffle bag, and most of his savings to cover her half of the house. She never even cried. Or that's how I saw her leaving in my mind. Dry-eyed in her pickup, with the radio on and a cloud of dirt-road dust, all the way from the Yukon to Alberta. Bet she never looked back, I thought. My uncle started to date one of the other cooks from the lodge. She had a university degree so everyone called her the professor.

My little sister grew up and moved to Calgary. She, like myself, inherited our family loyalty and looked Cathy up. My mom and I went to visit my sister at Christmas, and she told me Cathy would love it if I could make it out to visit her in Bragg Creek. But we got snowed in, so I called her the day before we left. Cathy's voice sounded the same as I remembered, except more tired. "I can't believe you're almost thirty years old. I remember you as just a little girl with that white hair and filthy hands, little chicken legs. You had such big eyes. My God, you were cute. Just let me grab my smokes." I could hear dogs barking and a man cursing at them to shut the hell up. A television droned in the background. She sounded out of breath when she got back on the phone.

"Here I am. Hard dragging myself around since my accident. Did Carrie tell you about my legs?" She had broken both of her femurs straight through a couple of years ago, and had pins in her knees. She still had to walk on two canes and couldn't work anymore. "I lost the trailer," she explained. "Couldn't get workers' comp because it happened on a weekend, and the unemployment ran out a year ago. Had to move in with Edward and lie about being common law even to get welfare."

"What are you saying about me?" I heard the man's voice again in the background. "Who you talking to anyway?"

"My niece. Turn down the TV for Chrissakes."

"You don't have any nieces. You don't even have any brothers or sisters." I presumed this was Edward. He obviously didn't understand family loyalty the way we did. Blood and marriage were only part of it.

"'Member that time you broke your ankle on the sled? You didn't even cry. You were my hero back then, you know?"

"Well, I cried when I broke my legs this time. I'm still crying. Some fucking hero I am now, huh?" I heard the emptiness in her voice and didn't know what to say. So I told her a story.

"Your old shed is still out behind John's, you know. Nobody ever goes in there. A couple of years ago. John said I should go and see if your leather tools were still out there. Might as well, since maybe I would use them, and so I did. It was like a time machine in there. Everything was still hanging where you left it. I took down your old bullwhip. It didn't really want to uncurl, but I played with it a little and it warmed up a bit. I took it outside into the corral and screwed around with it. On about the hundredth try or so, I got it to crack. I got so excited by how it jumps in your hand when you get the roll of the arm right that I hauled off and really let one rip. The end of the whip came whistling past my head and just the tip of it clipped the back of my ear on the way by, and it dropped me right into the dirt. I was afraid to peel my hand from the side of my head to see if there was still an ear there. Hurt like fuck. But I thought of you and made myself try a bunch more times until I got it to crack again, you know, so I wouldn't be too afraid next time. Like you would have done."

She was quiet for a while on the other end of the line. "You still have some imagination, kid. Always did. You gotta come visit me sometime. I'd love to see what you look like all grown up. I don't get into Calgary much anymore, only when Edward feels like driving, which is never. You'd have to come out here. Carrie could give you directions."

I've been back to southern Alberta twice since then, but never made it to Bragg Creek to see Cathy Bulahouski, the Polish cowgirl from Calgary. She can't ride anymore, she told me, and I couldn't bear to ask her if she had cut off her hair.

Love That Red

TRACEY LINDBERG

WHEN I WAS ABOUT NINE OR TEN, I told Lyle Mudd to fuck off. He had called my mom a squaw, and a squaw was not a good thing to be when you were nine or ten.

Being Indian is like that. You often have to act like you're ashamed or like you're protecting yourself when all you're trying to do is get by. The Lyle Mudds of the world would shit all over you if they had the chance. I don't think they really care that you're Indian. I think what they hate is that you're different. And no matter how many times your mom tells you that it's okay to be different you know that it's not.

I was trying to tell my boyfriend Leo that. He can't really understand because he grew up in Humboldt, Saskatchewan, a town full of Germans and daughters of Germans, and he doesn't know that much about Indians. When Leo and I met, he told me that he lived near a town called Reserve and that although all the Indians there were bad, he didn't believe we all were. That's Leo though; he is one screwed-up guy. Like having to tell me he had some connection with Indian people, but not telling any of his friends that I'm Indian. Amazing. He's so open-minded until you scratch the surface a bit. The thing I liked best about Leo was his sister Corrina. She's this big buffalo of a woman who has the saddest eyes you've ever seen.

The first time I met Corrina she had just finished applying a coat of Revlon's Love That Red lipstick. She kept puckering her lips while she talked and Leo's mom finally had to tell her to stop. That day sticks in my mind because it's the first time I had ever seen Mrs. Sturgensen cry. I didn't think anyone in that family cried but I especially didn't expect to see the swan-necked matriarch pealing off deepchested sobs. Corrina was incredible. She kept drawing those sobs out of her mom in a calm and purposeful way. At one point she stage-whispered to me that her mom had put her "away" when she was thirteen.

Leo had tried to prepare me for that afternoon. He told me that Corrina had occasionally been institutionalized for acute schizophrenia. Nothing could have prepared me for this 275-pound woman speaking so softly that you could barely hear her. And she was so truly intelligent that you wouldn't have thought there was anything unusual about her. On my way out the door, Corrina squeezed my hand and said to me in Cree, "Come again next week. We can be alone in the morning."

It became a ritual after that. We had this rhythm and this intensity that long outlasted Leo and me.

"He thinks you're crazy," she said to me one day.

I dragged my cigarette deeply, exhaling as I said, "You think he'd recognize a psycho by now."

That killed Corrina. People always danced delicately around her illness. I'd like to say that she wasn't crazy, but she was and I think that's why I loved her.

I never saw her out of control, although she assured me she had been on occasion. The nearest she ever came to it in front of me was at Leo's wedding. I arrived at the farm late and missed Corrina's entrance. As I sipped pink champagne and ate dry chicken Kiev from the corner of the natty velvet settee, I watched the after effects of Corrina's appearance. Leo told me later that Corrina had entered the room wearing Passion Plum nail polish, Very Cherry lipstick, a purple beret and a pair of matching flat shoes. The conversation in the room stopped, of course, and Lila and Wayne Sturgensen tried to rush her out of the room. Corrina would have none of that.

"Lucy," she spoke gently to me later of the event, "I bought that lipstick you told me about."

She then allowed her family to take her out of the room, smiling at guests as she left. That night Corrina was admitted at the Saskatchewan Hospital in North Battleford. The hospital was, and is, the principal mental institution in Saskatchewan for people with mental illnesses who are diagnosed as "at risk" patients. Just who Corrina was "at risk" to was undetermined.

I visited her about two weeks later and it was then she told me about Joseph Starr. Joseph was what they called a "term" at Sask. Hospital. He had been admitted eight years earlier at the age of eighteen and he was never expected to leave. He had shot a police officer on the reserve at Kochin. He then cut the officer's tongue out and put it in his pocket. Corrina seemed to think this was all very symbolic, and it might have been, but I was too far removed to understand it.

The first time I met him I was blown away. That was one good-looking man. He had a single black braid to his waist and the most startling black eyes I had ever seen. "A looker," my mama would have called him. What was perhaps his most attractive feature was his smile. He had the most beatific smile encasing a set of snow-white teeth. I just stared at his mouth and when he talked to me I didn't hear him.

"Pardon me?" I said in my barroom voice like we weren't at a psychiatric hospital and he wasn't a patient.

"Whore." He said from behind those teeth. I flinched and Corrina touched my shoulder and suggested we sit elsewhere in the rec room.

"He hates Indian women," she whispered, as if that was explanation enough.

I was a bit startled. I'd seen white men and white women look at me disdainfully, but I had never been overtly rejected by an Indian man. I was really hurt, but I was also determined to make him like me.

"Hello, Joseph," I would say dutifully every time I visited the centre.

"Fuck off," he usually replied.

Corrina and I would often sit in the library and speak in Cree during our visits. (It wasn't until years later that she told me she had learned it at the Regina General Hospital Psychiatric Centre.) Corrina could speak it better than I could, something she said that was indicative of an urban Indian's lack of exposure to it. She told me that most of the people she met at psych centres were Indian. She felt it was because people are more willing to institutionalize an Indian, and judges who let other offenders go with their families sent Indians to psych centres.

"The whole system is based on reinforcing the structural inequalities and ensuring that the economic wealth remains in the hands of the elitist few at the top of the social hierarchy," she told me one day.

Mostly, I didn't understand what she was talking about, but she was, in her "good periods" (as I came to refer to her drug-controlled state), as insightful as any teacher I had ever had. The day I went to sign Corrina out, she had to have a complete checkup and an evaluative session. I waited in the lounge for her and had been there for a few moments when I felt a tap on my shoulder. Expecting it to be Corrina, the smile pained my cheeks as I turned to face Joseph Starr.

"Hi, Joseph," I grimaced, waiting for the inevitable.

"Corrina's leaving," he said.

I probably muttered something about being glad that I would be able to see her more often. I don't really remember, because what he said next almost felled me.

"I'm leaving, too." I smiled and asserted how delighted I was, all the while trying to ignore the voice inside reminding me never to find out where he went when he got out. I had this little safety-encased world and somehow I knew Joseph Starr would be able to permeate my barriers around that world. I stood there in wretched discomfort, glancing furtively at the guard from the corner of my eye. Joseph Starr was not to be fooled.

"I'd kill you first," he smiled cheerfully, and I almost believed that he would.

I had just braced myself for an attack when Corrina, with that strange grace some overweight people possess, eased into the room. I noted that she had Orange Blossom lipstick on and I smiled. Lipstick meant she was in a jovial mood. As we left, Corrina brushed Joe's cheek and told him in Cree that she would watch the World Series for him.

He slapped at her hand and indelicately told her to leave him alone.

Two weeks later Joe Starr was released from Sask. Hospital. Corrina and I saw the news together the night we heard Joseph Starr was dead. He had killed a woman at gunpoint in Saskatoon when she refused to give him bus fare. Rather than surrender and face another long incarceration, Joseph ran toward a police barricade waving his gun. I cried and cried that night. Corrina rocked me against her mammoth chest and didn't say a word until the pain had seemingly drained from my breastbone. Finally, she said in her soft voice, "She didn't have a chance." I looked at Corrina, confused and startled. I was crying for Joseph.

Men Not to Be Fallen in Love With:

HELEN KUK

Gay men, if you are a woman.
Even if you are curious.
Even if you have healthy self-esteem,
and if scatological humour will only take you so far.
Especially not the one you approach to be a sperm donor.
Especially not if he thinks it's cute and lovable of you
and starts conversations with "So I hear you're in love with me"
and then says, "That's your story"
when you deny it.

Straight men
who claim to love Leonard Cohen.
A woman who loves Leonard Cohen has taste.
A man who loves Leonard Cohen has methodology.

Choose no man who reminds you of your father or your brother
or any male relative or anyone you've known—
you want no embarrassing incidences of mistaken identity
and no easy excuses.

Any man who introduces himself in the following way:
"My name is Steve. I write poetry."
Pity is no basis for love.

If you are Chinese, any Chinese men with mothers.
You will be arm-wrestling thousands of years of culture,
culture that will half nelson you.

Men with deadlines—
depending on the kind of love we're talking about.

Men of mystery—
Nancy Drew has been stuck at eighteen for sixty years.

Any man who reminds you of Holden Caulfield,
especially not if you find it endearing at first,
especially not if you are past sixteen.
Remember the phrase "without a cause."
Better to be beholden than to be held.

Men who want only one thing—
unless it's the one thing you're looking for, too.

Clinically depressed horn players,
with or without substance dependencies,
unless you want some starve with your groove
and your own pain accompanied
by the acute qualifier "exquisite."

Men in pain.
Pain is catching.

Any man who accuses you of being a bleeding-heart liberal
and who recites a list of the Bond girls and giggles
and who pauses in a bookstore's erotica aisle
and giggles
on the first date
and who subscribes to the theories of Erich von Daniken.

Erich von Daniken.

Your friend's ex, no matter how well you know him
because that would be a conflict of interest
and of lots of other things, too—
no matter how smart he is,
how intelligent his conversation,
how closely he listens to you,
how familiar he seems,
how familiar he smells,
as far as you're concerned, this man is committed forever,
to be gay, your father, fictitious, and dead—
but especially not within a week of the breakup.

Men who are cavalier with the heart,
their own or yours, but especially yours—
think what they'd do with other parts.

Any dead men, men in literature, or celebrities—
Imaginary friends always have at least one
serious deficiency.

Blue Knot

SINA QUEYRAS

They found the Painter hanging from a rope in his
warehouse   his brush dipped in blue on the floor
beneath him the walls his jeans and T-shirt splashed in
colour and I walked the streets for three days and three
nights touching the brick where his brush stroked
tracing each step as if we were in a video and could
rewind the moments to the exact spot where he had
knotted the rope   overwhelmed by the real of it
feeling the roughness of it on my skin replaying each
moment of us wondering when I could have spoken words
which would have told him how good it was to be walking
these streets with him touching these walls   pressing
myself against the walls as if I could hear the stories they
held   feeling only the hole he had created   the blue of
the sky a sad veil of all that was left unspoken

Theories

ROBIN BLACKBURN McBRIDE

Hysterectomy was said to fix a woman's problems,
cheer her up
settle her down.

In 1910 there was no replacement therapy.
Estrogen was a word in a foreign language,
the endocrine system
an uncharted sea.
After being ripped apart
a person feels uneasy.

Hysteria follows hysterectomy in the dictionary.
Not all cuts are by the knife.

In 1910 there were a lot of Latin names
coming over on ships and spreading.
Theories raised in the labs of Europe
grew wild at roadside hospitals;
it was said nothing much could be done.
Depression was a moral illness,
field guides were scarce.
Tending minds forced questions of flower or weed:
matters of perspective.
Certain varieties found conditions rough.

The Adulteress, Lunch, and Masturbation

NANCY HOLMES

Joking aside, she didn't get any.
Everyone was too busy.
If she eats only ink
much longer
she'll look anorexic,
faint like a Gothic heroine
on every page,
her hips a rusty anchor,
thrown away.

The ink is making her sea sick,
she complains.
Her skin rolls and buckles like paper.
Is meaning sinking into the silt of words
and slowing her down?

I cannot use
her naval metaphors.
I tell her
to go eat cream and bananas,
crush some garlic in her salad.
If she can't hook her hips into a man,
she should eat alone,
milk herself for a change,

as I do.

Mattie's Husband

ANNABEL LYON

ROBERT WAS THE HANDYMAN. He did odd jobs around the Kerrisdale house Sara's mother and sister, Mattie, shared: replaced the furnace filter, unstopped the antique upstairs toilet, shovelled snow, put up shelves. When Sara helped her mother with the household accounts at the end of every month, there had always been some little sum for Robert, nothing she had ever questioned. Now her mother was in palliative care and Mattie had phoned to say she and Robert were married.

"No, Mattie," Sara said. "You're not married."

Mattie had invited her for supper, to come see.

As she parked her car in front of her mother's big old house, Sara recalled she had met Robert, once, the previous spring. She had been getting out of the car, just as she was now, when he had come around the side of the house with a mangled squirrel on a shovel.

"Sara Landow," she had said, stepping onto the lawn, extending her hand, and they had shook, both of them strong-gripped, wary. He was late-forties to her mid-thirties, with curly hair cropped close to his skull, a nutty tan, thin lips, pale blue eyes. She intuited a dark, bitter sense of humour and a matching strain of intelligence.

"Ms. Landow." He nodded. "The younger girl, the professor." She suffered his clear, pale-eyed look and wondered what else he knew: about her divorce, amicable, years ago now; about her work, and the long, steady ascent of her career; about her ongoing refusal to come "home" and live rent-free in the Kerrisdale house.

Robert had not offered his own name in return, but explained about the squirrel, that Mattie and Mrs. Landow had found it that morning on the back deck, blood everywhere, and called him in a "bit of a tizzy." His words. A cat had got it, he thought; a coyote wouldn't have left so much behind. She watched him bag it and add it to the curbside can. "Now for the blood," he said, and for the next hour or so, while she drank tea with her family and received a fuller recapitulation of the discovery of the poor, poor squirrel, she'd been aware of him whistling and scrubbing the back deck, occasionally stopping to sip from the mug Mattie had carefully carried out to him. When he was done he rapped on the kitchen window and waved to let them know he was leaving.

The deck—Sara had checked—was spotless.

Now it was fall. She parked next to five clear plastic bags of leaves, and, when she got out of the car, smelled smoke in the air, pleasantly. Then she noticed it was coming from the Landow chimney.

"Mattie!" She ran through the front door. She could see her sister squatting on her heels in front of the hearth, firelight dancing on her face. "Mattie, get back."

Mattie looked up at her, astonished.

"You must never—"

Robert came through from the kitchen in socks, holding a drink.

"Sara," he said. "Don't worry about the chimney, I had it swept last week. Dinner won't be long. We made roast beef to celebrate, didn't we, Mattie-Battie? Roast beef?"

Mattie stood up and put her arm around his waist. He kissed her hair and looked back at Sara, waiting to see what she would do.

"She showed me the marriage licence," Sara told the lawyer the next day.

Mattie Landow had become Martha Dwyer last week, while Sara had been at a three-day conference in Seattle. When their mother went into palliative care, Mattie had been fine by herself at night and could do simple meals and baking; tea and toast, soup from a can, grilled cheese, salad, cookies, even pudding. She had her bus pass. During the day she had her job at the workshop and her crafts at the drop-in centre. At night she rented movies and talked with her workshop friends on the phone. Sara usually called her once or twice each day to make sure she was all right, and visited three or four times a week to help with cleaning and shopping, and to keep her company now that their mother was no longer there. Mattie couldn't drive a car or concentrate on a newspaper and she needed help with bigger sums of money, but after a short interaction with her you would not necessarily know these things. She was sweet and friendly and wore expensive, nice clothes chosen by Sara and their mother.

Robert, though, she told the lawyer, would have known.

The lawyer, a woman her own age, asked her about the conference.

"Genetics," Sara said. "I'm a geneticist."

The lawyer asked if Sara or her mother had ever had Mattie declared legally incompetent.

"No," Sara said. "We would have had to go through a judge. We thought it would be humiliating for her. She can do so many things; we didn't see any reason to define her by what she couldn't do."

The lawyer told her Robert Dwyer had a petty criminal record going back twenty years. Shoplifting, DUI, bad cheques, marijuana. She explained that if Sara had her sister declared incompetent, they could get the marriage annulled. Criminal charges were another matter.

"You mean fraud, theft?" Sara was thinking of her mother's assets. Mattie had her own bank account, enough for groceries and DVDs while their mother was ill, which she could more or less manage on her own, but the larger financial picture—investments and property taxes and so on—Sara now handled herself. She was pretty sure everything was still all right there.

"I mean assault," the lawyer said.

After dinner Robert had taken Sara aside. He had said he knew the situation was a shock, and if it helped ease her mind, he would be happy to leave the sisters alone and return in the morning. Mattie's face had fallen when they had told her Robert had to be away overnight.

"Where does he sleep?" Sara had asked when he was gone and she had locked all the doors and windows behind him. Mattie had blushed and laughed and hidden her face in her hands. Sara had never seen her so happy, so—that unavoidable word—radiant.

"Sexual assault," the lawyer had said.

"You cannot love her," Sara said.

She sat with Robert in her mother's kitchen. Mattie was watching a Danny Kaye movie in the den. They could hear the regular, inarticulate burble of voices and the odd burst of music when Mattie boosted the volume for a song she liked.

"No," Robert said. "I won't pretend. But I like her a lot and she's fond of me. We get along better than most couples. I'll guarantee you that. I don't mind how she is."

Sara said nothing. Those eyes again, pale and canny. Intelligence like an intimacy between them.

"I'm going to guess you've been a busy girl," Robert said. "I'm going to guess you've found out a few things about me. That's fine. Clean and straight for the last eighteen months, that's on my record too, but I'm guessing that's not foremost in your mind right now. That's fine. It's good to get these things aired out. Mattie knows what kind of person

I am, I've told her as much as she can understand. If it doesn't bother her, I'm going to suggest it shouldn't bother you."

"I could have brought the police with me today," Sara said. "That would have been my right. It was recommended to me, in fact."

"Well, then, thank you," Robert said.

Mattie came into the kitchen and asked if anyone else wanted juice.

"Just for you, I think, Mattie-Battie," Robert said. "Good movie?"

"It's my favourite," she said. "Next time you have to watch with me."

"You know I will," Robert said.

"I know," Mattie said.

When she was gone, Robert said, "Look around. Do you see a mess in this house? Do you see anything missing, anything out of place? I cleaned the toilets this morning. I raked the lawn, I made the beds. In a little while I'm going to start dinner. I've helped Mattie comb her hair and cut her toenails. Clean and straight, it's all clean and straight."

Sara told him about the annulment and the possibility of a restraining order.

"You think I should get a lawyer, Sara?" he asked. "Is that what you would do, if you were me?" He seemed genuinely to want to know.

Sara shook her head, then nodded, for Mattie's sake.

"Can you recommend someone?"

She said nothing.

"Sure you can," Robert said. "I'm sure you know some lawyers. I'm sure that's the kind of friends you have. I'm sure you get together with your lady lawyer friends for cappuccinos."

Lattes, Sara thought.

"All right," he said. "I'm not going to make fun of you. I'm not stupid, though. I want you to know that."

"No, you're not stupid," she said. "Mattie's the stupid one."

He leaned back in his chair. "That's an ugly way to talk."

From the TV room they heard Mattie laugh.

"Can I tell you a little bit about myself, Sara?" Robert said. "Can I? You've established some things already in your mind, I can see that. That I have a criminal record. That I waited until you were out of town. That I'm living here in this beautiful house and maybe that's fouling it for you. Am I warm?"

"It's not the house," Sara said.

"All right! It's not the house. Now we're getting somewhere. Tell me, Sara, tell me what it is. Let's talk about it and see if we can work it out. I can tell you I didn't go to university. Is that it? Do you hate me because I watch the Discovery Channel?"

"Stop," Sara said.

"My first wife had a master's in social work," he said. "I have a sister in the Kootenays and two nieces. Information, information. What else can I give you? I have high blood pressure. I take pills for it. When I was a kid I had a cat named Leo and a dog named Checker. My trade is carpentry. My favourite wood is cedar. I've been fired from every job I've ever had because I couldn't stand being told what to do. My bosses were always genuinely regretful. They knew my work was good, but they couldn't stand the way I talked back and made them look bad in front of the crew. That's not trouble, that's self-respect. Drinking is what gets me in trouble, and I don't drink anymore. I've been to jail three times, the longest time for five months. I've had seven girlfriends and eleven cars. I don't have to fight with Mattie, to prove myself to her every minute, like I'm doing with you now; that's why I want to be with her. What else?"

"Mattie's girlfriend number eight?"

"Number seven. Wife number two. What else?"

"The fact that there is an outstanding warrant for your arrest in Saskatoon?" Sara said.

He took a breath, and then let it out. Sara held hers. "I borrowed that car from its rightful owner," he said. "It was a legitimate misunderstanding but she turned vindictive for no reason. I don't want to go to jail again. I don't deserve to."

Sara allowed herself no expression.

"You would, wouldn't you?" he said. "I mean, you really would. I can see that. All right. I respect that. I do. You fight hard and you win."

She whispered, "Please leave."

He went upstairs. She knew this was the dangerous time, the time when smashing sounds might begin. A few minutes later he came back down with a large knapsack. "Don't be scared," he said, when he saw her face.

He went into the TV room and a moment or two later came back, pursued by Mattie in tears. "I hate you!" she told Sara.

"No, Mattie," Robert said, "you don't."

Mattie had been terribly upset, had cried for days, had blamed Sara no matter how many times Sara tried to explain. Their appearance before the judge, Mattie prettily dressed and uncomprehending, was a gentle horror: everyone so understanding, so respectful of Mattie's dignity. The judge spoke earnestly to Mattie, and Mattie had liked him, Sara could see. Mattie became confused by her own emotions—loving Robert, loving Sara, loving the earnest judge with the funny big nose—and when they asked her if she wanted to say anything, she got tangled in her own thoughts and blushed and shook her head. So easy, Sara had thought, hating herself then. Still, things seemed better after that, and the sisters cautiously resumed their old independencies: Mattie's carefully monitored, Sara's carefully guarded.

Then came the calamitous phone call from the hospital, scant weeks later, informing them of their mother's death. Contrary to all Sara's instructions, they had phoned the Landow family home, and gotten Mattie. When Sara, oblivious, dropped by two days later—her usual Wednesday visit—she found several phone messages from the hospital requesting instructions, and Mattie—hair matted, upper lip crusted with snot—hiding in their mother's closet behind the camphor-smelling dresses. Her face was so puffy from crying that at first Sara thought someone had beaten her.

At the funeral, Mattie and Sara held hands. They accepted condolences together, with a grave grace, and many of the mourners told them they had never seemed more alike, or like their mother. Afterwards they hosted a reception at the big house, Sara offering drinks and Mattie methodically approaching each guest with a tray of hors d'oeuvres, vegetables frilled with cream cheese that she herself had piped the night before.

"You are too unkind," their mother had told Sara not long before she went into the hospital. "I am not trying to smother you. You would have your own rooms here, your own office, everything you could want. You can even have your meals on a tray when you're busy with your work. You know what's coming as well as I do. Why do you fight it?"

After their guests had left and they had tidied the house, Sara asked Mattie if she would like to watch one of her movies.

"Will you watch with me?" Mattie asked.

It was dusk. Sara stood by the arm of the sofa, watching the men and women on the screen sing and dance in their flounced dresses and fancy pants. She wanted a good beer; she wanted salmon sashimi; she wanted her laptop on her lap—her work—in her own chair in her own living room, with her own view into the lit, stacked living rooms of the high-rise across the street and the other single lives being profitably led there.

"You're hovering," Mattie said. "You're making me nervous." This was something their mother used to say.

Sara perched on the edge of the sofa.

"Sit back," Mattie said.

Sara stood up. "Will you be all right on your own tonight?"

The musical number concluded with the entire cast striking an exuberant pose. Then everyone relaxed, and the dialogue resumed as though it had never stopped. Mattie turned away from the television and met Sara's eyes with a bleak look in which neither intelligence nor the lack of it had a place.

Thus ended the privacy Sara had sought so fiercely and protected for so long. She moved Mattie into the second bedroom in her West End apartment, which had been her office; she would work from now on from a small desk in the corner of her bedroom. Mattie learned new bus routes, learned to manoeuvre in Sara's tiny galley kitchen, learned to operate the coin laundry machines in the basement, learned to manage two house keys, one for the building, one for the apartment door.

Sara learned more about Robert in the months after he had left their lives forever. She learned that he had been a good cook. "Too soft," Mattie said now of Sara's indifferently stir-fried vegetables, and she asked more than once when Sara was going to bake some muffins or roast a chicken. She learned that Robert had been a tidy man, and thrifty. Mattie counted the money in her beaded wallet every night now before she went to bed, and when she couldn't afford some treat she wanted said, "Never mind," instead of begging from Sara. She folded her laundry now and put it away, packing it into the drawers of her new, smaller dresser with thoughtful intensity, like she was packing for a sea voyage. Sara learned that Robert had been a man who liked to touch, casually, affectionately: a pat on the back, a kiss on the head, a head on her shoulder during the TV news on the sofa before bed. There was no one else from whom her sister could have learned this behaviour; there had never been anyone else at all.

Sara learned how Robert had been in bed. Late every night, after Sara had turned her light out—long after Mattie had closed her own door—Sara would feel her sister slip into her room, slip under the covers beside her, and press her body against Sara's until Sara put her arms around her. They would lie this way for a long time, until Mattie turned away, backing herself against Sara so that Sara would turn and hold her that way, and then Mattie would sigh and busy her hands between her own legs. The doctor had assured Sara weeks ago that Mattie was healthy and her hymen intact. "You," Mattie would mumble after she was done, but Sara would only hold her. Every night after Mattie had fallen asleep Sara would promise herself to put an end to these intrusions: a gentle but firm talk, a lock on the door, a sharp, unequivocal word in the night.

But night rolled into day rolled into night, and she said nothing, did nothing. She had taken the sun and the moon from Mattie, as the old words went; they would not come again. Skin on skin, and not to be alone: didn't she owe her this, at least, if her own love was true?

Cup of Tea

JUNIE DÉSIL

Remember that tea you brewed for my sore throat
boiled lettuce water
dirty brown and hot it burned my tongue and throat
nothing soothing about that tea silencing my rebellion
my screams a lingering bitter aftertaste
a reminder scalding my already raw throat
from screaming and fighting at recess with some
white French kid

nigger he said quietly
first time testing the feel on his tongue
liking the feel of the forbidden word
second time letting it drip acidly like
the tea sloshed hot down my throat
burning my inside shame
(shame shame double shame now he knows
another name for me I wasn't christened
with)

girls
don't fight
good girls in dresses
don't fight
good christian black girls
in dresses born of immigrant parents
don't fight

I wasn't punished because I scraped
my knees and elbows or because my dress
hiked up exposed my white panties or
even because I clocked him so hard
his eye turned purple
black yellow and green no
you punished me
for being called nigger

Spitting out that vile concoction
that tea was supposed to coat
my throat and take the sting
and burn away the rest swirling
steaming in the chipped stained white mug
bits of lettuce leaves that escaped the strainer's grasp
staring at the muddy liquid punishment

Shelter

FIONA TINWEI LAM

They spurn you now, your teenaged judges
who shut out any tentative foray into their fortress lives
with sighs, rolled eyes, occasional grunts. No evidence
of the children they once were, ten years ago
at the campsite near Kelowna
where you settled them inside the sturdy frame
of your car, laid your own bed on the ground
in a precarious tent propped by the doors.

Hours later, the trees conspired with night,
rain and wind pummelling the earth. Then came thunder.
One kid scampered out, soon the other,
wriggling into the tent's narrowness
to root their limbs around you,
the three of you sheathed in the shifting skins
of a tent about to fold.

But only then could they sleep, anchored
at last to your breath and heat,
your alert heart's slow drumming,
one body in the forest.

Lament

EDEN ROBINSON

I.

A HELICOPTER CHOPS THROUGH THE CLOUDS, thumping like a grouse when close then fading, hollow taps as it traces the tower lines into the mountains. Logging roads seam the patchwork patterns of regrowth. One of the steeper mountains is untouched. Beneath the forest canopy, the dense moss muffles sound and rain leaks through in heavy drips. The gloom is broken by the pale grey rock of a lichen covered cliff. Midway up, the petroglyphs are, at first, a smudge of colour. The red paint has faded. The men have no faces; their stick arms hold spears and their stick legs are poised to run. The mammoth dominates by its size and its tusks, raising one of the men in the air, trampling another beneath its feet.

II.

The thin smile of the moon dimmed then brightened as high clouds slid across the December sky. Fat sparks spiralled above the bonfire, hovering near the smoke hole in the longhouse roof. The drummers struck a solemn rhythm. The chiefs were crowned with eagle down that spilled over their frontlets as they swayed. The down drifted like dandelion fluff, snow in firelight. Gloria chewed the edges of her fingernail and her mother nudged her, a hint to be more ladylike. In the close press of bodies, her regalia were hot and itchy and she wanted to lean against her mother's soft side and close her eyes, but she knew she'd be taken outside like a baby if she did. As the songs wound through the night, her head drooped and she rested her chin against her chest, nodding.

The first shouts startled her from sleep, but even then, Gloria thought maybe she'd missed the start of the *hamatsa* and sat up to get a better look at the cannibal bird masks. But her mother grabbed her by the upper arm and dragged her through the crowd. Gloria had always been taught that one could never leave a feast before it ended, that it was rude and disrespectful and only low people behaved with such a lack of manners, but then she saw the axes raised and shaken, heard women wailing and the heavy tang of metal hitting wood, and she was glad that they were hurrying out the door and down the beach, her mother breathlessly trailing her father, who untied their runabout and shoved it hard into the water. He picked her up by the waist and tossed her in and then he held his hand out for Mother.

"What's happening?" Gloria said. "What's wrong?"

"Nothing," Mother said.

"Why did they have axes?"

"Gloria, not now," Mother said, as she pushed off and they rowed hard for home, hugging the shoreline.

Their winter camp wasn't far, and by the time their boat scraped against their beach, her parents had begun to chuckle, shaking their heads.

"What? What's so funny?" Gloria said.

"If you were paying attention," Mother said, "you would know what was going on."

They could hear the distant shouting from the feast echoing over the water.

"Back so soon?" Oxasuli said. Her swollen hands held up a kerosene lamp as she waited for them in the cabin doorway. Mother's oldest aunt had come to live with them in the summertime. Mother took the lamp from her aunty, who limped back to her bed near the stove. Gloria gratefully stripped her regalia off and threw everything in a bentwood box.

"They're fighting over the damn masks again," Father said.

"I thought they settled that," Oxasuli said.

"Henry took an axe to one of them," Father said.

"Ha," Oxasuli said with great satisfaction, hunkering down and swaddling herself in blankets. The minty, oily smell of her ointments wafted to Gloria as she tucked herself into her cot and pretended to sleep.

"Henry never had any sense even when he was a boy," Mother said. "What a way to behave! And at his father's settlement feast!"

"Doug should have been chief," Father said.

"Why did you leave?" Oxasuli said. "Now I'll have to hear about the rest from Tslalum. You know how deaf she is. She never hears anything right."

"Oh, Aunty," Mother said.

"What else did they burn?"

"They hadn't burned anything when we left," Mother said. "Henry took an axe to a mask saying he was going to give a piece to everyone so they'd all shut up."

"What! He should have thrown it in the fire!"

"They should've given the masks to Doug," Father said. "His uncle carved them."

"They should've burned it then thrown more masks in the fire. That's how it's done."

"That's how it *was* done," Mother said.

"Are they so poor they can't afford to do things right?"

"I think some *gumpswa* wants to buy the masks," Father said, "and Henry wants a motor."

"Greedy, fat little seagull," Oxasuli said. She spat. "They should have made Doug chief, idiot that he is."

"Aunty!" Mother said.

"All the great chiefs are dead," Oxasuli said.

"Well, most of them were poisoned," Father said, and then lowering his voice, "by their wives."

Oxasuli and Father laughed, but Mother told them to shush themselves, pointing out that Gloria was trying to sleep and they should, too.

"Remember Jassee's last potlatch?" Oxasuli said. "*That* was a fight. All the coppers breaking and Jassee   "

"Oh, that man had a voice," Mother finished.

"Joseph still cries for his canoe," Father said.

"What were they fighting about?" Gloria said.

"Never you mind," Mother said.

"A woman," Oxasuli said.

"Aunty," Mother said, "don't fill her head with stories."

III.

The meth dealer's girlfriend gave Gloria an air conditioner for her birthday. The meth dealer lived across the hall in 208, and his clients were easily confused and kept banging on Gloria's door by mistake.

"Hush money," Summer, another of Gloria's neighbours, said. She tsk-tsked, shaking her head so her flat-ironed, waist-length hair shimmered and her large gold hoops swayed in her earlobes.

"Consider me hushed," Gloria said, fanning herself with a paper plate. She liked the meth dealer's girlfriend, a chatty woman with friendly black eyes, an easy laugh, and a grown son who never phoned. She was Haida from Masset, but Gloria didn't hold it against her. "Open it."

"I'll call Auggie," Summer said, reaching into the back pocket of her cut-offs and taking out a tiny pink cellphone. "Hey, baby. Can you come over to Grammy Glo's? We got an air conditioner we need set up."

"I was going to get a fan from Canadian Tire today," Gloria said. "But I think I'll get myself an ice cream cake instead."

"Wan' us to drive you to Dairy Queen?" Summer said.

Summer had totalled three beaters in the time Gloria had known her. She'd driven Gloria to the airport once and they'd been lost in Richmond for three hours. "No, no. If you drive today, your tires will melt to the pavement. I'll walk over to SuperValu."

Auggie quietly tapped on the front door.

"It's open!" Summer said. "Just come in, Auggie! Damn, I don't know why he's so unsociable. Remember to take your shoes off!"

Auggie loped in dressed in his usual black jeans and T-shirt, his wide brown afro bouncing to his every step. Summer's son had a narrow, dark chocolate face and overly large eyes that always looked shocked. If he wasn't bent over his Game Boy, he was usually bobbing his head to his iPod.

"Hey," Auggie said.

"Are you thirsty?" Gloria said. "There's Kool-Aid in the fridge."

"Nah," Auggie said. He bent his head, studying the box before he slit the tape with his fingernail.

"Didn't you hear about the guy who got jumped in our alley?" Summer said. "Police don't know who did it, but people are saying he couldn't pay up. You got to be careful with these people."

Gloria had seen one of the reports on BCTV's *Early Edition*. The guy had been attacked in the East Hastings Value Village parking lot sometime that evening and found the next morning. The back of their apartment building faced the Value Village. Gloria wondered if anyone had seen what had happened and just decided to close their curtains. Her apartment faced Frances Street, and she'd heard some little thugs using baseball bats to crack the decorative totem pole in front of their lobby. She'd shouted down at them that she was phoning the police, and one of them had thrown a flaming brown paper bag full of shit onto her balcony. People kept telling her she was lucky she hadn't got jumped. The whole south side of the apartment building had heard what the kids were doing, but she was the only one who'd bothered to call the police.

What had bothered her more was the next day, when two workmen in white overalls had come to their apartment building and rolled the totem pole into the shrubs before propping it up against the wall. She had found herself gripping the steel bar of the balcony, shaking.

"What do you think you're doing?" she'd said.

Both men paused, their heads swivelling toward her.

"Someone cut this pole down last night," the taller of the men said. Both of his earlobes were stretched to his neck in pink, stringy loops. "We're just here to get it out of the way. We aren't stealing it or nothing."

"Don't put it up again," Gloria said. "Once a totem pole falls, you have to let it rest."

"Ma'am," the other man said, "it's not even a real pole."

"Put it back down," Gloria said.

"You want it down," Earlobes said, "you talk to Vancouver Native Housing."

She couldn't get through to the office until that afternoon and the receptionist who answered kept putting her on hold.

"I know, I know, I know, Aunty," the woman said. "Just give me a sec. It's Friday and everyone that can deal with this is in a meeting."

She wanted to say she wasn't this woman's aunty, but Gloria didn't want to be branded a troublemaker so she hung up, still shaking with outrage.

"It's not how things are done," she'd told Summer. "It's not right."

"They just put that pole up to scare off white people," Summer had said. "Don't you come in here unless you ready to see some real injuns."

The pole was still propped against the wall, and every time Gloria passed it she felt lost in the way things were and what people today considered right.

IV.

When Gloria was feeling tired after her first week at the cannery and hadn't done her chores in the bunkhouse, Oxasuli had bathed her in ice water and prayed over her so she would be saved from laziness.

Wash the cobwebs from her eyes and let her see and be grateful for what she has been given. Wash the pride from her heart and let her find joy in useful hands.

She woke hearing Oxasuli in her dreams, her tremulous voice praying. Security lights shone lurid orange shafts through the curtains, lighting Auggie sprawled over a sleeping bag on her living room floor. Summer had claimed the couch cushions and Gloria had the place of honour on the sofa bed. She had invited them to stay and enjoy her air conditioning and had tried to insist they take the bed.

"You are the birthday girl," Summer had said.

Gloria turned her head. The red light on the answering machine was steady, not a single blink to say she'd missed a call. Both her girls had phoned her last year. But Shelley had the twins now and Dorothy had her court appearance next Tuesday.

Too much ice cream, Gloria decided, tasting the acid at the back of her throat, feeling the steady, bruised ache in her tummy. She pushed herself out of bed and felt her way along the wall to the kitchen. The mechanical whine of the air conditioner covered the sounds of her stumbling. Her wrists throbbed as if she were back in the cannery after a double shift. She must have slept on them funny. Usually the heat helped her arthritis.

She got herself a glass of tap water and went to sit on her balcony, watching the downtown lights twinkle in the evening air.

Oxasuli had been dead long before Summer was born. Oxasuli wasn't even the woman's real name—it was a nickname, a joke name, a name that compared her to a dangerous and helpful root that even scared ghosts. Gloria wondered if there were anyone else alive who remembered the old woman. She'd never asked why Oxasuli hadn't gone to live with her own children instead of staying with her niece and now she would never know.

They used to go blueberry picking in the summer on the mountain behind their winter camp. She dreamed of a cliff near a particularly good blueberry patch. Oxasuli said the Old Ones used to herd elephants off the cliff so they'd be easier to kill and Gloria used to laugh about that, saying there never had been elephants that far north.

"It's true," Oxasuli had insisted.

She regretted laughing now. She watched TV shows with mammoths thundering across the ancient world and she wished she could take it back.

The balcony door slid open and Summer poked her head out. "Can't sleep neither, huh?"

"Too much ice cream," Gloria said.

Summer laughed and stepped outside, flopping down on the plastic lawn chair beside Gloria and shaking out a cigarette. She offered one to Gloria. Summer inhaled deeply, letting out a satisfied breath. "Guess who's pregnant?"

Gloria paused. "Who?"

"Mabel in 415."

"No!" Gloria said. "How old is she?"

"Old. And her husband had a vasectomy last year."

"No!" Gloria said.

"It gets juicier," Summer said, leaning in close.

After a while, Summer went inside and brought them two glasses of iced tea. Gloria was glad Summer's apartment was an oven and that she had lively company for tonight to sit and share stories.

Skin of the Road

TANYA EVANSON

Una piel agrietada de sol se presenta en el camino, nos lleva a las dunas de pastel tiznado y mas lejos, un océano con provisiones interminables de agua saltado para llenarse el vaso y obstruir los poros al reves. Los flamingos en risa de una pierna y los foques con heridas de lancha, dientes felices y lamentos humanos. Las hembras siempre sobrepasan a los machos gigantes en movimientos maremotos de piedra y grasa. Un desierto de pura contaminación, conchas en pilas al lado del camino como tumbas, reluciendo en el sol central.

The suncracked skin of the road led us to dunes of sootcake. Beyond, an ocean with endless supply of saltwater to clog your pores from the inside out. Tiny Humboldt penguins, Chilean pink flamingos on one-legged laughter and colonies of sea lions with tour boat wounds, happy teeth and human cries. Female sea lions always outnumber giant macho males in tidal wave movements of rock and blubber. A pure pollution desert. Shells in heaps by the side of the road like tombs, glittering in centresun.

Islas Ballestas, Peru 10/27/99

Hanging

SUSAN STENSON

I hung myself out to dry. Swallowed the V of the clothespeg and twirled in the wind like some local trapeze artist with no net. The robins did not like this backyard spinning; in their voices almost cries, convincing me to give up, to go back in the house already.

When summer came, the neighbour children fed me with a long pole and a straw. The Hungarian lady thinned her goulash, understood it was laundry day. She'd heard of a woman still hanging in Budapest, her tiny feet so swollen, they'd called in the army but when they cut her down she folded herself into a perfect square and walked to the post office. The fire department would have done.

On Saturdays, my mother sits and talks. If it is still, she absent-mindedly gives me a spin between bra sales at Zellers and bowling scores. My husband says he'll never understand and when we make love, he gets caught in it, curses the little ones who poke him with sticks.

Are you dry yet? my children ask, not knowing the patience it takes. Do we test you with a fork like chocolate cake? It's your birthday, Mommy, won't you please come down?

There are nests in my hair. Little worms weave cocoons under each arm. In my pockets the light of routine is a minute, before you looked away and missed. Never seen light in oaks like this. A stray dog sleeps in the space below my feet.

Skin

ELIZABETH BACHINSKY

WHAT UPSETS CANDACE MOST about losing one hundred and seventeen pounds is that no one tells you what, exactly what, happens to your skin when you lose weight. Skin, she's discovered, consists of three layers—the epidermis, the dermis, and the subcutaneous tissue—and is remarkable in its ability to repair itself. Skin is the largest organ in the human body. North American women (and men, for that matter) spend more time and money caring for their skin than any other part of their bodies. This has to do with the immediacy of the skin. When we are naked we are not truly naked; we are in our skin. Many imperfections may take refuge in the body, but one good bout of acne and your gig's up. The world will see and the world will know your weaknesses. Imperfections of the skin are the first, and most overt, signs of illness. Around the world billions of dollars are spent each year on lotions, perfumes, talcs, and exfoliates to revitalize and refresh and renew: to reveal a better you.

And yet, Candace knows, there are times when all the alpha hydroxy in the world just won't cut it.

In the waiting room at the plastic surgeon's office Candace flips through a trade publication she's found wedged between a magazine rack and a potted silk plant. The publication looks innocuous enough with its tasteful fourteen-point cover font, but once opened is a gallery of the macabre.

The pictures that fascinate Candace most are the before-shots of what the magazine refers to as "problem cases": women with congenital defects, breasts that are hugely disproportionate, a left breast five times the size of the right, inverted nipples, implants gone awry, breasts that have drifted helplessly into armpits like ships that have lost their course. Candace's breasts have lost their course too, but the pictures in the magazine make her wonder if perhaps she isn't overreacting. The women in the publication are, after all, deformed. It says so right there on page thirty-seven.

And then, there on page thirty-eight, she sees her own breasts: pendulous and flat as day-old pop.

Candace tries to hold back the distressed little scream caught in her throat. She finds this hard to manage and the pretty blond receptionist looks up from her papers at Candace, who is now staring, slack-jawed, at the magazine in her lap. The receptionist smiles as if she knows the transformation has taken place. Candace can almost hear the sound of her brain calculating under all that pretty hair. *Cha-ching!*

The receptionist stands, smoothes her white lab coat over her perfect (non-deformed) breasts and puts a brown file folder under her arm. "Miss Carter?" she asks, as if she didn't already know her name.

Candace nods.

"The doctor will see you now."

Dr. Ian Pattel is in his early forties and is attractive in a salt-and-pepper kind of a way. He speaks with a slight, but charming, lilt in his voice. Dr. Pattel's office is nothing like her GP's office. There is no paper-swathed doctor's bench with stirrups tucked discreetly at the sides. There are no posters of the musculature of the back or ads for new medications taped onto off-white walls. There are no stainless steel instruments tucked into hanging wall-pouches or wooden tongue depressors or cotton balls stashed away in glass jars. In fact, Dr. Pattel's office resembles a small hotel lobby. If it weren't for the lab coat and the circumstances Candace would not have guessed she was in a doctor's office at all.

"So, Miss Carter," says Dr. Pattel.

"Candace," she interrupts. "Please."

The doctor smiles. He really is quite handsome. "All right then, Candace," he says and gestures to a steel-grey wingback chair. "Make yourself at home."

Candace feels awkward as she arranges herself into the chair. She had thought that losing weight would make her feel less awkward but it has not. This is another thing no one tells you about losing vast amounts of weight. Nothing changes except your dress size.

Dr. Pattel sits across from her in an identical wingback and crosses his legs. Between them is a glass coffee table with several of the kinds of publications Candace had been leafing through in the waiting room. These objects, along with the thin brown file folder she'd seen under the receptionist's arm only moments ago, are how she knows this is for real.

"So," begins the doctor. "What's on your mind?"

No one she knows has asked her this for a very long time. "I . . . uh . . ." Candace doesn't know what to say. The doctor leans forward, smiles encouragingly and Candace wonders if he was a therapist before he was a surgeon. She laughs nervously. "I want a boob job."

There, she'd said it, plain and simple.

Dr. Pattel smiles even wider and Candace feels herself pulled into that smile as if into an embrace. Dr. Pattel laughs easily and Candace decides she likes him very much. She smiles back with what she hopes is her most winning smile.

"That's not what I asked," says Dr. Pattel, suddenly serious. He opens the thin brown file and Candace instantly feels the fool. "No doubt a 'boob job' is on your mind, but I like to get to know my patients a little before we start doing any invasive surgery."

Invasive surgery. Candace cringes at the words. Together they reveal what she's been flippantly referring to as a boob job as what the procedure really is. Invasive. Surgery. Candace swallows hard.

"Would you like a glass of water?" the doctor asks.

"Yes," says Candace. "Thank you, Dr. Pattel."

"Call me Ian," he says. "Everybody does."

Twenty minutes and three glasses of water later the consultation is over and Ian leads Candace into a small room that, to Candace's relief, actually does resemble a doctor's office. There are the stainless steel instruments. There are the cotton balls. By this time Candace feels somewhat relaxed, having shared her painful story of weight loss and weight gain with Ian, all the while looking into his encouraging face. And, while she'd been candid as only a patient can be candid to her doctor, somehow Candace feels as if this was something more; she'd had the unmistakable sensation of being in confession to her priest. She was in need of transformation. No. It was more than that. She was in need of transcendence, and Ian was the man to lead her there.

Once inside the examination room, a female nurse joins them. Candace looks confused for a moment and Ian reassures her. "I always have a nurse present during my examinations," he says and Candace smiles tentatively. "For your comfort," he continues.

"Of course," says Candace quietly. "Thank you."

The nurse hands Candace a paper gown and Candace is left alone momentarily to get changed.

Candace hops down from her paper-covered perch, something she would not have been able to do a year and a half ago (hop, that is), takes off her pants and begins to unbutton her blouse. That's when she notices the key difference between this doctor's office and all the others she's stripped in. There's a full-length mirror on the opposite wall.

Candace feels her confidence collapse. She's never been much of a voyeur and this, she thinks, is hardly the place to start. Her hands shake as she pops each button free until she is standing in her bra and panties, unsure if she can go any further.

There is a knock at the door. "Miss Carter?" says the nurse. "Are you ready for us?"

Candace runs her hands over her breasts and her rib cage. She closes her eyes. Her waist feels small and strange. This is a sensation she has not become accustomed to: the hard ripple her bones make under her skin, the hollow before the jut of her hip bones. Candace worries constantly that her new, thin body will forever be foreign to her; still, this worry is not as great as the worry that she will once again be lost in it. That she will once again be fat.

She quickly reaches around her back and undoes her bra with one hand. The reflection in the mirror tells her all she needs to know. Her breasts hang off her body: flat empty packages striped with stretch marks. *Deformed.*

Candace pulls off her panties and wads them into a ball under the pile of clothes she's left on a chair. Then she puts on the gown.

"I'm ready," she says. And she is.

Breast surgery is a relatively simple procedure. This is what Ian tells Candace as he presses his hands to her breasts. He is checking for lumps in the tissue: unwanted bumps, cysts, imperfections in the skin. His hands are deft and sure. He is abidingly professional.

Having completed the physical examination, Ian steps back and reaches for a red felt pen from a jar full of red felt pens.

"The type of surgery that would best suit your needs," he says, "is a reduction mammoplasty. With a lift, of course."

"A lift," Candace repeats.

"It's a very common procedure," he says, brandishing his pen. "May I?" he asks.

Candace nods.

Swiftly and with astonishing accuracy, Ian begins to draw thin red lines onto Candace's breasts. Candace is very still as he draws.

"First," he says, "I'll make two incisions along either side of the aureola; that's the dark circle you see around your nipple. The incisions will run from where we would like the nipple placed during surgery"—

he points to a place high on Candace's chest and draws a small circle there to represent her new nipple—"all the way down here"—he points—"under your breast. Almost in the shape of a wine bottle." He draws this shape tenderly. "What will happen next," he continues, "is that I'll stretch the skin here, on your chest, down under your breast lifting the breast, as it were. I will then reposition the nipple, removing excess tissue along the way, and bring the skin back together under the breast with a series of stitches."

"Reposition the nipple," Candace repeats.

"That's correct," says Ian. "We'll have to remove your nipple in order to reposition it higher onto your chest."

Candace feels lightheaded.

The nurse puts her hand on Candace's arm. "You look a little faint," she says. "Are you going to be all right?"

Candace nods. "What about scarring?" she asks. "Will there be much scarring?"

Ian nods. "Unfortunately this type of surgery involves significant scarring, initially. But with proper care the scarring should become less pronounced over time."

"Less pronounced."

"That is correct."

Suddenly, Candace wants very badly to be out of this little room. The red ink on her skin seems obscene and Ian seems less and less charming with every passing moment. But, before Candace can make a scene and make a leap for her clothes on the chair, the nurse gathers Candace's file folder into her arms and Ian turns away toward the door.

"Of course you'll need some time to really think about this," he says. "This is a serious decision and nothing I can tell you will be able to sway you one way or another. But just let me say this: I've never had an unhappy patient. Breast surgery can change your life, but you have to be ready for it."

"Right," says Candace.

Then he's out the door.

That night when Candace gets home she finds her cat, Mr. Frisky, mewling in the kitchen for supper. She shoves a can of cat food into the electric can opener, spoons half of it into a dish and places it on the floor. Mr. Frisky attacks the mound while Candace shoves a can of tuna for herself into the can opener. She snips open a bag of prewashed salad greens and shakes some onto a plate. She grabs the tuna out of the opener and forks it out of its tin onto the lettuce.

"Bon appétit," she says to her cat.

Candace thinks about how tuna is the perfect food. Zero fat, zero carbs, and loaded with protein. Still, she hates it. Has to choke it down.

The neighbourhood is quiet this time of night. There are no kids playing outside on the street and her neighbours are all indoors huddled around their Trinitrons, loading disks into their new DVD players, or whatever it is they do, Candace doesn't care. The only sound comes from her refrigerator, humming soft and insistent. Candace thinks about Dr. Pattel's—Ian's—hands on her breasts. She dumps her salad down the garbage disposal and heads up the stairs toward the bathroom.

After she's thrown up, she feels better. She decides to take a shower but as she strips she sees the red marks the doctor left on her body and they make her feel queasy all over again.

Candace wishes there was someone she could call. Someone who would come right over and hold her, kiss her drawn-on, stretch-marked breasts and tell her they are beautiful. *You are beautiful*, they'd say. *You are beautiful*. But there is no one. Candace holds her breasts in her hands, stretching them and lifting them until it seems she can't even see them. In fact it seems her body has changed so much in the past year she doesn't recognize herself at all. *Who are you?* Candace asks, staring at her reflection in the bathroom mirror. The pale reflection stares back at her, replies, *I don't know*.

It says in the handbook, *How to Prepare for Your Surgery*, that patients should always be accompanied by a friend or loved one to and from the hospital. This is to ensure that the patient does not drive home post-op half hopped up on Zantax from the night before or completely looped from the local anaesthetic. Candace arranges for a home care aid from the Hospice Society to take her home.

Candace still can't believe they're going to be using a local anaesthetic. The idea seems somewhat medieval to her but Ian has assured her it's the safest option. Before the surgery Candace is not allowed to eat or drink anything—not even a multivitamin or a glass of water, which is fine with her, she hasn't been hungry for weeks—and she's been told that during the operation she may feel some slight discomfort. Happily, Ian has also informed Candace that she will not have to watch the operation being performed, despite her being conscious throughout the entire procedure.

"We have a curtain," he assures her, "to obscure your view. For your comfort," he adds.

And so, the worst part about the procedure is the sound: the sound of her flesh being separated from the wall of muscle in her chest, the sound of the lypo-machine suctioning away excess tissue. Candace, in her half-drugged state, believes she can actually hear the sound of the scalpel scissoring through her skin. At one point Candace's head falls to one side and she sees, clearly, one brown nipple lying like a coin on a bed of white gauze.

The nurse who has been stroking Candace's forehead with a cool white towel notices Candace staring at the nipple and gently turns her head away. Candace thinks of the ad for the SPCA she's seen on bus shelters all over the city: "Help us help those who can't help themselves." Candace wants to thank her but is unable to move her lips.

Candace thinks about skin. How skin wants to be whole, how skin is a covering and yet how, in it, we feel entirely revealed. Candace thinks about her skin and finds it remarkable. On it there is a map of her life: in the palms of her hands, in the whorls at the tips of her fingers. Her skin—its colour, its texture, its imperfections—tells almost all there is to know about Candace. She thinks how even absences on the skin tell her story. The absence of a love bite at the neck or a fingertip-sized bruise on the inside of one thigh.

What Candace's skin says about her right now, as she lies wrapped in gauze half-conscious on her bed at home, is that she is in pain but that pain is working its way out of her. It's made its way to the surface, to the skin where it can be seen. In four days the bandages will come off and Candace will see that the breasts she had thought unbeautiful will still be unbeautiful.

Our skin consists of three distinct layers—the epidermis, the dermis, and the subcutaneous tissue—and is remarkable in its ability to repair itself. But this information will not comfort Candace in four days' time. Her scars will be long and red and angry. She will not want to wait for them to fade.

Bolt

CHRISTINE ESTIMA

Last Night in Warsaw

YOU TAKE A BLOCK FROM THE BOTTOM and you put it on top. Nate takes a block from the middle and he puts it on top. It is at this instant you know that you will cheat on him.

You sit in the common room of the hostel with a Polish pint and this boy from Bath. Nate. Rugby player (scrum half?). Greasy hair. A bod. Insecure mannerisms. Eyes that linger too long. Shakes your hand with the delicacy of stroking a sparrow. Acne peppers his skin, seething red. You try to rearrange them with your stare. You enjoy all the piteous inadequacies. You have always been able to tell. You can anticipate his advances and will welcome them without reciprocating, exactly.

The hostel you sit in is a hive: feet pounding up stairs, doors slamming, fingers tapping Morse code into laptops, laughter and *American Top 40* rising from the pub, kitchen utensils clacking. Backpacks flung over sunken shoulders, heavy with unlaundered aromas, train ticket stubs, notes from Mum to be careful, plug adaptors, mashed travel toothpaste kits. Aussies. Kiwis. Canucks. Brits. Yankees.

For whatever reason, after graduation everyone flocks to the theatre of Eastern Europe. They migrate with the same high expectations. Nobody comes here to be bored. They want to be ghosts. To be anonymous. Disappear down the belly. Food to enrich their pre-nine-to-five lives. Except for you. You come here not to eat, but to be eaten.

The Swahili word for "to build." The tower wobbles, your fingers sticky with brew, and you lick them with a conscious sexuality. It's all a game. Today you will win. Nate doesn't see you run your knee up the table as he attempts a delicate slide of the block. You shake it as Nate steals the block from the tower. The structure topples, the wooden blocks making a delicious clunk as they collapse into each other.

You cheated. Now Nate has to chug his pint. He pauses to laugh over your continuous jab of *chug-a-lug*. Slang stuck inside your borders. They say *chug-a-lug* in Toronto. But in Bath, the term is *bolt*.

Nate makes a dent in his pint to be proud of. His eyes widen with far-off amusement when you tell him you plan to get laid in every city in Eastern Europe.

You know you will lose the next match.

Anatomical Cartography

Thought #1: Twelve months have passed since you were in Vienna. Met Gezim. Friends called him Gizmo. He wore a Mozart wig and *lederhosen* to sell Vienna Boys' Choir tickets. Originally from Kosovo. He asked what excited you. You said love. Left traces of himself on your body, infected your heart like a pathogen. Then screened your calls. You stood on the platform at Wien Westbahnhof, biting your lip until the last second. He never came. You sped away wounded without the pleasure of a scar.

Thought #2: Scenes from a short documentary. A woman approaches strangers on the streets of Toronto. Queen Street West, which morphs from a Gucci parade to nudist vegan yoga studios. She asks to enter their homes and cook them dinner for one night only. An urge to go beyond the boundaries. To want that kind of connection with another, but not an end product, not something to show for it. Just the urge for human contact. She never sees them again after that night and all they have is memories.

You think about #1 and #2 as Nate drops down. He's on his knees, but he's not praying.

The Warsaw nightclub swirls red lights, disco ball beams, plush velvet couches, sweet cocktails and liquors spilling onto the marble dance floor, a DJ booth shaped like a pair of puckered, swollen lips. Club beats, new and familiar. Oakenfold, The Chemical Brothers, Tiesto, Deep Dish. You are grinding in the thrust of the crowd, in the mash of bodies. You are dancing in an attempt to shake off your sins and become an angel. Gyrating like a ritual. When Nate falls upon his knees, he gathers your legs with his tongue. You momentarily consider trampling him, but instead allow his tongue to crawl up your knee, to your thigh. Lift up your skirt yourself. Warsavians pay no heed. He slides up. The map of your body is written in the crevices of his tongue. In the grooves. Anatomical cartography. Once at eye level, you see a flash of frustration in his job-well-done expression. You are surprised to see it on another face; you've worn it yourself many times. He's not getting the better of you. His charm is lost somewhere in the pressing of bodies all around.

"I know what you're thinking," you shout over the downbeat.

"What am I thinking?" He moves back one step. He's battling his attachments and presumptions.

"She's a con. She's a con. She's a con."

Nate snatches your hand, yanks you through the midnight mash. You tumble out onto the humid streets, so hot you want to sleep in the shower. Run past graffiti: Lenin. Trotsky. Che Guevara. He squeezes your hand before you sprint through chaotic intersections. Rages back to the marmalade-tinted hostel. He invites you to his bunk. He offers pistachios and a can of Coke. You wanted a different offer. Leaving for Kraków in the morning, anyway. You don't need an end result, anything to show for it.

Exchange e-mail addresses. Promise to write. Disappear.

Jesus Jeans

Scents linger in the angular streets of Kraków. What at first might seem like sweet breads and spiced cheese quickly devolves into the odious familiarity of spit gurgling on the sooty sidewalks. Black puddles and banana peels.

You arrive in the city with an unnatural craving for bread and margarine, black coffee. Like rations at a death camp. Take the Auschwitz tour. Suitcases piled, chalked names. Tattered shoes collected from the huddles: thin red straps, blue heels, silver buckles still vibrant. Clumps of hair, shorn, frayed, tied in elastics or braided, greying. Made into rugs. The twisted iron of spectacles, lenses cracked. Gas chambers and Zyklon B and barracks and guard towers and a sky so beautiful you might want to raise a family in these woods. You feel like a rose wound through the barbed wire. Thorn versus sharp metal, fighting for greatest infliction.

From a clock tower in Kraków's main square, a bugler plays a truncated tune as if an arrow pierces his throat. Nate shows up. He waits while the clop-heels of horse-drawn carriages pull tourists through the watered-down night. Bar patios and tour groups flow through. As you approach him under the gauze of night, he stands, hands shoved in his faded pockets. Your eyes travel along his green Adidas shirt. He's like Jesus in his daddy's jeans.

You thought you were safe on that train that broke from Warsaw like an ice chunk from the 'berg. No withdrawal from loss of Nate. No time for squirmy feelings, you didn't really feel the click anyway. It is your time that he must work ingeniously to reserve. Perhaps you knew his arrival in Kraków would be like this. Perhaps you almost invited him; his e-mails treat you like tiramisu. Technology and nature colliding in such a backlit way. But deep down, you know you've always been more inclined to run with the bullets that come flying toward you and see where they lead, rather than dodge them. Go fearward.

Nate is nervous, you can tell. His eyes dance around. His fingers bunch and unbunch. "Do you want to come sit on a patio? What would you like to drink? Are you okay in that chair? Too cold? Don't worry, I'll pay. No, no, I insist."

You attempt "*dziekuje*" to the server who delicately hands you your drink, but instead say "*dzien dobry.*" You and Nate laugh like it's the Funniest. Episode. Ever.

When you saunter over to a Brit nightclub—black leather couches, crocodile effigies, and Guinness pints—his pheromones chant louder than the club beats.

"You're such a pretty girl. You're different from the other girls. I love how I can talk to you about stuff. So smart."

This guy has the heart of a romantic and the severe head of ruthless Hermes. Recoup in the washroom. Stare at your creature-features in the slimed mirror. *Grain of salt, grain of salt, grain of salt.* Return to find a plump Aussie with stringy blond locks and dazed eyes falling all over Nate. You want to clear your throat, but it's too pathetic, so you stand there and drink your amaretto sour. He's too polite to tell her to piss off, but he can't find a way to slip out from her. Worried you'll get angry. Worried you'll think he's just not that into you. Shoots you looks of despair.

You blow bubbles with your straw, the amaretto spurts up your nose, and as he cowers under the weight of the smashed Aussie, you ridiculously snort.

The Compass

Nate gives you the compass. Little, round, a gold rim. Fits onto a watch band. You stand on the musky street before your Kraków hostel and play with your directions as Nate kisses your neck. His fingers play. Up your skirt, but your nylons a barrier. It's all a game. And he's cheating. When his hard-on punches through the denim, you think of Samson and Delilah. You want to cut off his hair and steal his power. You want to look victorious upon him as the Philistines put out his eyes.

You are leaving for Prague in the morning. At long last, an expiry date to aim for.

"Promise me we'll meet up in Prague." He won't let your eyes look away. "Promise me."

The beat box of your internal body rhythms pisses you off. You want away.

Prague Doesn't Let Go

The day is like a red mural that hints at a mosaic underneath the paint. The sky is an ultra-blue that can't decide whether to sizzle or whoosh. The city is a blade, rusting on both sides. The horseshoes are nailed into their feet, the leather sandals are strapped around your ankles. Prague. A tourist trap. An ice cream suppository. Flowers, flies, and flesh.

You woke up early, uncertain of how to spend the day other than going crazy. Meandered across the Charles Bridge, wishing it was empty like the daguerreotype depicting ancient foggy dawns. Carried yourself up into St. Nick's church, the gilt ornate idolatry of it wholly uninteresting. Bored tourists of the past with penknives scratched their names and dates into the wooden banister crawling along the balcony. 1850. 1890. 1875. 1820. 1835. So many engravings for you to run your fingers along. After all these cities, churches begin to blend into one steaming pile. Sat outside on the steps and ate red grapes, spitting the seeds when no one was looking. Swallowing when they were.

Lost in the Franz Kafka Museum later. His words displayed like an erotic swell upon a porno screen:

Prague doesn't let go.
Of either of us.
This old crone has claws.
One has to yield, or else.
We would have to set fire to it on two sides.
At the Vyšehrad.

And at the Hradčany.
Then it would be possible for us.
To get away.

You find the Mucha Museum, feel woozy at the sight of original Sarah Bernhardt etchings, a bewitching woman of herstory. Then impressions of Nate's lips break your inner monologue. You want to drink his spit for this moment. You will not change your mind on this.

Stitches Kiss

There is a slick drizzle, like October on Yonge Street, that stones the night as you meet up with Nate in front of the infamous Prague Astronomical Clock. Clanging bells. The marionettes of Death and Vanity frame the long and short hands. And Nate is wearing the same green Adidas shirt from Kraków. He only packed four, he says. You must kiss him on one side of his mouth; an infected pimple rests on the other side. Too tender for lips, he says. He laughs when you say pimple. "Spots, we call them spots."

He holds your hand while attacking Canada and America for corrupting proper British English. "It's not pants, it's trousers. It's not carriage, it's pram. It's not alu-min-um. it's *a-lu-min-eee-um*." You think of Patois and Bajan, the poetic developments of dialects like jewels for a restless tongue, and wish he'd shut the fuck up. No one ever bitches over a Shakespearian dialect.

"I know it's only been three days, but I missed you," he says, and looks for himself in the shine of your eyes. He waits. But all you do is kiss his nose. All you see are his lashes fall, his gaze moving down.

You dash across the Charles Bridge, the rippling water below black and quiet. He flips his grey hoodie up. He looks like someone new each time you see him. You run in and out of doorways, trying to stay dry. Awnings with steps are best. You sit on cold concrete, legs intertwined, and he tells you he will one day be a fighter pilot. A man in a long line. Dime a dozen. Order. Code. Cog.

Thought #3: A study you read about in *The Toronto Star*, where researchers asked kindergarten kids which of them could sing, dance, and draw. All said they could, every last six-year-old. The same question was then posed to Grade 11 students. Only a few said they could. Somewhere along the line, that desire, that howl, that urge to create is lost.

You decide to cheat. It's all a game. *What is the craziest act of fiction?* you ask yourself. Is your answer allowed to be fiction?

You tell Nate of exploits, of the men. Of the sex offers. Of giving head and hard tongues and thigh bruises. You show him your chipped teeth from Mr. Gizmo, whose kisses marked you up. You pull out your lip to show him the stitches.

But Nate leans in and kisses your stitches.

And you wonder what to do next.

"Why do I feel so much for you? How did this happen?" he breathes, his eyes painted like an ocean.

"Don't worry about *how*. Or *why*." *Don't look up. Don't look up. Don't look up.* "Because *what* is sitting right before your eyes."

"Anyone ever tell you you're downright happening in the department of accommodating handsome strangers?"

Did he say that or did you?

His fingers move between your thighs, but find your Kotex pad. "Aunt Flo," you sneer. His hands move back. Red-handed criminal. He looks at his palms for any marks. But it's you who feels an engraving on your body. Nate is getting in. You leave for Bratislava in the morning.

Slovak Exodus

You know nothing about nothing anymore. You're just scraping the bottom of the aquarium looking for bits of toxic waste to devour. Straggling goldfish without much of a rudder. A fucking wreck. The rain follows you across Eastern Europe, the Slovakians ambivalent. You're dying to run through this small capital city that looks like the leftovers of the Rapture. There's a nakedness on the streets. The houses scatter themselves over plateaus chipped out of the mountains.

At your hostel, you change your clothes with your dorm room door open. Waiting to see someone walk by, clear their throat. You'll recoil in modesty, blush, reach for your clothes. You're daring. Waiting for someone to see you ogle the peaks of your breasts in the mirror. Eavesdrop on you lightly singing "if you wanna be happy for the rest of your life, never make a pretty woman your wife . . ."

But from your personal point of view, get an ugly man to marry you.

No one walks by. You stare at the door frame until a clock tower—echoing the hour in the distance, beyond the dilapidated buildings and suspended construction sites—disrupts your quiet moment of lunacy.

Nate is arriving in Bratislava tomorrow, once again on your last day here. It was your last day in Warsaw, your last day in Kraków, your last day in Prague. You can't decide if he follows you with sincere emotion, or with the hunger of a rabid dog. What will you do with him once you get him? Or will he get you first? Today is the last day you're thinking about this, you decide.

You throw on your clothes, purposefully forgetting the panties, descend the winding staircase to the hostel pub. Aussies enjoying cinnamon coffees. Yankees clacking away on laptops. Canucks eating fried fish. Brits playing board games to one side. Kiwis playing card games to the other. No one is learning to bolt.

The man behind the bar has black hair. Styling product keeps it an unmoveable faux-hawk. You think you see faint charcoal smudged under his eyes. A nose ring. Leather wristbands. A band T-shirt you don't recognize. Italian?

You sit at the bar, arching your cunt against the plastic seat. Marking your territory. You inhale but can't immediately recognize the scent wafting by.

"I just peeled cinnamon," the Italian charcoal-nose-ring bartender says. Your back creases. You see him tossing the scraps into large coffee mugs the Aussies quickly snatch up while tossing a few hundred Korunas on the wet bar. "Here." He leans in toward you. "Smell me."

Don't sneeze, you tell yourself.

His name is Edmundo. From Rome. Ran out of money while backpacking. Working for train ticket money. Working for food. He's sly. He's a con like you. He's a rope that ties itself around you at one end, and unties itself at the other.

Dance the Poison

You are disappointed when Edmundo takes you to Starbucks. You would have loved an opportunity to experience a genuine Slovak cafe. However, there is comfort in knowing you will get your decaf double-tall non-fat Lactaid light-whip mocha. Edmundo talks to you about Italian dancing. The *tarantella*. A traditional dance, originating in the town of Taranto. Sounds like Toronto. Those bitten by the venomous tarantula spider are encouraged to dance all night until the venom is expelled through perspiration. People surround the victim while musicians play mandolins, guitars, and tambourines. Each beat has a different effect on the victim, causing various movements and gestures. Once the victim's clothes cling tightly to her body from sweating, it's certain she's cured. This image. Releasing an inner howl. To raise the sand all night.

No dime a dozen. No order. No code. No cog.

As Edmundo speaks, his five o'clock shadow present on purpose, you remove your thumb from the paper cup, see the Starbucks emblem. There's a woman with long flowing hair, like liquid black. Bearing a hint of a grin. Shadowed eyes. She wears a crown with three tines. Two tails emerge from her torso. A Melusine. The mythical mermaid. Half-human, half-serpent. Not one or the other, but both. Beautiful in her complexity. Slithers out of murky waters to entice, waiting for someone to see both sides. You mention this to Edmundo.

Edmundo pauses. Pause. Pause. Thought #1 marathons in your brain.

He then says, "You seem like you'll never want love. Only excitement, yes?"

Love bores you, you say. But in reality, it just disappoints you

Like a cat licking cream, he asks, "How do you manage this?"

If you had a mirror, you would describe your smile at this moment as nasty. "The secret is not looking back," you say without caution. You never spoke like this with Nate. *Nate would never understand this territory*, you say to yourself. Because he is the territory.

She's a Con, She's a Con, She's a Con

You are swallowing Edmundo. He slides the elastic band from your ponytail, takes fistfuls of your hair with him.

Press him into you. Pull yourself apart from Nate, who arrives in Bratislava in an hour. Edmundo rips out your follicles. Samson and Delilah, the dyslexic version. You believe the Talmud speaks of women cutting their hair when someone dies.

Small parts of you die, but stay stuck in the stone of your body. Edmundo stirs them into your womb. They feed off you. And you came here to be eaten, remember?

Nate's train is speeding him toward you. You're tonguing the stitches inside your lip. *Prague doesn't let go. Of either of us.*

His e-mail to you this morning said, "Go do whatever you've got to do today and if you're not in the hostel when i arrive i'll just wait for you. i'd wait as long as i had to to see you again, i'm so looking forward to holding you again, staring into your mesmeric eyes and kissing your beautiful lips."

It's all a game. You cheat. You want to sob for Nate, but you climax instead.

When you stop fucking, you're going to start thinking.

You're going to realize.

You'll point yourself out in a mirror and recognize the fall of your hip, the rise of your back, the dip of your shoulder, the peak of your collarbone.

You're going to know. That perhaps this is all for the best.

Leaving Edmundo's dorm, you pull the compass out of your back pocket and point your feet in the direction of the dancing arrow. It will tell you where you're going, but it won't tell you where you've been.

Morning after

ANNA SWANSON

A few hours of uncertainty by the ocean,
that's all. A blueberry seed rolling in the bowl
of an afternoon. But in a world where this summer
is allowed its momentum, I answer questions:
Your father? We laughed a lot. He had these eyes.
He knew I was leaving. Before you came along
I wondered what kept me so long, pushed my knee
against his under every table. There I was—
top floor of that old yellow house and summer
gone without me—when you burst in
through the latex. Not a care for our plans.
You always were stubborn, little blue.
I moved clear across the country for you.
Bought winter boots and sold the van with no heat.
There's not a lot can stand in your way, remember that.

I walked to the ocean, bottle in my pocket,
and lay in the matted crowberry. Four flat pills,
to be taken twelve hours apart. I let the wind
blow my hair into knots. The water was thick with colour.
The sun had made fat blueberries of the summer. The hours
went by one at a time and I spent them as something small
held in the world that would have me. It took most of a day
to swallow the first two. I stayed up late to take the others
I was lucky: No pain, no nausea, no cramping.
It's not as if I were pregnant. Only two small things
inside me, cancelling each other out. A summer
of suddenly unrelated events falling off a thread like glass beads.
Then I turned to what was left—the van with no heat,
the long highway home, that seed pod of the unhappened
rattling all the way.

Ghetto Feminism

AMBER DAWN

Coco and I peek through the yellowed blinds into the Rec Centre meeting room, assessing if we want to go in or not. It looks to be an amicable mix of community advocates, low-level politicians, and a few Downtown Eastside residents, all drinking coffee from Styrofoam cups and eating cheap pastries, so we push through the heavy glass door and find places at the round table.

As we sit, I see a woman who once strangled me because I wouldn't give her a cigarette. We have since made peace, or at least made peace the way that street workers do—we pretend it didn't happen. This was long ago, when I worked low track. I assume she doesn't recognize me since now I am twenty pounds heavier, my clothes aren't from a church donation box, and I don't keep my head perpetually bowed. When she greets me, I almost say "Hey bitch, you strangle anyone lately?" but I stop myself, for it is my understanding that community advocates and low-level politicians are uncomfortable with this sort of banter.

The meeting is to discuss changing the Criminal Code regarding prostitution and how to push for this issue in the upcoming election. I quickly learn that most people present, or those doing the talking, are pro decriminalizing both prostitution and solicitation.

There was a time when I still believed that laws and policies actually promote social change, and during that stage of optimism, I too would have been for decriminalization. It's a bit unsettling to think that I've grown into an age of pessimism, but I really do doubt that laws, alone, will improve working conditions for sex workers. I've come to this meeting with more questions than opinions.

My head unconsciously begins to shake in both agreement and disagreement as the advocates speak. I blurt out "Well, actually . . ." a couple of times, trying to insert myself into the conversation when someone has a mouth full of croissant, only to be interrupted by the next person.

When I do get a turn, I explain that while some relatively affluent sex workers could benefit from legally being able to solicit clients and work from their homes, many women will remain on the street or with their pimps because that is both what they know, and more accurately, that is where society wants sex workers to remain, in unlit streets and alleys, out of sight. Changing the laws doesn't mean working girls will be able to change their lives accordingly.

"No one seems to be able to tell me if the right to solicit will work both ways," I continue, still shaking my head even though I now have everyone's attention. "Will clients suddenly be allowed to approach any woman they believe to be a sex worker and offer to buy sex from her? Could this possibly turn into a legalized form of sexual harassment?

"And I like our discreet, coded lingo like 'half-and-half' and 'all-inclusive.' That is our language." I stress the words "our language," hoping I'll gain credit if my position echoes cultural conservation. I receive only blank stares from around the table. "I wouldn't want some guy to ask how much to penetrate my ass," I offer—perhaps too colourful of an illustration. One of the men, the representative of an NDP candidate, clears his throat a few times.

"And could trafficking rise?" Coco asks, tapping her acrylic nails on the tabletop. I notice everyone leans forward as she speaks. Coco is considered an "unheard voice": an Asian immigrant sex worker who is willing and able to articulate (in English) her experiences. "Vancouver is already one of the top cities for trafficked women in North America. I don't want to confuse trafficking with sex work, but could decriminalization have an impact on both?"

"Just because something's not criminal does not mean there will be justice," I add. "Rape is illegal, and a woman is raped every two minutes or something. Laws don't guarantee safety."

"Fuck the police," my old strangler friend shouts out. "They don't fucking protect us no matter what. If you want to do something, make the police protect us from getting raped and beat up all the time."

"We need services, like advocacy and medical clinics. Will decriminalization mean more support services for us?" I ask. Coco nods.

These points receive nods and "hmms" from the advocates and politicians. I am certain we've been clear (and maybe a tad offensive). However, after a brief pause to reflect, the meeting loops back to the same agenda: how to make decriminalization an electoral issue. By the end of the meeting the entire group, except for Coco and me, dub themselves the "Change the Code" committee.

This meeting is not the first time I've involved myself with politics, nor is it the first time my opinions have clashed with other politically minded people. Calling myself a feminist has posed problems since I joined an anti-violence feminist collective in 1995. As a member, I learned the power of identity—the idea that even an uneducated woman like myself, who hadn't read Mary Wollstonecraft or bell hooks, could be an expert on feminism simply because of her identity as a woman. Phrases like "as a woman of colour" or "as a lesbian mother" qualified every opinion.

While being valued "as a young, poor woman" seemed miraculous to me, the miracle was hampered by my awareness of how different I was from my sister collective members; I was the "bad" sister. I wore a miniskirt and had scraped knees in a room full of sensible pants and makeup-free faces. The collective also taught me that sex workers, from street workers to phone-sex operators, are "servants of the patriarchy." I learned immediately that the phrase "as a sex worker" is not met with the same gravity as other women's qualifiers. Debate arose when I suggested we, as an anti-violence collective, stop vilifying sex workers and start offering them much-needed support. Some members listened, some agreed we should assist sex workers if they were trying to quit, and some acted as though I had spoiled their fortress of womanly empowerment. We took a vote: Should we or should we not help sex workers out of violent situations? I remember crumpling into the purple beanbag chair in the meeting room as I watched the show of hands in favour of no. I left the collective with the bitter realization that "prostitute-ism" and "whore-phobia" were not words in the feminist lexicon.

I've witnessed a great deal of change over the past decade, however. I've seen an alarming number of survival street workers from the Downtown Eastside go missing; their photos currently haunt newspapers as the Pickton trial begins. The north end of Commercial Drive—the very street where I worked for years—has been exposed by the media as Vancouver's kiddie stroll. Dozens of massage parlours with names like the Lotus and Shangri-La have sprung up throughout the Lower Mainland. In response to this, it seems every community and feminist organization has slowly, yet steadily, added assistance to sex workers to its mandate.

I underwent my own evolution too: I left the streets and started working high-end fetish jobs and escorted for midway celebrities employed by our "Hollywood North." I stopped spending my money on cocaine and men who didn't love me and put myself through university instead. I grieved for the women I knew who have died or disappeared, and grieved for myself for having survived some of the tough experiences I faced. But I never stopped wanting to work in solidarity with other sex workers. In fact, coming out the other side, mostly unscathed, I wanted to help more than ever.

Coco and I met at an HIV prevention project that hired us to do safe sex outreach to massage parlour workers. Like me, Coco had lasted a couple of rounds with feminist organizations and was not willing to go back for more. We both started volunteering at health-related organizations during the syphilis comeback and hepatitis surge in Vancouver. We bonded over this and because, unlike most of the long retired sex workers-turned-advocates, Coco and I were still hustling clients here and there to pay the bills.

Our job was to reach out to immigrant and Asian massage parlour workers—a difficult demographic to connect with. At first, the parlour owners wouldn't let us through the door. Coco and I would stand outside parlour doorways joking, in our best spy voices, "We've got to infiltrate the building." Next we pretended to be applying for jobs; this got us as far as the softly lit lobbies. Then, we were invited in because we came with big fruit baskets and sweets from a Chinese bakery. Finally, after months of this dance, we were welcomed in to hand out free condoms to the girls, teach safe sex, and get women appointments with doctors who wouldn't discriminate. I was doing something that had a direct impact, and it felt damn great to be doing it.

The project suffered from a lack of funding and within a year was scooped up by a UBC doctoral student who forged a quick partnership with the board of directors. We were told the project could continue for several more months if we helped the doctoral student collect data, including blood samples, for her thesis: basically a study of how HIV is spread by Asian prostitutes. Accustomed to duking it out in the name of sex workers' rights, Coco and I threw some good punches about how this was stigmatizing and blaming the women, and how it would ruin the relationship we had with them, and that blood samples were a thing most Asian women, for cultural reasons, would not simply hand over. Never mind the fact that sex workers are one of the most researched peoples in Canada, and as far as I can see, these studies aren't helping anything except the researchers' CVs. In the end, Coco and I walked out.

Having already tried feminism and health services, I suggested we give legal issues a go. This is how Coco and I have found ourselves rolling our eyes as the advocates and politicians draft a plan of action to Change the Code.

At the end of the meeting we slink away, angry. "How sad is it when the workers themselves don't even get a say in the laws and policies that affect them?" I complain. This is when Coco tells me she hasn't made any money in two weeks. She is broke: not eating at a soup kitchen broke, but broke enough to be scared.

"None of my regulars are calling." Coco asks me to hit the kiddie stroll with her. "I just need a hundred bucks or so," she says.

I take her to my old corner beside the fish factory. We scan the beat-up trucks that circle the block to check us out before going home after their workday. "Factory workers are okay," I tell her. "But only on a Friday when they get paid."

Soon a police cruiser is circling us too. "We're just out looking for a girlfriend of ours. We haven't seen her for a couple of days," I say to the officer, and he drives off without further questions.

When a good client does come around, I recite the numbers and letters of his licence plate as Coco gets in his car. I sit on the stoop of the fish factory and wait for her to return as the setting sun lights up the shards of broken glass embedded in the pavement. I've stood watch, like this, many times for other girls; come running when I've heard a woman scream; stuck around to listen to the story of why she was screaming. I realize this is the place where I have discovered a kind of ghetto feminism, a street social justice. No debates, no mandates, only survival.

The Fourth Decade

Volumes 31 – 39 (2008 – 2016)

Translating Intention into Action: An Interview with *Room*'s Former Managing Editor Rachel Thompson

KAYI WONG

Since 2010, Rachel Thompson has been a member of *Room*'s editorial board, and at different points has also been the magazine's managing editor and web designer. Rachel is an editor, writer, communications consultant, and an avid contributor to the CanLit community and supporter of emerging writers. In the same year she joined the Growing Room Collective, she won SFU's First Book Competition and published her first book of poetry, *Galaxy*, with Anvil Press in the following year. In our interview, Kayi Wong spoke with Rachel about Souvankham Thammavongsa's poem (p. 308), languages, and what it takes to push a forty-year-old institution into becoming more diverse and inclusive.

KW: What made you decide to join *Room* in 2010?

RT: I was having a hard time in my personal life and needed something to do to stop dwelling on things. Also, I really wanted to do something in the literary community and in a feminist environment. It is kind of a funny story, and you can choose to put it on or off the record, but a big motivation was also that I had submitted to *Room* twice at that point and had never received a response of any kind. I even chastised one of the editors at Word on the Street and still had no response. I thought, obviously they need some volunteers that are pretty organized, and I'm an organized person, so maybe I should volunteer [*laughs*].

KW: How do you think the publication has changed since 2010?

RT: We've been much more deliberate around diversity. As a rotating collective, we don't have a lot of institutional memory so we don't have a really good sense of who was on the collective before, but when I joined there was a lack of visible diversity. At that time I was wringing my hands about what to do—textbook white privilege, in that I knew it was a problem but didn't want to rock the boat as a new member. More and more people joined and it was something that also bothered them. I think it bothered older Roomies, but they also just didn't know what to do.

Eventually, we got more proactive about it and became more deliberate in our recruitment strategies and practices, as you know. And a lot of that culminated in the Women of Colour issue, a threshold issue for us. It was an essential issue that had to happen, but it also had to be the beginning of something, not just ticking off boxes like we "did" diversity.

KW: Was the subject of feminism treated very differently by *Room* then?

RT: It was surprising to join and not find intersectional feminism at the forefront, but it's hard for me to say exactly because I was just learning what was going on. Six years is not that long in the grand scheme of *Room*, but since I started, by coincidence, feminism became all of a sudden mainstream. Before, celebrities were always saying, *I'm not a feminist, that's a dirty word, but I believe in women's equality*, when we know, uh, that's what feminism is! So, for the first time as a lifelong feminist, I heard many people embracing the term. I guess the point I'm trying to make is that *Room* was all of a sudden in the middle of an arena where people were saying *Feminism is cool* and *It's okay to be a feminist*, while within *Room* itself, we became more intersectional or definitely more aware of intersections and inclusivity. So while "white feminism" is now almost mainstream, we're now pushing feminism to be more. The cool thing that has always been part of *Room* is that there are so many voices—the decision-making is done collectively. And we are pretty agile; in six years change has happened pretty quickly. I can't think of a lot of institutions that would start without an intersectional focus and be where *Room* is today. It's not like we are a new, young, upstart organization. We are a forty-year-old institution with a rotating roster of decision-makers, who all have equal power. Maybe that's what made it easy for us to change so fast. Though, of course, it was about damn time!

KW: Before I joined *Room*, and even when I first started, the idea that diversity is important was very clear but also abstract. And now that we have been doing it for a few years, it's like, *Oh, we're actually doing it. There are actual ways to do it.*

RT: Yes! It was important to get editors trained, and in this volume (39), we have women of colour playing a big part in the decision-making process. Having more diversity within the collective means we're going to have so much more diversity in the magazine. I agree that influence started earlier, but now we're deliberate about it. Like, one of the reasons we did translation as a theme in volume 38 was to invite more linguistic diversity and then—we hoped—more ethnic, cultural, and regional diversity. But, while it's all fine for me to edit an issue like that, it's even more paramount that we have editors who come from different cultures and perspectives and who can crack things even wider open.

KW: Do you still remember why you picked Souvankham Thamma-vongsa's poem "Pregnant"?

RT: Speaking of cracking things open, that's what that poem really does. I used that as the opening piece because it's so powerful. The whole translation issue is about the joy of language, learning different languages, and how words work within a culture. These are conversations that I have all the time now, because after I joined *Room* I left Vancouver and have lived in places where English is not the main language. This is a part of what the poem explores, and it's so well carved out. It cracks open the issue, cracks open the idea, and cracks open your head in terms of opening up your mind to how words work in different places and for different people.

KW: Do you have a philosophy when it comes to editing an issue?

RT: Staying loose is a philosophy, I suppose: letting the work guide you and seeing how all the pieces fit together. For me, I want to hear the music. I come to it as a poet, so I hear a lot of music within writing, especially in poetry but even in prose. I read things aloud; the music is a metaphor, and also literal. I try to hear how things resonate together as I juxtapose and pick pieces that fit within the ecosystem of the journal. When you start it's just a blank slate, so I'll first pick a few works that really do something for me and are truly unique, and Souvankham's poem was definitely one of those.

KW: What direction do you hope *Room* will take in the next forty years?

RT: It would be so cool if we're still around [in forty years]. And the only reason I say "if" is because media is changing so much, so we don't know. I just hope that *Room* remains agile and that we maintain the kind of integrity yet flexibility that we have now so that we can carry on. Who knows what the cultural and media landscape will be like then! It'll be great to have another volume of this anthology. Maybe it'll be in a virtual reality format where you can talk to each of the authors in the issue or something.

The River Phoenix Social Club

MONICA PACHECO

Fiona

IT HAPPENED IN THE MORNING. Fiona turned on the kitchen tap and let warm water run over the back of her hand, through her spread fingers. The water pressure is low in all of our units. A month ago one of the pipes burst. It's supposedly fixed now but none of us can feel the difference. With the water running, Fiona answered a knock at the door. When it was all over she was left on her back in the living room listening to the water. The sound reminded her of an old folktale her Swedish grandmother used to tell her—*Bäckahästen*, which means brook horse. He appears near rivers in foggy weather and whoever decides to ride on his back is unable to get off again. The horse then jumps into the river and slowly drowns the rider.

Mary

Mary was on her way home from work. There's an underpass near our building that the neighbourhood kids call the cave. If they need a place to kiss for the first time or smoke their parents' cigarettes they simply look at each other and say "cave." It's a dark, meaning-making place for kids, but a non-place for adults because most of us drive. Mary doesn't have a car. She usually takes the bus, but it was summer and she'd been trying to lose weight. So, she walked from Broad Street over to Hudson and Hudson onto Chester, beneath the underpass, and that's when it happened.

Kirstin

She was wearing her leathers. Kirstin bought a Moped last year. We used to think that if anything bad happened to her it would be a vehicular accident. This just goes to show that you can't prepare for the worst because nobody has any idea what the worst is going to be. She was in the parking garage when it happened, steadying the bike on its kickstand. The greatest danger of riding a moped is not speed, or over-braking or running wide on a curve or under-cornering, it's other vehicles not noticing you. Bright clothes help other motorists spot you, and that's why Kirstin got red leathers instead of black. She was noticeable. She had prepared for the wrong worst.

Sara

They moved into the building a week ago. Sara and her husband carried furniture in on their backs like ants. It was her idea not to hire movers. The corner of her television stand gouged her shin. A bruise bloomed around the scab. From far away it looks like a tattoo, which in turn makes her look like a different sort of woman. She is not that sort of woman. She is a birdwatcher, though not a very good one due to a crisis of confidence. She doesn't trust her eyes and ears to make correct identifications. Out on our building's rooftop patio she thought she saw an orange-breasted falcon, but it could have been a kestrel. As she was watching the bird, he had been watching her from the sidewalk and made his way up to the roof. That's how we know he has a key.

FACT

We are all over the age of thirty-five. This is an important clue. The police officers assigned to the case jot it down. It becomes part of the suspect's profile. "It's rare in a case like this," they marvel, as rare as a killer with a signature. We try not to be insulted. "He most likely has issues with his mother," they say.

FACT

None of us are mothers.

Zoe

It was Zoe who suggested we meet weekly. It happened to her on a Thursday and she made flyers on Friday. We meet in our building's rec room. As far as we know, the only victims are those from our building, Skylar Commons. Yet instead of leaving, we become shut-ins, quarantined, the thing that happened to us a curious case of the measles that must be contained. Zoe brought a coffee urn and a printout of the police sketch. It confounds us how all the details of the sketch can be exactly right and the picture all wrong. Zoe says we should perhaps make some adjustments. She is taking a drawing course at the Living Arts Centre because she's dedicated to self-improvement and trying new things. Last summer she learned how to bake French bread with Le Cordon Bleu in Ottawa. This summer she is learning perspective, volume and form.

FACT

The police created the facial composite using a computer program called Identi-Kit 2000.

FACT

There is a tip line. Call 1-888-224-8477 if you recognize this man and have information leading to his whereabouts. The police can't tell us what, if any, tips they have received, but they can tell us they are following up on a few leads.

FACT

In the elevator, men no longer look us in the eye.

Diana

As Zoe jots down our ideas for the new sketch, Diana admits something that we've all been thinking but didn't dare say because it felt like a kind of betrayal, though against whom or what we're not entirely sure. Our attacker is gorgeous. With wavy blond hair and lips shaped like a cinnamon heart, he is the spitting image of a teen heartthrob we loved when we were girls. Perhaps this is why none of us were alarmed when he first touched us. If he wasn't gorgeous we would have realized what was happening sooner, we would have gotten away or at least had a head start. Diana is not gorgeous. She has a plain, freckled face and is wearing a pink dress with a tea stain on the skirt. We picture her wearing this the day she was attacked.

Linda

Linda has a theory: mass hallucination. She read about a case in an all-girls' school in France where the girls, suffering from a lack of iodine in their diets, all reported having been strangled in their beds at night by a man in a yellow coat. They were so convinced of this fact that they asked the prefects to set up cameras in the dormitory to prove it. The result: an hour after the girls fell asleep, a bright amber beam from the nearby lighthouse shone through their window, and the girls, almost in unison, began writhing around in their beds gasping for air. We think carefully about this. Are we missing anything from our diets? Is there something in the water? What is our iodine? Where is our lighthouse?

Natalie

There is a competing theory. Natalie wonders if our attacker hasn't actually killed us all, and if Skylar Commons and our meetings in the rec room aren't some kind of purgatory where we're supposed to figure out who harmed us and why before we can move onto the next realm. We really like this theory, and if we didn't still have to load the dishwasher and shave our legs every day, this would be the clear winner.

FACT

We've all been to church at least once.

Nancy

Before the attack, Nancy had a recurring nightmare in which a man stabs her and throws her down the garbage chute. She had never lived in an apartment building before and found the idea of hundreds of bodies stacked on top of each other "frankly, terrifying." Our attacker didn't stab her or throw her. They were out back behind the building in the hydrofield. He pressed her face into the sun-scorched grass. She did not feel like she was falling. She was keenly aware that there was nothing between her and the earth. In her most recent nightmare the garbage chute is how she escapes.

FACT

We all live in Skylar Commons, an apartment complex which is thirty-six stories high with four hundred and fifty-one units.

Elaine

Some women like walking alone at night. Some women watch the news and instead of thinking, "Thank God that wasn't me," think, "If only it were me, he'd be sorry." Elaine was one such woman. In her purse she carries pepper spray, a rape whistle, and a Wild Kat Keychain—brass knuckles in the shape of a cat head with two pointed ears for stabbing.

FACT

Elaine scratched his face. She left a scar in the shape of a horseshoe beneath his right eye.

Stella

Zoe's drawings look as distorted as the police sketch. Stella has a better idea. "Everyone is the spitting image of someone else," she says. "There isn't a person on earth that doesn't resemble another person, living or dead. We know who his doppelgänger is, so why don't we just use a picture of him?"

FACT

We were all in high school the year River Phoenix died. Six of us cried. One of us wore black for a week.

Kate

Kate adds the scratch in Photoshop. She brings the file to the printer's and asks for five hundred copies. We divide the stack into smaller piles, one for each of us. Kate, who has stared at the photo most of the night, wonders if it is right to link the deceased actor's image to that of our attacker. Many of us feel it is in poor taste, others think it will merely lead to confusion. In the end we figure that, since he was vegan, and a human rights activist, he was the sort of person who would let us use his image if it were for a good cause. Kate staples his face to the notice board in the lobby. An elderly woman looks on as she does this. Kate asks her if the face looks familiar. The woman says, "No, he has the face of an angel."

FACT

River Phoenix died on Halloween in 1993. He was twenty-three years old. The same night one of the largest wildfires in California's history swept across North Malibu, eventually burning more than 16,516 acres of land.

Ingrid

Ingrid has been collecting all the headlines about our case in a large black binder. She slips the article about our River Phoenix posters into a clear plastic sheath. Having all the pieces in one place gives her a great sense of calm. There is a new piece about our case in the *Post*. It's an op-ed about tax hikes and rape culture. Ingrid doesn't get the *Post* so she walks to the convenience store to buy a copy. But when she gets to the newsstand it is the *Star* that catches her eye. They found him. Someone recognized his face from one of our posters. Our attacker was spotted at a bus stop scratching a lottery ticket, methodically unearthing a sequence of symbols and dollar amounts with the now defunct Canadian penny.

FACT

We each have a case number. We memorize this number instantly. It goes from being a number to the number, climbing the shelf in our mind where our mothers' birthdays sit, alongside our old landlines and the street numbers of our childhood homes.

FACT

We use our case numbers to call the station and find out what happens next. The police tell us there will be an identity parade, which sounds both Freudian and festive. Individually, we will have to pick him out of a lineup. Most police stations have one-way glass, so he will not be able to see us.

FACT

We have the right to attend the bail hearing and give evidence about why we think he should not be released.

Stephanie

"The end is a different kind of beginning." When we learn that the police have him in custody, we come together in the rec room to discuss our feelings. Stephanie stopped calling him "our attacker" and started calling him "Phoenix River." He is the opposite of the actor we all loved growing up. But opposites are opposites because they exist on the same plane; they are different in a precise way, one that links them together. When we were girls, he was older. We would have done anything to have him, but we didn't. Now we are older, and he did everything to have us, and he did.

Emily

Our attacker did something to each of us when he was finished. It was perplexingly kind given the circumstances. We hid this fact from police because it's an embarrassing, small detail, and ultimately irrelevant. When we watch the clip of him being taken into custody on the news, we don't think about the attack, all we think about is the thing. Everyone hates that the thing happened and we are afraid that it will all come out now that he's been caught. Everyone except Emily. She thinks that if we can understand the thing we can understand why he did what he did and why he chose us. "Why me?"

Jenny

Jenny hasn't said a word in any of our meetings. When we see her being interviewed about the case on TV it's like watching a ficus come to life. The reporter is not interested in the attacks. She is interested in the way he was caught. She holds up the picture of River Phoenix with the Photoshopped horseshoe scar beneath his eye. Jenny takes a sip

of water. She calls what we did "a cool solution to a very uncool problem." "It's cool to liken your attacker to a cute celebrity?" the reporter
asks. "A picture is not a person," Jenny says, "it's an idea." "Precisely."
When the reporter tells her that our attacker's new nickname is "the
heartthrob," Jenny looks down and blurts out the thing, and now it's
the reporter's turn to take a sip of water.

Ajala

Ajala wants to say something: she will not be pressing charges.

Barbara

She can't sleep with her husband anymore now that she knows that
he knows everything. Sex is not over for all of us but something is
acutely different. Barbara thinks our attacker breached the terms of
the victim/attacker contract. There is a story we should be able to tell
ourselves as victims and he has changed that story. We know now
why sex is difficult. The problem isn't that we were hurt, it's that we
weren't hurt worse, by someone worse.

Kelly Anne

She has decided to move out of Skylar Commons. Like many of us,
she was attacked in her own apartment. He forced his way in as she
arrived home from the gym. In addition to moving she is also giving
away her cat. Bijou was there when it happened. He sat atop the side
table unconcernedly batting his big yellow eyes. The cat couldn't have
understood what was happening but his eerie presence bothered her
all the same. Bijou never used to sit on the side table and now it was
his go-to spot after mealtimes and before bed. What did he mean by
this? If Kelly Anne had a dog, everything would have been different.
He would have barked, bit the attacker. A dog, she is sure, would never
sit on that spot again.

FACT

Our attacker is 5'11". His middle name is James. In his pockets, police
find a half a stick of gum, a wedding band, and a winning lottery ticket

for five dollars. He has no prior arrests and no high school diploma. He is not married.

FACT

Though our attacker is not employed by the Skylar Commons rental property, his father, Dean, is. He's a plumber. When tenants complained about low water pressure, Dean shut off the water in the entire building in order to pinpoint the problem. Once he located and fixed the burst pipe, he personally tested the water pressure in each unit, from top to bottom, in reverse numerical order.

Lulu

Lulu thinks we need to forgive our attacker, not for his sake but for ours, so we can move past what happened. This is irrefutable daytime talk-show logic, so we agree; however, we should mention that none of us really believe that Lulu was attacked. We suspect she comes to these meetings for the company. She wants to hear our stories, even though they make her cry. Perhaps what she really wants is to feel like she is a part of something bigger than herself. Lulu has wheeled in a DVD player. She thinks we should watch the movie where River Phoenix plays a male prostitute. She says this will be cathartic. In the movie, Phoenix's character, Mike, lives on the street and sells his body to older women and older men for money. He has narcolepsy and when he's asleep he dreams about his mother, a hotel maid. Other characters do what they want with his body. Like most narcoleptics, he can't control when he's about to have an episode and does so at inopportune times. While asleep the plot inches forward and Mike wakes up not knowing what happened, where he is or why. That's how the movie ends.

A Precise Benefit

MATEA KULIĆ

well, that's men for you
that's men for you
well that's men
that's men
that's well, men
well that's, that's for you
that's, that's for you
that's well, well
for you, well
that's you

Everybody Out of the Pool

NAOKO KUMAGAI

Formative Waters

EACH POOL HAD A DISTINCT ODOUR. Westhill stunk like pungent industrial bleach. Rocky Point Park pool, overlooking the Burrard Inlet, carried tidal saltwater smells. Clumps of grey and white bird shit sometimes floated in the water. Once I found a purple starfish in the pool gutter, and took it home in an empty Dairyland ice cream bucket with a wire handle. The starfish died in the bathtub and its body turned brittle. Easthill pool was indoors, in a townhouse complex, and the water came over us like a warm, soothing chemical brine. It got hot inside like a tropical greenhouse. We were parched and yawning within an hour of drills.

A typical morning practice when I was eleven: 20 sets of 50-metre freestyle (2 laps 20 times), 30 sets of 100-metre backstroke (4 laps 30 times), 20 sets of 100-metre breaststroke (4 laps 20 times), 10 sets of 25-metre freestyle sprints (10 laps fast). Then flutter kick drills with a kick board. Then freestyle arm stroke drills with a pull buoy, which was a flotation device made of two short tubular pieces of round white foam connected together with an adjustable rope. I shoved it between my inner thighs, squeezing the muscles to make it stay put, and stroked through the water with my arms, keeping my legs still and floating. Finally, a breaststroke cool down, eight laps. Turn ankles out, kick like a frog. My bathing suit was a second skin, a fabric tattoo. Its imprint on my body remained at night while I slept.

My teammates hummed while they swam, blowing bubbles out of their noses. We were swimming in our collective snot. We wore rubber swim caps lined with baby powder so that the caps would slide on our heads easily. Our faces were half-masked by plastic Speedo goggles, yellow, blue, and red. Tara Connell had arms like the wings of an albatross; Christy Brown, with the overbite and long legs, had the happiest, tallest parents in the world; and Trina Neal, who always wore a navy-coloured bathing suit, showed me how to draw a vagina in the margin of a comic book, while we were sitting in the grass on our beach towels between races at semifinals in Coquitlam. It was as simple as sketching an inverted triangle with a soft pencil.

We swam, back and forth, indoors and outdoors, across 25-metre-length pools in Port Moody, from May to August, sealed in silent camaraderie in the water. We kept swimming until the pool wall opened, until the cavernous tunnel appeared, until we reached the California sea near Santa Catalina Island, where Natalie Wood had drowned. She was the reason my mother signed me up for the Port Moody Aquarians swim club, with its red and white killer whale logo painted on the wall by the communal outdoor shower at Westhill pool, where the boys pissed into the drains.

"I don't want any of you to drown," my mother said to my two brothers and me, so we were all put in the club, only I ended up staying in it the longest, from the age of six to twelve. "You just never know." My brothers moved on to other sports. Natalie Wood was small and had dark hair like me.

In the midst of a choppy crawl, my arm sometimes caught on the lane rope, a thick plastic red spiral that looked like the long, rounded back of a centipede. This happened when I had swum too far over in the lane, in the middle of a long set. It was like being shaken from sleep when I caught myself on the rope. I'd snap upright in the water, like a frantic, disoriented animal, centre myself in the lane and keep moving. Swimming in the deep end could bring hallucinations, like the woman who had butterfly swum the English Channel and experienced shifting illusions underwater: leafless trees, giant towers emerging from the waves, grotesque grey sunflowers thrusting toward the sky. The pool floor sloped and fell away. Diving deep might mean drowning, a dance with an undercurrent.

When I turned my head to the side to take a breath, my ear would leave the water and briefly connect with the world again. Our coach's voice from the deck, music blaring across the pool from the radio and a medley of other dissonant sounds punctuated the distance between land and water. The familiar became alien. The skin between my fingers grew webbed, my legs sealed together in scales, and my giant fish tail pushed out through the soles of my feet. I would never walk on dry land again.

Then came my father's voice, fragmented and urgent, dismayed at my bodily transformation. Was that really him? Was he there on the deck, cheering me on? Had he actually stayed to watch after dropping me off at the pool? He never appeared. It was part of the trance.

You're Just Like Me

Dad was proud of my swimming. He didn't compliment me much so it was something I clung to, like a charm on my wrist.

"You're like me," he said to me once, when I was swimming well. "You come from my side of the family. You're just like me."

A brief inventory of the traits shared with my father: short, stubby fingers, dry, raw skin that flared into eczema under stress and when the weather changed, oddly shaped kneecaps that looked like small, fleshy islands, thick legs, medium bone structure, a flat left foot, bad eyesight, and bruxism, grinding teeth during sleep. Growing up, I could hear him through the wall at night, making a grating sound like he was a nocturnal cannibal, chewing through his jaw and cheekbones. We also shared addictions and black depression. We were short for our respective genders.

You're just like me. A mantra for my formative years. If I was going to be a man, I wanted to be like Muhammad Ali, who shot off his mouth, threw his Olympic gold medal into the river, dodged the draft and talked dirty about other people's mothers in the ring. Or Marlon Brando, who could sob like a baby and rip apart his T-shirt like he did in *A Streetcar Named Desire*, but could also play a regal Napoleon. Or Jack Nicholson, balding, grinning, drawling, self-indulgent with a gigantic pot-belly, and smoking a fat brown cigar. There were already two boys in the family. I should have been the third.

Skin

Six years old in grade one. We were creating a ceramic imprint of our right hand. Mrs. Singer had frosted blond hair, green eye shadow, and her skin smelled of apples. She saw me hesitating over the wet clay.

"Why aren't you putting your hand down?" she asked. I wanted to use my left hand instead of my right. The eczema on my left hand wasn't as bad today. But I was too shy to tell her. Maybe to outsiders the rawness of my skin was invisible, which was hard for me to fathom because I was so self-conscious and always felt discomfort when my skin encountered random surfaces: droplets of rain while holding the plastic handle of an umbrella, the oily neck of a bottle of salad dressing, dishwashing liquid, pickle juice. Ceramic clay. Mrs. Singer firmly pressed my right hand into the white paste.

"Go wash your hands," she said. The imprint took a day to dry. My mother hung the mold on the living room wall beside a photo of my father. Was he responsible for my skin? It was like chronic, ferocious anger coursing through the body, receding, then returning in a rage, erupting in ancestral, cellular fury. Skin never calm. Attack pending. I examined my oddly shaped, imprinted fingers hanging on the wall, then at my father's photo. It seemed to be something we were doing to ourselves. What were we both so angry about?

Dad fell asleep after dinner, stretched out on the ugly black and white nubby weave couch, with my mother's homemade pillow under his head. Mouth slightly open, hands on stomach. Jet black hair, symmetrical brows, short eyelashes, a lean nose, cheekbones, and chin smoothly shaved. A nice face. My dad's face. His stocky, solid body in a pressed blue shirt and jeans. His feet in navy socks. Dry, red patches around his knuckles. He never smiled much inside the house, but he did at strangers when we were out. I'd overhear my mother's friends telling her how kind and gentle he was, and that she was lucky. He slept on the couch—mythical, elusive, duplicitous, and towering in my mind.

"Don't bother him," my mother said, entering the living room. "He's working so hard these days."

Baseball

The ball came hurtling at me, a spinning white orb. I raised my arm up and caught it with the soft caramel brown glove, which I had received as a gift for my twelfth birthday. When the ball landed hard in the centre of the glove, the impact was solid, a jolt up my wrist.

"Curve ball," I said. I tossed it back to my father. We were in the backyard. The ravine behind our house was rushing water from weeks of rain. Spring had triggered my eczema and the skin on my hands was more cracked than usual. My fingers throbbed, as if they had tiny, urgent heartbeats of their own.

Dad threw another ball. He had been an amateur ball player in Japan and he made sure that I recognized baseball pitches. He seemed to think that this was important information for a girl to know. We couldn't just toss a ball around on a Saturday afternoon and have a conversation. It had to be another drill.

"What about that one?" he said.

"Slider." The ball landed in my glove, a hard punch. I imagined removing my glove and seeing the skin on my hand darkening. I could toss my decaying hand into the ravine and have nothing but a blackened hand-stump left. Our neighbourhood had coyotes. One would find my hand among the wet leaves and twigs and carry it away in her mouth to feed it to her children.

Another ball. This time I had to run for it, since it floated in the air, suspended, before it careened straight down. I was too slow to catch it and the ball rolled through the grass.

"You missed," he said. "What was it?"

"Knuckleball," I said. "It's not fair."

"What's not fair?"

"One more," he said. It came faster than the others, too fast. I ducked. The ball hit the grass and rolled. My father was shouting, so I ran after it. The ball popped over the edge of the grass, down the high, muddy slope and into the deep ravine. It sat in the running water, lodged in some wet leaves and pebbles, trembling on the gravel bed. I hoped the coyotes would get it.

Jane Fonda

At twelve, I had aches I had never felt before. Knees were sore after swim practice.

"You're getting fat." Dad smelled of beer. It was nearly dinner and we were in the kitchen.

"If you're thin, you can wear anything," my mother said, standing at the stove, cooking. She didn't look at me when she was saying this. She served me several helpings of broccoli that night.

When swim season ended in August, I exercised in the basement to my Jane Fonda workout video, which had been dubbed for me by my mother from a library copy. Girls at school said that Jane Fonda had had a rib removed to look thinner. Her twisting and bending torso in shiny, tight blue spandex was mesmerizing, but it was hard to tell if a rib was actually missing. She had feathery hair and lean muscles with turquoise sweatbands around her wrists. Legwarmers collapsed around her ankles, and her svelte white sneaker toes peeked out from under the cuffs. She wore a sparkling blue leotard. The synthesized music was upbeat. Bits of her voice floated in my head during the day: "Don't forget your sunshine arms."

What did they use to saw her rib off? Did it make a buzzing noise, like the way my father's electric razor did in the morning? What did they do with the rib afterwards? I would put the fine white powder in a saltshaker so that Dad would accidentally sprinkle it on his food. Then I would say to him, "You ate Jane Fonda's bones." Or, I would add water to the powder to make chalk, and write all over the sidewalk, rants that would wash away in the rain.

Fish Cowboy

My father worked in a fish factory all his life, processing salted salmon eggs, the ones you eat with sushi. Sometimes I imagined him standing on the riverbank by the Seven Seas fish factory in Ladner, where he worked. In my mind, he transformed into a cowboy, a fish cowboy, looking at the rushing water. The fish swam upstream, leaping high over cascades, as if propelled by a spring in their tails. My father held a thick rope, waiting for the moment when a fish jumped high enough. He had the loop ready, and when the fish leapt, the rope closed around its middle, and he snapped the fish back toward him. He had a club that looked like an old table leg, rough and blunt at the ends. He struck the wriggling body, until it lay still. Then he slit the abdomen with a dagger, stuck his hand inside and tore the bulging egg sac out. Slicing the head off was quick. He raised his knife and cut through the gills. He kept the fish heads in clear plastic bags in a separate freezer in the garage. They were well preserved in death. silver skin, glass head eyes, inky pupils and open mouths, still stunned from the beating.

My father went wherever fish eggs were abundant, up along the coast of B.C., sometimes Washington state. It depended on the season. He never wore a wedding ring. It interfered with the use of his hands. He needed his fingers to be nimble, not weighed down by a band of gold. A wedding ring didn't fit on the hand of a cowboy. It didn't belong there. The fish were beautiful. Even though he beat them, slit them open, took their eggs, he was astonished by the way they fought, how much they wanted to live.

It's All a Test

I was sixteen and studying for a biology lab exam. My mother didn't bother to knock.

"He's not answering the phone," she said. "I think he's with someone." Dad was on a business trip and she had called his hotel.

"He could just be out," I said.

"If something's happened to him, I'll die."

"No, you won't," I said, then felt bad for sounding unkind.

My mother wiped her eyes. She was a tiny woman with a short, pixie haircut, like a boy's. Her helplessness overwhelmed the room. I hated seeing her cry. *Cytoskeleton and microtubular organelles. The cell has a supporting network of thin fibre-like elements called the cytoskeleton.* The cold language of the biology textbook was comforting, a clinical distraction. A crane-necked lamp was on my desk. It shone in the room like an interrogation light.

"I'm studying. I have a test tomorrow," I said.

She sat on my bed, on an old, striped cotton bedspread she had made for me to comfort my skin.

"Sometimes he comes home at night smelling smoky," she said, her voice rising. "And you know he quit smoking, long ago. One of the women was a family friend but I don't want to tell you her name because you know who she is. She's divorced now."

Microtubules are hollow tubes made of repeating protein units. They appear to give the cell structure to anchor certain organelles in place and to act as tracks along which certain organelles and vesicles can move.

"There was the other woman who called our house at 6:30 in the morning. She wanted to know where your father was. I wished I'd told her to go to hell."

Microfilaments are very thin chains of protein actin, which can change shape when provided with energy.

"When I tried to talk to him, he said nothing. Grandma said ignore it. That's what she said. Your father's father once said a real man only says three words a day. Three words a day and then nothing. Makes you crazy living with someone like that."

My mother had never confided in me like that before. I failed her that night, and flunked the biology test the next morning, but maybe that would have happened anyway. Biology was not one of my stronger subjects.

When my parents immigrated to B.C. in the 1970s, my mother didn't speak English and had been completely dependent on my father. Over the years, I fantasized that she would evolve into someone fierce and eccentric like Yoko Ono, and jettison this life. Pack up my brothers and me, get us all on a plane for Japan, where we would be raised among a huge extended family. From Japan, she would write a letter to Dad, telling him he was no longer needed, that he had struck out. She would emerge defiant, triumphant, and independent.

"I married the wrong person," she told me, years later. It was a complicated mistake.

Other Women

Here was the heat of swimmers in the race, all the women who were vying for my father's affection, the ones I knew about:

Lane One: a co-worker at the fish factory
Lane Two: a friend of my mother's
Lane Three: the woman my father took on a date to a hockey game
Lane Four: Tiger, our family cat
Lane Five: my mother
Lane Six: me

All the women were Japanese except our cat. She was an orange tabby who loved the baths my father gave her for her fleas. She coveted his attention, his tenderness, his hands on her fur, and she was successful. She didn't mind the water, and she didn't have to compete, like I did. She earned his affection naturally, without having to improve her split time on the 50-metre butterfly. All she had to do was hold still in the water and purr. Tiger, with her four legs and seductive tail, was non-threatening and likely the best member of the family to ask my father the questions that I longed to ask but lacked the courage to do so: Tatsuya, who were all these women? What was your pickup line? What did you say about your life? Did you love any of them? Maybe if you loved them, even one of them, I would have understood. After all, we all dove willingly into the pool.

Return to the Water

My father and I were floating in Westhill pool, surrounded by a chain-link fence and pine trees. We were alone. Whenever he swam, his arms thrashed about and he would be tired after one lap. I gave him a black inner tube so he could rest. I was treading water. My father's black hair had gone grey, and the lines on his face were deeper.

"What are you talking about?" he said. "I don't know what you're talking about."

My father was placed firmly inside the thick inner tube, remote and protected, so I couldn't get that close.

"Your affairs. I know all about them. You don't know what it's like, knowing what I know about you." I kept treading water. "I'm a feminist."

"I don't know what that means," he said.

"I think you hate women."

"You think too much. You think way too much."

"Were you unhappy in your marriage?" I asked.

"Huh?" It sounded like a question he never considered. "I've worked hard all my life. When a man works that hard, he gets to do what he wants."

"Is that what you think?"

"I've worked very, very hard. A man should get to do what he wants."

"Why did you even get married?" I asked. He was moving his feet gently, trying to get away from me. I kicked closer to him. Anxiety was creeping into his face.

"My life has nothing to do with yours," he said, finally. "I did all I could to provide for you. I worked hard. I worked very hard. I provided for you. That's all I could do. My life has nothing to do with yours. Ask your mother. I can't help you with anything else. I never could."

He'd never been that honest with me before. I swam away.

Love and Other Irregular Verbs

SIGAL SAMUEL

I. My dad speaks ten languages

No, REALLY, HE DOES. In order of acquisition, they are:

1. English
2. French
3. Hindustani
4. Arabic
5. Hebrew
6. Mughrabi
7. German
8. Latin
9. Greek
10. Japanese

I should probably explain that my dad is the professor type. His specialty is mastering foreign languages—the more arcane, the better. If you ask him, he'll tell you that he does this in order to be able to read the Great Books of Human Civilization in their original, unadulterated forms. If you ask me, though, he picked up half those languages in order to gain access to the women he loved, and whom—given enough practice with participles, plosives, and possessive pronouns—he might persuade to love him back.

II. Hum tumku boht pyar karta

My dad was born to Jewish but secular parents in 1950s Montréal. As a result, bilingualism was a given: he grew up immersed in both English and French. He also grew up surrounded by the strange sounds of his great-grandmother's patois—a peculiar blend of Arabic and Hindustani words. Granny was a Baghdadi Jew who had immigrated to India in her youth, caught the eye of a rich Bombay businessman, and stayed there to raise her brood. She spoke Arabic because that was the language of Baghdad, and Hindustani because that's what her Indian servants spoke.

My father was fascinated by Granny. Unlike his own meek mother, Granny was a tough old broad, a pigheaded matriarch who was always bursting into your kitchen, tasting whatever was simmering on the stove, and proclaiming, "Too much *haldi*! Too little *cotmeer*!" He was enthralled by the movement of her gnarled hands as she spoke, cutting through the air like branches in a windstorm; he was in love with her way of chewing tobacco and spitting into the spittoon with a soft *tu-tu-tu!* He wanted desperately to hear her stories of India—supposedly she'd owned a pet monkey, a baby leopard, and a goat named Peter— but of course she spoke no English and refused to learn.

So one day my father approached his mother, who (as she tells it) was washing dishes at the time, and begged her to teach him Arabic and Hindustani.

"One phrase every day," he pleaded.

"Shouldn't you be focusing on your schoolwork?"

"I want to talk to Granny," he insisted.

She studied his stubborn little face for a minute before agreeing. "Here's your first lesson. Go and tell Granny: *hum tumku boht pyar karta*."

Obediently, he shuffled off and told her. Her face lit up; she kissed him on the crown of his head and sighed a soft *tu-tu-tu!* He returned to his mom and asked, "What does that mean?"

She said, "I love you very much."

III. Mazel Tov!

At around age seventeen, my father began to take a serious interest in Judaism. A social isolate from pre-K onward, he found himself hungry for some form of authentic connection—preferably one that didn't involve fraternizing with the stoner kids at Wagar High—and religion seemed to offer just that. After his first year of university, he dropped out and announced that he was going to live in Jerusalem, where he would study at an Orthodox yeshiva and learn how to live an observant Jewish life.

As it turns out, a big part of living an observant Jewish life in that setting meant, well, finding an observant Jewish wife. *How hard can it be?* thought my father, who'd never even had a girlfriend, never mind a potential life partner. It turned out to be harder than he'd thought. In the end the head rabbi of his yeshiva appointed a matchmaker to help him find that special someone.

The story of how my father met my mother is one he often used to tell me as a bedtime story when I couldn't get to sleep. It runs a bit like *Goldilocks and the Three Bears*. The matchmaker showed up at his door on three separate occasions, each time with a different candidate in tow.

Candidate #1 was a Yemenite Israeli with big bones and an even bigger personality. She scared my father half to death, raining questions down upon him like burning sulphur on Sodom and Gomorrah. With each question his answers grew quieter and quieter until he was speaking in a virtual whisper. Which, apparently, was a pet peeve of hers, because she proceeded to throw a fit right there in my father's living room. Too hot.

Candidate #2 was a wisp of a woman who looked like she could be blown off her perch if anyone so much as exhaled in her direction. She rivalled even my father in shyness, and answered his questions in such delicate decibels that he couldn't make out her words. For the duration of the meeting he simply sat on the couch, looking at her and trying hard not to breathe. Too cold.

Candidate #3 was my mother. She was a pretty Moroccan girl with high cheekbones and sleek dark hair. She spoke at a normal volume and even made occasional eye contact. Her name, my father discovered with delight, was Mazel Tov—literally, good fortune. With a name like that, how bad a match could it be? After she'd left his apartment, he turned to the matchmaker and confided that he thought this last woman might be just right.

In the coming weeks, the matchmaker arranged a few more meetings between my father and mother. He travelled to Beit Shemesh, a town one hour outside Jerusalem, to meet her parents. Within seconds, my dad discovered that none of his languages—not even his fledgling Hebrew—would allow him to communicate with this wizened couple, who sat on their patio shrivelling in the sun like a pair of overripe prunes. They'd moved to Israel from a tiny village in Morocco which no longer exists, and the language they spoke was a weird mash-up of Hebrew and Arabic known as Mughrabi. My father listened to their morphemes and phonemes clinking around in his ears, and was charmed by their dialect as much as by their daughter. To this day, I'm convinced that his meeting with my mother's parents is what really cinched the deal. A new language was being offered up to him like a dowry.

Three months later, they were married. A few hours before the wedding night, the head rabbi of the yeshiva called my dad into his office and told him to take a seat. The old man then proceeded to give a strange demonstration: he brought his thumb and middle finger together in a loop, and thrust the forefinger of his other hand in and out, in and out. Mortified, my dad realized that the rabbi was instructing him in the art of losing one's virginity. He was being subjected to the Orthodox version of Sex Ed.

For a couple of years, the marriage ran smoothly. My dad's Hebrew and Mughrabi improved dramatically. As time passed, though, his passion for the religious lifestyle began to wane. He started reading forbidden books—books that his yeshiva deemed treif, intellectually unkosher. One day he picked up a copy of Nietzsche's *Beyond Good and Evil* and was captivated by the ideas he found in its pages. Soon enough the linguist in him emerged, demanding that he study German in order to read these texts in the original. And so he did. For the first time, a new language drove a wedge between him and the woman he loved.

IV. Être, Avoir, Aimer

After my parents split, my sister and I grew up with my dad in Montréal. As the male head of a single-parent household, he was sometimes at a loss for how to connect with two little girls. At a certain point, though, it occurred to him that he could use languages as a way of getting closer to us, just like he'd done with my great-great-grandmother and my mom. Other girls got dolls and dresses; we got diphthongs and dangling modifiers.

We already spoke English, of course, but no matter: when I was eight years old, my dad told my sister and me that he'd pay us a dime for every picture book we read and a quarter for every chapter book. We had to discuss the books with him before he'd pony up the cash. Budding entrepreneur that I was, I polished off entire series of books that year—*Nancy Drew, Boxcar Children, Goosebumps*—as fast as my money-grubbing paws could flip the pages.

In Grade 2, my dad started helping me with my French homework. I still remember standing barefoot on the cold kitchen tiles and licking a cherry popsicle while he quizzed me on verb conjugation.

"*Je suis, tu es, il est,*" he declaimed, the *Bescherelle* propped open on his knees.

"*Nous sommes, vous êtes, ils sont!*" I recited between slurps on the popsicle.

"*J'ai, tu as, il a.*"

"*Nous avons, vous avez, ils ont!*"

"*J'aime, tu aimes, il aime,*" he said, and I froze, because the use of the first-person term of affection followed by a second-person pronoun was not something I was used to hearing. I looked down and saw that the popsicle was dripping onto my hand in sweet, sticky trails.

As a teen, I attended a Jewish high school where everyone had to learn Hebrew. I brought my homework into my dad's study sometimes, and even though by this point his bookshelves betrayed his atheist leanings, we worked on my Hebrew by studying the Bible together. Nietzsche and his giant moustache smiled down on us forgivingly.

By the time I became a student at McGill, I was still living at home, but my dad was spending more and more time cooped up in his study. Dictionaries encased him like a child's snow fort. As he sat poring over auxiliary verbs and adverbial clauses, I started to feel increasingly elided, like a weakly aspirated *h* at the beginning of a Greek word. So I did what I had to do to become audible: I enrolled in Arabic classes. I knew it would mean long afternoons of paging through the Arabic dictionary with him—and it did. By the end of my second year, I was wearing the gloss off its pages. The substance melted onto my hands, sweet and sticky. *Nous aimons, vous aimez, ils aiment.*

V. Tadaima

Earlier this year, my father met a woman on the Internet. He lives in Montréal and she lives in Tokyo; they met in a chatroom. Started talking books. She's a Comparative Lit student. Japanese and English folktales, or some such thing.

I live in Vancouver now, but my sister, who lives in downtown Montréal with her new husband, still goes over to our old house in the suburbs every Friday to have dinner with my dad. I get weekly phone calls from her, reporting on the status of his Internet relationship. She says she can gauge how well it's going by the height of the pile of Japanese language books on his desk. Ten books or less means it's just a crush; twenty means it's getting serious; thirty or more and they're in love.

A week before I was due to fly home for winter break this year, my dad taught me the Japanese phrase *Tadaima*, which means "I'm home!" Sure enough, that's what I said when I turned my key in the lock and stepped back into the house I grew up in. Before he could even respond with the traditional rejoinder (*Okaeri*, which means "Welcome home!"), my eyes landed on the Jenga tower of Japanese books that he'd just gotten out of the library. That's when the question popped into my head: Does my dad learn foreign languages in order to gain access to women he loves, or is falling in love an excuse for him to learn another language? Either way I looked at it, the answer was yes.

To be with my great-great-grandmother, my dad learned Arabic and Hindustani. To be with my mother, he learned Hebrew and Mughrabi. Now, to be with his Internet girlfriend, he's learning Japanese.

To be with me, my dad tried to learn the language of tenderness, of fatherly affection, but he stumbled over its intimate grammar, how to conjugate *to love* and other irregular verbs like *to miss a daughter without making her feel guilty for leaving home and to not live in a fort made of dictionaries*. I think, now, that I can spot the source of his trouble: his love for language grew so strong that it began to strangle the human love it was meant to nourish, the same way an umbilical cord can asphyxiate a baby on its way out of the birth canal.

VI. I speak five languages

Well, almost. I'm still working on number five. In order of acquisition, they are:

1. English
2. French
3. Hebrew
4. Arabic
5. Spanish

Four of these five languages, I learned in order to get closer to my dad. One of these languages, I learned in order to distinguish myself, to set myself apart.

This summer, I started learning Spanish. On the first day of class, our teacher, Enrique, taught us how to say I love you. *Te amo.* Strangely, my first thought was: as in ammo? Like, ammunition? My second thought was: oh, of course, *amo* as in *amour*. Enrique quickly moved on to the verb *hablar*, to speak. He asked us to open our Spanish textbooks to the appropriate page, and began leading the class in a resounding chorus of *yo hablo, tu hablas, el habla* blah blah—I stopped listening. I was thinking about how there was something right in that first thought, in that etymology that linked love with ammunition, with warfare. Beneath my palm the textbook radiated heat, full of plosives preparing to detonate at the slightest pressure from my tongue.

The Marrying Kind

AYELET TSABARI

IT'S YOUR WEDDING DAY, and you're barefoot in a deep blue sari, hunched over a cigarette outside a North Vancouver home. It's a cold, wet December day, and the snowy path had to be shovelled before guests arrived. You take a few urgent puffs, like a high school student in a bathroom stall, and flick the cigarette onto the pavement. You rub your henna-painted hands together and breathe into them to keep warm.

Your brother-in-law pokes his head out the door. "You're okay?"

"Yes," you say, forcing a smile. "Just getting some fresh air. I'll be right in."

You're not going back in. Not quite yet.

Inside this house, thirty-odd guests you just met are pretending to be your family. Looking at them through the steamy windows, you're almost fooled. They could be your family—a bunch of olive and brown-skinned people with dark hair and dark eyes. From where you're standing, it's hard to tell that the women wear saris and that everybody looks more Indian than Israeli.

You look Indian too. You look Indian to Indians in Vancouver who ask you for directions in Hindi or Punjabi on the street. To the girl who yelled, "You fucking Punjabi!" when you didn't give her a cigarette on Commercial Drive. You even looked Indian in India, where the locals thought you were a slut for dressing like a Westerner and walking around with white boys.

You've never looked more Indian than you do today. Your wrists are heavy with elaborate bangles, and you're neatly tucked in six metres of shimmering silk embroidered with gold and red stones. Your boyfriend's cousins helped with the sari, wrapping it around you as if you were a gift with many layers, draping one end over the shoulder and stuffing the other into your skirt. You're only wearing a thin line of eyeliner, and your fingernails are chewed down and unpainted. You're barefoot, because you don't wear heels. You catch your reflection in the window and eye it with satisfaction, tossing your hair back like a Bollywood starlet on the red carpet.

The door swings open, letting out warmth, broken conversations, and the smell of curry. Your boyfriend steps out and looks around suspiciously, as if expecting to see someone else. "What are you doing?" he asks.

"Nothing, I'm coming in."

You take one more look at the empty suburban street. It is frozen still: the snow-topped houses, the parked cars, the cotton ball bushes, the slushy road. Your feet start to feel numb. If you had shoes on, you might have walked away, down the trail, up the slushy road. Your bangles would jingle as you strode off, and the free end of the sari would flutter behind you, a splash of blue against all this grey and white.

"Are you coming?" He's holding the door open for you.

When you met two years ago, you weren't thinking marriage. You were sitting outside your bungalow in southern India when he walked by. He looked a bit like Jesus, skinny and brown, long-haired and unshaven. He carried a guitar case and a small backpack slung over his shoulder. When you started talking, you discovered he was an Indo-Canadian from Vancouver who didn't speak a word of Hindi.

One night you shared a bottle of cheap whiskey around a beach bonfire, and talked until everybody left and the fire died out. After one week, you were throwing around I love yous in both Hebrew and English. After two weeks, you called your families to announce your state of bliss. You wandered through India delirious and glossy eyed, made love in guesthouses infested with rats and monkeys and cockroaches as long as your index finger, cooked food outside straw huts, shared sleepers on overnight trains, and licked acid stamps at parties on sandy beaches.

You separated at a crowded train station in Pune, a classic scene from a Bollywood film: a woman holds on to her lover's hand, extended from between the metal bars of the train's window. They utter declarations of love and cry. They vow to meet again. The train conductor blows his whistle, and the train starts chugging away slowly. The woman runs alongside the train until she can't continue. The train fades away into a cloud of smoke.

You spent the next seven months waitressing in Tel Aviv while he planted trees in northern British Columbia. You wrote each other long sappy love letters, and sometimes, when he was out of the bush, you spoke on the phone. When you made enough money for a ticket, you flew to Canada to be with him, lugging a suitcase filled with Hebrew books and tie-dye tank tops you'd bought in India. You were hoping to travel in B.C. for a while and then find a job. Maybe you'd stay for a year or two if you liked it. Who knows? You'd been living like a nomad for the past four years so you wouldn't mind the change.

Vancouver was beautiful that summer, warm and golden, and the days long and lazy. You'd never seen the sun setting that late before. You found a one-bedroom apartment in the West End, facing English Bay and a daily display of sunsets, bought IKEA furniture and a foam mattress. An old American car. A set of Teflon pots.

One night after dinner, you started talking about the future. "Maybe I could go to college here," you said.

Your boyfriend eyed you carefully. "Here's the thing," he said. He had done some research these past few days. Apparently, the only way you could stay in Canada, get a work permit, study, was to get married.

You tensed up.

You were twenty-five. You never planned on getting married; never really understood why people bothered. Growing up, you didn't throw white scarves over your head for veils or gazed dreamily at wedding dresses in magazines. You blamed your father, who died when you were ten, for your textbook fear of abandonment and string of bad relationships. But your tourist visa was running out and so was your money, so you knew you had to make a decision. Fast.

"I don't want to get married," you whined over the phone to your sister in Israel. "Why do I have to? It's not fair. Why does it even matter? It's just a stupid piece of paper anyways."

"If it's just a stupid piece of paper," your sister said, "what difference does it make?"

"Okay," you told your boyfriend as you lay in bed that night. He looked up from his book.

"Okay," you repeated with a sigh. "If we absolutely have to get married then I want it to be really small, just us, no big deal. Nobody has to know. We're doing it for the papers. That's all. And . . ." you paused for emphasis, "there's going to be no husband-wife talk. You're my boyfriend. Not my husband. Is it clear?"

Your boyfriend grinned.

A few days before the ceremony, your boyfriend called his father to tell him about the wedding and inform him that he was not invited. In fact, nobody was. It was just a little thing you had to do to sort out the papers. You heard his father yelling on the other end (you could make out the words *customs*, *tradition*, and *community*) and watched beads of sweat gathering over your boyfriend's brow as he struggled to throw in a word. Finally, he slouched onto the couch and nodded into the phone, drained and defeated.

"My dad is throwing a party," he said after he hung up, rubbing his temples. "Just close family members, nothing big."

Within days, his father arranged a catering service, a cake, and an outfit for you to wear. Fifty guests were invited, and your boyfriend's aunt volunteered her large North Vancouver home. He wanted you to have real wedding bands, replace the 150-rupee rings you'd bought each other in India, but you refused; you liked yours, his was shaped like an Om and yours like a flower with a moonstone in it. You called your mother in Israel and assured her that there was no need for her to borrow money to fly to Vancouver. That it was just a formality. Your mother sighed but didn't push. You figured she was so relieved to see you marry off that she chose to pretend it was the real deal, or at least hope it would turn into one.

On the morning of the wedding, you woke up at 3 a.m., flushed with sweat, remembering a visit you made to a fortune teller in the mountains of Israel the year before. You and your best friend had driven her beaten VW Bug two hours north of Tel Aviv and up precarious mountain roads just to see her. It was a hot day and the car wasn't air-conditioned. The fortune teller greeted you in jeans and a T-shirt, not quite the mystical character you had expected, and led you to her living room, which had no crystal bowls or velvet curtains. Children's toys were scattered on the carpet. She opened your cards on a table marked with crescent-shaped stains left by coffee mugs, and then leaned over to examine your palm. Her brow wrinkled, and then her face lit up. "Good news!" she announced. "You're going to be married by twenty-five!" You leaned back, laughed a long, healthy laugh and explained to her that that was impossible, that you did not intend to ever marry.

"She really doesn't," your friend affirmed. "She's not the marrying kind."

The fortune teller smiled a knowing smile and said you must invite her to the wedding. "What a waste of time," you muttered, rolling your eyes, as you stepped out of her house and into your friend's car.

You woke up again at 9 a.m. with a jolt, heart racing as if you'd been running all night. It was raining outside. It took forever to put on your sari, and it ended up looking stupid: the front pleats were uneven, and the part that draped over your shoulder kept loosening up. You pinned the fabric to your blouse with safety pins. It would have to do until your boyfriend's cousins fix it later this afternoon. Your boyfriend came out of the bathroom wearing his brother's suit. "It's too big," he groaned. A red dot adorned his cheek where he cut himself shaving. You swore he looked fine and helped him tie his hair in a neat ponytail. Your maid of honour, a male friend of your boyfriend's, showed up with a bottle of champagne, and you downed a glass with your morning coffee.

The wedding ceremony was held in your living room. The only guests were your maid of honour and your boyfriend's brother. A poster of a contemplative Bob Marley was your backdrop as the justice of the peace, a grey-haired lady you'd picked from the phone book, performed the ceremony. You'd picked her because you liked the sound of her name, and because she was a woman. Jewish wedding ceremonies are traditionally performed by men, so having a choice was just one advantage to marrying out of faith. Not that either of you cared much about religion. Your spiritual affinity was the kind one picks up on one's travels, along with mass-produced Buddha statues and incense sticks. It was summed up by statements such as "everything happens for a reason" and "the universe takes care."

The early morning glass of champagne made you tipsy and you giggled like a teenager at a school dance and avoided your boyfriend's eyes. You felt silly repeating these English lines you'd heard a million times in movies. Eventually, you fixed your gaze on the justice of peace. She had icy blue eyes, like frozen puddles.

You exchanged the same rings you had been wearing for the past year and a half. Then the woman said, "I now pronounce you husband and wife," and your stomach turned. Your boyfriend smiled at you. You kissed quickly and hugged.

Now your boyfriend is holding the door open, looking at you narrowly. "Are you coming or what?" he says.

You walk in. He follows.

Inside, the house is warm and smelling of turmeric and steamed rice, coriander, and perfume. The guests wander around, taking dozens of variations of the same photo, lining up by the buffet table to heap vegetable samosas and lamb curry on their plastic plates. Your boyfriend's buddies form a row of white boys as they sit against the wall, on their best behaviour, clad in suits, empty plates in their laps. There is no alcohol served, which you find peculiar and cruel. Your boyfriend's young cousins chase you around the room, admire your henna, and grab the free end of your sari. Finally, you escape to the washroom. You lean on the sink and stare at your reflection.

"You're married," you say. "How does it feel?" Your reflection shrugs. The truth is you feel nothing, except for a dull pain over your right eyebrow, a remnant of a champagne-induced headache.

"You're married!" you continue. "You're someone's wife!" Your reflection flinches. For a few seconds it's hard to breathe, as though a foot presses on your chest, but then it passes.

After the buffet, everyone gathers around for the ceremonial portion of the day. You enjoy the traditional rituals for the same reason you like wearing a sari; you see them as an anthropological experience, like some weddings you attended in your travels; only now, you're the one on display. You let your new family feed you Indian sweets and shower you with rice. You and your boyfriend break little clay cups with your foot while the guests cheer. The custom is that whoever breaks the first cup will be the boss of the house. For the next three years, you will both remember breaking the cup first.

In the late afternoon a cake is brought out, a massive creamy thing, with your names written on it in pink. At this point you're exhausted, your cheeks ache from smiling, and your eyeliner is wearing off, along with the effects of Advil. The party reminds you of a distant cousin's bar mitzvah you'd been dragged to by your parents. You feel like pulling on your mother's sleeve and nagging her, "Is it over yet? Can we go now?"

The guests gather around, prepare their cameras, and wait for you to cut the cake, holding the knife together as you bend over the cake smiling, and feed it to each other as newlyweds do. This is the one ritual in the party that you recognize from your own family weddings, from movies and television. As you stand by the cake, your sari suddenly tightens, clinging to your skin, making it difficult to breathe. You feel nauseated just looking at the cake. You breathe in deeply and slide two fingers between your petticoat and your skin to allow for air circulation, startled by the cold touch of sweat. You lean toward your boyfriend and whisper, "I'm not cutting the cake."

He turns to you. "What? Why not?"

"Because I think it's stupid. That's why. I'm not doing it."

"It's not a big deal. We're almost done."

"I'm not doing it. And I'm not feeding it to you or being fed either. Anybody who knows me even a little bit would know I hate this shit."

He doesn't tell you you're being ridiculous. He sighs. His aunts are whispering into each other's ears. A murmur spreads around the guests, growing louder as moments pass. Nobody is sure what is going on. But you won't budge. You have given up enough. You never wanted to get married in the first place; you never wanted a party and now you want a drink and you can't have it, and you will not cut the fucking cake!

Your boyfriend (as you'll call him for the next three years, never your husband) ends up cutting the cake with his brother, not quite the photo-op the guests hoped for. You stand beside them and smile like a bride should, feeling as if you won one battle amid many defeats.

A couple days later you pick up the wedding photos and browse through them quickly, pausing only to admire your outfit or to discard the ones of yourself you don't like. You're posing besides strangers you cannot name, smiling the same smile in all of them. Except for one. In the picture, your boyfriend leans over a cake with a knife, smiling goofily, his brother pretends to fall over it, while you stand in the shadow looking smug, the smile you thought you mastered so skilfully appears frozen and forced. You feel that pressure in your chest again, but this time it stays. It's like someone has your heart in his fist.

You call your brother in Tel Aviv that night and recount what forever will be known as "the cake story." You do it in a light, amused tone, as if it were some funny tale for dinner parties. You think you're being clever and charming. You expect him to appreciate the hilarity, to share your distaste, knowing well enough that you're better than those cake-cutting brides. But your brother isn't laughing.

"I don't get it; it was just a cake," he says. "What was the big deal?"

You're quiet for a moment, while your mind races in search for an answer, then say, "Whatever," and change the subject.

You hang up the phone and look over at your boyfriend; he's stretched out on the couch, switching channels on TV. He catches your gaze and smiles. Your husband. From this angle he almost looks like a different man, a handsome stranger, the kind of man you'd meet on a tropical island for a holiday fling.

Your husband.

You feel that weight in your chest again, and this time you know: it's doubt. This won't last, it tells you. It's not the cake, it's you. It won't last. You're going to screw it up. Can't you see? He likes the cake; he likes the husband-wife talk, he *is* the marrying kind.

"What?" Your boyfriend's smile turns to a frown. The moment is gone. You bully doubt into a dark corner and shut the door.

"Nothing," you say. You wear a big smile and join him on the couch.

Even if you wanted to be good, the night would stop you

JEN SOOKFONG LEE

You have done many bad things,
the kind that reek of vanilla vodka and slutty underwear and the alleys
behind bars where you've thrown up before going in to drink some more.

There is a stray eyelash on your cheek. You pick it off,
balance it on your finger, close your eyes and blow.

So. What do you wish for?

Babies, an A-frame cabin on a cliff above the white-edged ocean, the
skin you had when you were twenty-five, rain on your bare arms, a
room filled with helium balloons, a cat, long-haired and suspicious.

No, of course not.
There is a shadow list,
one saved in your head
where its grime is obscured
by work and sandwiches and the weather tomorrow.
Some days, you forget.
In the night, you never do.

You want a man to love you.
You want him to run the first kiss and the eleventh kiss
and the last kiss through his head, parsing each breath
and lazy, stuttered beat because he is just so manic with longing.
After you leave him, you will fuck him one last time.

You want a dog who hates everyone but you. A car that makes noises
that sound like sex. You want to know what your pubic hair is supposed
to look like. You want a newspaper just for the horoscopes. Pork rinds.
A short leather skirt that pulls across your ass.

And all of it in the night. The stakes are higher then.
The smells stick to your hair. The streets are slippery
with beer and piss and what people are ashamed of.
You were born to be the girl in the tall heels on a cracked sidewalk.
The one who says, *yes*, who has never said, *I should leave.*

Oh, naked whispers at dawn, French toast with strawberries, lemon
verbena hand cream.
That was you, for a while, in a green house on a nice street
where blue jays sang, perched in the maple trees, and you wondered
who was screaming.

It was half-easy.
But the other half almost killed you.
Remember?

The eyelash is gone. You imagine it floating through dust and fruit flies,
watching for married men on business trips
or young men who will never guess your real age. It will land, eventually,
someplace dirty and limp with a saturated damp
that cannot be described. Maybe you'll cry in disgust. But so?
It will be night and no one will ever know the difference.

Walk a Mile in Her Red High Heels

MARIE ANNHARTE BAKER

native women version of Oz unusual
comparison so wonderful to be a wizard
opportunity to decode exotic message display
revealed in designated special Elder gathering
granny circles may offer great straight forward
advice or personal insight shared by those present
make sense of collective past plus extravagant promise
self praise as usual granny speaks only of her own past
government designated funding makes worthy women
excellent role models to emulate a shared vision of plenty
words clue in the crowd about every step of arduous path
yet diversion happens in a blink of eye as heads turn toward
one granny who alone shows off red suede stiletto heels
not for the purpose to make her ass stick out far enough
catch attention whenever she wobbles by horny old guys
no these feet adorned sans moccasin shout take a gander
retrieve inside self fond memory shoe shopping spree finds
who doesn't recall fashion max celebrated like snag pride
history no longer low budget bargain shoe but ritzy style
saved by now bowl of strawberries full circle passed around
encourage each woman to chomp on this fruit shaped like her
heart anticipating frequent stretch toward prosperity windfall
however humble high heel could prophecy class upward mobility
no kidding who would think one granny makes swank accessible

Drowning Not Waving

M. NOURBESE PHILIP

WHAT DID HAPPEN THAT BRIGHT SUNNY WINTER'S DAY? On the bridge. A bridge spanning a ravine in the heart of a city. In retrospect my mind turns to the poet Stevie Smith, who writes: "*I was much further out than you thought/And not waving but drowning.*" I had seen him from below—purple jacket neatly folded and laid on the ground beside him. He had put one sneaker-shod foot into the iron fretwork of the railing and bent over to tie a shoelace. Or so it seemed to me. Perhaps, he was pretending. *What is that man doing?* was what I had asked myself as I looked up. What was it that attracted my attention? That bright morning. Thinking of instances where people have dropped items over bridges, I had moved to the edge of the path.

If I had my cellphone with me I would call the police was what I was thinking as I walked past him on the other side of the bridge, giving him wide berth. If I knew he was drowning, not waving, what would I have done? Would I have run up and tried to save him? I might have shouted. Even if I had called them, I tell myself later, the police would not have got there in time. And what would I have said? *Hello, Operator? There is a man here on the bridge and he's not waving, he is drowning. He is too far out and not waving. Not doing exercises or yoga postures. As I had thought. He is drowning.*

What if I had left home earlier or later that morning? What if I had stayed and had my morning cup of coffee and not set off in a somewhat irritated mood, having just had a testy exchange with a family member? What if I had stayed longer in the store selling Italian products where I had bought a lovely, round box with a black and white rococo design in which to pack a Christmas cake to send to a friend? What if, what if, what if?

What if I could erase the sound? The sound of a body hitting frozen ground from several metres up. What if Newton's apple hadn't fallen to earth but instead was borne up by angels, as I wish had happened with this man. Who was drowning. Not waving. Whom I did not know, but whom I will remember. Always. And the sound of a body hitting the ground. He did not so much jump as fall. Over. Out of the corner of my eye as I turn again to see what he is doing—there is a flash. Of his pants, perhaps, and he is no longer there. The only thing remaining the sound. The thud. How soon after did it come? I do not believe what my eyes record—he is no longer there. Only the thud and I am running. Back down the bridge to where he had been. Drowning. Not waving. Not exercising. Or, perhaps, he was. Practising the fall. His Fall. Because when I first look back—after passing him; after thinking: *If I had my cellphone, I would call the police*, I see him lean over the railing, then come back to ground. Was he testing his courage? His fear? His commitment, perhaps?

Past him, down at the other end of the bridge, I see another man. He's doing push-ups against the railing. Are they together? A moment of relief—the brain always hardwired for illusion. A respite from the anxiety—perhaps, they are together. Exercising, not falling. Or jumping.

He falls—headfirst. To ensure his commitment. To that which levels us all. His fall, like Newton's apple, would accelerate due to gravity— a force exerted on an object or body moving downwards as the earth rushes up to meet his weight. But whether he jumped or fell, the sound would have been the same. The same thud. The same moment of looking back. Freezing. Glimpsing. The flash of his pants. In retrospect, I think that perhaps he was throwing us off—me and the other two people on the bridge that day.

What is that man doing? I take the question with me as I climb the wooden stairs from the ravine below to the bridge above. These are the stairs people use to exercise—running or walking up and down. As you climb you see the underbelly of the bridge, the iron struts that hold it up, the concrete footings. *What is that man doing?* I am breathless as I pass another walker on the stairs and pause at the top to catch my breath. *What is that man doing?* I speak out loud—to myself, to the morning air, to anyone who will hear me. He stands where I first saw him from down below, except he has both feet stuck in the iron railing. He appears to be doing exercises, every so often turning his head to look at where the only other people on that bridge are. I am there— catching my breath; there is the woman I passed on the stairs and there is another man. He does not answer but turns away after hanging his bag on a light pole. As if turning his back on me and my question. *He is a man*, I think; *better able to approach another man. Why doesn't he do something? Why does he turn from me and my question?* The woman turns—is she turning away from the man at the railing, or simply doing what she had intended to do all along—head back down the stairs.

There are three of us on the bridge that bright morning, three of us and the man who is not waving. Who was drowning. Although none of us knew. *What is that man doing?* To no one in particular except myself. *People should be careful; that's how accidents happen*, is her response. She, like me, did not see that he was drowning not waving.

The day is one of those hard, bright winter days with the typically big, open sky, the air like a crisp, clipped accent. Although winter has not bitten as deeply as it usually does, the cold is recalcitrant. I recall the bridge. I also recall that although we had not had a lot of snow, the ravine had been frugal, keeping what little there was, and within the shelter of the slopes, the ice, keeping faith with winter, had made the path slippery. That was why when I got to the footbridge, I decided not to venture any farther into the ravine. I would climb the steps to the upper level, cross the bridge, and return home. What if, instead of climbing the stairs when I did, I had continued walking farther into the ravine? What if I had brought with me my crampons I use for walking on ice? I would have continued walking into the ravine and not climbed the stairs. On my return I would have come upon the event in the past tense. Stopped by the yellow police tape, forced to retrace my steps. To find another route home. Not past the man on the bridge who makes me nervous, too nervous to walk close to him. I would not have thought, had I walked into the ravine and not climbed the stairs when I did: *If I had my cellphone with me, I would call the police. Now.*

Addressed to myself, to the morning air, to the bright blue sky, to the trees you can see extending all the way to the east: *What is that man doing?* The sort of question a child would ask. A caring parent might respond: *What does it look like he's doing?* Perched like some giant bird over the railing, hands grasping the rail as he leans slowly forward and backward, stretching as in some bizarre type of extreme exercise. His well-developed forearms stretch as he leans over in some form of extreme yoga. *He's too old to be doing this sort of thing . . . what is that man doing?*

I have walked across this bridge for at least a decade. Built in the early 1900s, it connects the well-appointed homes that lend heft to the mantra, "location, location, location," on both sides of the ravine. It took me a while to walk the ravine alone, afraid, as so many women are, of being in isolated spaces alone. Countless are the times I have stood on that bridge and exhaled. Over the years I have photographed it in every season, and as the earth tilts gently on its annual journey around the sun, it was mine to enjoy—one of the secret pleasures of Toronto. Up high I would often look across at the tree canopy, a bright, tender green in spring, abundantly lush in summer. From the moment it first stipples the trees, the long, slow blush of fall gathers momentum until the tipping point when, tipsy with tippling the sugar, the leaves become one long, red roar that heralds the severe white of winter. Here I have seen the odd fox, red bushy tail waving in the distance, a pair of serene and sleekly shining ducks gliding on the little stream running through the ravine. For years I crossed paths with a birdwatcher, gaunt and silent, treading his way quietly through the ravine. The only two species I recognize are the red-winged blackbird and the scandalously red cardinal. Tall and gaunt, pussy willows line the path while languorous irises rise out of still water. Red osier dogwood is everywhere. There are runners, walkers, and talkers; there are dogs on and off leash; babies in carriages pushed by nanas, nannies, and parents. I know this place intimately. It takes me one hour to walk from my home to the end of the ravine and back. There are fellow walkers whom I have seen for years, noticing subtle signs of the passage of time such as greying hair, wondering whether I too display them.

This particular winter morning I see nothing but the bridge and the man on the bridge. *What is this man doing?* Why does he keep turning his head to look at us? Was it the second or third time I look back, once past him, that I see the flash—a streak of colour as of a bird swooping by? I know I heard the sound of something hitting the bare earth and I am running back down the bridge, back to where he was only a minute ago. I do not believe the evidence of my eye—he is no longer there. Three words—*Oh my god!*—beat against the air, repeated three times as I run. I look over the railing and see what I've always seen—a broad path below the bridge: *It was a trick; he was playing games all along; he's not there!* (The mind, always hard-wired for illusion.) But I did hear something, didn't I? The sound of a body hitting the ground. Where is he? Quickly I move farther down the bridge, scanning the ground and suddenly—*If thou be the Son of God, cast thyself down from hence: For it is written, He shall give his angels charge over thee, to keep: And in their hands they shall bear thee up, lest at any time thou dash thy foot against a stone.* This is the second temptation of Jesus by the Devil as told by the disciple Luke. Christian or not, how many of us have not been tempted at times to shake off this burden that is life and, even if not wishing to take one's life, longed for death as a respite to living. Not even caring whether or not there would be angels to bear you up? Where were the angels to bear him up? Instead of wings, red ribbons unfurl against the white, hard-packed snow.

At the far end of the bridge, the man who had turned from me and my question has heard my cries and begins to move up the bridge. I turn and begin running to the homes at the other end of the bridge hoping to find someone with a phone to call for help. A woman pushing a baby carriage hurries toward me and my shouts as she calls 911 on her cell. *Someone's jumped off the bridge!* On the corner two men, hearing my cries, jump from a pickup truck and race down the bridge, down the steps, phones pressed to their ears. I cannot stop myself crying.

Except he didn't so much jump as fall, sneaker-shod feet nestled in the diamond-shaped spaces of the railing—leaning over and falling. Headfirst. Was he screwing up his courage to fall? Was that what his pseudo-exercise movements were all about? His surreptitious glances? Perhaps, he was checking to see if we would intervene, waiting for me to pass him by. Before he jumped or fell. Does that offer me some comfort? What I do know is that he wasn't waving, he was drowning. Does it matter? That he jumped or fell? Why do I make a distinction? Why didn't he climb on the railing and jump? Had he done that there would have been no ambivalence. On my part, that is. Would we, the woman who answered my question—sort of, and the man who was exercising and hadn't, and myself, have rushed him, tried to grab him? Had we known? That he was drowning not waving?

There are few positive connotations to the word fall, except in relation to that beautiful transition season in temperate climates when leaves burst into a hallelujah of colour. One of Christianity's deep roots is the Fall—the expulsion of Adam and Eve from the Garden of Eden giving rise to the idea of original sin. This originary belief is a crucial aspect of the Judeo-Christian culture that continues to dominate the world in its asseveration that this act has corrupted all of humankind. In these days of melting glaciers and other grim evidence of climate change, I wonder whether that was the beginning of us swimming out too far—according to the Western, Judeo-Christian myth, that is, and that ever since, we have been drowning not waving, our pre-lapsarian innocence notwithstanding. In the aftermath, there are times when I feel as if I fell with him. Did I? Have I myself swum out too far, as I consider my own sadness, at his and my own despair? I have, at times when it was darkest and there seemed no way out, summoned the subjunctive—if this is life—toxic combination of growing old, dead, decomposing dreams, the lassitude and mourning after completion of a major work—then let death come. Is it courage, bravery, or despair that brings you to the edge—the bridge of life, and the realization that you have swum out too far and are not waving. His fall mirrors my own. A fall away from something all too well known but toward something that is still unshaped and undefined.

Women and angels become fallen. Icarus, wings melting as he comes too close to the sun, falls to earth: falling appears its own punishment. But Billie Joe McAllister didn't fall; he jumped off the Tallahatchie Bridge. The song surfaces a few days after my witnessing the suicide—the laconic tone of the ballad by Bobbie Gentry playing over and over in my head. Somehow the act of jumping appears more active, more purposeful.

I choose to see odd correspondences and synchronicities: Ernest Hemingway walked this ravine when he lived in Toronto in the early '20s, no doubt under this very bridge. He too would have witnessed the slow, steady burn of the trees in fall, the ravine raging at the encroaching death; in winter the snow hanging tatted lace on trees; the fragrance of spring in bud; the bold summer green that colludes in the pretence of nature in the heart of the city. He, too, would swim out too far and he was not waving, but that would come much later.

In *La Chute (The Fall)*, Albert Camus, the Algerian Nobel laureate, has his protagonist, Clamence, crossing a bridge—Pont Royal in Paris— to the Left Bank. At night. A darkened bridge. As dark, perhaps, as the one I crossed was bright, etched in my mind's eye in the winter's stark colours. Clamence is a lawyer by training with a vaunted sense of himself. I, too, am a lawyer. On this particular November night he passes a woman leaning over the bridge. She too was not waving and was out too far. Clamence does not look back when he hears the sound of a body hitting the water, nor when he hears a cry, *"repeated several times."* There was no scream that winter's day on the bridge. Only a thud. Clamence keeps walking; I turn back. *"Too late, too far,"* Clamence thinks. He was out too far, I think later, and not waving but drowning. Clamence tells no one. My cries are addressed to no one. And everyone. "I never cross a bridge at night," he would later tell a drinking companion when he recounts the event. His act of omission will haunt him, but he also seems relieved that he will not be tested again. *"O young girl, throw yourself again into the water so that I might have a second time the chance to save the two of us! . . . It's too late now, it will always be too late. Fortunately!"*

When they arrive on the bridge, the police officers—four men and a woman—are an almost textbook representation of Toronto's multi-ethnicity—one African, one Asian, one Eastern European, and two Anglo-Canadians, one male and one female. All except the female officer appear somewhat chastened by the event. She's all girl gone guy—hands in her pockets, she swaggers more than the male officers and refuses to make eye contact with me as the other officers do. She's pretty sure she knows him, I hear her say casually as she looks over the railing at the body below. He's still lying on his stomach, so she can't be completely sure, she continues, but if it's who she thinks it is, he slit his wrists a couple of weeks ago. *Yep, that's him,* when they finally turn him over, hands still in her pockets. She stands out among her male colleagues as showing no feelings for the loss of this life. So abruptly, so violently. Changing forever the serenity of the ravine.

There is another genealogy to this place, one deeply rooted in the political and having as much to do with its present-day existence, one could argue, as that original glacier. This green sigh in the heart of a city, this oasis of calm in the hurly-burly of a bustling metropolis strutting its parvenu stuff would not be, had it not been for residents in the sur-rounding neighbourhoods pushing back at planners in the '60s who could, and would, only see expressways shuttling people to and from shopping centres. The planned expressway would have, like that originary glacier, gouged its way through the ravine, truly turning the "burning would" into "a dance inane" had the provincial government not stopped it in 1971.

Places acquire resonances of words and acts. Twelve thousand years ago the Wisconsin Glacier, in its retreat, first gouged out the ravine. Through erosion and deposit, the lacustrine period that followed laid the groundwork for an abundance of wildlife including wolves, bears, and deer, much of which has disappeared as the ravine has become more park-like. After a visit to Lake Superior one summer, the ravine appears too tame, too conquered. I miss the wild, untamed beauty of the north, but the ravine is home—it is where I walk day after day, one step at a time into my future. There are times when I sense the presence of the First Nations of the area, the Mississauga, who might have walked or hunted in this ravine. Long before the bridge. Their presence, despite efforts at erasure, a tangible link between the now of then, and the then of now.

The ravine speaks to me as I walk, triggering my recall of certain details or events from recorded books I have long ago listened to. At a certain spot, I recall the precise moment when *Heart of Darkness* felt like a large, dark pool. A curve in the path and I recall an admonition from Machiavelli. I understand, perhaps only faintly, what the Australian Aborigines mean when they talk about the land generating stories. This is the place I have gone walkabout for at least a decade—conquering my fear of being alone in isolated places as a female.

Over the years I have dreamt up characters here; convincing myself that I could sense their presence, I see them slipping through the bush—one African woman brought as a slave and later freed, and two men. Her name is Gwyniad, meaning white or snow, and she appears in an essay I wrote over a decade ago. Whatever the reason, the ravine conjures her up and we have long conversations as I traverse back and forth across what was then nothing but a trail, now a broad path. We've never talked of those who swam out too far. What would she have to say about that, I wonder. No doubt she has seen many who choose to fall.

Many other things fall from the bridge: television sets, computers, and even pumpkins, thrown under the cover of darkness. (A young friend maintains that there is a wild nocturnal life in the ravine, and not just that of the wildlife.) None with the same consequences. I should return to the ravine as quickly as possible, the victim impact team advises, but it feels as if his fall has exiled me from the space. In the city of Oshogbo in Nigeria they tell a story of the revered founder-king, Timohin, who ended his life by descending into the ground—a transformation from man to god. I wish I could view this act as an equivalent act—his fall from the bridge commensurate with an ascent to another state.

"Why did you go back?" The question hits me like a bucket of cold water thrown in my face, shocking me into wordlessness. I stare at her. The question feels like an abomination. An insult, not to me, but to something larger—life perhaps. More so, given that she is a health care practitioner.

"What else could I do?" My tone challenges.

"It's just that you seem upset."

This response is different from the usual, which comes via the questions: *What is the lesson here for you, or what is the lesson you need to learn?* Another tells me that that is the path of his soul and that I shouldn't let it affect me. Perhaps she is attempting to protect me from the horror of it all, but the lack of compassion for a life so brutally and abruptly ended leaves me uncomfortable. The zeitgeist of contemporary life encourages us to feel entirely responsible for everything in our lives—the pernicious legacy of New Age beliefs such as *The Secret* and what I call the Oprahfication of society, as governments increasingly make themselves responsible for less and less. So, living in poor housing or being unemployed has more to do with your thoughts and less with government's actions.

There is also the woman on the bridge who, in the immediate aftermath, looks at me and although she doesn't say it, she may as well have said, *Take a pill*. As if a man jumping from a bridge in a ravine on a bright winter's morning is as normal as ordering a cup of latte at Starbucks. Like Clamence, I could have kept walking; left him for some person on the path below to come upon. Or, I could have gone back, looked over, seen him and then walked away. Or, I could have done what I did, which was first to disbelieve the evidence of my eyes—lying down there, then to call for help, not to God but to 911. Was what I did instinct or reasoned choice? And if, indeed, there was no choice, was what I did a moral act? Can there be inherent morality in reactions or instinctive responses?

I am haunted by the too-late realization that he was much further out than (we) thought/and not waving but drowning. Falling not exercising. The sheet they pull over him is orange. It covers his entire body and face. He hadn't died instantly—the men who had earlier run down to where he lay had called up to me that there was still a faint pulse. Looking down at the orange-draped stretcher, a policeman at my side taking notes, a thought rises swiftly and strongly to the surface of my consciousness: *They will have to pull me kicking and screaming out of life*. A more prosaic version, perhaps, of Dylan Thomas's exhortation to "rage against the dying of the light." It was a thought that had pushed back against the sight of the orange sheeting; a thought that attempted to honour the simple and not-so-simple fact of life measured in the inhale and exhale of our breaths—mysterious, magical. A thought trying to get at the feeling I often have that the ravine breathes, has a rhythm and that what drew me to it almost every day over the past decade was an attempt, only just understood, to get in sync with that rhythm, that breath; a thought that acknowledged that underneath it all, life is a crackle of an electrical charge jumping across a synapse; a thought that understands that sometimes we are so far removed from that, we care not whether we jump or fall—not waving but drowning.

Who bears witness for the witness, Celan asks in the aftermath of the charnel house that Europe became for European Jews and other discounted minorities. Who bears witness for my witness? Do I bear witness for myself? Perhaps the ravine bears witness for me—absorbing the maelstrom of despair that must have been the reality for the man who fell to earth that morning in the ravine, obeying the law of gravity that always ends with a thud.

Words like God, salvation, redemption no longer have the heft they once had. Today we talk of being in the Now—whatever that is—and the Universe (what message was the Universe giving you?) the way we once talked of God. As if this great mystery, despite all that we know about it, replete with black holes, dark matter, red dwarfs, and galaxies, is a personal deity. I have not thought that there was any particular lesson to be learnt from this event. I have mourned the act of this stranger that ruined a space that was of inestimable value to me—a place of respite from the unceasing rush of the surrounding city. A space that people used for recreation, exercise, and healing became a space of violent death. The anger would come much, much later, rising with a force one morning as I prepare myself to walk around the streets in my neighbourhood, not being able to return to the ravine. I rage at him—how dare he ruin the ravine for me.

How do I restore what the ravine meant for myself? Can I? Do I even wish to? When I think of returning, I wonder whether I will always think—*This is where I saw him. Swimming out too far. This is where I turned back. This is where I first heard the thud. This is where he lay on the ground.* I think of the earth and how it has had to absorb so much violence and outrage and yet because it is all that we have, we always return to her—must find respite in her.

Coda

I promised myself that I would only return when I was done writing about the man who was out too far and "not waving but drowning." Two years go by before I'm able to do so and I do think—*This is where I first saw him.* This is where he lay. This is where I heard the thud. It is spring and the ravine, serene, intimate, and patient as ever, appears shrunken, not as big as I imagined it. I complete the walk I should have that morning—walking to the end of the ravine and back, not climbing the stairs, not walking into his future but my own.

Face

EVELYN LAU

A writer once said, *Face it,*
no one's ever going to give you a second glance.

A judge once wrote,
Your face is like a lotus blossom,
your lips like an exotic orchid.

You live in every reflective surface,
snag my gaze in a shop window,
a polished picture frame, a teaspoon.
I must see you twenty times a day, yet somehow
I missed the moment you came unpinned
from the framework of bones that stretched you
taut like a canvas, and slid—
settling into your current motley state
of pouches and hollows, as if invisible fingers
had prodded and pulled at the flesh,
scattered sunspots across your cheeks
and chin, pawed the skin around your eyes,
pinched a tag or mole out of pure malice.
White hairs zigzag from your temples,
streak the childish fringe you've maintained
since your first haircut, as though
this could keep you a child.

Yet there are days you still surprise me,
seen from an angle in flattering sunset light—
times I would secretly agree with the judge's verdict,
glance around for confirmation
and realize no one's looking.

Brain

EVELYN LAU

There might be something wrong with you.
Or is it all in your head?

Migraines flash across your landscape
like electrical storms, scorching trees and shrubs.
Anxiety torches your neuron pathways,
obliterating names, faces, human language.
You stare at a line of poetry for hours
before stuttering to a stop
like a seized-up computer.
You search so ardently for the right word
you implode in a shower of sparks
and scrolling numerals. Some days
you are shrouded in fog like a coastline—
a horror-movie fog that creeps in
like poison gas, like lethargy.
Other days you are on fire—
when I touch my forehead my fingertips
leap away singed—
I can almost smell you burning,
a tofu scramble left on high heat on the stove,
swelling against the stricture of the skull.

The middle of the night is your favourite time—
you replay reel after reel of embarrassments,
spark lame conversations with a Round Table wit
that evaporates in the morning light.

Skin

EVELYN LAU

You came into this world a sheet of blank paper,
fresh linen, a bowl of almond milk.
My life has left its marks on you—
the puckering of scars, railroad tracks
of stitches, the needle pricks
and tic-tac-toe forearms
of a wayward adolescence.
Your keloid tissue shines silvery
as snail slime, meandering
down the scratching posts of my limbs.

Now I am in preservation mode—
moisturize after every shower,
stay out of the sun, avoid parabens
and parfums, leaf through magazines
in search of the latest miracle cream,
functional food, do everything
to prolong youth. To give you
that satin texture, that radiant glow.
Line the pockets of Estée Lauder,
the dermatologists at Clinique, even when
there's no money for the mortgage.

These days, you don't need a punched window
or a razor blade to register damage—
a mosquito bite, a scratched hive
will leave a stain that takes six months to fade.

Pregnant

SOUVANKHAM THAMMAVONGSA

The words we use to describe it in Lao is *teu phaa*

It means to hold a split, to hold a splitting, to carry around a split

Whatever you think you are or was, split

Not split open and broken away, but the split that is still hinged
   there, the coming-apart that hadn't caught on to anything to
   break off

To have never carried that split, to not know

What then do you know you have:

A sanding-down, a knowledge of repair and mechanic, how to keep
   wood to wood

Amah

DEVYANI SALTZMAN

I FOUND HER IN LITERATURE ONLY ONCE, hiding in Salman Rushdie's short story "The Courter." London, 1962, an Indian nanny walking down a street in Kensington with the edge of her "red-hemmed white sari" in hand. Amah did the same as she cut through the pedestrian pathway at the end of our street, making a beeline for the 7-Eleven. But unlike Rushdie's Kensington ayah, Amah never met and fell in love with the Eastern European hall porter of her employer's building. She never had liaisons that involved a shared love of chess.

Amah came to Canada when I was eight weeks old. I was told that her husband beat her and drank, although I never met him and she never talked about the beatings. Romantic love was of no interest to her, and whenever she saw a couple kissing on television and in the movies, she'd say "*chee chee*" in disgust and turn away. She arrived in our lives through the recommendation of an aunt in Delhi. Her previous charges had been the children of diplomats, although I couldn't imagine Amah rotating through the three-year cycle of embassy employees. All we knew was that she had come from a village outside Bangalore in the south Indian state of Karnataka. She was illiterate, the mother of five daughters, and didn't know her own age.

Amah flew back to Toronto with my parents in January 1980. Canada required a work permit and a passport at that time, neither of which she had. My parents applied for both. As they filled out the work permit application before leaving India, my father explained that she would feel jet lag in the weeks after they arrived in Toronto. The city was ten hours behind Delhi; a different time zone, a different season. Amah just started laughing, her round belly heaved. "Sahib, everyone knows it's the same time everywhere."

My parents' first home was in a neighbourhood of red brick Victorian houses, professors, artists, and ex-hippies. It had two bedrooms, theirs and mine. Amah slept on the floor of the dining room, on a dark brown shag carpet between the radiator and the heavy wooden legs of the mahogany dining table. My first memory of her was as she slept, taking afternoon naps with the sunlight falling across her head, which lay cushioned on an outstretched arm. She kept her long black hair tied in a bun, and her belly gently rose and fell beneath a cotton sari. After she woke up, Amah would let me sit next to her under the dining table and look at the symmetrical tattoos on the tops of her hands and feet. Geometric designs in deep indigo, fading into her dark skin. One of our earliest conversations was about how she got them. Amah spoke broken English, Hindi, and the south Indian languages of Tamil, Telugu, and Kannada. She pointed at her hands and poked at the skin with her finger. The tattoos had been done with a sewing needle when she was very young. When she didn't sleep on the dining room floor she slept on a mattress that slid out from beneath my white IKEA bed.

In her twenty-three years in Canada, Amah had only two friends. Her first was Lucy, the Italian cleaning lady who came to our house once a week. Lucy was married, but she wore fitted black skirts and sleeveless black blouses as if she were a widow. They would sit on the stairs and talk during Lucy's lunch break, heavy Italian and Indian voices gossiping and complaining about the church. Both women were Catholic. Amah's patron saint was St. Anthony of Padua, a Franciscan always pictured with a child—the infant Jesus—and white lilies in his arms. Amah would sometimes walk the two blocks to Bathurst Street to visit Lucy in a little walk-up across from Steven's Grocery Store. She wore leather chappals on those walks, even in early winter after the first snowfall.

After a few years, we moved up the hill to a neighbourhood with detached houses. It would be where we lived until I went to university, and the last home Amah would know in North America. She graduated from her space on the dining room floor to a stucco apartment in the basement. It suited her—private and dark, with enough space for her two favourite possessions, a television and an altar. She spent her time saying the rosary by candlelight and watching *Magnum P.I.*, her favourite show.

The bedroom opened into a small, windowless antechamber that housed a cedar closet for her cotton saris and luggage. I hung three Indian prints on the wall in an effort to make it more home-like. As a teenager I thought she lived in near poverty; she thought she lived a life of privilege and thanked God every day. Her food, shelter, and medical expenses were taken care of, and she made weekly phone calls to her daughter Rita in Delhi to make sure the remittances had been received. I had no idea where her other four daughters lived or what they did. Their names were Violet, Mary, Iris, and Rose. We heard that

Amah's husband died at a home for disenfranchised men in New Delhi a few years after she immigrated, and that Violet died of cancer soon afterwards. The only photo Amah had in her room was a preschool photo of me wearing blue OshKosh overalls. She kept it in a plastic frame, nailed into the stucco between the television and the altar.

Eleven years after Amah's immigration, my parents divorced. Mom moved into a townhouse down the street, and for the next seven years Amah, Dad, and I would form an unorthodox nuclear family—a south Indian Catholic, a Jew, and a lonely child. My bedroom was two floors above Amah's, at the front of the house. In summer the ivy would grow thick, and I could barely see outside my bay window. Amah's room became my escape, a safe haven that smelled of must and the betel nut mixed with tobacco that she would chew for a mild high, staining her mouth a permanent red. She became my family then. "*Ro mat, beti*," she would say, the only woman there to urge me not to cry as she folded her betel nut and tobacco into a paan in the darkness of that basement room.

We spent time together in the kitchen, she on a worn wicker chair pushed against the wall below our wall-mounted phone, me eating her homemade *rajma chawal* at the white kitchen counter. During Christmas dinner and Passover she refused to eat with us at the same dining table she used to sleep under, instead taking her plate of food to the privacy of her basement room.

Amah decided to retire when I was too old to be fed every meal and when I preferred the company of friends to our shared space in the kitchen. I never thought that she would leave us. It was devastating, but I had little time to consider the vacuum created by her departure to Delhi. Our family friends and neighbours asked after her: "How's Amah?" But my father had already begun searching for a replacement, and I just felt hollow whenever her name was mentioned. She had lived in Toronto for thirteen years, a landed immigrant who never chose to sponsor her children.

Amah was replaced by a Jamaican woman named Angela. She left her six-year-old son behind in Port Antonio to inherit Amah's basement apartment with attached cedar closet. She made the best spaghetti and meat sauce, but she didn't love me. Amah had raised me, rubbing my infant arms with Johnson & Johnson baby oil to stimulate growth, putting gold jewellery aside for the dowry she imagined I would have as an adult.

Amah-less, I began to notice women always on the move outside my bay window—pushing children in light-framed strollers, helping them out of minivans along with bags of groceries, answering the door in striped cotton T-shirts and flip-flops. They drove and had friends and went out on weekends (to sing karaoke at the strip malls at Bathurst and Wilson). They were a new kind of Amah, supported by social networks, mobile. Young. Ninety percent of domestic caregivers in Canada were Filipino women, brought into the country by nanny agencies and church networks, Olivias and Joannas who, in the words of one British journalist, "rubbed in the sore point that the feminism of the 1970s would have been broken by the insoluble problem of how to continue career and family if domestic servitude hadn't been neatly passed from one group of women to another."

A young Filipino man was interviewed in *The Georgia Straight* about the difficulties reconnecting with his mother after she sponsored him to Canada. She was required to work twenty-four months in a three-year period before applying for landed immigrant status, and only then was she able to sponsor him. He was six when she left him, twelve when they reunited. The difficulties of their lost time haunted him even in adulthood.

A BBC photographer did a photo essay on a Filipino nanny named Josie Pingkihar, working in Hong Kong. Of the US$470 she made a month, $390 was remitted to her family. With $80 a month in pocket money, she cared for a six-year-old Chinese girl and slept on the floor of her bedroom, much like Amah and me. Her own children had started calling her "Aunty." In 2005 Filipino nannies sent home US$10 billion from around the globe. According to the Central Bank of the Philippines, women caring for other women's children contributed 13.2 percent to the country's economic growth.

Amah came out of retirement when I was fifteen. She phoned my father from Delhi and told him that she missed me. She moved back as if she'd never left. However, the Amah who came back to a half-empty stucco house was no longer the woman who rubbed my arms with baby oil, but someone I would begin introducing as my grandmother, out of a combination of guilt for having a nanny and pride for someone I loved. She had lived for two years with her daughter Rita and Rita's husband, Cheena.

It was unclear if the money she had earned in Toronto was in her own bank account or theirs.

Amah had aged, and as a result she no longer had specific duties. She would come to my bedroom in the mornings of my years in high school, letting in the dog as she told me to wake up, balancing on the thick soles of her bare feet, which were made rough by years of not wearing shoes. Her place in my room was a pine rocking chair with a quilted floral pillow. She would sit down in the chair and undo the massive bun carefully pinned to the back of her head. Her hair was still black, but thinning. Amah would pull it down past her shoulders and place strands of hair across her lap. She had bulked it up with extensions, bought at a Jamaican hair salon on St. Clair Avenue, down the street from the 7-Eleven. Since none of us knew her age it was estimated to be somewhere around sixty. A birth date was chosen randomly—December 1—halfway between my father's and mine.

As soon as I got my driver's licence, I began driving her to Gerrard Street on the weekends. Saturdays had been her market days, when we would go to Little India for vegetables and *bhel poori* at Bombay Bhel. Now she would sit peacefully beside me in a sari and green jacket as I drove the two of us down the Danforth. We drank south Indian coffee and ate *dosas* at the Madras Dhaba. Afterwards we would cruise the video stores for the newest Bollywood titles. It was my way of reconnecting her with her south Indian roots, the next level after hanging Indian prints on her bedroom wall.

After graduating from high school, I was accepted into a university in England. The year I left was the year that my father's girlfriend moved in. Amah's work now involved making the occasional cup of tea and cooking whenever she felt the desire to. Her monthly wage remained the same. She continued her walks to the 7-Eleven and Loblaws, but she stayed in her basement room more and more. My father and his girlfriend were both empty nesters who had inherited my nanny, and Amah's Tupperwared Indian food remained untouched in the fridge. It was in that year Amah made her second, and last, friend, in twenty-three years.

Joanne was completing her doctorate in economics at the University of Toronto. She worked part time as a teaching assistant and part time in my father's office. During my school terms in England, it was Joanne who earned Amah's trust and offered the support I wished I could give her. In the middle of winter, thin, blond Joanne would help Amah, increasingly arthritic, into her second-hand Saab, which smelled of cigarettes, and drive her to Loblaws, or the bank, or Little India.

One holiday, Amah began rubbing her knees and told my father that the flights of stairs had become too much. Whenever I was at home I sat at the foot of her wicker chair and rested my head on her legs, offering to massage them. After all, it was my growing up that led to her redundancy. When I went back to England, it was Joanne's idea that Amah join the South Asian Women's Association. Joanne drove her to a community centre near Bloor and Lansdowne once a month. After the tenth time Amah told Joanne and my father that she didn't want to go back. Why waste her time with a bunch of old women gossiping about their husbands, she said. Hers was already dead. Anyway, he was someone she would rather forget. Amah returned to her basement room, the monthly remittances to Rita, and her daily contact with love—Joanne.

Dad told me he was letting go of Amah in the fall. The ivy covering the house had turned and the neighbourhood's nannies were busy seeing their wards off to school. Amah didn't want to go back to India. At twenty-three, I didn't want her to go either. I resented my father for forcing her retirement after two decades of service. She was my grandmother, our responsibility—Amah to countless neighbours and friends. How could she be sent away? But there was no choice. Even though she had savings, she couldn't manage an apartment on her own. Amah had no other friends and family in Canada. No network beyond our house, the 7-Eleven, and the discount shops on St. Clair and Gerrard where she would haggle for goods. But there was another reason she had to leave, more painful than the logistics of surviving on her own. I too wanted my own life, and there was no room for my nanny in a grown-up world. I related to Rushdie's narrator in "The Courter": "For years now I've been meaning to write down the story of Certainly-Mary, our ayah, the woman who did as much as my mother to raise my sisters and me." Twenty-three years after immigrating, Amah would go home to India. Remitted. Returned.

Laxmi Nagar lies in the north end of New Delhi, on the eastern side of the Jamuna. The lower-middle-class neighbourhood is squeezed between a congested roadway, funnelling traffic from the bridge, and the exposed sandy banks of the river. It takes forty minutes to reach Amah from my maternal grandparents' home—Amah, my other grandmother, now living in an apartment with her blood daughter.

The market below her apartment is crowded with clothing shops and general stores selling her beloved betel nut and tobacco.

The taxi stops in front of a low-rise block of apartments. Rita is waiting at the bottom of a concrete staircase. She is now in her late thirties; a little younger than Amah was when she came to Canada in 1980. She has dark skin and sad eyes. Whenever I phoned for Amah, I spoke to Rita, and now, greeting her, I feel the shame of a cowering dog that knows it has transgressed. Somewhere, I always knew I took this woman's mother away from her. Now, at our convenience, it is this daughter who will care for the aging mother who never wanted to return.

Rita leads me up the stairs to a double entrance, a locked iron gate with a wooden door behind. A young woman answers the door wearing a salwar kameez and dupatta tied as if she's been working, sleeves and hair pulled back. She is Amah's maid, Sangeeta. Amah's own domestic servant. Sangeeta lets us in. The apartment has three bedrooms and a narrow living room painted cream. A small balcony overlooks the telephone lines and market below. One bedroom is Rita's, one is Amah's, and the third is devoted to Rita's shrine—an extensive collection of Hindu, Christian, and Buddhist images placed in an aluminum mandir.

"Devyani *ayaa?*" I can hear Amah ask if I've come as Rita leads the way.

"*Hah,* Amahji." I've come, I say. The only reason my Hindi is alive is because we've spoken it together since I was a baby.

She's excited, sitting on her single bed, much thinner than I remember. It has been two years, and although I've spoken to her on the phone, I've never met her outside of the home we shared together. Our home.

"*Bheto, rani. Bheto.*" She pats the bed as she barks orders. "*Arre* Sangeeta, *chai banayo!*" Someone else can make the tea.

There is a white dog tied outside on the balcony, barking incessantly. Rita's Pomeranian, Lily. There's an Alsatian as well, a large female named Nancy. She sits loyally at Amah's feet and reminds me of the golden retriever Amah left behind. Rita disappears into the kitchen. Only then do I feel comfortable hugging Amah, but what I really want to do is put my head on her lap and sleep like a baby. Instead I examine her room: a television, her own bathroom, a ceiling fan. Screwed into the wall is a white shelf, and on it is her altar, a perfect reproduction of the one in her stucco Toronto room. At least St. Anthony and the Virgin protect her in Laxmi Nagar, I think. There is only one photo on the wall, above a light switch glowing red, and it's of me. It's the same preschool photo in blue OshKosh that has always been in her room. I wish I could give this woman everything, but I cannot blame my father for wanting his freedom.

"Daddy *thik hai?* Patricia *thik hai?*" She listens intently to news from home.

"Are you okay, Amah?"

"*Kya Karo?*" What can I do? she says. She gives her shoulders a disheartened shrug as she takes betel nut out of a plastic case normally used for film. "Daddy *nahin rakha.*" Daddy didn't keep me.

I listen as she tells me how much she detests India. The food is expensive: rice, meat. The phone gets cut if she doesn't pay extra. She misses Canada. But I look around, and she owns this apartment, she has people to care for her, we send her money to help her out, and I realize it's more than food and comfort she craves, it's being Amah. Her home hasn't been taken away from her; her purpose has.

Rita comes in with tea and snacks, and I let go of Amah's hand. Amah gives me a gold necklace with a pendant shaped like three Victoria head coins. She asks me when I'm going to get married.

"When you have a home and husband. I'll come and stay with you," she says, smiling. She chews her paan and refuses to eat, insisting I do. Rita sips her tea and tells me that Amah loves to watch the Discovery Channel. When Amah's busy packing away her betel nut and tobacco, Rita looks right at me for the first time, and asks me the only thing she will ever ask me.

"Sponsor me."

Writing, In Transit

NAJWA ALI

I. Possible Causes

Because women's graves in my family's small graveyard in Zanzibar bear no names, no writing. The men's names curl on the gravestones in Gujarati above verses in Arabic, Urdu, and Farsi.

Because I spent too long a time figuring ways to resist easy narratives but instead found myself in a corner, silenced.

Because this tongue, English, was never my own. I fall in and out of love and turn it to my use.

Because English speaks Empire. Thus my story and its own translations.

Because translation, sediment, betrayed origins, whisperings is what I learned in my four corners of the world. And I paid attention.

Because new imperialisms, globalization, *The New York Times*, CNN, CBC, and all the world's writers are hunting for stories to sell. The difference now, is in the telling. Who, out there, is listening?

Because I do not want to be told.

Because they said *Shant bes! Modhu bundh rakh—Sit quiet! Shut your mouth!* and I, afraid, escaped to another tongue thinking they could not follow me. I was wrong. Wrong to have escaped. Wrong to think they could not follow me.

Because escape to English built new walls around me. It took years of work to figure a way out.

Because Gujarati, my mother tongue, was already lost to me in writing, as was my mother. We were thrice displaced and there was never just one breast to drink from.

Because tongues gathered in my mouth and sometimes I grew mute with their quarrels. I was hungry for books and had never known land.

Because I learned early on that art has consequence. Faiz exiled in Beirut; Ngugi's escape; Darwish's endless wandering; Fahmida crossing the bloodied border of her tongue; Forugh reviled, her poems banned. *Bol*, I heard Faiz say in Urdu, *Speak!*

Because language bears more than its own history. And writing, we force it up against what is untranslatable. That is what interests me.

Because men from Toronto's mosques came to my father's house and made plans to burn *The Satanic Verses*. I had to serve them tea.

Because I spoke out. A man, stranger to the house, told me to shut up. My father first said *let her speak* but then interrupted me mid-sentence and said *that's enough.*

Because one day they found my love letters, written by a woman. Someone said *she should be raped and killed.* I crossed two states to escape a line.

Because a threat is a powerful incentive—to writing and to silence.

Because there are things I alone know that no one has talked about. But also, I invent.

Because here, in this part of the world, they can simply ignore you, or imagine they have reinvented you.

Because war begins with words—only some words survive but they change all meaning.

Because writing is the one place I can move borders, reach out to the living and the dead.

Because writing, I am always ahead of myself.

II. Routes, Byways, Borders, Deflections

A literary agent in Toronto says: *What's hot these days is Bombay. Everyone in Europe wants to read about India.* She suggests nobody would want to read about immigrants in Europe. As she speaks, a young man from my hometown appears in my head. He is cleaning a toilet in Stockholm. I listen to her speak but the man in my head grows stronger than her words. I imagine his dark hands scrubbing the white porcelain; I imagine his curiosity about the city he has entered. I try and hear the way Swedish words sit on his tongue, the way the grey boats in the harbour are like nothing he remembers. I watch him learn the edges of his skin. I wonder if he writes letters home to his mother. I wonder how his Swahili changes its inflections, if his memories of home are disappearing. The man teaches himself English in an Internet cafe at night. He dreams of joining his sister in Toronto. He is starting to write down all that he is afraid he will forget. The agent is now saying *Europeans are not interested in Black writing from Canada.*

Dilemma for the transplanted migrant writer: Will you now become a tourist guide to the place which you have lost?

The writer's business is to contemplate experience, not to be merged in it.[i]

Bombs explode in Bombay. Youthful gunmen terrorize hotels. Tourists seeking *shanti* are hurt or killed. As are Indians—guests, waiters, cooks, those passing by. Frantic, I tap out messages on my cellphone, try to reach my mother still visiting relatives in Bhavnagar. In two days she is due to arrive in Bombay.

When we see two similar events separated by time, it's as if we are watching an intriguing pattern unfolding before we know exactly what the pattern is.[ii]

Two decades ago, my uncle's body on fire in Dongri, the poor Muslim quarter of Bombay. Twelve years ago, over two thousand Muslims killed in Gujarat, a right-wing Hindu stronghold.

The writer writes, immersed, unnerved. Distance is metaphoric. Words cross. As do love, terror, and longing. But distance is real. Geographical. She counts the kilometres, the stretch of water and land. The money it costs to cross actual boundaries. She writes, interrupted. Receives phone calls, watches the news on television, sends emails. She knows the story will not end here. She waits beside electronic instruments, watchful, listening.

∽◦

What do you know? the writers ask the would-be writer. *Write about the everyday*, they urge, *describe things accurately. Learn your genre. Your gender*, she translates. *Your proper form.*

It was never a lack of things to write about. What stopped her was a kind of dread, an exhaustion at having to translate, to explain what, for her, was ordinary. The ones who understood, who shared her sense of story, were too busy working long hours—driving taxis, packing boxes in factories, selling cloth or machine drills. The ones with leisure for literature had arrived to this country in vastly different ways. They structured their gaze with a different code, their mouths set into English long before their arrival here.

Sometimes she wants to shelter her stories behind words—a niqab of sorts. The English language, foreign yet intimate, would never be transparent. The thought is oddly comforting.

∽◦

A writer looking for subjects inquires not after what (s)he loves best, but after what (s)he alone loves at all. Strange seizures beset us.[iii]

Strange seizures beset us. This morning, waking once again to a street, half-imagined, half-memorized. Crows flying out. The sound of *adhaan*. The tap-tapping of a cane down the street. The whole body heaving awake with this. Pain solid, somewhere in the region of the heart. Pain familiar. Nothing to be shared.

Writing may rise from this, but inherently mobile, it moves, dislocates such pain and oddly abstracts it by beauty.

Strange seizures beset us. Through English, words come from a place she has never visited. A poet, Chilean:

> *We asked the ocean for its rose,*
> *its open star, its bitter contact*[iv]

Seven years ago, my aunt died in Dar es Salaam, still struggling with forty years of exile. Like my mother, she was not allowed to go to school after she reached puberty. She taught herself from the books of brothers and sisters younger, luckier, than her. She read voraciously: Swahili newspapers, Gujarati novels, the Qur'an in Arabic, Farsi and Arabic novels translated into English that her son mailed from Vancouver.

A writer's work is important to the extent that the ideal bookshelf on which (s)he would like to be placed is still an improbable shelf, containing books that we do not usually put side by side, the juxtaposition of which can produce electric shocks, short circuits.[v]

Her conversations with me about the things she read, her stories of her own life, of the lives of those she lived in such deep community with— her words flood my mind at her death.

Orality and Literacy. So much of what we have lived through is unwritten. Powerful censors still prohibit the telling of certain tales— what gets told at a kitchen counter or while squatting on a cement floor, slicing onions and green chilies.

After her death, the family gathers on the carpet of her home, the only place constant in our various exiles. A relative, an old woman, visits to console us—when I ask her questions about her own life, she holds my hands. Only then does she speak.

On my table, dictionaries—English, Kiswahili, Gujarati, Urdu, Arabic. Nights I scour the Internet gathering news of all I was never able to learn before. Histories of my birthplace. Of the places I lived before I ended up here. I read words written by those privileged enough to choose travel, those able to select objects of study. Sometimes I feel like an object, an artifact, something to be written about by others more sophisticated, more powerful, more "at home" in this, their native tongue. Writing, they enter a vast library that they and their forefathers have constructed about people like us. It is one among several libraries I dream my words will gather within, dislodge texts, unsettle old phrases with their presence.

Not knowing enough, crafted "inauthentic" by multiple migrancies, I invent instead, building worlds out of gathered fragments and incomplete archives. Art, I believe, comes out of the possibilities of a different recollection. An unexpected angle of vision. Accidental juxtapositions that become charged with truth. Authenticity becomes yet another story and I open its seams, check out its making, its lineage of makers.

Other libraries are oral, held in gossip or rumour. She has heard these gather in Gujarati, Urdu, or Kiswahili, sometimes in creolized mixtures of these tongues. She has listened to recitations in the courtyards of mosques, in homes, alleyways, and graveyards. Writing, she knows she will be unheard, unread, ineffectual in such gatherings. She dreams her stories will get translated by gossip, will travel and arrive in mouths and ears like unintended rumours. She knows she will lose control over her endings. She knows scandal will follow. That there may be consequences.

A literary situation begins to get interesting when one writes novels for people who are not readers of novels alone, and when one writes literature while thinking of a shelf of books that are not all literary.[vi]

Wittgenstein wrote: *The limits of my language mean the limits of my world.*[vii] Incomplete in several languages, I grow heartened in the places I rub against the edges of different tongues. The world's languages push against this English I write, they work their way in, ingeniously trespass. Writing, I imagine my text will become a conduit for illegal traffic, a body to incubate a different type of future—fractured, polyphonic, cacophonous, but sutured with silence, with all that remains impossible to put into words.

Things aren't all so tangible and sayable as people would usually have us believe, most experiences are unsayable. They happen in a space that no word has ever entered and more unsayable than all other things are works of art, those mysterious existences, whose life endures beside our own small, transitory life.[viii]

Another library, endless rows, enough space: the shelves are populated with volumes of complicated questions phrased with uncommon beauty.

༄

Finally, concentration is one translation of "dhyana," the Sanskrit term—source of the Chinese "chan" and Japanese "zen"—that describes the one-pointed mind of meditation.[ix]

Reading, I find myself interrupted. A word in another language, and immediately, a whole new string of connotations, of sentences extending in ways unmeant by the author.

Dhyan raakhjo, my mother says, as I leave her house. *Take care*, she says, afraid of what the outside will hold. *Dhyaan rakh*, I tell myself as I start to write. Take care, concentrate, focus. The invocation in both instances is toward pure survival. Keep your wits about you; the world is hostile, full of distraction, full of accident.

But sometimes, writing also means submitting to chance, to distraction, to unexpected dislocations. I write a poem, a good one, I think. It is built entirely out of chance connections, found fragments of language. What holds it all together is a profound, concentrated anger hemmed by grief. But I have taken care, *dhyan raakhine*, not to let this leak into the poem. Instead the language is sparse, distant, carefully collected and assembled. The anger is coded, it feels like ice. I share the poem with readers; some are excited by the radical polyphony of the form, others prefer individual fragments.

Anger need not be mentioned by name. But it must be embodied in the movement & texture & pitch of the recollection.[x]

I listen to comments on form, on words, on technique. I notice that few of my Canadian readers catch my references to medieval Arabic literature, to contemporary torture techniques, or to processes of secret rendition. All these seem obvious to me, embedded carefully in the lines. A gap opens between the text I have written and these well-educated, sensitive readers. We meet within a specific field of a specific language only to discover that we have been produced as readers and writers by vastly different but deeply connected historical processes. I find myself refusing to translate the references, reluctant to make the poem so easy to access, consumable, I think. In the process, I know I lose some readers.

Literature is not school. Literature must presuppose a public that is more cultured, and more cultured than the writer (her)self. Whether or not such a public exists is unimportant.[xi]

III. Limits

The writer knows (her) field—what has been done, what could be done, the limits . . . Only after the writer lets literature shape her can she perhaps shape literature. The art must enter the body too.[xii]

I begin by writing essays, trials in thought. An editor at a magazine reads one and decides to call it "literary journalism." Another calls it "literary non-fiction." A lover of Montaigne, I prefer the old word, I essay out, searching. A poet reads it, says "your lines are like poetry." Encouraged, I begin to study the genre, unfamiliar with its possibilities in the English language. In poetry, more than anywhere else, I find myself reaching the limits of my language, stumbling in my mouth for words; I find myself constantly, imperfectly, translating. The purity of a lyric voice becomes increasingly impossible and my poems become assemblages, cut up from a reality too insistent in the present. In another vein, I return to translating Urdu ghazals, Swahili proverbs, with dictionaries under my arms. I cross genres, write critical elliptical ghazals in English, cryptic aphorisms. I note how certain images recur in my poems. Coastal objects, ephemera from particular moments in the 1970s in Tanzania, in Pakistan. I make lists in my notebooks. Gather. I realize this may not be useful here, but elsewhere. Things to carry over.

Crossing: the Novel. I begin one, what instinctively I know will be my second one. Its method resembles the poems I will later write and learn from. But here, starting, the project grows wildly, uncontrollable. I quickly learn I don't yet know how to do this. I return to what I think is my first novel.

Working with old notes, abandoned poems, fragments, ideas, an insistent constellation of questions about movement, about place and time—and so a story grows. But first, a voice enters my head: insistent, singular, lyric. I am uncomfortable with this. Suspicious of first-person narratives, of linearity, of the world seen through one person's eyes. But the voice, oceanic, obsessive, refuses to leave. I type it down and stories emerge.

I begin to question the genre into which the stories manifest. A girl-child, moving, narrating, growing *Bildungsroman,* I recognize, exasperated. The story of the consolidation of the Western subject. What use is this to my Third World girl-child telling? I grow anxious. I do not want her to consolidate. Movement, I believe, will make her shatter. I want her to shatter but she coheres nonetheless through all the catastrophes she endures. She listens, my mini-Scheherazade, she collects. She gathers the memories of others like shells and holds these to her ears. She narrates and, obedient, I write.

Reality intervenes. In the city where I write, a girl dies, murdered by her father. Interrupted, I write an essay rapidly, grief-stricken, my own memories wakened. I know too well how the Western media will tell the story. Writing, I realize I do not want to tell the dead girl's story. I write a piece in fragments, sentences float unmoored in my text. I want my writing to deflect, to radiate, to enact the way my own mind wanders through its grief. This essay, written, revised, languishes on my desk for two years. I find myself reluctant, frightened to publish it.

Aware that it reveals brief but startling details about my own life, my family's threats, my deep fears. I know how easy it would be to misread this, to turn heartfelt truths to stereotype and dogma. I know too well the recuperative power of a reader too quick to pity, too full of her own cultural certainties.

The novel with its effort, its pages, its careful concatenation of voices, its journeys through time and space, becomes refuge. Fictional, I find myself carried by the narrative's own patterns, its waves eddy and fall. Story opens and leads to places I could not have imagined, each line opening to another. Hope resides in this, I think, writing freed from the real world's constraint.

I swear to myself I will never write another essay. And if reality threatens or intervenes, poetry, I imagine, might allow me a different way to approach life's immediacy, its insistent present.

There are no safe territories. The work itself is and has to be a battleground.[xiii]

ENDNOTES:

i. Flannery O'Connor, "The Nature and Aim of Fiction" in *The Writer's Craft*, ed. John Hersey (Knopf, 1974), 56.
ii. Charles Baxter, "Rhyming Action" in *Burning Down the House: Essays on Fiction* (Graywolf Press, 1998), 146.
iii. Annie Dillard, *The Writing Life* (Harper and Row, 1989), 67.
iv. Pablo Neruda, "Love For This Book," trans. Clark Zlotchew and Dennis Maloney. <http://www.poets.org/viewmedia.php/prmMID/16755>.
v. Italo Calvino, "Whom Do We Write For? Or The Hypothetical Bookshelf" in *The Uses of Literature* (Harcourt Brace & Co., 1986), 82.
vi. Ibid, 82.
vii. Ludwig Wittgenstein, *Tractatus Logico-Philosophicus: proposition 5.6* <http://www.iep.utm.edu/w/wittgens.htm>.
viii. Rainer Maria Rilke, "Letter One" in *Letters to a Young Poet*, trans. Stephen Mitchell (Vintage, 1986), 4.
ix. Jane Hirschfield, "Poetry and the Mind of Concentration" in *Nine Gates: Entering the Mind of Poetry* (Harper Perennial, 1997), 7.
x. Dennis Lee, "Polyphony: Enacting a Meditation" in *Body Music* (House of Anansi, 1998), 52.
xi. Italo Calvino, 85.
xii. Annie Dillard, 69.
xiii. Italo Calvino, 88.

Listing

CHIMWEMWE UNDI

in dog years, I am dead. in black years, alive.
so: exceptional, increasingly so. I ask strangers
for directions on pocket scraps and build myself
a map home as cohesive as a litany
I am having trouble remembering.

there are too many bodies in this room built for bodies
we are magic typecast as disappearing acts. History
whispered into memories.

and easier things:
1. the prime ministers in chronological order,
2. My Very Educated Mother Just Served Us Nachos,
3. the angle at which the earth leans, shaking us off like water

there is too much to say for this mouth built for praying
there are too many names to unhear
so I don't have to remember
or truly, repeat to meaninglessness
or truly, forget them,
outrage a poor mnemonic device

I am forgetting and that is the worst part
I cannot hold a name long enough
to know it. even the faces are growing statistical,
the write-ups into archives. I know guilt better
than grief, as well as a restlessness,
better than a black body breathing still

Reading this list of names, I find myself

CARA-LYN MORGAN

sticken.
An infant lost in the wild prairie,
thistles and thorny grass
bloodying my skin. Tonight,
li noosim,
the granddaughter, I
am relearning my tongue.

I speak their names,
a stumble in this tongue
I know, the *moniyaw* tongue
the white man's tongue
that rejected their spirit names
replaced them with bible names
incorrectly spelled.
I ask them to return to me
in the smudge of sage
let me not be abandoned.

Ni nokoms, long abandoned, all
but these dustsoft pages,
these air-blurred photos,
stern, heavy women.
I want to hold their black braids
like an ox-tether, I want
to wrap their woolen
shawls across my shoulders.

I call to my body the curl
of their old fingerprints, that they may
enter me like thunder, *li toneur*
that shakes the barns
and flickers the lights.

In my most quiet calling,
I speak their grandmother names
the left behind names
the only names that remain.

Sophia Bird, born 1792
Catherine, second wife
of Henry Hallet (first wife
unnamed, call "Indian"), Catherine,
daughter of Marie Pruden,
Suzette born 1815, Clementine,
mother of Catherine, who married
a Scotsman, Margrette Monkman
born 1832, Nancy Bird, mother
of Charlotte, dateless,
Caraline Cote born 1847,
Mary Inkster born 1848
come awake.

Come awake Mabel Monkman, born 1853,
my mother's grandmother
Mabel Monkman with the white bone lighter,
who clipped horse-shaped barrettes
in my mother's hair
remember to me the warm salt smell
of bannock in the outside oven
the smoke of walleye
on the river stones
enter me like the poplar
fluff that whitens the roadsides
and covers the grass
remember to me
my spirit name
let me not be forgotten.

As Long As You Look Hurt

KELLEE NGAN

MONA HAS BEEN GONE FOR NINETEEN HOURS. True, she's been away longer before, but this time feels different. She took the leftover pizza from last night, box and all. She never stays away long enough to miss more than one meal. Not until now.

Mona just turned seventeen. She's too old for an Amber Alert, and too messed up for our mum to make a call. Mum never panics. She folds socks and prunes her bonsai tree.

"Mona is being Mona," she says. "And Mona always comes back."

"How do you know for sure?" I say.

"I feel it in my bones. Now, don't you have something better to do?"

I should probably study for my physics test tomorrow. Cram my head with facts about velocity, distance, and relativity. Mona has the test too, but no one expects her to show up for anything but lunch or third-period biology lab. Mona likes dissecting animals and drawing human body parts. I like numbers and theories. Sometimes it's hard to tell that we're related.

I point to the window seat that has a view of the front walkway. "I'll read in here."

My mother eyes me over the edge of her ever-present coffee cup, the one with the cracked handle she got at Expo back in '86. "Study in your room," she says. "Mona won't care if you're up."

Mona misses me when she goes away. She wouldn't come home if she didn't. We're family—an unconventional one, but still. We were born forty-three weeks apart, as close as two sisters can be without being twins. Mona was a mistake my mother made. I was made to make up for that mistake. But my dad ended up leaving anyway. Mona's dad did the opposite. He never considered staying.

Something in Mona's blood makes her restless too. She paces a lot at home. Her footsteps thunder along the hardwood, and she howls about how she hates every minute of being alive. Then there's the dramatic crash and squeal of glass against glass and glass against floor and glass dragging against the skin of my sister's forearms. Her blood looks like mine, bright and thick like maple syrup, but there are secrets running through her veins that I just don't get.

Mum reacts the same way every time. She forces Mona over the sink and turns the cold water on. Bit by bit, drop by drop, my sister spirals down the drain.

"I'm making you a doctor's appointment," Mum will say.

Mona just laughs in her "so what?" kind of way, and we know that it won't make a difference. Mum patches her up and then lets her go. "You're just like your father," she says.

Mona first disappeared when she was twelve. She did it again at thirteen and has taken off a million times since then.

The last time she left, I helped myself to her hairbrush. It's an antique from our grandmother, made of sandalwood and wild boar bristles. Gran gave it to Mona one Christmas. All I ever get from her are extra-large sweatshirts and other things to grow into.

When Mona came back that night, I smelled her before I could see her. She reeked of hot dogs, seaweed, and cigarettes. I hugged her anyway, squeezed her until the stink on her skin sank into mine. Her shoulders softened for a second until she saw the brush on the nightstand.

She jerked back and untangled herself from my arms. Then she grabbed the brush and tapped me repeatedly on the forehead with the handle until I blindly swatted at her to stop.

"Chinese water torture," she said. "Who said you could touch my stuff?"

"I was just borrowing it," I said. "Mum thinks we should share."

"We don't share anything," she said. "None of my shit is yours."

She ripped handfuls of my hair from the bristles and scowled. "You couldn't even clean it out?"

I shrugged. I didn't think it meant anything to her. She would've taken it with her otherwise.

Mona stopped picking at the brush and stared at the reddening depression between my eyebrows. She pushed on it, scrubbed it with her fingers as if trying to remove a stain.

"Ouch," I said. "That stings."

"Sorry," she said. "I didn't mean to hurt you."

I believed her, even when no one else did.

Mona has been missing for twenty-two hours and I'm done learning about gravity from a textbook.

Mum is asleep in the living room recliner. The TV is still on, the evening news giving way to talk shows and infomercials. I guess important things don't happen after eleven o'clock at night. The empty coffee cup lies by Mum's feet, overturned and facing outward. There are brown stains on the inside of the cup, pink lips stamped to the edge. The telephone rests in her lap. She snores lightly, the tension in her forehead easing with every breath. Her mouth softens into a straight line, an almost smile.

I leave a note on the kitchen table and take ten dollars in case of emergency. I put the money and a granola bar in my jeans pocket, along with Mona's hairbrush. I've left a few of my black hairs tangled in its teeth. I want her to see them and to yell at me. It'll be nice to hear her voice again.

The neighbourhood is quiet, which is normal for a school night. I roll my bike out through all the sets of doors between our apartment and the sidewalk. My plan is to ride around to all the places I think Mona might be, all the places I'm not allowed to go. Not at night, anyway. Not alone.

I check the schoolyard, the hockey rink, and the twenty-four-hour convenience store. There are people out, but none of them are Mona. The rink and the school parking lots are empty, except for the cars of the overnight cleaning staff and shopping carts filled with plastic bottles and pop cans. Some homeless guys root through the recycling, pulling leftovers from takeaway bags. I leave the granola bar on a bench, broken in four but still in the wrapper.

Then I walk into the convenience store and watch the clerk rearrange the Ruffles bags, alphabetically by flavour.

"The ride stays outside," he says.

I prop my bike against the magazine rack. "I don't have a lock."

He eyes me suspiciously until I pull Mona's high school ID card from my pocket.

"Have you seen her?" I ask.

"She buys licorice and Red Bull," he says.

I nod. "She stays up late a lot."

He adjusts his black-rimmed glasses and lowers his voice. "Is she in trouble?" He shifts from one foot to another and shuffles a couple of lighters in his hand like poker chips. "I didn't have anything to do with it."

"I know," I say. Something in his discomfort hits me. He doesn't even know Mona but he feels guilty. But it's not him. He's not the man she's looking for.

Mona sits behind me in biology lab. We're arranged alphabetically. My first name beats her by one letter. We both have Mum's last name, although Mona asks for teachers to change the roll call and use her dad's. He comes at the beginning of the alphabet while Mum comes at the end. No teacher has separated us yet.

Last week, while Mrs. Lum lectured about Gregor Mendel, Mona threw a pencil at the back of my head and inched her seat forward to talk to me.

"Amazing, eh," she said. "This shit about gene variation?"

"I didn't think you cared," I said.

"Are you kidding me?" she said. "It explains everything."

Then she grabbed the metal compass from my pencil case and slashed open her palm.

I passed out immediately. When I came to, I was in the nurses' office. Mona hovered nearby, still holding up her now-bandaged hand for me to see. The blood had seeped through the gauze and formed a purple spot in the middle that looked vaguely like a nucleus splitting in two.

"What did you do that for?" I said. "Mum's going to kill you."

"Scientific proof," she said and pointed to her wound. "Half the shit in here is from him."

It's nearly impossible to find a phone book in this city. There aren't many public booths anymore, and the ones that do exist are filled with tumbleweeds or psychos. The first two I stop at are occupied. The woman in the second one is trying to rip off the machine. She gives me an evil stare as if I'm after the quarters too, as if I'm just waiting for her to fail. She bangs at the number pad repeatedly and screams, "Try your call again!" at the top of her lungs. Then the man in the booth beside her comes out, licking his palms. I keep riding.

I go to the hospital. I should've come here in the first place. It's quiet and no one ever questions why you're there as long as you look hurt. There's a sign saying "no cellphones," but tons of people are texting or trying to look inconspicuous by burrowing their heads into their jacket sleeves while they talk. I leave my bike by the hand-washing station, walk into the empty phone stall, and pick up the White Pages. I leaf through the Cs to the listing of the last name

Mona wishes were hers. There's only one in the book. It's the one Mona has been trying to find.

Mona has been missing for twenty-three hours and I have been missing for one. Mum is probably awake by now. She's probably noticed that I'm not there and kicked her cup in a panic. I bet she's tried calling my cell, then heard it ringing in my bedroom. But she shouldn't worry. I left her a note. I only had a torn corner of a piece of lined paper to write on, but I think I managed to say it all: *Dear Mum. I can't sleep. I need to see Mona home. L.*

I speed across the bridge alongside the late-night traffic. I head farther and farther north, away from the ocean toward the monster homes with three-car garages that our place could fit into three times over.

I ride up to the Tim Hortons drive-through and ask the lady for directions. She points to the closest hill and then points at my bike. "You should have lights on that thing," she says. She sounds just like my mother.

I don't stick around for a lecture. I thank her and speed off. Change gears to climb up the never-ending slope. Finally, I get to the address printed in the phone book. It's a giant brick box guarded by two carved lions on either side of the driveway. Here is where the other half lives.

A gate snakes around the perimeter. The sky-high steel bars have been painted with fake rust spots to make it look less imposing. They still shout "Stay out!" to me. I lean my bike against the closest lamp-post, then walk to the gate, press my face between two of the bars. Some porch lights are on for security. The Range Rover parked in the circular drive looks dusty and unused. There are no signs of life, except for a black dog sleeping near the doorway.

I kick the gate, frustrated. The metal vibrates and the pitchy creaks get louder and louder. It sounds like I'm trapped in a bell tower. I hold my breath and wait. Wait for the lights to turn on inside the house. Wait for the cops to show up. Wait for the dog to bark bloody murder.

But the dog's not making much of a stink, even as it lumbers toward me. I feel bad for waking it up. I should just leave it be. Back away, run home, and climb into bed before Mum sends out the search parties. The dog keeps coming, though, standing higher with each step until it's almost upright. I stare at its shape and try to figure out the breed. Maybe it's not even a dog. Could be a bear. A grizzly or a Kodiak. Something less domesticated.

Next there's a grunt and an outstretched arm. I match the gesture. I reach out, too, and grab the tips of her skinny fingers.

"Mona," I say. "What are you doing?"

She's hidden by the hood of her black sweatshirt, shrunken into the dark folds of fabric. But I can still see her. Still make out her familiar face. Her hair is twisted in static-y ropes, and her sad eyes look like Mum's, lost and disconnected. There's a smear of red sauce by her lip that I mistake, at first, for blood.

"I'm waiting," she says.

"Your dad's not here, is he?"

"I'm waiting," she repeats.

Mona slides down to her knees in front of the gate. I lower myself across from her and take the hairbrush from my pocket. I hold it up for her to see, my hair tangled in its teeth, but she doesn't complain. She just nods and puts her hand on my face. The scar on her palm scratches against my skin. She runs it across my forehead and down my cheeks, traces the visible veins, then stops at my temple and feels my heartbeat.

"Take me home?" she asks.

"Whenever you're ready," I say.

Mona's shoulders sag and she sinks into a heap again. She's too tired to stand. I sit beside her and run the brush through her knotted hair, trying my best to undo the snares.

Maheen's Collage

NILOFAR SHIDMEHR

Murder me if this is all it takes to make me beautiful
—Iranian proverb, only used by women

My mom loves us, loves to
make us beautiful,
make my sister and me
into one girl—
a pageant of Persia.

For this, she is going to slaughter us,
then select and refine
the body parts, which are good
for the marriage contest and bind
them together in a package
she proudly calls,
the daughter of Islamic Republic
of Maheen, ready and present
for judgment day.

The unwanted parts go to the garbage
like our umbilical cords did.
It brings no pain
to get rid of the undesired.

My mother first cuts off my breasts,
re-rounds them so that they'll pass
the pencil test and stick them
to the torso of my sister,
adorned with a flat belly that needs
no further trimming,
small from many years
of strict dieting.

Our legs have to be joined together
to be long enough, and she'll add
my slender arms, unwanted
black hair removed by laser.

The chosen face is my sister's:
she has already got a nose job
and made her cheeks stand out,
with the extra flesh she had
the surgeon remove from her behind.
But mother gouges out my eyes
to insert into the sockets
of that other daughter she fashions
for the jury's final decision.

My mother's ideal model
for each body part comes
from *Desperate Housewives*,
but not eyebrows—
they should be elaborate
and thick, like those of all thin Persian women
from classical miniatures.

Ass is not hard enough, my mother sighs,
as she lays our corpses flat,
side by side like twins
on a white and hard sanitized bed,
and cuts us part by part,
while with the gaze of a former judge—
my father's—she makes
her careful and hard choices.

Fishing

SERENA SHIPP

I HAVE NEVER FELT SO MUCH AND KNOWN SO LITTLE about anything as I do this.

Some days your pupils are two graphite-dirty holes where a geometric compass punctured the paper: a hardly visible sacrifice for a perfectly executed circle. On these days, when your pupils are hardly anything more than well-centred freckles, smaller than 2.8 mm if I had a tool to measure, there is a lot of room for colour. And you fill it well. Green mixed into green, scratched with blue and gold, dark and thicker than the Pacific. On these days I've come to recognize you are high on opiates.

Some days, those same pinholes wax too wide. They consume almost all your colour, leaving slight rings of gold to wrap around black sinking holes, left to hang limp like inverted moons in a bleach-yellow sky. On those days, I admire my own reflection in your fish-eye pupils and rarely trouble myself to guess what made them expand that way. Cocaine. Crack. Shitty ecstasy. Crystal methamphetamines—*batu*, Hawaii's drug of choice, thankfully not yours, but I know some days you dabble.

It seems these days, you take what you can get. And you can get a lot.

Our lives together have always been salted. Then roasted.

There are some aspects of our relationship that will never change. You are my brother, born four years, four months, and twenty-two days before me. We share our father's narrow feet, our mother's thick thumbs. We share the same blood flow, the same origins. You and I are so alike; some days it scares me.

I've always envied you; your sea-smarts; your lashes, like a camel's, black framing green; your native Sioux nose and skin tone; your mind's collected memories of our now-dead father—my mind whitewashed, too young, too long ago. I've always envied your courage and your goddamn charm.

The salt: the bloodstains on your hands, your blood or fish blood I'm never certain. I admire your hands, covered in scars and tattoos as they are. Your fingers, stiff and swollen from one too many bad breaks. Your calluses are thick yellow and your scars dark purple, never properly healed. On the topside of your right hand, there's an outlined map of the Hawaiian Islands, just in case you get lost. You will always have a map of home. And on your left hand, black ink looped around your second finger, as a wedding band of sorts. I keep expecting you to come home one of these days having chopped that finger off altogether.

"Fishing accident," you'd lie. And I'd encourage you to keep it in a Mason jar, pickled in formaldehyde, as a souvenir from a marriage that never actually happened. But you'd probably feed it to the fishes instead.

I've collected all the *Maui Time* newspaper clippings with you on the front page: local fisherman brings in 80 mahi mahi; local fisherman reels in 555-pound marlin; local fisherman hauls in over 1,000 pounds of bigeye tuna. I especially love the photos. You always look so god-damn pleased with fish hung from chain all around you.

My brother: (I used to brag) Jesus of the Fishes.

I obviously don't remember my own birth.

I don't remember waking up to the hospital's glaring lights, to my mother's radiant, tired smile.

I don't remember my father taking my brothers fishing that morning instead of pacing the whitewashed hallways, leaving my mother alone to her task.

I don't remember how fine she was with their absence, how glad she was to let the boys go fishing. When they did arrive, smelling of salt water and fish scales, she let them take turns holding me. She let the boys choose my middle name. I don't remember this.

But I do remember your daughter's birth.

I remember it in that deep-breath, dizzy-headed kind of way. I remember you wrestling me awake some time far before dawn. And the humour we somehow upheld, crammed in the front seat of your truck, your lover panting labour pains, wide-eyed and constricted between us. You were thrilled with the excuse to speed in the pre-dawn streets, hauling a hundred, running reds, daring a cop to pull you over, dialogue prepared: "My girl's in labour, we gotta rush." Rush rush.

You have been rushing for as long as I can remember, roaring around in lifted trucks, loaded high with racy chicks, snorting whatever drugs. Rushing out to sea on your boat, and rushing back to sell the fish, rushing to party-burn through the cash. You rushed out of childhood and into this fictitious adulthood. You've been rushing after pills and needles and powders with a passion I've rarely seen in any other aspect of your life—desire, desperation, finally physical cravings seem to be the only thing that drags you off the couch lately, into parking lots, bushes, backyards, back alleys, wherever it is people meet to slay drugs.

I remember your daughter's birth with a sort of concocted stillness, a full-bellied breath in the shallow-water gasping of our every day.

My hands were shaking, a shudder that stemmed from my elbows and tightened into my wrists. And the nurse came in, confused at my role in the room. There was already one man, one baby, one post-labour lady. And me.

Who's this? She asked with a look. Oh, me, the over-delighted woman-child slobbering kisses on the scene. The nurse thrust the clip-board at me.

"Fill this out, yeah honey girl?" she asked. The birth certificate form: quit shaking dumb hands, this document needs to be perfect. Date, time: hour, minute, second. Her name: her mother's middle name, and our last name. Malia: Hawaiian for calm waters. Malia. My niece. My goddaughter. I cried when you asked me to be that for her.

From my view over her mother's shoulder, I watched as she rose and fell, rose and fell, with every bare-chested breath. Swaddled and chalk-white with afterbirth, tiny eyes squinting, I have never seen anything so goddamn pure. I watched you watch her, tight chested and ready for this calm.

"Promise her," I said to you when your lover and tiny baby slipped to sleep, "promise to be calm, for her. No more storms. Still waters. For Malia."

I have begun to think of your pupils in different ways.

As copper bullets, I take them from you willingly and swallow them each. An ache behind my navel, heavy metal fish swimming in my gut-pool.

As someone else's teeth, digging into my lips, into my gums, bitingly.

As a syringe in my tongue. I can't close my mouth.

As a syringe in my neck. I can't turn my head to look at you.

As two oxygen-starved wasps, trapped in the layers of a windowpane, dizzy with the lack of air, beating useless against the layered glass.

Hawaiian proverb:
When the frigate bird flies out to sea, the rough sea will grow calm.

I've only been seasick that one time. I was so mad and embarrassed
even though it was only you and me out there. We were out bait fishing
and it must have been 2 a.m. The ocean was so glassy it reflected the
constellations flawlessly, fashioning us into a spacecraft tiptoeing
through some endless, speckled universe.

A beer and a bag of Doritos was all I had in me.

"Chumming the water for us," you said. "Thanks, baby sis."

I wanted to jump overboard.

Green and orange fluorescent fish emerged from the deep to nibble
my vomit, suspended on the surface, gliding through the stars. I
watched it come apart.

I tried to focus on the stars in the sky. I tried to focus on the stars
on the surface of the ocean. The constant movement churned my gut.
I looked to the contour of Maui in the distance. Huddled lights on the
south shore, swaying—nothing solid, not even land.

"Do you want to turn back?" You asked.

"No." (Even though I wanted nothing else.)

You readied the rods. I paused to churn and chum again. Then we
fished.

The nurse came in to give your lover a spinal tap, holding a juicing
foot-long noodle to prick into her backbone, to ease the labour pains, to
help numb the experience.

"Fuck this," you'd said, kissing her on the forehead and walking out
of the room. You've always hated needles. I've never minded them. So
I stayed, held her hand as the nurse poked her, doped her up. Her body
so contorted in agony, and you barfing up McDonald's breakfast in the
back parking lot.

I have two repetitive dreams:

In the first, I'm an *iwa*—grease-black Hawaiian fishing bird—flying
over your toy boat. You and I are fishing the same game.

In the next, I'm walking down the hallways of our childhood home.
Our father is dead, his body frozen in the bathtub and I sit on the toilet
lid, letting my fingers skate across the iced surface.

"Wanna watch?"

"No." (But I stay.)

You slouch, sinking into your crummy couch. I haven't seen you leave your den in weeks. I brought you breakfast—a bowl of cereal without a spoon. Mom says no more spoons for you; she says she's running out. You laugh your lucky laugh and put the bowl aside. From the creases of the couch, you fetch your kit.

A spoon you've used and reused, its bottom burnt black, its inside pale blue and crusted like elephant skin. You pull out your orange safety-capped needle, still half-full of red-black liquid, a blood-drug mixture. You dig your hand into the folds one final time and come up with a jar of little blue pills. I shrink onto your bed, burrowing in the dirty sheets. My head hangs limp next to yours. I reach out and stroke your unshaven chin. Your face gaunt, shallow breath, scabbed. Grunting and uselessly high, brother dear, you are so goddamn handsome.

You ask for your Gatorade. I pass you the almost-empty bottle, a cigarette butt floating inside. You reach your needle to the bottom and suck the Blue Frost into its tip, like a spring-hungry hummingbird sipping on sugar water. You find your rubber band and strangle your upper arm, teasing out a vein. A prick and the frosty-blue oxycodone syrup dyes black.

"It's coagulating," you say.

"Big word," I joke.

How can I joke? I turn away from you, but keep one hand on your shrunk face.

"I'ma do more." Drug-induced pause. "Wanna stay?"

"No." (But I do.)

You've taught me things I've truly needed to know in this life; like how to tie my shoes. I was five; you were ten. And you didn't teach me that bullshit bunny-ears method either, you taught me how to tie them proper, like a big kid. We ate ice cream afterwards to celebrate. When I was ten and you were fifteen, you taught me how to surf. You'd paddle me out to the break on your longboard and you'd catch the waves for the both of us. When I got my own board, you taught me how to dive under the big waves, tuck, and turtle roll. And out at the break together, you'd push me into the little waves, and whistled encouragingly when I did stand.

You taught me how to drive standard, let me ruin your truck's clutch, and mostly, you stayed calm. I was fifteen; you were twenty.

You've taught me things I never thought I would need to know, like how to cut a clean line of cocaine with a credit card, and make that little straw with a dollar bill. I was twenty; you were twenty-five, on Christmas Eve in our mother's garage. You taught me how to be an undetected junkie, how to shoot up between toes and fingers—to leave no trace. But you said if you ever caught me with a needle mark, you'd barbecue me. So I stayed clear.

The fish was only maybe eighteen pounds, but it took all my strength to reel it in. You helped me pull it up out of the water and swing it onto the back net of the boat. That damn fish was so desperate to get back to the water, I think that if fish made any noise, any whimper or cry, I would have had to let it off the hook. But it was all silence, just squirming back and forth between our feet, its glass eyes reflecting.

Not at all accepting of its death, but powerless to it. Your bare foot pinned it down, so it wouldn't slip back to the sea. My very first mahi mahi. You got someone to take a picture of us with the fish, "before it fades"—you had said.

I hadn't known what you meant about fading. But then I watched the fish die, watched the vibrant blues and yellows drain from its scales. Fade to grey. The colours seemed to drip off the fish, leak back to the Pacific.

Marble-eyed, clear and black, reflecting you and I, fishing together.

Mountain Pine Beetle Suite

CHANTAL GIBSON

i. Dendroctonus ponderosae

They come with axes between their teeth. Pioneer beetles,
females hungry for trees, ready to carve an instant town . out

of the wilderness. Somewhere in the needling green sprawl
between Darwin & God, an edict etched deep & tingling

beneath the skin, they believe this stand of old pines will last
a lifetime. By nature, they desire. A species wants

nothing more than to procreate. Back home,
a pheromone-frenzy stirs a gnashing appetite

for industry. The new believers wake & uncross
their legs, hell-bent on leaving this unholy land

of hollow trees. How soon they forget the splinter's prick
between their lips. In unison, they hum, the blue-

stained settlers, young males itching to leave this once-
Eden girdled & snap-necked. A ghost town rusting, their dead

pitched out of the trees. Meanwhile the humans look
petrified, like butterflies shocked in resin, arms wide,

palms flat against the front-room window, disbelieving
the FOR SALE sign on the lawn, wishing away

the dust on the toys piled up in the driveway.

ii. Summer: Mating Season

the female plays house   between
the bark & the sapwood   she is
hardwired for love   in the phloem
her scent on the walls   she rubs
her Avon wrists together   & waits

the male finds her   intoxicated   they
make love   under the trees   legs become arms   hands grow fingers   nails
scratch   tiny love notes   in the bark

summer is short here   little time
for courtship in the North: the cold-
blooded retreat to the woods   veins
pumped with antifreeze   the female
bores deeper   into the sapwood   she
drags her smokes   & her big belly   up
the tree   carves her birthing chamber
and her coffin with her teeth

iii. Homo sapiens

There's a red stain on your floral dress
trying hard to look like a rose. Usually,

you don't bleed this much.
It just takes a minute, to stop:

a dab of Vaseline, a greasy piece
of rolled-up toilet paper shoved up

your nose, the tissue bent
and twisted a few times

to reach the broken blood vessels.
In the back of your mind, you know

you'll have to see the Doc, probably
have it cauterized. Tell him it was just

an accident, no need to fill out a report (no
big deal). It's a small town, after all.

Everyone talks. But no one told you
it would look like this, marriage:

your high-school sweetheart, a sawmill job,
a house, two kids, a camper, a truck,

and a severance check.
You borrowed

your mother's fairy tale, a ponytail dream
you can get with a Grade 12 diploma.

It all started with a forest and a knife
and an old pine tree with your name on it.

Remember? The hands
that lit your smokes first,

that wooed the knot from your halter top
and filled the back pockets of your jeans,

that drew circles on your round belly
and caressed your pink baby scar,

have somehow forgotten
how to touch you without leaving

a mark. A little foundation and some lipstick,
and you're good as new, right? Tell the kids

you'll be out in a sec. It's time
to get ready for bed. Tuck in

your pocket an extra white tissue, just in case
the bleeding starts. *Daddy will be back soon*

to tell you a story. Is that what you'll say—
this time—when you open the bathroom door

and try to smile away the swelling, when you find
a kitchen chair in front of the fridge, and your 4-year-old

daughter holding out a bag of frozen peas?

How to Keep Your Day Job

REBECCA ROSENBLUM

DO A DRY RUN ON THE BUS a week before you start, at the right time of day, carrying the right amount of stuff, in the stiff, uncomfortable black shoes you can't run in. If you don't own such shoes, buy some. Don't get paint on them.

Also, buy a second alarm clock. Set it half an hour early. Promise your boyfriend that you'll turn it off as soon as it goes off, and that you'll get ready really quietly. In the dark if you have to.

You can wear most reasonable clothing to an office; it isn't as bad as all that. Just nothing with paint or an amusing slogan on it, and nothing that makes you look either really attractive or really awful. Probably nothing purple, either. If in doubt, put a cardigan over it.

Smile as you turn off the alarm. Smile on the bus. Smile in the lobby. Smile at your desk.

Put your full name on all paperwork, even though your boyfriend makes fun of your middle name. Accept whatever desk you are given, even if it is in a hallway and someone seems to be asking if that is okay with you. Laugh at whatever jokes you are told, even if they seem sort of mean to gay people. Work hard.

Don't work so hard that you don't take a lunch. The first day, bring something interesting to eat, although certainly nothing with a weird smell, or even any smell at all if you can help it. Then wait and see if people invite you eat with them. Interesting food will give people something to talk to you about if they invite you to eat with them. If they don't, eat your complicated, odourless sandwich alone at your desk at 2:30.

Smile in the hallways, even when people don't smile back. Smile at the photocopier, even when it's jammed and smears toner on your cardigan when you try to unjam it. Never smile in the washroom.

Don't do anything that could draw attention. Your goal should be to be anonymously indispensable, like a photocopier that never jams. Examples of attention-drawing activities include: putting up posters for your art show, getting loudly angry at your boyfriend on the phone, falling down the stairs, or crying when someone yells at you.

Use Post-its, all the different colours. Use a mechanical pencil. Use

Excel spreadsheets, Internet radio, Google Earth, and a speakerphone. Use Xpresspost and bicycle couriers and the colour scanner and too many paperclips. Revel in all that is yours to use, though you don't need or want to.

When you talk about your boyfriend, start saying *partner*, even though you know he would give you a dirty look if he could hear. In an office, everyone is assumed PC and judgey until proven otherwise.

If ever you arrive late, don't say a thing, least of all an excuse. Act like you thought the workday really started at 9:47. But don't eat lunch, as penance.

Do not moan to your partner that you are imprisoned away from your real life, squashed and stifled, unmotivated and underappreciated, stationary and over-stationery'd. He'll only tell you to move the canvases out of the living room if you're not going to work on them. Your partner hates whiners.

Watch your step.

Watch the movie *American Pie*, particularly that girl from *Buffy* with the "This one time at band camp . . ." refrain. Avoid becoming the loser who is cool somewhere else, not here, and wants people to believe it. You can talk about your surreal still-lifes and your partner's band, but keep in mind: most people don't care. And how cool are you even elsewhere, really?

Even in summer, don't stress about tattoos. Everybody has one now; a butterfly on your shoulder isn't even interesting anymore. If in doubt, put a cardigan over it.

If, because relationships are stressful and his band has been fighting and the summer's been hot, your partner knocks you into a wall and it leaves a bruise, a cardigan will cover that too. You might be able to call the Employee Assistance Program, but they probably report everything to management. Nobody likes a whiner.

Do not complain to your colleagues that you are imprisoned away from your art, that your partner is cold and distant, that the photocopier is broken. Your co-workers have problems, too, and will not feel sorry for you. And—remember—nobody likes a whiner.

Your colleagues might not like you even if you don't whine, but you have to pretend they still might. If someone says your clothes are "interesting" because they are "apparently" reversible or that they "can't help but notice" that you are "able to resist" hairstyling products, give them the benefit of the doubt.

If your yogurt disappears from the fridge, give everyone the benefit of the doubt.

If, at 4:07, a superior finds something that must be completed by the next morning, say you can't stay if you can't stay. Explain that to do overtime, you'll need some notice because you have lots of responsibilities (use the words *overtime* and *responsibilities*—they are more imposing than *work late* and *stuff to do*). If your superior doesn't respond, explain about the show, the workshop, or your partner's desire to have you home by six. Then look sad. Then go sit down and do the work.

Breathe.

If your partner tells you he needs the space to stay out all night, try to understand, but also explain that you feel lonely and worried when he does this.

Then try to be sexier. Then look sad. Then go to bed alone.

If people ask you for things that aren't part of your job, try anyway. If you can't do those things, find out whose job it is and tell him or her to do it. If he or she implies that you are lazy, assure them you are not. If they disagree, go sit down and do their work.

Despite your best efforts, you still might fall down the stairs. That's natural. We are all hurtling through space at alarming speeds and those stiff, shiny shoes are without tread and not designed for grip. And life is complicated enough that stairs might not be the first thing on your mind.

Accept the possibility of the fall. To be prey of gravity is to be human. But if falling, do stop when you can. *Don't* be seduced by the free fall, the absence of responsibility from the complications of life, the new angles at which a broken leg can bend. Weigh your body hard on each step until you come to one on which you can rest.

Rest.

It's okay.

Check if you are breathing. You might have stopped, for the pain or the shock of the drop.

Breathe.

Check for breakages: limbs, spine, heart.

Are you breathing? Are you broken?

It's okay. Whatever the answer, it is okay.

Breathe.

Open your eyes, even though stairwells are unattractive places, and illuminating windows are unlikely. Regard the grey or beige or greyish-beige walls. Concentrate on their solidity, immobility, inability to do you any harm . . . or help.

Help, or something like it, will come. Heavy footsteps on the landing above you indicate a man with some sense of his own authority. Whoever it is, it's probably no one whose presence can comfort you. You will want your partner, but remember: he doesn't want you, and just signed the lease on a bachelor apartment. You'll want to sob like a rock star, or scream like a soccer mom, or curse like a CEO, but don't.

Wait. Wait and see what happens next.

Don't throw the baby out with the bathwater.

Don't cut off your nose to spite your face.

Don't get too big for your britches.

Don't quit your day job.

Wait on your stair, whatever stair you've managed to stop at. Lie still.

No matter who is up at the top of the stairs, don't bother to try to look business casual, to stop crying and straighten your clothes, tuck your hair behind your ears, to stop being hurt or heartbroken or human. Don't even wipe your face—you'll just smear snot, tears, and blood across your nice clean cardigan. Blood stains everything, you know.

What is going to happen happens, and that's, "Hey, you okay?"

Don't let the colloquial diction fool you. This query is not light. He can see blood on your shin, on the side of your mouth from the fall, and the bruise on your collarbone from last weekend. Even the old bruise hurts now. Your calm, even breathing does not obscure the pain. You aren't fooling anyone, you know.

He will probably touch you, on the shoulder or arm perhaps, because the bubble of business casual propriety has already been breached by injury, tears, snot. And instead of irritated or sexually harassed, you will feel very slightly comforted by this stranger's touch, and then profoundly ashamed of that.

Think about your ergonomic chair upstairs, the strength in your spine.

He'll say something strikingly banal, like, "Fell?"

Something will clog the back of your throat: maybe blood, or vomit, mucus, dignity. You open your lips and nothing pours out, which is something. But no words, either, just the silence of your bloodied lip, a tooth-bitten cut, not internal hemorrhaging. Remember that you've made your own damage.

The man's tie dangles into your eyeline, and then he lowers onto your stair. He puts his hand back on your shoulder, and says, "Well, don't fret, I'm on the health and safety committee—I know what to do. We gotta assess the damage." He reaches into his jacket pocket.

Your leg is probably broken, just above the ankle, where the bone is close to the surface. Something there is digging and jagged, you feel it without looking down.

Don't look down.

Fine, if it will make you feel better: adjust your cardigan to cover the bruise, but remember that this man doesn't care.

What he pulls from his pocket is not a splint, bandages, sedatives or liquor. It's a cellphone, just like yours, the one that comes free with the two-year contract.

If you are still woozy from the drop, it might help to focus on something solid and singular. Focus on this man's flushed face, his stubble under the silver cellphone as he presses it to his big, flat ear. His voice bounces loud off the hard stairwell walls, "Hey, Steve-o. Gregster here. We've got a faller on the southwest stairs, below three, damage to the . . . the fe—"

You know he wants to say *femur*, because that's the famous interesting bone on television medical dramas. But that's the thigh bone. That's not the one you broke.

Watch him think and think. He doesn't know what bone you broke. But he comes up with something; he is a man doing his job and he does it okay. ". . . Damage to the shin bone, plus pretty shaken up. Call it in, wouldja? I'll get'er down. Bring a car . . . yep. Ten-four. Roger. Okay. Bye now." He does it smooth and fast enough, you have to give credit there.

He meets your gaze. He has swimming-pool-coloured eyes. He says, "We have to document this," and you think, suddenly, of all the documents on your desk, things undone. A certain number will never be needed, true, but certain mailings are important, pressing, will be noticed if undone.

You have a headache that could be a concussion. Your lip is bleeding onto your cardigan. You think your right top incisor is loose. And your leg is broken. You feel dangerously close to whining.

There's an invoice that needs to be sent out. You should do it. You probably could do it, if you could lean on this gentleman beside you, or someone. You've been trying to get a hold of your ex-partner all week to give him back the guitar picks and combs and Kerouac of his that you've found. But you think he's screening, or he's changed his cell number.

Don't be too concerned about what's been left behind.

The phone is still open, silver bright. The man isn't speaking on it anymore. He speaks to you instead. He says, "Hike up your hem, please." Staring into the depths of his chlorinated eyes, you wonder what he means, until he looks down at your strangely angled ankle, and you understand what you have to do.

You have to.

If you think to say *tibia*, don't; he'll find out. If you think to ask him how many sick days you are entitled to, don't; you'll find out. If you've been thinking about calling your ex's mother, his bandmates, that Dominion checker he sort of likes, and telling them all of his crimes, don't—they'll find out.

Be a class act. Be the bigger person. Be a model employee. Pull the cuff of your Gap on-sale dress pants gently, smoothly, away from the jut of bone. Don't worry about making the folds even. Don't worry about what this man, Gregster, is thinking, or seeing, or judging. You are colleagues collaborating on a project, the project of accident documentation.

He is saying, "We just gotta record this, you know, for the accident report." It seems that this is not a written report, though, since he doesn't ask you a single question—not your name or your pain threshold or why you find yourself in this strange, lame building. Not even whether you are single, if there isn't someone who loves you that should be called on the health and safety cellphone. He won't require a word from you, just flick the phone until it's a camera. He doesn't care, and neither should you.

Then, before you fully realize the state of your blood-painted face, your rucked-up clothes, blood-smeared mouth, akimbo angle of your leg and the edge of collar where that bruise might show, he will have taken your picture. Frozen forever, bleeding in the stairwell, in your cardigan.

Don't cry.

Don't even hate him. What else could he do? For you, a stranger with eyeliner running down onto your clavicle, breath all hiccupy, tears tangling your hair, his best emotion is probably only pity. For you in a similar nest of misery last week, your ex couldn't even manage that; only rage. You aren't what he wants, though he thought you were.

Let it go, all of it. You don't really have a choice, anyway. The Gregster is already sliding his palm round your shoulders.

When he says, "Allyoop," push up on your unbroken leg, but let him take as much of your weight as he will. Let your body press into him to keep from falling. It's ok; this isn't sexual, though it's hardly professional. Though he might be blushing as you try to balance, you have no cause to be embarrassed; his job is to help you in this, your hour, or week, or month, of need.

Don't cry.

Just walk down the stairs.

Don't think about the severity of the breakage, the horror of crutches on public transit, improper stairwell maintenance, or invoice day on Thursday. Don't think about the drawers in your dresser that are empty because he took all his socks and underwear, but don't think about the time he called you a waste of space in front of your brother, either.

The short-term disability and gift baskets will all come through to you, just like the forms you filled out so carefully back at the beginning promised. You will wind up with six weeks of full pay before you must return to your overdue-invoice-encrusted desk. As the fragments of your tibia slowly knit back into place, so will a lot of things, or at least begin to. In the meantime you have only to hop down the stairs, straighten your blouse, cry if you must but delicately and without snot. Be the person Steve-o expects to see when he brings the car around.

Breathe.

Keep going forward.

You have a job to do.

Wolves, Cigarettes, Gum

AMY JONES

ANNALISE AND HER MOTHER DRESS EXACTLY ALIKE. Short denim skirts with fraying hems, pink tank tops, platform sandals: too old for one, too young for the other. They stand in line at New York Fries, looking out over the food court in opposite directions, one chewing on nails, one chewing on hair. From the back, at this distance, it's actually hard to tell them apart.

Annalise's hair is crimped like it's the '80s, which she told me is back in style, according to all the magazines. She doesn't have a crimper though, so every night she goes to bed with tiny wet braids that make her pillow wet. I imagine haphazard geometric patterns crisscrossing her skull, red marks on her neck where the elastics have dug into her skin while she sleeps.

Annalise's mother's hair is in a ponytail, her bangs curved up in a preposterously high inverted *C* shape plastered into place above her forehead. Red with large swaths of platinum running through them. Gravity-defying bangs.

"Bangs you could shatter a bottle over," Troy says, like he's given this a lot of thought.

It's hard to believe Annalise's mother has even seen the inside of a bank, let alone robbed one. She just doesn't look like a bank robber. She looks like she might be able to hold up a Mac's, maybe, a balaclava pulled over her freckles, a dirty syringe waving in the air, maybe rip an old lady's purse out from under her arm at a bus stop, maybe even a smash-and-grab at a mom-and-pop electronics store. Something street level, no security, no finesse. But not a bank robber. Those are not the bangs of a bank robber.

"It was actually a credit union," Troy tells me, taking a bite out of his sub, wimpy shreds of lettuce falling out onto the tray from between two slabs of bread as hard and white as Styrofoam. "She used a paint-ball gun. No one got hurt."

"They just got . . . what, decorated?" I ask. Troy just stares at me, gives me that *you're so dumb, Robin* look, a dollop of mayonnaise smeared across his lower lip. He still doesn't get why I'm pissed. I pick up a piece of fallen lettuce and pop it into my mouth without thinking about it. Then I think about it all at once: *When was the last time they washed those trays? What kind of cleaner did they use? What was on there before? Whose fingers? Which bodily fluids?*

I stick my tongue out, let the lettuce fall.

Troy met Annalise's mother, whose name is either Joy or Joyce or maybe just Jo, at the bowling alley. Troy is very serious about bowling. He is on a team called The Gutter Sluts and they play in a league every Tuesday and Friday night, talk about their scores the way other people talk about their kids. Annalise's mother worked at the bowling alley bar until she got caught stealing bottles of Wild Turkey and selling them to kids in the parking lot on her smoke break. Shortly after, she robbed the credit union.

"No one suspects her, because she looks so trashy," Troy told me this morning, smoking cigarettes in bed even though I keep telling him he's going to burn the building down. Secretly, though, I like it, the way the sun comes in through the slatted blinds and makes a pattern on his bare chest, the way the smoke flickers in and out of the light. But I'd never tell him that. He'd just take it as permission to ash on the floor.

"So what are you going to do?" I asked, fiddling with the drawstring on his pyjama pants. I wasn't nervous or anything, just curious. I'm never nervous for Troy. There is something about him, the way he licks his lips or juts his chin forward that makes you feel like he knows what he's doing all the time. It's comforting, being with a man who makes you feel that way, even if it's not entirely true.

He swatted my hand away, taking a long drag on his cigarette. "Drive the car, mostly," he said.

"Mostly?"

"I might be providing some of the firepower."

"I'm guessing you don't mean paintball guns."

He looked at me through narrowed eyes—that look that he gave me when he wanted me to remember the distance between us. "You don't want to know."

He was right. I didn't want to know. I didn't want to know what he meant by firepower, just like I didn't want to know why suddenly he had the need to progress from breaking and entering to armed robbery. I also didn't want to know if he had slept with Annalise's mother, this random Jo-Joy-Joyce he was ditching me for. Instead, I tried to think about about how much I missed his goatee, that surprised *O* of hair, the little bristly wreath framing his mouth.

He shaved it off a few weeks ago, and now it was like I was kissing a different person. A smoother person, someone who didn't care about hiding any part of his face, like, *Look at me world. Here's my fucking chin. Deal with it.*

"And why can't I come, again?" I asked.

Troy didn't say anything. He just stubbed out his cigarette and let the last bit of smoke curl away from his lips in a slow, thick stream, his eyes closed, one hand rubbing over his smooth, hairless chin.

Annalise and her mother come back to the table with their tray, a giant container of fries and two oversized cups of soda. "Holy Christ," says Annalise's mother, sitting down next to Troy. "How hard can it fucking be to get French fries, right?"

Annalise sits down next to me, earbuds shoved in her ears, fingers flying across her phone's touchscreen. Without slowing down, she leans forward and takes a sip from one of the giant cups, then makes a face.

"That one's yours," she says to her mother, stopping her texting just long enough to exchange cups and shove a handful of fries in her mouth. She looks like she hasn't eaten in weeks—and mows through that handful of fries like it, too—but doesn't eat any more after that.

Her mother picks through the fries like she's trying to find a four-leaf clover in a field of corn. She finally decides on one and bites down delicately on one end.

"I fucking hate these things," she says, dropping the fry back in the container. "Annie, where's our fucking ketchup?" She kicks her daughter under the table. Annalise kicks back, eyes still focused on her phone.

I try to make eye contact with Troy. This should be something we do, as a couple—make eye contact in meaningful ways when other people around us are batshit crazy. But Troy ignores me, reaching around Annalise's soda cup and grabbing three little packages of ketchup.

"Here ya go, geniuses," he says. Annalise takes a package and rips it open with her teeth, then squirts the contents directly into her mouth.

I can't help it; I gag.

Annalise stares at me, then opens her mouth and sticks out her tongue, ketchup smeared like blood across her teeth. She reaches for the other two, but I grab her hands and we have a little slap fight until I finally tear the packages away from her, holding them up over my head so she can't reach. Eventually, she rolls her eyes and sits back down with a huff, grabbing her phone and typing again.

"Ugly skank," she says. Tap tap tap. I try to imagine what she's texting. *This bitch at the food court won't let me eat fucking ketchup. I'm probably going to starve.* I look at her mother, but she's digging through her ugly red sequined purse for something. I wonder if she keeps the gun in there. I wonder if it's heavy.

"Troy," I say. "I can't do this."

Troy balls up his sub wrapper with one hand. "You can't do this? Fuck, Robin. You've got the easiest job of all." One leg bounces under the table, his eyes shift from the top of my head to a point in the distance, restless and unfocused, and I know it's too late. There's no pulling him back from this, not now. Not this time.

Annalise's mother pulls a tube of lipstick out of her purse and runs it over her mouth. Cherry red, like her purse, caking into little globs the minute she applies it. She looks at me for the first time since we arrived at the mall. "Don't let her into Claire's," she says. "She'll steal everything she can get her hands on."

Troy and me, we burgled for love. At first, I just wanted my diamond ring back. Percy had taken it when I broke off our engagement, forcibly ripping it from my finger while crying like a little girl. We broke into Percy's house when I knew he was away on business, a smashed basement window, our black hoods pulled up over our hair, taking not only the ring but some gold cufflinks, a watch, an iPod, some antique coins, and a wad of cash we later discovered was Canadian Tire money, schlepping it all back out the window in a garbage bag that might as well have had a giant dollar sign painted on it. Then we ran, until our hearts stopped and our lungs exploded. We ran until we collapsed against a park bench fifteen blocks away, giddy and coughing, our lungs screaming for air, our vision blurred with euphoria, our skin sparking with electricity, and Troy pushed me down against the cold wooden slats and fucked me right there under the street light, the animal desire on his face backlit by the soft yellow glow.

The next weekend, we sat on our couch and watched a movie and drank beer and tried to forget about it. But both of us were antsy. We couldn't sit still. We couldn't concentrate. We couldn't even agree on a movie to watch. We should have seen it coming. How could we go back, after that first rush of the window breaking?

"You wanna do it again?" Troy asked.

I nodded.

We were so stupid in those early days, so reckless. We didn't stake out. We didn't track the neighbours or scope out security systems. We didn't even wear gloves. We just smashed windows and hoped for the best. That we were never caught is still shocking to me. That we never felt guilty about it, possibly less so. When you're in the middle of it, when you're standing in a stranger's house and everything is dark and silent and there are things everywhere—all this stuff that someone has because they traded some little pieces of paper for it, stuff they don't even use anyway, which just sits around being looked at, being owned, not fulfilling its true destiny as a functional object—it doesn't feel like you're doing anything wrong. It feels like the way it should be: that everything belongs to everyone and that you are just making it right. We restored the balance to the universe. We took other people's stuff and we felt like goddamn fucking superheroes.

And now, somehow, I've become nothing but a babysitter.

"Wolves, cigarettes, gum," Annalise says to me, suddenly, one earbud hanging out of her ear.

"Huh?" I'm slumped over, one ear down, listening to the beat of the piped-in music reverberating through the plastic of the table, the muffled sounds of people talking around me. It's oddly soothing. Troy and Annalise's mother have been gone for twenty minutes. Twenty more minutes to go before we leave the mall to meet them at the rendezvous point at Mission Marsh, where we divvy up the money and go our separate ways. This is the part of the plan I am most excited about, the part that I have been looking forward to ever since Troy told me what we were doing.

"Don't you know anything?" She sighs, tapping away on her phone. "Wolves, cigarettes, gum. It's a game. What do those three things have in common?"

"Uh . . . they're all things that you shouldn't swallow?"

Annalise rolls her eyes. "Like there's anything you won't swallow."

I look down at my own phone. Nineteen minutes. "I'm going to get a coffee," I say. "Stay here."

There's no one in the line at Tim Hortons except for two fat women in front of me who can't make up their mind about what kind of muffin they want. And when they do, the cashier runs out of the little paper squares they use to pick up the muffins and has to go in the back. "I think I should have a bagel instead," one of the fat ladies says while she's gone.

On my way back to the table with my double-double, I don't think about Troy, but about Percy, my ex, and how he used to make up little songs about his food before he ate it. He thought it was cute, that it would make me laugh. *Macaroni and cheese, macaroni and cheese, nothing else can fill me up like macaroni and cheese*, he'd sing, to the tune of "Winnie the Pooh," and I would roll my eyes, or ignore him, get up and leave the room. Thinking about it now, Percy and those stupid little cheerful songs, it just, I don't know, makes me want to cry.

Stupid Percy loved me with every soft round part of his heart. Troy loved me with all the sharp, jagged edges.

I mean loves. Loves me with all the sharp, jagged edges.

When I get back to the table, of course Annalise is gone.

Troy and I fell in love over burgers and coffee at the Coney Island Westfort on a Friday afternoon. I had just got off my shift and was counting my tips when he came in and sat down at the counter. He had his workboots on, splotches of paint over all over his Carhartts, his cheeks windburned and shiny. He'd been in before, ordering takeout, and I'd watch him open the greasy brown paper bag on the sidewalk, rip into the burgers like a starving animal right there in front of the window. This time, though, he ordered two burgers and two cups of coffee and when I asked him if there was someone joining him he said, "You are," with this wide grin, and in that instant I saw both the boy he had been and the man that he would be and I wanted all of it, all of him.

So even though I was supposed to go grocery shopping with Percy I folded up my apron and sat down beside Troy. His legs were open wide and I had to tuck mine to the side to make sure they weren't touching his. He wiped his face with a napkin and swivelled his stool to face me, his eyes resting on my left hand.

"Nice ring," he said.

It isn't Claire's, like her mother said it would be, it is The Body Shop, her Hello Kitty purse weighed down with little tubs of lip gloss, smooth, cool vials of perfume, bars of glycerine soap wrapped tightly in plastic. I can smell her fruit salad stench the moment I step into the security office.

"Who are you?" the security guard asks. He is round, rosy-cheeked, bored. It occurs to me that he has gone through this with Annalise before. Annalise sits in front of the security desk, texting. For some reason, the fact that she is still doing this infuriates me. Why would he let her do that? Why wouldn't he take her phone away?

"I'm her babysitter," I say.

Annalise makes a little puff of air through pursed lips. "No she's not," she says, without looking up. "I've never seen her before in my life."

"Of course you haven't," I say. "You've been looking at that phone the entire time I've known you."

"Whatever," says Annalise, slouching down in her chair. One of the straps of her tank top slips down her arm. She pulls it back up and scratches her shoulder with so much force I feel like she must have ripped through the skin, but when I look there's nothing but a light pink streak across her tanned skin.

The security guard hands me some papers to sign. I sit down on the chair next to Annalise and search through my purse for a pen. The security guard hands me one. It's a blue ballpoint that skips when I try to write with it. I want to stab the security guard's eye out with it.

"Can I go now?" Annalise asks.

"No, you can't go *now*," the security guard says, mimicking her tone. "This is the fourth time we've caught you shoplifting. The cops are on their way."

Both of us go rigid, and even though Annalise rolls her eyes and gives another "whatever" I can see it in the tips of her fingers turning white against her phone's keyboard, in the sudden straightening of her spine: terror. I know, because I feel it, too. The security guard turns to his computer, shaking his head. That word, *cops*, clangs around in my brain for a good thirty seconds before I'm leaning in to Annalise's ear, my mouth nearly on her earlobe before I whisper.

"Run."

It's not the way I remember running. In the gas station parking lot across the street, I stop the car and close my eyes, my hands shaking on the wheel. The windshield is still partially frozen, thick blades of frost reaching upward from the tiny half-moon of defrosted glass above the dash that I had to lean forward to see through as I drove. My breath comes in tremendous gulps. Maybe running is different when there's someone chasing you. Maybe it hurts more, somehow.

Annalise seems unfazed, of course. She turns on the radio, flips to a Justin Bieber song. Stares out the window for a moment, her phone forgotten in her lap.

"They all come in packs."

"What?"

"Wolves, cigarettes, gum. They all come in packs." She shakes her head. "Jesus, Robin, keep up." She turns to me, and the sudden sight of her eyes is startling, wide and blue and utterly hopeless. She opens her hand, and I see she has held on to one of the glycerine soaps, red and glistening in her palm. "Wanna smell it?"

I take the soap, sweaty from Annalise's hand, and press it to my nose. It's strawberry, or a soap company's interpretation of strawberry. But it smells good. I breathe deeply, then pass it back to Annalise, who has already turned back to her phone. When the song on the radio ends, I realize I can hear the distant wail of sirens, and I wonder if they're for me and Annalise, or if they're for Troy and Annalise's mother, or if they're for someone else stealing something from somewhere else, or if it really even matters, if we're all just moving stuff around.

"Bagels, buttons, blue whales," I say. Annalise is silent for a while. "Annalise?" I say. "Bagels, buttons, blue whales. They all have a hole in them."

Annalise sticks her earbuds back in her ears. "That's stupid," she says, eyes down even as the cop cars race through the intersection in front of us, cherries flashing. "Everyone has a hole in them."

And Then We Let Ourselves In

AISLINN HUNTER

This is the glad havoc
    of my childhood:
patchwork, mottle, as if my life had no
    thread in it—
an eagerness to steal
    other girls' stories, to wear
their skirts and collared blouses.

I have never been called
    beautiful, am instead the blunder
whose name was scratched in blue ink
    on toilet-stall walls:
Bitch, Slut, Whore
    which was far worse, at twelve,
than Stupid or Boring.

We have, all of us, some wound
    coiled up inside and waiting,
the way a dog curled in her basket
    anticipates the sound of keys
or the tread of feet on the floor,
    or a voice that will say
not to worry—

things, by their very nature,
    unravel—
and every entry into error
    is still an entry.
And how well you've done,
    Dear Girl,
to find the door.

Failed Séances for Rita MacNeil (1944 – 2013)

LUCAS CRAWFORD

I.

Rita, you requested that your ashes
be held in a teapot—"two if necessary"
Low days, I browse plus-size caskets
(They are all pink or blue)
But you took death with milk and sugar, long steep
       Rita, we are both members of the fat neo-Scottish diaspora.
       Don't tell me it doesn't exist, sweet darlin'
       until *you* are the only fat transsexual
       at a Rankin Family concert in Montréal.
       Until you feel more at home than you have all year
       when Raylene (1960 – 2012) thumbs-ups
       your 400-pound dance moves in the front row
       during that last, last, encore.
          Fare thee well, love.
          Will we never meet again no more?

II.

In Grade Two, I sang with your coal mining choir, "The Men of the Deeps"
There is something terrifying about one hundred pre-pubescent squirts
squeaking out the high falsetto tones of "We Rise Again"
over the miners' sea of too-knowing bass tones.

The highest note of the song comes at the word "child"
and we screamed it. We didn't yet have the sadness
that keeps you from even trying the high notes in that tune,
which take you from ours to other worlds and back again.

One of the miners comes forward in concerts for a mustachioed solo
I heard him on the CBC the day you died, having an open cry
They all wear helmets onstage. They are all Henny Penny
ever hardhat-ready for another falling sky.

Rita, did I ever tell you my great uncle Miley died in the mines?
My mother and I drove to Glace Bay last year
The old company houses are split down the middle
Each half is a different hand-painted hue and empty

We bowled candlepin alone in the basement of a church
It did not strike us to genuflect upon entry

III.

Rita, I heard the RCMP trailed you in the '70s!
They were not good Arts reviewers, those Mounties:

*She's the one who composes and sings women's lib songs. 100 sweating,
uncombed women standing around in the middle of the floor with their
arms around each other crying sisterhood and dancing.*

They didn't know the *gravitas* required of a fat woman with a microphone.
They didn't see you as a teenager with a baby decades before *Juno*
Or the surgeries you had for cleft palate in your youth
Not even the abuse you sang through

They don't believe in ghosts like we do or know those family spirits
that can refill a rum tumbler when your back is turned.

IV.

Rita, do you remember the "Heritage" commercial about mine collapse?
An actor swears that they sang   those   hymns
Even drank their own *you know*
At seven, this frightened me
But now I've seen a bit
I've watched Ashley MacIsaac (1975–) discuss urination during sex
I still toe-tap to his first crossover hit
Still watch the bit on Conan O'Brien
where Ashley kicks up his kilt
while going commando.
Yes, to queer kids watching at home
a kilt can become a portal to another life
not yet witnessed or understood.
Step we gaily, on we go!

Heel for heel and toe for toe!
I want to feel him move his bow, dab at his brow,
wash his feet, or at least buy him a pedicure
so that I can tell him that the queer, rural Nova Scotian diaspora
        (don't tell me it doesn't exist, b'y)
needs him to survive because
my accent is buried in Banff now
and he's the last member of my trinity still,
last I checked, alive.

V.

One of my fat aunts resembles you, Rita.
Once, at the liquor store, someone cried:
I didn't know that you're in town for a show!
My aunt grabbed her rye and tried to smile
She drove home angry foot to floor
had her niece pour the spirit
until the ice would float.

Now she's on the wagon.
Her niece is a nephew.
Things change, Rita.

       Rita, say anything! Tell me we can break biscuits
       with blueberries and Devonshire cream.

       Say that you'll let pitch-free me
       hum along as you sing me to sleep.

       Just don't tell me we didn't exist
       Don't tell me you don't

                    feel the same way too

Our Lady of San Juan River

CARMEN AGUIRRE

MARUCHA WAS SWAYING HER HIPS to ChocQuibTown's "De Donde Vengo Yo" when the last of the crystal ware arrived. The clock at the other end of the big kitchen read one thirty. She loaded a rack with the cognac glasses, then pushed it through the machine until it caught on the conveyor belt that pulled it through the wash cycle. The music blasting from her headphones brought with it a third wind; the second had moved its way up the soles of her feet hours earlier when, as a batucada played on her iPod, she'd been presented with stacks of stubborn sauté pans.

The restaurant was hosting a private function for the film festival tonight and the floor staff was aflutter with the presence of Hollywood royalty. Marucha had heard them say that Johnny Depp and Leonardo DiCaprio were in the room, but when she'd peeked through the swinging kitchen door, careful to stay out of sight in her soiled white apron and filthy pink crocs, all she'd managed to make out in the crowd of expensive black suits and sequined gowns were the backs of the restaurant's owners (a couple in their thirties), and the manager's aquiline profile. Extra security had been hired to protect the tony crowd; the private cops had even come into the kitchen at the start of the night and peered into its corners, conducting what the manager referred to as a "sweep." iPod silenced, Marucha had leaned against the counter, mouth shut, face neutral, avoiding eye contact with the cameras that lived where the walls met the ceiling.

Her back was turned to the blur of activity lit by rows of hanging lights, so she could lose herself in her playlist. Tonight, like every night, she let the music take her back to El Choco. Once, she'd heard the sous-chef refer to Sierra Leone when pointing her out to a new line cook. She hadn't corrected him. She communicated with the staff mostly through hand signals and low clicks and murmurs, even though her English was at an advanced level, according to Señor Yoon, the old Korean man who owned the grocery store on the corner of her building and could always be found at the cash register. Except for slang, she understood quite a bit. But she revelled in the freedom of playing dumb, nodding and smiling the odd time someone talked to her or gestured in her direction. There was no need to tell her story, no interest from anyone to hear it. She could live in a bubble not entirely of her own creation, and, like the hot blood that rushes from the core of the body to the extremities when one is freezing to death, there was a warmth to the numbness that came with it. She nodded at herself now, in surrender to the certainty that this would be her last such night. A smile formed on her lips when she thought of the paradoxical undressing that comes at the final moment of hypothermia, the action of disrobing calling on death to come quicker.

She'd been surprised at how much she loved being invisible. When she left the confines of the bustling kitchen and took the bus and then the streetcar to her home in Regent Park, her tall frame, black skin, and Afro hairdo were perceptible, but people dropped their gaze if she met their eyes with hers. Sometimes young black men in her neighbourhood were beaten or shot by police, their grieving families denouncing racism on the evening news, but she herself hadn't experienced it, although people sometimes cut in front of her in a lineup, claiming not to have seen her when she piped up. In El Choco she hadn't been invisible, but rather inconspicuous in a place where most of the population were descendants of slaves from Guinea, Ghana, and Nigeria. Eye contact was the norm, and being whistled at by the men was not only expected, women felt insulted if their swinging hips didn't elicit catcalls. She smiled at the memory of carnival dancing in her tight, white jeans during a weekend getaway to Barranquilla with her girlfriends, at a lover's tongue between her legs on the beach at the break of dawn. Here, men seldom flirted with her, and no man had ever asked her out. She sighed and wondered how she'd ended up in a country where Saturday nights found her swaying alone in a hairnet under fluorescent lights.

As she loaded a new rack with champagne flutes, she envisioned her parents, sitting in the doorway of their home on the shores of the river at dusk, swatting at flies. Like most of her comrades, she'd shielded them from the darker aspects of her life. Her heart still contracted at the image of her father coming home from singing praise at the Evangelical Christian Church, taking in the scars on her face, swallowing hard and stepping back. Marucha brought her rubber-gloved hand up to the mark on her temple, an indentation left by a cigarette burn. The glowing tip had been aimed at her pupil, but she'd managed to break free of the hands that held her head in place, turning away at the last second.

Stevie Wonder's "For Once in My Life" travelled from her eardrums down her arm and to her hand pushing the champagne flutes onto the conveyor belt. She pulled down a wineglass. rack and conjured the smell of the plantain frying in the afternoon, her children licking their lips around her. In the three years she'd been in Canada, they had grown from teenagers to adults, and they thrust their Hollywood assumptions onto her Northern refugee life. She couldn't blame them—she managed to send money back home every month even on her kitchen worker's wages. She'd been a doctor in Colombia; Canada had reinvented her as a dishwasher. She wondered at the immigrant dream, at those who wanted nothing more than what people in this country referred to as a "high standard of living" or a "good quality of life." She saw no meaning in it herself. Perhaps that was why there had been no inciting incident to convince her that she had to burst the bubble before she paradoxically undressed and mistook the consuming of goods for a good quality of life. She wished she could say that something terrible had happened, whether it be a violent act of racism, or insurmountable poverty, or lack of opportunity in this richest of countries. But no. Nothing like that. It was just a piling up of inconsequential days referred to as "peace and safety" by those who looked upon the likes of her with pity, if they bothered to look at all.

Her imperceptible life in Colombia had become an underground one after the paramilitary ambushed her on the way home from the clinic. During a gang rape, they'd not only put out cigarettes on her skin, they'd knifed her. The scar ran across the right side of her face, from the root of her nose to her jawbone. The attack came because she'd spoken out about the Canadian gold mine upriver. Day after day she'd treated patients who were suffering from mercury poisoning. They'd arrive gasping for breath, complaining of nausea, vomiting, diarrhea. Some of them were miners, others were women who washed clothes in the San Juan River. There were no safety standards at the mine, either. A few miners had already been killed in accidents and others had been injured. Several union leaders had been murdered by the paramilitary, who worked off a list of names provided by the Canadian embassy in Bogotá. Marucha was filled with rage at all of it, but as a doctor, she had concentrated on the mercury, demanding that the government declare the poisoned water a public health issue. She'd travelled to meetings with health workers from other regions encountering the same conditions, had appeared on radio shows and granted print interviews, until she'd been intercepted by the paramilitary on her way home that day.

Afterwards, she'd staggered to one of her colleagues' homes. He'd disinfected her wounds, sewn her cheek shut, and then hidden her through a network of helpers, moving her from home to home almost nightly for a month. If her political conscience had been born during the months leading up to the attack, those weeks of hiding had provided her with political education. She'd concluded that, given the current situation, one must sometimes work underground to be more effective in bringing about change. That her public outcry had not been in vain, but that working to protect the river and its people by fighting for zones free of multinational control was more useful if done in secret, organizing outside the public eye, where one was a moving target. She watched her new-found comrades refer to each other by fake names, leave through back doors, refrain from sharing personal information, and talk in hushed tones about tactics and strategies, while she smoked her Pielroja cigarettes and stared out a window at the sky. Before being smuggled to Bogotá in a clinic van, she stopped by her parents' house. Her heart squeezed again now, at the memory of her mother holding her face in her hands, at her children's shocked expressions when seeing her scars, at her father retreating into the other room.

She placed the final wineglass on the rack, pushed it through, and sang out loud for the first time. Still singing, she turned around and observed the choreography of the winding-down kitchen from her background post, the clatter and banging and yelling, the swinging door, the leaning staff, and, while she sang along to the last verse of the Stevie Wonder song, she placed her palms together, bowed her head, and inwardly gave thanks to this machine that melted away grease and grime and spat out kitchenware shining like new under the lights.

The staging area on the other side of the dishwasher was full. The first rack she'd pushed through pressed against a lever and the whole operation stopped. Marucha peeled off her gloves and hauled over the rolling rack, straining to get it over the rubber mat she stood on, muddy with her footprints now, so she could stack the racks of clean glasses and then wheel them down the aisle to put them away. Sade sang "Your Love Is King." The restaurant had emptied out by now, and a glance toward the other end of the kitchen told her that things would wrap up in about half an hour. The junior sous-chef, a young man about her son's age, was wrapping and labelling food, the porter Anil, a Sri Lankan immigrant who also kept a low profile, was about to start mopping the floors, the corporate chef, the chef de cuisine, the sous-chef, the line cook, the pastry cook, and the servers—all young, all pretty, almost all white—were standing in a circle, boisterous in their gossip about the celebrities they'd served. It was a rare moment of camaraderie between the floor staff and the kitchen staff. Even the executive chef was smiling.

"Holy shit, man! The shrimp tartare with avocado citrus sauce was a genius palette cleanser," one of the male servers kissed ass, his offer to high-five the corporate chef falling flat.

Not to be outdone, a blond server who always snuck Marucha dessert (she'd explained through a hilarious slapstick routine that ended in a pratfall that she herself had been a dishwasher in Fort McMurray the summer before, so she knew how horrible the job was) exclaimed that the ivory oyster mushroom soup with stewed rabbit had been a hit, and that the Nunavut caribou hind had inspired Katy Perry, who was sporting lavender dip-dyed hair tonight, to take a selfie and tweet it to her fifty million followers.

"We almost ran out of the Manitoba wild rice pudding, though," said the corporate chef, throwing an accusatory glance in the pastry cook's direction.

"Only because so many people asked for seconds!" chimed in a petite Québécoise server.

"How were the motherfuckers tonight?" inquired the executive chef.

"Worse than ever," responded a tall male server with McDreamy hair.

The manager entered through the swinging door, a morose expression on his face, followed by six of the burly private cops, walkie-talkies in hand. They planted their feet firmly apart, in a crescent moon around the manager. A chill went up Marucha's spine. She pulled off the headphones, stuffed them into her pant pocket where she'd placed her folded final paycheque, wrapped her fingers around the rolling rack handle, inhaled, and stayed put.

"Everyone take off your aprons. You have five minutes to grab your things and get out. You're all fired," the manager said in a menacing tone.

The owners walked in and stood behind the security guards, their skin pasty under the bright kitchen lights.

A stunned silence overtook the room.

The corporate chef, known for his arrogance, finally found his voice. "What are you talking about?"

"You have four minutes to take off your aprons, grab your things, and go. You're all fired."

"Is this a joke?" asked McDreamy, who was usually bragging about the big tips he got from women he referred to as cougars.

"Do I look like I'm joking, motherfuckers?" The last word was delivered with barely contained fury.

The staff's jaws dropped, the colour drained from all their cheeks. Some of the guards widened their stance, others smirked, the owners' faces remained blank.

Marucha let her hands fall to her side.

"You now have three minutes," the manager snarled.

The owners crossed their arms and set their jaws. With trembling fingers, Marucha reached behind her and began to untie her apron strings. Eyes on the floor, diverted from the glaring lights and gleaming stainless steel.

The kitchen staff in front of her removed their hats, undid their aprons, balled them up and left them on the counter. The strings of hers dangled parallel to her legs, still rooted to the tiled floor. The servers pulled off their vests. McDreamy's Adam's apple quivered, tears filled the blond ex-dishwasher's eyes. Anil balanced the mop handle against a counter and began to untie his apron at the other end of the kitchen. He and Marucha watched the staff file into the break room, fetch their jackets and bags, and exit through the back door with heads dropped. It was an act of respect, to await their turn, which they knew was always last. When they were the only two left, Anil and Marucha looked at each other and started to walk down their respective aisles, past the hanging copper pots, pans, and ladles, the gas stoves and ovens, their knobs turned to "off."

"Oh, no no no, Marucha, you don't have to go. Finish putting away the dishes and come back tomorrow. You can stay. You too, Anil," the owner ordered through a forced smile. She was wearing a black lace pantsuit and emerald droplet earrings like the ones Marucha had seen on Julia Roberts in *Us* magazine, her favourite tabloid. She devoured each new issue while sitting on a milk crate in the alley during her breaks, headphones on, cigarette wedged between her lips.

Alone with Anil in the massive kitchen now, Marucha rolled the rack up and down the aisles to finish putting the glasses away. Ears free of headphones, her job was performed to the swish of his mopping, the cameras aimed at the backs of their exposed necks.

She walked in a daze down Yonge Street, pulling on a du Maurier Light Regular, her pupils adjusting to the billboards and signs ("Guess," "Sears," "Hard Rock Cafe," "Roots," "7-Eleven"), her optic nerve transmitting this final onslaught of flickering lights to the memory folder of her brain. A knot formed in her throat.

When she opened the door to her apartment, she found her construction-worker roommates Marcos and Jaime sprawled on the couch.

"Aren't you guys at El Convento Rico picking up white chicks and dudes?"

"We were, señora, we were."

"Stop calling me señora, you idiots."

Jaime, an undocumented Oaxacan, slept on the living room floor. Marcos, a Chilango gay refugee claimant, on the couch. The three of them would smoke cigarettes and drink Negra Modelo deep into the night and tell jokes. When a silence would pass between them they'd say in unison, "An angel has passed," and keep on being silent, each lost in the realm of recollection, evoking their loved ones with eyes fixed on a distant horizon.

Marucha cracked open a beer and sat heavily at the Formica dining room table. After a moment of contemplation—the young men contemplated her, she contemplated the ceiling—Jaime asked:

"How was work?"

"Fine. They fired everybody but me and the Sri Lankan and forced everybody off the premises."

"Illegals?" Jaime asked with alarm.

"No. It wasn't the migra. It was the private cops the owners hire when they have a big do."

"Stealing then," Marcos concluded.

"No. The fools didn't know the kitchen's miked. All they ever did was slag the owners and manager and call them names behind their backs. Guess the powers that be finally got sick of it."

"Oh."

She aimed a stream of smoke at the Colombia-shaped stain on the ceiling, the one she'd lost herself in on so many winter nights.

"How did you know about the microphones?" Jaime asked, leaning forward on the couch.

"Those expensive places always spy on their workers."

She looked at them both now, careful not to let her eyes water.

By four in the morning the two young men retired and she stared out the window at the occasional passing streetcar. In the bathroom, she worked a handful of aloe vera through her hair, ran the tip of her index finger along the scar that ran like the San Juan River along her cheek, and went to bed.

A siren woke her. She looked at the clock and saw that her alarm was about to go off anyway. She got up, finished packing her bag, and placed a note and cheque on the table before slipping out.

Looking out at the city below once the airplane took off, she pondered the underground life that was coming, and all the ways in which it would differ from the invisible one she was fleeing now. How being obliterated by the North was the opposite of being destroyed by the South. By the time she disembarked in Bogotá, the bubble she lived in would burst. She crossed her arms over her womb, lifted her eyes away from the window, swallowed, and looked straight ahead.

trans womanhood, in colour

jia qing wilson-yang

with love to all of us in life, spirit, remembrance, and struggle

i. *for St. Marsha P and every Miss that took hits*

i am the flower that grows out of the cliffside
overhanging the lake on thin soil
birthed by lichen that digested rocks
that i might bloom in her body

i am the flower growing out of the cliff
will you pick me as proof of where you've been?
moved by my beauty
inspired by my resilience

will you display me so that you may walk forward
on your helping path
telling the world about flowers on cliffs
in thin soil
as you wait for recognition
          politely
in practical cloaks of humility and common goodness?

will you dry me out
pressed in the pages of a book
hidden from the light and wind
that once fed me

but now would destroy me?

or will you leave me behind
lying on the ground
my strong stem
broken
my careful bloom
withered

i am the flower that grows out of the cliffside.
a beacon. a prayer.
a target.

ii. *the many metamorphoses of white butterflies*

mechanic musician messenger mail
   "men" who
teacher trainer technician trade
    overcame
doctor dentist dealer dean
   the cocoon
engineer electrician elected elite
   to face
cyclist clergy caretaker cop
   the camera

reflecting on the metamorphoses of white butterflies
and where the camera finds focus. tells me
white butterflies can do anything

the colourful ones are just pretty.
that's why you catch them.
pinned up collections dusty in museums.
   these lost tribes gave special place to transvestites,
   why they were even revered.

but white butterflies flock to cameras like milkweed
centring themselves for the benefit of others. tells me
white butterflies can do anything in this modern world

the colourful ones are just pretty.

the metamorphoses of white butterflies
with all their possibility
tells me
a narrow path
with the brightness up
and the contrast high
sharper lines and brighter whites

tells me
these cameras aren't helping me
nearly as much as they are entertaining you

iii. *the stars are not courageous for shining,*
        they always do;
we must turn out the lights to see them.
OR i'm having second thoughts about being on your panel.

please.

i know your intentions are good
it's just that i don't trust them.

stop telling me i'm brave and courageous
courage implies consent.

Free Fall

DANIELLE DANIEL

I SHOULD BECOME A PROFESSIONAL WRESTLER. My name would be Mad Justice. I would stitch MJ on my chest and tie a tomato-red satin cape around my neck. It would flap behind me as I bounced in the ring. I'd wear badass boots and have really big hair teased on all sides.

Instead, I'm an incensed domestic, stacking plates on the counter, squeezing too much soap under hot running water, clenching my teeth in silence as the sink foams.

It was weeks since the incident, but I couldn't let it go. Anger was something I was comfortable with, like slipping on my favourite pair of jeans. I wasn't sure if it was growing up with my dad that made me that way or everything else that came after. We'd gone as a family to the local Remembrance Day ceremony, the first one since the accident. Steve wanted to take Owen. He said it was time. I told him we'd go together.

That morning, he rolled out of the bathroom wearing his green wool uniform. My body throbbed with grief as I forced a smile, my tired eyes gazing past his. He still looked like a soldier. I busied myself by counting the medals on his chest. One. Two. Three. Four. One for every six months we spent oceans apart. His jump wings sewn above them. Wings wide open like a bird about to take flight. Golden. I watched him leaning over, putting on his boots in his wheelchair, with the brakes on. Black laces gripped in hands calloused from wheeling himself around. He laced them tightly, like he had done all those times before, even though he'd never walk in those boots again. Then he sat up tall in his chair and positioned his maroon beret on his cleanly shaved head. I had married such a handsome man.

Owen wore his good pants, black with a thick sweater under his winter jacket. I wore black pants as well, with my grey turtleneck and black wool coat. Funeral clothes. All three of us with poppies pinned like splotches of blood to our chests.

Since we would all be separated on November 11, we decided to go to the local ceremony the day before. There, at least, we could remember together. But the hardest day we would spend apart. Ontario did not recognize Remembrance Day as a statutory holiday—thanks to the Legion, who had voted against it. On November 11, it would be business as usual where we lived.

As we approached the community building, a parade of cadets was already sliding into formation. Legion people strapped with medals and banners paced with equal parts of purpose and pride. This was their day.

My eyes scanned the perimeter of the building, looking for the way inside.

"Steve, do you think there's another way in?" I asked.

"There better be. I see stairs, and a lot of them," he said as he pulled into the parking lot.

I felt my jaw clench, my teeth grinding front to back. For god's sake, not today.

"Just relax, Dan. We'll figure it out."

He'd barely brought the car to a stop when I swung open the car door and jumped out of my seat. At the back of the car, I clutched his wheelchair frame, attaching both wheels and rolling it toward the driver's side. Slowly he transferred into the chair, the spasms in his legs shaking his body like a vibrator. When his legs stopped shaking, he picked them up with his hands and positioned his feet on the plate at the front of his chair, strapping the feet in with a bungee cord so they wouldn't fall off without him knowing. We'd learned this the hard way: his feet had flopped over while his arms propelled the chair forward, jamming his feet under the metal frame. Several times, he could have fallen out flat on his face. And then, there were the times that he did. He pulled down on his jacket and straightened his beret, squeezing it against his head into proper placement.

"Let's go," he said as he wheeled ahead toward the cadets, legionnaires, and other spectators who had started to arrive. Owen and I followed hand in hand.

They looked at us like we didn't belong—the only ones with Veteran plates in the parking lot. Empty faces looking on with no welcome or salutations as though Steve had not been prompted and persuaded to attend the ceremony by a local man who belonged to an Airborne Association.

"Excuse me," I asked an older woman legionnaire. "Where is the wheelchair access to this building?"

She looked around before answering me. Her eyes skimmed past

Steve, then Owen, then me. Then she scanned her surroundings from side to side. A man stepped forward and spoke before she could open her mouth.

"I'm sorry, but I don't think this building is wheelchair accessible, Miss. We'll send someone in to find out."

"What the hell," I murmured under my breath.

Steve shot me a glare. I knew he wanted me to be careful with my language in front of Owen.

"Well, my son is about to get quite an education then," I said, ignoring his warning.

We waited for five never-ending minutes. I spoke to Owen in French while we waited, telling him the world still had so much to learn and this was one of those teachable moments. He just shook his head and agreed with me. He knew I was angry. Steve waited patiently without saying a word.

"I just spoke with the custodian and I'm sorry, there is no handicap access," he said, looking directly at Steve.

"This is unbelievable! How can you host a goddamned Remembrance ceremony in a building without wheelchair access?"

"I'm sorry, we didn't know."

"You didn't know? You didn't know veterans might want to pay their respects to the Fallen—our friends? What about other wheelchair users who want to attend? Shame on you. Shame on all of you!" I yelled.

"Dan, that's enough. Let's just go."

I took a step forward.

"You have no idea how hard it was for my family to come here today," I said as I jabbed my index finger into my chest. This was the first time since the accident that we've been able to come as a family and we just got kicked in the face by the people who are supposed to know better."

"We could carry him in," the man who had invited us hollered as he approached us. Did he know about this before? Was this his intention all along?

"Carry him in? He's a human being, a grown man!" I shouted.

"I just thought—"

"You thought wrong."

"Let's go, Dan. Now," Steve said. And I knew by his tone it was time.

"Mama, you were not nice to that man," Owen said in the car as we drove away.

"No, Owen, I wasn't. But sometimes you have to tell an asshole that he's an asshole."

Steve eyeballed me, shook his head, and kept driving.

We were back home before eleven in the morning. I couldn't wait to take off my funeral clothes. I kicked off my boots and threw my jacket on the chair.

"Aren't you going to say something?" I said.

"What do you want me to say?"

"Something. Anything! Aren't you pissed off?"

"Today was a really shitty day," he said.

"That's it?"

"Dan, I don't want to hear you bitch about this anymore. This day was—is—hard enough. I just want to forget about it."

He rolled back into the bedroom to take off his uniform, his boots, and his poppy. He had long ago removed his beret. It had been sitting in his lap, an empty shell. I closed our bedroom door and led Owen to get changed, throwing his clothes into a heap beside his hamper. I knew it would bother Steve, but I left them on the floor anyway. I pulled Owen in close, his long legs dangling off the bed, and I held him against my chest, rocking him back and forth like when he was a baby. He let me hold him without saying a word.

December had arrived quickly, despite my ongoing resentment with November. I was unpacking the Christmas decorations, cradling the glass ornaments I had purchased our first Christmas as husband and wife—the one when Steve was serving in Bosnia. I remembered how we spoke that Christmas morning. He had called me on a satellite phone from the field, a rare occasion. He was in the mountains and eating beans from a can. He said they had decorated a small tree with various items from army kits to make it more festive while he was on OP (Observation Post). His voice was still cheerful. But that was before.

"I don't think I can do it again," I said.

"Do what again?" He asked.

"Host Christmas. It's the last thing I want to do. It ruins the entire holiday for me. I used to love Christmas."

"Dan, please. I don't have a large family like you. They're all I have."

"I know, but I keep feeling like I'm betraying myself. I can't hold my tongue while I pass the mashed potatoes anymore."

"It's just one day. I want Owen to know his grandparents. I never had the chance to know mine."

Two years ago we'd given Steve's dad the proper wood to build a ramp for their home, but there was still no ramp and there never would be. His younger brother, who had bought a house with a ramp next door to his parents, had removed his. Without explanation. No one ever spoke of this in the Daniel family. And I was forbidden to.

Christmas was on me. I was tired of giving what I didn't have. I could not pretend for one more day that this was acceptable. I could not open my home to this family anymore. But I did—for Steve. I kept the peace on the outside as my insides twisted with rage.

"Dear Heavenly Father, thank you for this meal we are about to eat. We pray for mercy and forgiveness. We pray for those who are not here and those who are unable to eat a meal like this on Christmas Day. Bless the hands that made this meal, Father, and all those who are here tonight. We give thanks for the birth of your Son on this joyous holy day. In God we pray." *Amen.*

I tried not to choke on my food as my father-in-law's divine words lingered over the table like fine ash. I wanted to tell them all to eat shit—*you're all a bunch of hypocrites.* I wanted them to know how much we struggled, every day, to get around in this world while they walked into their rampless homes, said grace, and prayed for us to accept Jesus—only then would Steve's suffering end. I wanted to tell them all to have a Merry-fucking-Christmas-and-a-Happy-fucking-New-Year as I launched the turkey out the back door and into the deep snow. But I didn't. I smiled. I hosted. I dug into my insufficient reserves to give them a pleasant Christmas, then, as I had so many times, I picked up the crumpled paper from the gifts they had opened. I faked it while I watched my sister-in-law, who had just married into the family, open her gift from my in-laws, a remote car starter (installed), while my car would continue to sit, frozen every morning. My performance was Oscar-worthy. And after all this, after they had gone home, I went to pour myself a glass of wine, the same wine I had asked his brother and wife to bring (after years of coming empty-handed), but it was no longer in my fridge. Even the opened bottle was gone.

For almost a week after the holidays, I reminded Steve daily that I wouldn't be hosting his family's Christmas again, not for the next five years. He didn't fight me. But he did ask me to stop complaining about it. He was sick of hearing me go on. It was over and I should stop being so negative. I better change my attitude soon because I was becoming really hard to live with, he said.

I wanted him to call his mother, but he wouldn't. He said he would tell her next year. Why call her now? It would just make things awkward, he said. What I really wanted was for him to be on my team. To demand respect for me. To tell them to build a ramp or else.

But all of that was in the past. Now was now. And right now, I needed a change of scenery. Steve and I booked a trip to Las Vegas. We had never been there before and we couldn't wait to leave the snow behind. Owen was to stay with my mom for five nights. It would be our first trip alone since he was born. We needed this time together.

We had to run some errands before driving to the Toronto airport the following day. I watched as a large man pulled into the only vacant wheelchair parking spot. I watched as he leaped out of his vehicle and sprinted toward the store entrance, while we circled the lot trying to find a wheelchair-accessible spot. We were unsuccessful. The snow was wet and heavy. I pushed Steve through the thick slush.

"Can you believe that guy?"

"What now?"

"That guy who took the wheelchair spot and strolled into the store. I'm going to find him."

"Can't we just get some light bulbs without causing a scene?" he said.

"I'm sick of people like him. He needs to be called on it."

"You're right, some people are jerks, but you can't change them all."

"That's your opinion."

We bought the light bulbs, extension cord, and windshield wiper fluid. I was holding the bags when I saw the man climb into his truck.

"Just let it go," Steve muffled under his breath, hoping for once I could hold myself back.

"Someone's got to tell him," I answered. My heart was pounding so hard I could feel it in my throat. I couldn't wait to spit my words into his face.

"You know you're parked in wheelchair parking?"

"I—uh, just ran into the store for like—a minute," he responded.

"Well, buddy, other people who really need it could use that spot. Hopefully karma doesn't bite your big, fat ass," I said, lifting my bags in the air.

He closed his door and started his truck. I watched him drive away and spin his tires onto the wet road. I heaved the chair back into the trunk after removing the slush from the wheels and we rode home in silence.

"See, there are perks," Steve said to me, as we were led first onto the plane. "Being a handicap has its benefits, we're like VIP."

I watched him transfer out of his wheelchair and into the airport aisle chair. I looked the flight attendant square in the face and said: "Be careful with that wheelchair. Last time Air Canada broke it."

Steve stared at me. I turned away unapologetically. We waited for the next 150 people to pile into the plane. I was tired already. I thought about *Star Trek* and how I wished we could transport ourselves to the American desert. I looked over at Steve. He seemed calm and content.

"So, are you ready for Veee-gas?" he asked.

"Yes, I am. Bring it." I said as I closed my eyes, wishing all the people would disappear.

We were the first ones on but the last ones off. I needed to pee. I watched as the flight attendants thanked every single person leaving the plane, smiling with their brightly painted lips but not with their eyes. Finally, two airport attendants came in with the aisle chair. Steve transferred into it, his legs trembling after not being able to stretch or move for seven hours. They pushed him out of the plane as I grabbed our carry-on luggage and followed him. We eventually made our way toward the baggage carousel. Some guy rushing to get somewhere almost knocked Steve over; Mad Justice gripped his shirt before he connected with the chair and sent Steve to the floor.

"Hey, watch where you're going. Open your freakin' eyes!"

Steve was still wheeling forward. He didn't see what happened. He didn't hear the repulsion in my voice.

"I'm so sorry. I didn't see," the young guy said. He seemed sincere. I continued to glare at him until he walked away. We got our luggage and went to find a cab.

There was a lineup. Finally it was our turn, but the taxi driver seemed confused.

"You need a handicap taxi?" He asked.

"No, my chair breaks down, but can I sit in the front?" Steve said.

The driver nodded.

Steve transferred into the front seat while I hauled the luggage into the trunk. I went to get the chair as the driver reached for it. "I got this," I told him. "Just hold the wheels." I detached them from the frame and watched to make sure the chair didn't get crushed as he closed the trunk.

Steve shouted from the shower of our hotel suite.

"Our roles have reversed!"

"What do you mean?" I asked, knowing full well what he was implying.

"Well, I used to be the hard-ass when I was in the army."

"Yup," I answered.

"Remember when I would go visit you in Ottawa with my buddies? We were such hotheads."

"Ya, you Petawawa boys, always full of trouble."

He turned off the water. "Now you walk around wanting to throw a heavy all the time." He got out of the shower, transferring from shower bench to wheelchair. I don't know how he manages to move his entire weight, all day long.

"I guess so," I said. He was now the kind and patient one, the one who chose to see the best in everybody, the kind of guy who would end up with his own TV movie-of-the-week. I was the one looking to throw down a body slam.

If only he would have known to skip the 160th parachute jump.

"Ready to hit the slots?" he asked, sliding the room key off the desk.

Vegas was a circus show for adults. Everything about it was grand.

"This is a perfect world," he said, beaming. "Everything here is so accessible."

He felt welcomed there, like he belonged in society. It made me sad the only place on earth that made him feel welcomed was the city with no heart and no soul. We managed to get tickets to Cirque du Soleil's *O*. The show was sold out, but they usually reserved wheelchair seats. Perks. We watched the show and it was so beautiful I wanted to weep.

But I breathed in deeply instead, worried that if I started, I would not be able to stop.

"In my next life, I'd like to be an acrobat," he whispered to me wide-eyed. "That's pushing your body to the extreme."

I nodded my head, remembering how much he loved to free fall from ten thousand feet.

We rolled toward the elevator to get back to the main floor, and watched a family of twelve pile into the elevator without even glancing our way.

"You have got to be kidding me," I said, the familiar rage rising within me.

"Just leave it! We'll get the next one," he said.

But Mad Justice could not let it go.

"Hey, all of you with legs," I yelled. "Use the goddamned stairs!"

They looked at me, gobsmacked. Steve wheeled sharply away, distancing himself.

My cape flapped against my back and my teeth clenched inside my mouth. He wheeled back to me, and I stood behind him, like a shadow. And we waited.

Best Practices for Time Travel

DORETTA LAU

I.

"Time travel," Ogun says, "is something I want to do, but like Louis C.K. says, if you're black you can't really go back in time further than 1980 without it sucking pretty badly."

"So time travel is something you've thought about," I say.

"Extensively," he says. "I've been thinking about this since childhood."

"You were alive before 1980, but I guess you were too young to know how terrible it was," I say.

"It was only two weeks," he says. "I was born mid-December."

Annette says, "I once tried to explain to a white male friend from high school why it wasn't possible for me to travel anywhere in the world and no matter how hard I tried, he just didn't get it. He just could not accept that women don't receive the same treatment as men. He didn't understand that sometimes I'm afraid to walk down the street I live on when it's dark out because some guy might rape and kill me. I didn't even attempt to discuss the race factor."

"If you had tried, he probably would have told you that he doesn't see race," I say.

"The thing is, he is *literally* colour-blind," Annette says. "His sister has an opposite condition—she's a tetrachromat—so she can see many more hues than a regular person."

There are four of us having dinner together: Ogun, Annette, Van, and me. We are at Ogun's apartment in Vancouver. We are not drinking, which is why we can talk about race and gender without anyone getting butthurt.

A few days before I was lying on Ogun's bed. He showed me papers belonging to his German grandmother: letters to the Nazi government and a Berlin U-Bahn map from 1938. One of the stops listed was Adolf Hitler Platz, which was called Reichskanzlerplatz when it was built earlier that century and again after the Second World War. In 1963, it was renamed Theodor-Heuss-Platz. Last year, by mistake, Google Maps reverted the square's name to Adolf Hitler Platz; the error was corrected within a few hours. Representatives for Google still cannot explain how this happened.

Even with this U-Bahn map in hand, if the four of us landed in Berlin in 1938, we'd become lost.

II.

I am sitting by myself in a cafe in Seoul, in a neighbourhood west of the palace. I do not drink coffee, but I can appreciate a good coffee shop for its ambience, by which I mean ample natural light and good music. The Grimes album *Visions* is playing at an unobtrusive volume; this makes me feel like I'm in my own apartment in Vancouver. The Blue House, the seat of South Korean presidential power, is a short walk away, and as a result, police officers in neon yellow jackets stroll back and forth on the outside pavement in a continuous fashion, alone and in pairs. Not one has stopped in for refreshments. It is snowing, but as I did not drive and I do not have dinner plans I am unconcerned.

Just moments before, I was reading Javier Marías's *Dark Back of Time*—the sequel to *All Souls*, one of my favourite Oxford novels— and encountered for the first time the word *coprophagy*—the eating of feces:

> It was rumoured that on one occasion, upon learn- ing that a university in the United States was about to offer some succulently lucrative position to an un- grateful or insufficiently obsequious disciple of his, the tactic he came up with to keep this from happening was to accuse this disciple, *sotto voce*, of coprophagy, no less, which sufficed to make the moneyed South- ern puritans cancel the nauseating contract, appar- ently without even wondering how Rylands could be in possession of such reliable information on practices and activities which, if they truly exist (and I doubt they do; these are figments and affectations of litera- ture and cinema), would certainly never be spoken of openly by anyone, still less in the city of Oxford where almost nothing is overlooked and what isn't known is created or invented.

If I am ever caught up in political intrigue, I shall denounce my enemies in this fashion: *Oh him? You didn't hear it from me, but I have it on good authority that he practises coprophagy.* A friend's ex-boyfriend—who isn't prone to hyperbole, this is important to note, but once told me I was the most racist person he'd ever met—recounted that he once took a shit at a fast-food restaurant along Granville Street in Vancouver. (There is a discount shoe store there now.) He stood, and right before he was about to flush, someone reached under the stall, grabbed a log of his poo from the toilet bowl, and ate it in a gulp.

III.

"If you were to travel back in time, where would you want to go?" Van asks.

"I've been trying to determine whether it would be safe for me to visit Egypt while the pyramids were being built," Ogun says. "Apparently it's a myth that they used slave labour, so I think I'd like to go there."

"I'd like to see dinosaurs," Annette says.

"That doesn't seem safe," Van says. "You'd become a meal."

"A prehistoric destination is probably safer than some parts of the world right now," she says. "I'd rather take my chances with a brachiosaurus than with an ISIS zealot."

"Are we playing *Would you rather?*" I ask.

"Would you rather deal with racism or sexism?" Van asks.

This question causes both Annette and I to pause.

"I'm not sure anyone can answer this one," Annette says.

"If I really had to answer . . . sexism," I say. "For me, it hurts less to be called a *stupid bitch* than a *stupid chink.*"

The sound of a siren drifts up from the street. It is just distant enough that I don't feel it vibrate in my chest.

"What if the technology was so good you could just beam in and out of time?" Ogun asks. "So that if a dinosaur came for you, you could beam to safety."

"If time travel were that simple, it wouldn't be safe for public use—it would be a military-grade weapon," Van says.

"I wish we could just beam out of racism and sexism," Annette says.

"That machine would be better than a time machine," Ogun says.

"An empathy machine," Van says.

We all look like we're dreaming the best dream as we each imagine how an empathy machine would change our world.

Ogun makes a pot of tea.

"I'm not sure I'd want to go anywhere into the past because I'm afraid of causing a rift in the space-time continuum and erasing my own existence," I say.

"Is that even a real thing?" Annette asks.

"I don't know, but I've seen *Back to the Future* at least twenty times, and that's my main primer on time travel," I say. "My ideas aren't based on science or anything like that. But what if I go back in time and step on a bug and it sets off a chain reaction that wipes all of us out and destroys the Earth?"

"You know, I don't think you're quite that powerful," Van says, and we all laugh.

IV.

Van and I are at a coffee shop in Toronto, talking about porn. He's gay, but his primary fascination is with female stars. He reads about them, but that's not really the same as watching them in action.

Mariah Carey's "Dreamlover" is playing over the coffee shop's speakers.

"I was just reading about Alina Li," I say. "She said in an interview she'd never 'do interracial,' even though she's Asian and all her scenes are with white men. It's creepy that *interracial* is a porn category meaning sex with black men. It's creepy that *Asian* is a category. The next time someone tells me that racism doesn't exist anymore, I'm going to point them to the narrative framework that presently exists in Western pornography."

Van laughs and says, "Asa Akira published a memoir."

"I saw her Reddit AMA about that," I say.

"I read that too. She has three definite boundaries: she won't eat shit, fuck a child, or fuck an animal," he says.

"I think those three things are no-go for most people."

"But, Rule 34—if something exists, there is porn of it."

"Sometimes I feel like such a second-wave feminist when it comes to porn," I say. "In theory, I'm like whatever. I mean, this generation of stars seems to have much more control over their careers. But if there are coprophagic child bestiality videos, I just can't."

"In the case of those sorts of videos, with the exception of shit-eating pedophiles who live for that kind of thing, we're *all* second-wave feminists."

"You know, I don't like the way Asa Akira does her eye makeup—like she's a white girl, making it clear that the fantasy that's unfolding on-screen is curated for a white male gaze—so I can't watch her," I say. "When I told my roommate about this, he told me I must not like sex. But porn is about aesthetics, fantasy, desire, and power as much as it is about watching people fuck and getting off on it."

"Maybe you think too much when you're watching porn," Van says.

"That's my new Tinder tag line: 'I think too much while watching porn.'"

"Keep it simple. Make it: 'I watch porn.'"

"I think 'I watch sports' is more attractive."

"But that would be a lie."

"I do watch sports documentaries though."

"You do?"

"It comes in handy during Tinder dates."

"You're depressing me now."

"Am I sadder than Grindr?"

"At least Grindr has dick pics."

"Okay, let's stick to porn," I say. "I interviewed Annabel Chong, when she was the title holder of the World's Biggest Gang Bang—actually maybe someone else had already topped her number by then. It was during the time the documentary about her was screening at film festivals."

"What did you talk about?"

"I asked questions about her family and about feminism—"

"No!"

"Because she was doing graduate work in gender studies."

"Still."

"Before the interview started, she took my list of questions and read them before I said anything," I say. "We didn't have much of a conversation. My friend Kate ended up talking to her for two hours and after that they kept up an email correspondence for a few years."

"What would you ask her now?"

"If I did it all over again, I'd probably ask her what kind of porn she likes to watch, or if she even watched porn before she shot her first scene. I wonder if she watches porn now."

"Maybe she's like one of those writers who don't read," he says.

V.

Annette is serving us cupcakes that she baked. "I think my favourite stand-up comedy take on time travel is Aamer Rahman's takedown of the idea of reverse racism," she says.

"That's the best," I say. "A perfect three minutes highlighting that racism is structural rather than interpersonal, plus the joke involves a time machine."

"Why are people so uncomfortable when the word *racist* comes up, as if accusing someone of being a racist is more of a crime than being the victim of *actual* racism?" Ogun asks.

"It's you-smelt-it-you-dealt-it logic," Van says.

"Don't get me started on people who say things like *you're playing the race card* when there's a discussion about inequality," I say.

"You know people who say things like that?" Ogun asks.

"I read the comments on gymnastics blogs," I say.

"Never read the comments!" Van and Annette say at the same time.

"Too late, I've already caught canceraids from reading comments," I say.

"What if I told you I had the power to transport this entire apartment, with us in it, to another time and place?" Annette asks.

"We're not going to enact Aamer Rahman's script, are we?" I ask

"Nah, that requires us to colonialize Europe," Annette says. "I'm not into an eye for an eye. That's way too Old Testament."

"Are you going to take us to the Triassic period?" I ask.

"If we go too far back in time, this apartment won't exist," says Van. "How would we return?"

"Trust me," Annette says.

VI.

Belle and Sebastian's "The State I Am In" is playing in the Seoul cafe and the sun has begun to set, turning the light outside grey. The snow has subsided. I am thinking about Marías again. The opening sentence of *Dark Back of Time* has been haunting me:

I believe I've still never mistaken fiction for reality, though I have mixed them together more than once, as everyone does, not only novelists or writers but everyone who has recounted anything since the time we know began, and no one in that known time has done anything but tell and tell, or prepare and ponder a tale, or plot one.

Often I think about the line between fiction and non-fiction and all the ways in which we're trying to tell stories in writing or film or art or music so we can communicate how we see the world to other people. In *Dark Back of Time*, Marías is playing with authorship and autobiography. By meshing the unreal and the real, he exposes fiction for what it is: an interpretation of the human condition that is rooted in specific experiences. We don't necessarily write about what we know—words permit us to construct the grandest of characters and settings and narratives—but we write about what we know to be true.

Once, at a photo shoot with a group of writers, I asked a man in his sixties about his work.

"I write poetry, essays, and fiction," he said. "What about you?"

"I write fiction," I said.

"What do you write about?" he asked.

"Life," I said.

"So you write women's fiction," he said.

"No, I don't," I said.

I wondered if it was pretentious to say that I wrote *literary fiction*.

"Are all your main characters women?"

"No," I said.

"Oh," he said. "I've been hearing about this thing called chick lit."

"If I wrote chick lit, I might actually make money from writing," I said with a laugh.

"Less than one percent of writers make their money from writing," he said, as if he were speaking to a dim child.

I said goodbye and walked away.

Ten days ago I was riding in Lee's car in Singapore, where it was so hot despite it being January that I was wearing summer clothes. Her sister had left *Tigermilk* and Jay Chou's *Still Fantasy* in the CD player. Music is the closest I'll ever come to time travel. Whenever I hear an old album, all the feelings and the technology employed to play that music come back to me. I have owned a record player, a tape deck, a Walkman, two CD players, a Discman, four iPods (they seem to malfunction after a year or two), an iPad, an iPhone, a MiniDisc recorder, and more than twenty pairs of headphones. These days, I listen to a lot of music on my laptop, which has terrible sound quality but it doesn't matter to me because I'm not an audiophile.

Still Fantasy was released when I was living in New York. I listened to it on the stereo an ex-boyfriend had bought for me and tried to learn Mandarin by memorizing songs. My mother learned English this way, by reciting the lyrics to hits by Elvis and The Beatles. Through pop music, both of us have learned many metaphors to talk about love and loss and pain, but still we are silent about our feelings. Sometimes the only thing you have in common with another person is a language and even that tremendous advantage is not enough.

VII.

The four of us are making a production of our possible time travel. I insist that we all use the bathroom before the journey. Ogun searches through a closet for a backpack and outdoor equipment. Van fills up our water bottles and wraps up the remaining cupcakes. Annette types out an action plan that details emergency rendezvous points and best practices. She fills five pages and prints a copy for each of us. I play *Black Messiah* on an iPad just in case we need music to help us find our way back home to the present day.

"The three of you are definitely on my apocalypse team," I say.

As the men take care of the dishes and final preparations, Annette and I stand outside on the balcony for a moment. The light of the moon wavers on ocean water.

"Where are you taking us?" I ask.

"You'll like where we're going," she says.

"Are we going to the future?"

"We're always travelling forward in time."

VIII.

I liked that one stretch of Granville Street better when it was always closed to cars. Then, there were more sex shops advertising twenty-five-cent peep shows and movie houses with Hollywood, foreign, and independent programs. I saw a Care Bears flick at the Capitol 6—that was the first time I remember seeing a film that was in English in a theatre. These are some of the other films I remember seeing somewhere in dark venues along Granville that no longer exist: *Double Happiness* (with my parents and brother); *Ringu* (I was afraid of my television for an entire week after seeing it); *Crossroads* (a miscommunication—I made a joke about Britney Spears, and my friend, who is now a movie producer, bought the tickets before I arrived); *Teenage Hooker Became a Killing Machine* (which is one of two movies I've walked out of partway through . . . I felt no need to achieve narrative closure); and even *Cowboys & Aliens* (why did we think it had the potential to be a sly post-colonial commentary on what we have done to Aboriginal communities across North America?). I have never once entered one of the sex shops, not even out of curiosity, but there is something reassuring about the one or two that still remain because they run counter to the glossy fiction that Vancouver is trying to present to the world that involves beaches, pristine ski slopes within driving distance, yoga, farm-to-table restaurants, and crowded nightclubs housed in former movie theatres.

Is this nostalgia I am feeling? Am I being sentimental?

"We dismiss sentimentality in order to construct ourselves as arbiters of artistry and subtlety, so sensitive we don't need the same crude quantities of feeling—those blunt surfaces, baggy corpses," writes Leslie Jamison in the essay "In Defense of Saccharin(e)." In the months before I read this sentence, I had been thinking about why I felt an accusation of sentimentality was so galling. I wondered, what is so wrong with expressing emotion in art?

I find myself in a Catch-22. If I betray too little feeling, then I am nothing more than an Asian. If I exude too much feeling, then I am nothing more than a woman.

IX.

The four of us are standing by the door with our coats and shoes on.

"We're there," Annette says.

"How do you know we're there?" Van asks.

"I feel it," she says.

I don't feel any different. Everything in the room looks the same—except the view from the window may have changed. Or am I imagining that? Has the apartment transited space and time?

"Where are we?" Van asks. He walks to the window. "I can't see anything."

"We can see for ourselves if we leave the apartment," Ogun says as he picks up one of the backpacks.

"Is that a good idea?" Van asks.

"You trust me, don't you?" Annette asks.

I have many questions, too: What's outside? Is a dinosaur about to tear me apart?

I try to take in even breaths. I can't let fear stop me from discovery.

"Ready?" I ask, peering at their faces. Van looks nervous. Annette is calm, while Ogun is excited.

Everyone, including Van, nods.

I open the door and cross the threshold.

No Comment

ALESSANDRA NACCARATO

I've heard there is a room where hooded
women enter, writing dates on the wall
with the torn edge of their finger. I've heard
you can cipher the numbers to bodies, to
the graceless edge of some men's beds. Is
this what you call justice? If so, why not
pull back the hood. They say the room locks
from the outside. Just wondering how you
got out? If you could show us, on your body.
For example, one man we publicly shamed.
He's tied up in court, if you're looking for press
credentials. How many women stand
in this room? Where do they piss and how
often? Can you comment on the man suing
your spokeswoman for slander? How close
was your body to his mouth? Did you choose
his name by lottery or straws? How will you
answer if you're sued for this poem?

Somewhere in Between

EMILY COOPER

Somewhere in Between by Emily Cooper
Photography, 40.64 x 66.04 cm

It was an artistic block that became the inspiration for this body of work. I felt like all the creative doors of my mind had been slammed shut, and I was trapped inside a tiny box. When I went to Mexico to find a way out, I started to photograph with my gut, and found myself drawn to these beautiful pieces of crumpled-up paper. I realized I was literally photographing my creative block. I took this instinct, and brought it with me through my travels in Asia, picking up paper as I went along. We became reflections of one another, and as I emerged from my artistic block, the paper slowly unravelled. The words swirl around the page as my thoughts swirl in my mind. Once I had finished the series, every artistic bone in my body was alive.

The Future of *Room*

CHELENE KNIGHT

ROOM CHANGES LIVES. And when it comes to what the future of *Room* looks like to me, it's pretty simple: we need to *continue* changing lives.

When I published my first book and did interviews with newspapers and other magazines, the number one question I was asked was where I got my MFA. I cringed because I don't have one, nor have I ever had the urge to take my education to that level, and, let's be honest, it's not and never will be financially possible for me. But this questioning about my education made me think about my role in the writing, publishing, and teaching world and how this role would most likely break a few moulds along the way. How do I fit in among the people who— according to every other Canadian literary magazine—should be doing the job I am doing? Every opportunity that has been offered to me came attached with the inevitable question: Can I do this? Yes. And I am doing it.

Because of the serious focus on diversity and mentorship at *Room*, I decided to jump at the offer of managing editor. In my opinion, I was too inexperienced, but I knew *Room*'s former managing editor Rachel Thompson would guide me and make sure I was supported. I don't know many other magazines that operate like this, that take chances like this and say "don't worry, we've got your back, we'll figure it out." There's a trust within *Room*, and there's a need to uplift not only the writers we support and publish, but the people that make up this very important collective. This is the real diversity and the first step toward real change. It starts here.

One thing I have come to realize is that we are in a constant tornado of diversity hashtags. Trying to fit in, trying to fill gaps, trying to accommodate, but are we? Are we a literary community providing a safe place for our writers to speak? Are we constantly self-evaluating ourselves and the way we interact with our community? This is where *Room* shines. We never stop trying, we never stop taking risks and chances on the "unknowns"—I know this for a fact because *Room* took a chance on me.

Growing up in a single-parent household facing adversity, with a mother who struggled her entire life with addiction, violent abuse, and prostitution, I never felt like I had a safe place to share my story, her story, or any story. The future of *Room* has space for women like me. Women who've come from nothing, and brought more than their fair share to the table.

The future of *Room* is about providing that safe haven for stories, all stories. From the first decade with Cyndia Cole's "No Rape. No." to the fourth decade with Alessandra Naccarato's "No Comment," you can see, feel, and hear the necessity for amplifying voices and speaking up. The voices of those who were and are afflicted by physical, emotional, and sexual abuse need to be heard too. We can't shy away from that. And we haven't. After over forty years the threads are still connected, holding on tight without the threat of unravelling.

When I first heard about Meghan Bell's idea for this anthology project a couple of years ago, I was brand new to the collective and had no idea the effect this project would have on me or how important it was until I started reading through the archives. It's very evident that people trust us as a platform to share stories that are not easy to tell. As a survivor and witness to some very disturbing sexual and violent abuse—something I've never had the courage to say out loud until I penned this—I find solace in knowing *Room* exists and will continue to exist.

Empowered. I feel it every single day. We still have work to do, but when diversity stops being a hashtag and instead becomes a natural instinct, an everyday organic occurrence, I will happily say real progress has been made. I see *Room* growing in many ways, and this is beyond what we publish. We have always been a place for women's voices and we can still continue to add to that, but my vision goes above and beyond the pages of *Room*. I hope that other magazines will mirror our progress. Let's sit down and have these never-ending conversations. It's time. There's room.

—Chelene Knight, December 2016

On the Making of *Making Room*

MEGHAN BELL

WHAT YOU HOLD IN YOUR HANDS IS A LABOUR OF PASSION. I've been a part of this project from day one: I proposed *Making Room* (then referred to as "the Anthology") at a meeting in December 2013, and applied for the first grant to make the book a reality a year later. I still can't believe that the rest of the collective—at the time, all volunteers—were willing to throw their energy into what felt like a pipe dream with me.

This project has involved a lengthy digitization process (including hunting down missing issues from libraries), hundreds of volunteer hours reading through these archives to create a longlist of works to consider for publication, and then dozens more hours of reading, plus a two-day retreat, to cull our longlist down to seventy-five contributors.

In addition to showcasing some of the best work the magazine has published, one of the goals of this anthology was to explore how Canadian feminism has evolved since *Room* was founded in 1975—and how *Room*, under the ever-shifting Growing Room Collective, has changed as well. We tried to pick writing that best represents feminist discourse in CanLit for each of the four decades of the magazine's existence. We envisioned creating a unique publication in Canada's literary landscape: a historical document, a political statement, but, above all, a collection of writing by some of the finest authors our country has produced in the past forty years.

On behalf of the Growing Room Collective, I am grateful for the support and enthusiasm of the Department of Canadian Heritage through the Canada Periodical Fund, Vici Johnstone from Caitlin Press, Amber Dawn, Eleanor Wachtel, Gayla Reid, Mary Schendlinger, Lana Okerlund, Rachel Thompson, Chelene Knight, accounting superstar Mindy Abramowitz, our IndieGoGo donors, and all of the amazing authors and family members of authors who gave us permission to republish the incredible writing that appears in this collection. And a special thank you to the dozens of women who have volunteered their time to publish *Room* since 1975 (named on the next page). We couldn't have done this without you.

—Meghan Bell, December 2016

Room Collective Members and Guest Editors, 1975 – 2016

COMPILED BY CLÉLIE RICH, TARYN HUBBARD, & CARA LANG

Thank you to the many people who have volunteered their time as a collective member or guest editor of *Room* over the past forty years.

Mindy Abramowitz
Mary Anderson
Sylvia Arnold
Helena Ashcroft
Virginia Aulin
Laurie Bagley
Patricia Bartle
Tanya Behrisch
Meghan Bell
Robin Bellamy
Tanya Berish
Olivia Bevan
Penny Birnbaum
Gail Blayney
Terri Brandmueller
Mary Breen
Cynthia Brooke
Ruth Brown
Cullene Bryant
Danielle Bugeaud
Rachel Burns
Monica Calderon
Mary Cameron
Anne Camp
Thyrza Cohen
Christina Cooke
Susan Cooper-Sylvestre
Viktoria Cseh
Lucille Dahm
Nancy Dautovich

Amber Dawn
Stephanie Dayes
Joanna Dean
Shawna Delgaty
Jennifer Delisle
Margo Dunn
Melissa Edwards
Judy Egerton
Kim Elhatton
Karen Elkan
Jane Evans
Verna Feehan
Sylvia Fenichel
Candace Fertile
Linda Field
Adrienne Fitzpatrick
Barbara Fletcher
Jayne Forbes
Victoria Freeman
Jasna Ganibegovic
Sierra Skye Gemma
Elaine Bougie Gilligan
Leah Golob
Caragh Goudie
Paula Grasdal
Maja Grip
Joy Gugeler
Jane Hamilton
Zoya Harris
Enid Harrop

Sonya Hirschberg
Amber Hitchen
Serena Henderson
Shannon Henderson
Beverly Hornal
Taryn Hubbard
Dawn Johnston
Nailah King
Jónína Kirton
Caroll Klein
Melanie Klingbeil
Chelene Knight
Karin Konstantynowicz
Irina Kovalyova
Lindsay Glauser Kwan
Bonnie Lane
Cara Lang
Laura Leach
Rebecca Lee
Fiona Lehn
Mica Lemiski
Sue Leon
Lora Lippert
Karen Loder
Brigid MacAulay
Susan MacFarlane
Kathryn MacLeod
Maureen Mahoney
Lisa Manfield
Alissa McArthur

Amy McCall

Xan McCallum

Audrey McClellan

Lora McElhinney

Jade McGregor

Melva McLean

Laura McNairn

Lorrie Miller

Emily Milliken

Karol Morris

Rose Morris

Amy Dunn Moscoso

Sachiko Murakami

Bonnie Murray

Nav Nagra

Heidi Nagtegaal

Janet Nicol

Bonnie Nish

Lana Okerlund

Liz Orme

Madelen Ortega

Dorothy Ellen Palmer

Ruth Panofsky

Naomi Pauls

Monica Penner

Janice Pentland-Smith

Nita Pilans

Janet Pollock

Helen Polychronakos

Susan Prosser

Wendy Putman

Gayla Reid

Poppi Reiner

Karen Rempel

Clélie Rich

Patricia Robertson

Patricia Robitaille

Susannah Rohloff

Helene Rosenthal

Samantha Rousseau

Rebecca Russell

Susan Safyan

Mary Schendlinger

Carrie Schmidt

Chloe Sekouri

Geffen Semach

Elizabeth Shaffer

Muriel Shey

Margaret Shore

Sandy Shreve

Laura Sibbery

Nadine Simcoe

Ikbal Singh

Jo Sleigh

Cathy Smith

Mikey Smytho

Arielle Spence

Maria Stanborough

Christine Stefanitsis

Bonnie Stewart

Carolyn Stewart

Cathy Stonehouse

Amanda Sun

Joy Tataryn

Betty Taylor

Eunice Tempest

Madeleine Thien

Rachel Thompson

Carol Tidler

Ana Torres

Anita Ungar

Robin Van Heck

Yvonne Van Ruskenveld

Gail van Varseveld

Eleanor Wachtel

Kim Wakeman

Andrea Warner

Nancy Weaver

Gerda Wever-Rabehl

Jeannie Wexler

Jean Wilson

Kayi Wong

Betty Wood

Susan Wood

Lisa Xing

Kam Sein Yee

JM Young

Jennifer Zilm

Contributors

Carmen Aguirre's *Something Fierce: Memoirs of a Revolutionary Daughter* won CBC Canada Reads 2012 and is a #1 national best seller. *Mexican Hooker #1 and My Other Roles Since the Revolution*, a *Globe and Mail* best seller, was published in April 2016.

Najwa Ali's fiction, non-fiction and poetry has appeared in *Room*, *World Literature Today*, *Warscapes*, and *Wasafiri*. "Writing, In Transit" won *Room*'s CNF prize in 2013 and was short-listed for the Canadian National Magazine Awards.

Gail Anderson-Dargatz is a two-time Giller finalist. Her latest book, *The Spawning Grounds*, was released in September 2016. She mentors writers around the world through her online forums. For more, visit her website at gailanderson-dargatz.ca or on Twitter @AndersonDargatz.

Elizabeth Bachinsky is an arts administrator and advocate, educator, and the author of five books of poetry including *The Hottest Summer in Recorded History* and *Home of Sudden Service*. She lives in New Westminster, B.C.

Marie Annharte Baker envisions with sideways slant for continuance and survivance in her poetics. *Being on the Moon*, *Exercises in Lip Pointing*, and *Indigena Awry* bear witness to her walk and talk. Her challenge is a mutant métissage method. Currently, she is working on the murdered and missing issue as she lost her mother in the fifties. She is a winner of the Blue Metropolis award for Indigenous writing. She is off-rez Winnipeg from Little Saskatchewan First Nation.

Juliane Okot Bitek lives and loves in Vancouver. She is a doctoral candidate at UBC and an avid reader, essayist, poet, and occasionally a short fiction writer. Her poetry collection, *100 Days* (2016), is published by University of Alberta Press.

Monique Bosco was an Austrian-born Canadian journalist and writer. She received the Governor General's Award for French-language fiction in 1970 for her novel *La femme de Loth*.

Kate Braid has written and co-edited twelve prize-winning books of poetry and non-fiction. In 2015 she received the Mayor's Award for leadership in the literary arts in Vancouver. Visit katebraid.com.

Nicole Brossard is a poet, novelist, and essayist born in Montréal in 1943. Her work has been translated in ten languages. She has won, among many other prizes, the Governor General's Award twice. She has published more than forty books, including *Mauve Desert*, *Notebook of Roses and Civilization*, *White Piano*, and *Ardour* (Coach House Books).

Cyndia Cole is a member of Quirke, the Queer Imaging and Riting Kollective for Elders. Her work can be found in Quirke's forthcoming book, *Basically Queer: An Intergenerational Guide to LGBTQA Lives*, co-authored with Youth for A Change. She lives with her Soka family in Spud Palace in Vancouver.

Emily Cooper's art has been published in *Applied Arts* magazine, the *National Post*, the *Vancouver Courier*, the *Toronto Star*, and has received the Communication Arts Award. Her work includes fifteen covers for *The Georgia Straight*, photo illustrations for Shaw Festival brochures, book covers for HarperCollins, and editorial illustrations for *The Boston Globe*. She is currently working on a project with the National Film Board. A selection of Emily's work can be found at the Doctor Vigari Gallery in Vancouver.

Ivan Coyote is the author of eleven books and a seasoned stage performer. Coyote is a third-generation Yukoner who now lives in Vancouver.

Lucas Crawford is from rural Nova Scotia and lives in Fredericton. Lucas's *Sideshow Concessions* (Invisible Publishing, 2015) won the Robert Kroetsch Award for Innovative Poetry. Lucas was Critic-in-Residence of CWILA (2015) and is Assistant Professor of English at UNB.

Su Croll has published two books: *Worlda Mirth* (Kalamalka Press, 1992) and *Blood Mother* (Signature Editions, 2008). A novel, *Image Hungry*, and a poetry collection, *Someday*, are seeking publication. She lives in Edmonton.

Lynn Crosbie is a PhD and professor. Her new collection of poetry, *The Corpses of the Future*, will appear with House of Anansi in 2017.

An Officer of the Order of Canada and the winner of the Governor General's Award, **Lorna Crozier**'s most recent book of poetry, *The Wrong Cat*, won the Raymond Souster Award for best book of Canadian poetry and the Pat Lowther Award for best book by a Canadian woman. She lives on Vancouver Island with poet Patrick Lane, many fish, and two cats who love to garden.

Danielle Daniel is the author of two children's books and *The Dependent: A Memoir of Marriage & the Military* (Latitude 46 Publishing, 2016). She is completing an MFA in Creative Writing through UBC and lives in Sudbury, Ontario.

Amber Dawn is a writer living on unceded territory of the Musqueam, Squamish, and Tsleil-Waututh First Nations (Vancouver, Canada). Her memoir *How Poetry Saved My Life: A Hustler's Memoir* won the 2013 Vancouver Book Award.

Junie Désil is a Haitian-Canadian writer. Born in Montréal, and now living in Vancouver, Junie has performed at Under the Volcano, Vancouver's International Storytelling Festival, and other venues. Her work has appeared on CBC's *Definitely Not the Opera, Room*, and in other print media.

Sandy Frances Duncan lives on Gabriola Island, British Columbia, where she continues to incubate ideas in a semi-retired fashion. She has collaborated with George Szanto on a mystery series set on islands, published by Touchwood Editions.

Dorothy Elias is a retired printer and photographer, currently living and gardening on Vancouver Island.

Marian Engel (1933 – 1985), OC, was a Canadian novelist most famous for her novel *Bear*, about a librarian who keeps intimate company with a bear. She was the founding member of the Writers' Union of Canada.

Based in Toronto, **Christine Estima**'s work has appeared in *VICE, The Globe and Mail, Metro News*, CBC, *Bitch Magazine, The Antigonish Review, subTerrain, The Puritan, Grain, EVENT, The Malahat Review, The New Quarterly, Descant, Matrix Magazine*, and many more. Visit ChristineEstima.com.

Tanya Evanson is a Montréal poet, performer, producer, and director of Banff Centre Spoken Word. She performs internationally and has published widely in journals and anthologies. Her fourth album, *ZENSHIP*, launched in Fall 2016.

barbara findlay QC is a fat old white cisgender lesbian feminist lawyer with disabilities, raised working class and Christian, who has been fighting for queer legal rights, organizing unlearning oppression work, and writing, for forty-plus years.

Cynthia Flood's most recent book, *Red Girl Rat Boy* (Biblioasis, 2013), was shortlisted for the Ethel Wilson Prize and longlisted for the Frank O'Connor Short Story Award. She lives in Vancouver's West End.

Chantal Gibson is a writer and visual artist living in Vancouver. She teaches writing and design communication in the School of Interactive Arts & Technology at Simon Fraser University.

Leona Gom is the award-winning author of fourteen novels and poetry collections. She was the editor of *EVENT* magazine for many years. Five of her novels have been translated into other languages. She lives in White Rock, B.C.

Jane Eaton Hamilton is the author of nine books of short fiction and poetry. She has been shortlisted for the MIND Book Award, the BC Book Prize, the VanCity Award, the Pat Lowther Award, and the Ferro-Grumley Award. Her memoir was one of *The Guardian*'s Best Books of the Year and a *Sunday Times* best seller.

Wasela Hiyate's work has appeared in literary quarterlies and anthologies across Canada and in the U.S. The title story of her fiction collection, *Travel Is So Broadening* (Quattro Press, 2015), was nominated for the Journey Prize. She has lived in Asia, Europe, and Latin America and in neighbourhoods in Canada that felt like Asia, Europe, and Latin America. She is currently at work on a novel.

Nancy Holmes has published five poetry collections, most recently *The Flicker Tree: Okanagan Poems* (Ronsdale, 2012). She edited *Open Wide a Wilderness: Canadian Nature Poems* (Wilfrid Laurier UP, 2009) and teaches creative writing at the University of British Columbia Okanagan. She lives in Kelowna.

Anna Humphrey is an author of books for young readers, including *Mission (Un)Popular* (Disney-Hyperion, 2011) and the *Clara Humble* series for middle grade readers (OwlKids Books, 2016 – 2018). She lives in Kitchener, Ontario.

Mindy Hung's writing has appeared in *The Toast, Salon, The New York Times, Joyland, PANK, The New Quarterly*, and many other publications. She received a New York Foundation for the Arts fiction fellowship in 2010. Her debut novel, *Trip*, was published in 2012 by Outpost19. She writes romance novels as Ruby Lang.

Aislinn Hunter is a poet, fiction writer, occasional essayist, and the author of six books. *Linger, Still,* a new collection of poems, will be published by Gaspereau Press in 2017. She lives in North Vancouver, B.C.

Carole Itter is a Vancouver-born artist who has spent decades of summers up the coast. She has worked in performance, installation, and film. In "Ten Sketches," she is writing about her daughter, Lara (1972 – 1995). Itter published Lara's journal writings, "I Might Be Nothing," in 2004.

Amy Jones won the 2006 CBC Literary Prize for Short Fiction and was a finalist for the 2005 Bronwen Wallace Award. She has published a collection of stories, *What Boys Like* (Biblioasis, 2009), and a novel, *We're All in This Together* (McClelland & Stewart, 2016). Originally from Halifax, she now lives in Thunder Bay, where she is associate editor of *The Walleye*.

Helen Kuk's poems have been published in magazines such as *Descant, Matrix, EVENT,* and *Room*. She lives and works in Vancouver, B.C.

Matea Kulić lives in Vancouver, B.C. Recent writing appears in *Poetry Is Dead, Room, the ti-TCR* (a digital imprint of *The Capilano Review*) Stuff Issue, and *The Rusty Toque* blog.

Naoko Kumagai has been published in *Room, Ricepaper,* and *EVENT*, and was also longlisted for the CBC Nonfiction Prize. She has an MFA from the University of Guelph and lives in Toronto.

Fiona Tinwei Lam has authored two poetry books, *Intimate Distances* and *Enter the Chrysanthemum*, and the children's book, *The Rainbow Rocket*. She co-edited *Double Lives: Writing and Motherhood*, and edited *The Bright Well: Contemporary Canadian Poems about Facing Cancer*. She teaches at SFU Continuing Studies.

Doretta Lau is the author of a short story collection, *How Does a Single Blade of Grass Thank the Sun?* (Nightwood Editions, 2014). She lives and works in Hong Kong and Vancouver.

Evelyn Lau is a Vancouver writer who has published eleven books, including six volumes of poetry. Her poetry has received the Milton Acorn Award, the Pat Lowther Award, and a National Magazine Award. Evelyn was the 2011 – 2014 Poet Laureate of Vancouver.

Jen Sookfong Lee lives with her son and dog in North Burnaby. Her books include *The Conjoined*, *The Better Mother*, a finalist for the City of Vancouver Book Award; *The End of East*; and *Shelter*, a novel for young adults. Jen appears as a contributor on *The Next Chapter* and is a frequent co-host of *Studio One Book Club*.

Tracey Lindberg is a citizen of As'in'i'wa'chi Ni'yaw Nation Rocky Mountain Cree and hails from the Kelly Lake Cree Nation community. She is an award-winning academic writer and teaches Indigenous studies and Indigenous law at two universities in Canada. She sings the blues loudly, talks quietly, and is part of a long line of argumentative Cree women. Her first novel, *Birdie*, came out with HarperCollins in 2015.

Dorothy Livesay was a Canadian poet who twice won the Governor General's Award in the 1940s. In 1983 she was made a Doctor of Athabasca University, and in 1987 she became an Officer of the Order of Canada. Livesay was awarded the Order of British Columbia in 1992. In 1989, the B.C. Prize for Poetry was renamed the Dorothy Livesay Prize after her.

Annabel Lyon is the author of seven works for adults and children, including the novels *The Golden Mean* and *The Sweet Girl*. She lives in Burnaby, B.C. She is currently working on turning "Mattie's Husband" into a novel.

Vera Manuel was a Ktunaxa/Secwepemc writer. Her poetry has appeared most recently in *ROCKSALT: An Anthology of Contemporary B.C. Poetry*. She was the recipient of a World Poetry Lifetime Achievement Award in 2006. She has one published book, *Two Plays about Residential Schools* (Vancouver: Living Traditions, 1998).

Daphne Marlatt, poet, theorist, novelist, and co-founding editor of *Tessera*, received the George Woodcock Lifetime Achievement Award in 2012. Her most recent publications are *Reading Sveva* (Talonbooks, 2016) and *Rivering*, selected poetry edited by Susan Knutson (Wilfred Laurier UP, 2014).

Robin Blackburn McBride is a writer, teacher, and transformational life coach. Her books include *In Green* (Guernica, 2002) and *Birdlight: Freeing Your Authentic Creativity* (2016). Robin's debut novel, *The Shining Fragments*, will launch in 2018. She lives in Gatineau, Québec.

Carmelita McGrath is a writer of poetry, fiction, and children's literature. Her most recent book of poetry is *Escape Velocity* (icehouse/Goose Lane Editions, 2013). She lives in Montréal.

Cara-Lyn Morgan hails from the prairies and now lives in the Toronto area. Her debut poetry collection, *What Became My Grieving Ceremony* (Thistledown Press, 2014), was awarded the Fred Cogswell Award in 2015. Her work has appeared in a variety of literary journals and was included in Tightrope Books' *Best Canadian Poetry in English*, 2015. Her second collection of poetry is due for release in Spring 2017.

Erín Moure is a Montréal poet and translator. Her most recent book is *Kapusta* (Anansi, 2015). A forty-year retrospective of her poetry, *Planetary Noise*, will appear from Wesleyan University Press in Spring 2017, edited and introduced by Shannon Maguire.

Susan Musgrave has published close to thirty books—poetry, novels, non-fiction, and books for children. She lives on Haida Gwaii, where she owns and manages Copper Beech Guest House, and teaches poetry in UBC's Optional-Residency MFA in Creative Writing Program.

Alessandra Naccarato is a writer, performer, and teacher based on Salt Spring Island, B.C. Winner of the Bronwen Wallace Award for Emerging Writers and the Readers' Choice Award for the CBC Poetry Prize, her writing has appeared across North America. She has toured nationally and internationally as a spoken word artist.

Kellee Ngan lives and works in Vancouver, B.C. Her writing has been published in such literary magazines as *Geist*, *Grain*, *Room*, *Witness*, and *Poetry Is Dead*. She holds an MFA in Creative Writing from the University of British Columbia.

Lana Okerlund was on the *Room* collective from 2002 to 2007. Now a partner with West Coast Editorial Associates, she edits, writes, and indexes non-fiction books and is an instructor in Simon Fraser University's Editing Certificate program.

Monica Pacheco was nominated for a 2016 National Magazine Award for her short story "The River Phoenix Social Club." Her fiction has appeared in *Room* and *The Minnesota Review*. She lives in Toronto.

M. NourbeSe Philip is an unembedded poet, essayist, novelist, playwright, and former lawyer who lives in the space-time of the City of Toronto. She is a Guggenheim Fellow and the recipient of many awards, including the Casa de las Americas Prize (Cuba). Philip's most recent work is *Zong!*, a genre-breaking poem that engages with ideas of the law, history, and memory as they relate to the transatlantic slave trade.

Helen Potrebenko and her husband are landed gentry living in Burnaby. Ten years ago, she gave up all her jobs and went to play ball. She has written ten books, including *Taxi!* (New Star, 1975); *Sometimes They Sang* (Press Gang, 1986), recently reprinted by Publication Studio in 2011); and, most recently, *Winter Words* (Lazara Press, 2007).

Sina Queyras is the author of *Lemon Hound* (Coach House, 2006), *Expressway* (Coach House, 2009), and *MxT* (Coach House, 2015). She lives in Montréal.

Now enjoying retirement, **Gayla Reid** spends the northern summer in the Comox Valley, B.C., and the southern summer in Australia.

Eden Robinson's 2000 novel *Monkey Beach* is in its twentieth printing in paperback. It was shortlisted for the Governor General's Award and the Giller Prize. Her most recent novel is *Son of a Trickster* (Knopf, 2017). She lives in Kitamaat, B.C.

Constance Rooke (1942 – 2008), unsparing CanLit champion, widely published essayist and fiction writer, long-time *Malahat Review* editor, university and PEN Canada president, author of *Fear of the Open Heart* and many other works, has a magnolia tree and plaque honouring her name in Toronto's Gwen MacEwen Park.

Rebecca Rosenblum is the author of two short story collections, *Once* (Biblioasis, 2008) and *The Big Dream* (Biblioasis, 2011). She lives in Toronto. Her first novel, *So Much Love*, is forthcoming in March 2017 from McClelland & Stewart.

Devyani Saltzman is a Canadian writer and curator. She is the author of *Shooting Water* (Key Porter, Penguin, 2007) and is the Director of Literary Arts at the Banff Centre as well as the Founding Curator, Literary Programming, at Luminato. Her work has appeared in *The Globe and Mail*, *The National Post*, *The Atlantic*, and *Tehelka*.

Sigal Samuel's writing appears in *The Daily Beast*, *The Rumpus*, *BuzzFeed*, *Electric Literature*, *The Walrus*, and the BBC. *The Mystics of Mile End* (Freehand Books, 2015) is her first novel. Originally from Montréal, Sigal now lives in Brooklyn.

Mary Schendlinger is a writer, editor, comics maker (as Eve Corbel), and retired teacher of publishing. She was Senior Editor of *Geist* for twenty-five years. She lives in Vancouver.

Nilofar Shidmehr, PhD, MFA, is a British Columbia Book Prize-nominated poet with four books. Shidmehr was the 2015 – 2016 Writer in Residence at Regina Public Library. She lives in Vancouver and teaches in the Continuing Education Program at Simon Fraser University.

Carol Shields published ten novels, three collections of short fiction, three volumes of poetry, four published plays, and two books of literary criticism. Honours included the Canadian Authors' Association Award, the Arthur Ellis Award, the Governor General's Prize, the National Book Critics' Circle Award, the Pulitzer Prize, the Orange Prize, and the Charles Taylor Prize.

Serena Shipp was born and raised on Maui, Hawaii. She attended the University of Victoria, graduating in Creative Writing with a focus in non-fiction. Currently, she is living in a tiny home with her partner and travelling through North America, unremittingly in motion, seeking inspiration.

Carolyn Smart is the author of six collections of poetry and a memoir. She is the founder of the Bronwen Wallace Award for Emerging Writers and lives near Kingston, Ontario.

Susan Stenson is a poet and holistic practitioner living in Victoria. She has a beautiful room for writing and working with clients. Her forthcoming manuscript is *Joining the Dogs*.

Anna Swanson is a writer and librarian living in St. John's, Newfoundland. Her debut book of poetry, *The Nights Also*, won a Lambda Literary Award and the Gerald Lampert Award for best first book of poetry.

Souvankham Thammavongsa is the author of three poetry books, *Small Arguments* (2003), *Found* (2007), and *Light* (2013), all published by Pedlar Press. She lives near Toronto.

Audrey Thomas was born in Western New York, but has lived on Canada's West Coast since 1959. She has published eighteen books and is working on numbers nineteen and twenty. She is a past chair of the Writers' Union of Canada and a recipient of the Order of Canada.

Ayelet Tsabari's first book, *The Best Place on Earth* (HarperCollins, 2013), won the 2015 Sami Rohr Prize for Jewish Literature and has been published internationally. She lives in Toronto.

Chimwemwe Undi is a Black poet writing on Treaty One territory in Winnipeg, Manitoba. In 2016, she graduated university and was featured in the the Edinburgh International Book Festival.

Eleanor Wachtel is the host and co-founder of CBC Radio's *Writers & Company*, which is now in its twenty-sixth season. She also co-founded and hosts *Wachtel on the Arts*. The author of five books—most recently *The Best of Writers & Company*—she's been widely honoured for her contributions to Canadian cultural life, including as the recipient of eight honorary degrees and as an Officer of the Order of Canada.

Betsy Warland is a Vancouver author of twelve books, most recently of *Oscar of Between: A Memoir of Identity and Ideas* (Caitlin Press, Dagger Editions, 2016). Warland received the Vancouver Mayor's Award for Literary Achievement in 2016. She is also a creative writing teacher and manuscript consultant: see betsywarland.com and vancouvermanuscriptintensive.com.

jia qing wilson-yang is a mixed-race trans woman living in Toronto. Her first novel, *Small Beauty* (Metonymy Press, 2016), won an honour of distinction from the Writers' Trust of Canada as part of the Dayne Ogilvie Prize for LGBT Emerging Writers. More information about her work can be found at littleqing.com.

Copyrights

In addition to appearing in *Room*, several pieces in this book were published elsewhere. They have been reprinted with permission:

"These Hips" by Kate Braid. Also published in: *Rough Ground Revisited* (Caitlin Press, 2015).

"My Hero" by Ivan Coyote. Also published in: *One Man's Trash* (Arsenal Pulp Press, 2002).

"Failed Séances for Rita MacNeil (1944 – 2013)" by Lucas Crawford. Also published in: *Sideshow Concessions* (Invisible Publishing, 2015).

"VillainElle" by Lynn Crosbie. Also published in: *Villain \ Elle* (Coach House Press, 1994).

"Free Fall" by Danielle Daniel. Also published in: *The Dependent: A Memoir of Marriage and the Military* (Latitude 46 Publishing, 2016).

"Ghetto Feminism" by Amber Dawn. Also published in: *How Poetry Saved My Life: A Hustler's Memoir* (Arsenal Pulp Press, 2013).

"Was That Malcolm Lowry?" by Sandy Frances Duncan. Also published in: *Vancouver Short Stories* (UBC Press, 1985).

"The Smell of Sulphur" by Marian Engel. Also published in: *The Tattooed Woman* (Penguin Canada, 1985).

"Twoscore and Five" by Cynthia Flood. Also published in: *The Animals in Their Elements* (Talonbooks, 1987).

"Grade Three" by Leona Gom. Also published in: *The Collected Poems of Leona Gom* (Sono Nis Press, 1991).

"Kiss Me or Something" by Jane Eaton Hamilton. Also published in: *Hunger* (Oberon, 2002).

"The Adulteress, Lunch, and Masturbation" by Nancy Holmes. Also published in: *The Adultery Poems* (Ronsdale Press, 2002).

"Ten Sketches" by Carole Itter. Also published in: *Whistle Daughter Whistle* (Caitlin Press, 1982).

"Wolves, Cigarettes, Gum" by Amy Jones. Also published in: *Journey Prize Stories 26* (McClelland & Stewart, 2014).

"Musing with Mothertongue" by Daphne Marlatt. Also published in: *Touch to My Tongue* by Daphne Marlatt (Longspoon Press, 1984), and *Two Women in a Birth* by Daphne Marlatt and Betsy Warland (Guernica Editions, 1994).

"Theories" by Robin Blackburn McBride. Also published in: *In Green* (Guernica, 2002).

"Notes on the Sexual Division of Labour" by Carmelita McGrath. Also published in: *To the New World* (Killick Press, 1997).

"Reading this list of names, I find myself" by Cara-Lyn Morgan. Also published in: *What Became My Grieving Ceremony* (Thistledown Press, 2014).

"Sleeping Together" by Susan Musgrave. Also published in: *What the Small Day Cannot Hold: Collected Poems 1970 – 1985* (Beach Holme Publishing, 2000).

"Maheen's Collage" by Nilofar Shidmehr. Also published in: *Between Lives* (Oolichan Books, 2014).

"The Orange Fish" by Carol Shields. Also published in: *The Orange Fish* (Random House, 1989) and *Collected Stories* (Harper Perennial, 2005).

"Straight Talking" by Carolyn Smart. Also published in: *Swimmers in Oblivion* (York Publishing, 1982).

"Hanging" by Susan Stenson. Also published in: *Could Love a Man* (Sono Nis Press, 2001), retitled "Laundry Day."

"Morning after" by Anna Swanson. Also published in: *The Nights Also* (Tightrope Books, 2010).

Editorial Team

Meghan Bell joined *Room*'s editorial board in 2011, and is currently the magazine's publisher and graphic designer. She lives in Vancouver and can be found online at meghanbell.com.

Terri Brandmueller is a journalist and poet currently working on a book about family secrets and Internet genealogy. She has an MA in Media Studies and lives in East Vancouver.

Candace Fertile teaches English and creative writing at Camosun College in Victoria, B.C. She has a PhD in English from the University of Alberta.

Leah Golob is a Toronto-based journalist and member of the Growing Room Collective.

Taryn Hubbard joined *Room*'s editorial board in 2012. Her writing has appeared in magazines and anthologies across Canada. She lives in B.C.'s Fraser Valley and online at tarynhubbard.com.

Chelene Knight is managing editor at *Room*, and author of two books: *Braided Skin* (Mother Tongue Publishing, 2015) and *Dear Current Occupant*, forthcoming with BookThug in 2018.

Lindsay Glauser Kwan joined the editorial board for *Room* in 2014. She is a graduate of The Writer's Studio at SFU and is currently completing her Master of Arts in Professional Communications degree at Royal Roads University.

Cara Lang joined the Growing Room Collective in Spring 2016. She is currently the assistant online editor for roommagazine.com as well as the events intern. She splits her time between Vancouver and Kelowna.

Brigid MacAulay has been a member of *Room*'s editorial board since 2009. She is a freelance editor and sustainability consultant living in Vancouver.

Alissa McArthur joined the *Room* editorial board in 2015. She has an MA in English Literature from UBC and writes out of her adopted home, Toronto.

Nav Nagra joined *Room*'s editorial board in 2014, and is currently the magazine's ads coordinator. She lives in Vancouver, where she writes and reads.

Bonnie Nish sat on the editorial board for *Room* from 2014 – 2016. She is Executive Director of Pandora's Collective and is currently pursuing her PhD in Language and Literacy Education at UBC.

Rebecca Russell is a freelance editor, teacher, and arts administrator. She has held various positions in publishing, ESL education, and film and theatre, and currently calls Toronto home. She holds a BA in English and Women & Gender Studies from the University of Toronto.

Kaitlyn Till and **Patricia Wolfe** are proofreaders for Caitlin Press.

Rachel Thompson joined *Room*'s editorial board in 2010, where she has also served as the magazine's managing editor and poetry coordinator. She shares tools and stories to help writers build the writing lives they want at LitWriters.co.

Kayi Wong has been an editorial board member and the coordinator for all the art and writing contests at *Room* since 2013. After living in Hong Kong and Singapore for many years, she is currently writing, editing, and doing graphic design in Vancouver.

Lisa Xing has been reading submissions for *Room* since January 2016. She is a creative writer and a full-time journalist who has filed from South Korea, London, U.K., and from across Canada.

About *Room* Magazine

❧

Room was founded in 1975 by Mary Anderson, Laurie Bagley, Pat Bartle, Penny Birnbaum, Lora Lippert, Gayla Reid, and Gail van Varseveld as *Room of One's Own*. *Room* has been run by an editorial collective based in Vancouver for over forty years, and currently publishes fiction, poetry, creative non-fiction, book reviews, interviews, and artwork by women (including authors who identify as trans and genderqueer). Works originally published in *Room* have been anthologized in the *Journey Prize Anthology*, *Best Canadian Poetry*, *Best Canadian Stories*, *Best Canadian Essays*, and have been nominated for National Magazine Awards.

To learn more about *Room* magazine, including information on how to subscribe or submit your own writing, please visit roommagazine.com.